These Days of Large Things

THESE DAYS OF LARGE THINGS

The Culture of Size in America, 1865–1930

Michael Tavel Clarke

THE UNIVERSITY OF MICHIGAN PRESS   Ann Arbor

Copyright © by the University of Michigan 2007
All rights reserved
Published in the United States of America by
The University of Michigan Press
Manufactured in the United States of America
⊗ Printed on acid-free paper

2010   2009   2008   2007   4   3   2   1

A CIP catalog record for this book is available from the British Library.

Library of Congress Cataloging-in-Publication Data

Clarke, Michael Tavel.
    These days of large things : the culture of size in America, 1865–
1930 / Michael Tavel Clarke.
       p.   cm.
    Based on author's thesis (Ph. D.)—University of Iowa, 2001.
    Includes bibliographical references and index.
    ISBN-13: 978-0-472-09962-7 (cloth : alk. paper)
    ISBN-10: 0-472-09962-0 (cloth : alk. paper)
    1. Popular culture—United States—History—19th century.
2. Popular culture—United States—History—20th century. 3. United
States—Civilization—1865–1918. 4. United States—Civilization—
1918–1945. 5. Size perception—United States—History—19th
century. 6. Size perception—United States—History—20th century.
I. Title.

E169.1.C546   2007
306.0973'09034—dc22   2006100128

Grateful acknowledgment is given for permission to reprint "Virginia," from *Complete Poems of Hart Crane* by Hart Crane, edited by Marc Simon. Copyright 1933, 1958, 1966 by Liveright Publishing Corporation. Copyright © 1986 by Marc Simon. Used by permission of Liveright Publishing Corporation.

For Sarah,
who made this possible,
and Abraham,
who reminded me daily of the value of small things

Acknowledgments

My sincere thanks to Ed Folsom, who provided invaluable feedback on the early drafts of this book and a wealth of support, of various kinds, over many years. Thanks also to Bill Brown and the anonymous reviewers who provided detailed and insightful criticisms of the manuscript (any flaws in the book are failures to live up to their astute recommendations and are therefore wholly my own). I am grateful also to Barbara Eckstein, who encouraged me many years ago to pursue the questions that led to this book; Doris Witt, who was a steady source of encouragement throughout the writing of the manuscript; Ken Cmiel, who provided invaluable assistance in the early conception of the project; Brooks Landon and Bluford Adams for their suggestions on chapters of the book; and Martha Patterson for helpful conversations during revisions. Thanks also to the University of Iowa for a generous fellowship to support the writing of this work, the University of Calgary for a research grant to help with its completion, and the interlibrary loan staff at both universities for their help in acquiring research materials.

Contents

Introduction

Several years ago, at the time I began this project, an advertisement appeared on television that provided both an implicit confirmation of several of the ideas that were beginning to cohere in my mind and an explicit confirmation of the links between my incipient study of turn-of-the-twentieth-century America and our own turn of the century. The advertisement featured a large truck, the Chevy Tahoe, driving through an expansive western landscape. The camera was situated above the truck and at a distance, a device that did more to elevate the viewer than to diminish the size of the vehicle. As patriotic music played in the background, a quotation from Teddy Roosevelt appeared in white at the top of the screen. "Like all Americans," it said, "I like big things."

Those of us who drove automobiles smaller than the Tahoe may have questioned the universality of Roosevelt's and the advertisers' claim. But the presence of the advertisement nevertheless encouraged me at a time when I was beginning an examination of a recurring theme in American culture: the celebration of and identification with large things. This book investigates the American obsession with bigness and the effects of that obsession on national identity. It is, more specifically, an attempt to understand the forms and formulation of attitudes toward physical stature in a key moment of U.S. history—a moment when a variety of discourses and institutions coalesced to make size a subject of central ideological importance.

It is fitting that the Chevy advertisers looked to a figure from the turn of the twentieth century to sanction their values. As Louis Brandeis intimated in 1913, when he characterized his era as "these days of large things,"[1] the American obsession with size may be nowhere more pronounced than in the Progressive era (conceived broadly here as the period between 1865 and 1930).[2] The obsession was fueled by a variety of developments—what one might refer to collectively as a culture of expansion—that had far-reaching implications.

The nation itself grew tremendously until the presumed closing of the frontier in 1890, and overseas imperialism in the 1890s added a new dimension to the country's program of manifest destiny. Fueled by record levels of immigration, the U.S. population expanded more than three times between 1870 and 1930.[3] Cities expanded even faster than the population; whereas in 1890 only 30 percent of the nation's 63 million citizens lived in cities, by 1920 half of the population, now swollen to 106 million, lived in urban areas.[4] Between 1870 and 1930 the number of cities containing over one hundred thousand people expanded from fourteen to ninety-three.[5] Buildings within cities—railroad stations and libraries, for example—grew in scale as monumental architecture became the prevailing national style. Schools burgeoned as the populace converged on cities and more and more states passed compulsory education laws. Mass entertainment assumed new dimensions with the establishment of vast national parks and the construction of immense world's fairs, giant sports stadiums, and amusement parks like New York's Coney Island. Technological developments in communications (including the telegraph, radio, and telephone) and transportation (the steamship, automobile, train, and airplane), along with improvements in the production and distribution of mass periodicals, transformed American society from a collection of relatively isolated island communities to a unified culture that began to conceive of itself not just in national terms but in global terms.[6] Businesses increased rapidly in size with the growing monopolization of industry; individual businesses employed more people than ever, industrial production increased at an unprecedented pace, distribution systems (e.g., railroad cars) expanded to accommodate the increase in production, industrial machinery grew to a gargantuan scale, the scale of consumer marketing expanded with the introduction of giant department stores, advertisements increased in size and volume, huge billboards appeared, and corporations raced to erect the tallest of a new form of corporate icon, the skyscraper. At the turn of the twentieth century daily life in the United States had assumed a scale unlike anything previously known; gigantism seemed to express the nation's self-image as never before.

Expansion was not a new phenomenon in the United States at the turn of the twentieth century, of course, and there are other periods in American history in which bigness has been embraced as a virtue. One could argue, for example, that the enormous geographic expansion of the early nineteenth century, and the associated ideology of manifest destiny, reflected a deep-seated desire for growth. The popularized notion of manifest destiny (a term that did not originate until the 1840s), however, obscures the genuine uncertainty and debate over U.S. expansion and cohesion before the Civil War. Montesquieu had argued in 1748 that a republic could not survive over a large geographic area, and his theory found widespread support among the founders of the Republic.[7] The very formation of the United States, which was born out of the British failure to maintain its far-flung colonies, seemed to confirm Montesquieu's theory, and during the Revolution it was far from certain that the States would remain united after the war.[8] It is easy to understand why antebellum Americans might have doubted the possibility of maintaining an extensive nation; the technological developments in communication and transportation that enabled a democratic state to function effectively did not appear until the late nineteenth century. Similarly, there was intense debate over the Louisiana Purchase and the various territorial acquisitions of the 1840s that brought the United States close to its current size;[9] even those who were most enthusiastic about continental expansion often embraced it as a means of preventing other forms of growth. Thomas Jefferson, who arguably did more to promote American expansion with his purchase of the Louisiana territory than any other single American, for example, regarded westward extension as a way of forestalling industrial and urban expansions that he feared would lead to a concentration of power and wealth in metropolitan areas.[10] For Jefferson, expansion took place in the interests of smallness, and for Americans generally before the Civil War, the desire for continental enlargement did not converge with other celebrations of growth. Most important, all geographic expansion before the Civil War occurred under the constant threat of secession. It was not until the Civil War that Americans were convinced that expansion could occur without fragmentation. "To see the growth of the nation as the inevitable filling of obviously predestined bounds is to miss the peculiar confusion, the peculiar hope, and the peculiar promise of American thinking about the national future" in the period between the Revolution and the Civil War, argues the historian Daniel Boorstin.[11]

This study begins at the end of the Civil War, therefore, because it marked the moment when the United States demonstrated it could sustain its vast region as a unified nation-state.[12] It ends at the Great Depression because this was the moment when many Americans seriously began to contemplate that national growth (particularly in the economy and population, which fueled many of the other forms of growth) had reached its end.[13] Thus, while a culture of expansion and a corresponding infatuation with bigness were not unique to the period between the Civil War and the Great Depression, that era witnessed an intensification of both of these phenomena that deserves special attention. What was unique about the turn of the twentieth century was the strength and duration of the expansionist ethic and the diversity of its incarnations.

There is a danger, of course, in accepting the words of contemporary observers as simple truth. But if their remarks are to be trusted at all, it seems clear, too, that Americans at the turn of the century felt as though they were in the grip of unprecedented changes in social scale. As the environment in which people lived—the cities in which they resided, the buildings they occupied, the vehicles in which they traveled, the stores in which they shopped, the businesses in which they worked, the machines that helped them complete their work, and the places they ventured for entertainment—changed, so too did their understanding of American identity and their ideas about the relationship between self and society. People spoke of feeling as if they resided in a suddenly new world, a change that was often accompanied by a profound sense of disorientation. "The modern man is not yet settled in his world," wrote the social critic Walter Lippmann in 1914. "It is strange to him, terrifying, alluring, and incomprehensibly big."[14] Lippmann, writing of the ideological barriers inhibiting Americans in the shift from a village to a global culture, steered a precarious middle course, neither celebrating the social transformations nor condemning them. Others were less circumspect. Extolling the virtues of modern architecture, the skyscraper builder and enthusiast W. A. Starrett believed that "We Americans like to think of things in terms of bigness; there is a romantic appeal in it, and into our national pride has somehow been woven the yardstick of bigness."[15] In the opposing camp stood the socialist Henry Demarest Lloyd. Writing in the tradition of the American jeremiad, he excoriated the antidemocratic tenor of America's culture of expansion. "Our bignesses—cities, factories, monopolies, fortunes . . . are the obesities of an age gluttonous beyond its powers of digestion," he wrote. "Our size has got beyond both our science and our conscience. . . . America has grown so big . . . that the average citizen has broken down."[16] In whatever camp they may have positioned themselves, however, all of these writers understood that the confrontation with modernity demanded, among other things, an accommodation to a new scale of life. Perhaps Ernest Poole expressed it most directly when, in his best-selling novel of 1915, he pondered, "Was everything modern only big?"[17]

Recent cultural historians have generally agreed that divisions and contradictions were emblematic of the era,[18] so perhaps it should be no surprise that Americans like Lloyd and Starrett were divided in their feelings about the scale of modern life. (Even in the works of Lippmann and Poole one detects a conspicuous note of ambivalence.) To the generalized picture of cultural schism that has emerged in the writings of recent historians we might add that discourses, such as those circulating around issues of size, are inherently fractured and contradictory. (Following Michel Foucault, I use the term *discourse* to mean "a set of ideas and practices which, taken together, organize both the way a society defines certain truths about itself and the way it deploys social power.")[19] Because discourses are characterized by internal division and contradiction—and because separate discourses may present irreconcilable conflicts—they are amenable to manipulation and change. The ideas and practices that constituted the turn-of-the-century discourse of size were seized and deployed in various ways, therefore, and one of the purposes of this project has been to identify and investigate those multiple deployments.

Like the writings of previous scholars, then, this work proceeds by examining the antinomies that characterized American society in the Progressive era. I have adopted a cultural studies methodology as the best means of addressing a theme that found expression in various forms, from literary works and other written texts to architecture, photography, and international fairs. This book is an interdisciplinary study aimed at understanding the political signification of various texts in their relation to discourses of size. The general vision that will emerge is that, while America's turn-of-the-century culture of expansion developed in ways that solidified the authority of dominant powers (the European-descended, male, corporate elite), it also provoked various forms of dissent and resistance that helped shape its development.

This work, however, was motivated less by a desire to offer a new interpretation of the cultural history of the period than by a desire to understand a key moment in the history of American attitudes toward the body and physical stature. The dizzying set of material changes brought about by Progressive America's culture of expansion had decisive implications for American ideas about embodiment. On one hand, dominant ideologies insisted that changes in bodies would correspond to social transformations; the tall, growing body came to signify the American evolutionary, industrial, and social progress that was an integral ideological component of America's culture of expansion. Bigness (by which I mean specifically tallness), as a bodily characteristic and a national cultural trait, became a key component of American identity and a peculiar sign of American progress in this period.[20]

On the other hand, in the presence of massive corporations, enormous urban crowds, vaulting skyscrapers, and gargantuan machines, many Americans felt both actually and figuratively diminished. That the unprecedented material and social changes were associated with a new scale of social conflict and inequality (the bloodiest labor conflicts in U.S. history, for example, or the dramatically enlarged gap between rich and poor) and precipitated new social problems (problems related to urban housing, transportation, and sanitation; immigration management; business organization; regulation of industrial production; food processing; architectural construction; the reconceptualization of American citizenship in more pluralistic terms, etc.) made the apparent diminishment of the powers of individuals all the more ominous. As in other historical periods, the human body became a site for imaginatively negotiating a variety of problems coincident with the tumultuous social and institutional changes of the day; but to a greater degree than in other eras, the size of the body played a key symbolic role in this ongoing negotiation.

Previous scholars have recognized the Progressive era's fascination with sheer bigness, and there have been brief attempts to study the phenomenon, typically in relation to limited, specific developments, principally architecture and the scale of business.[21] A few scholars have recognized the broader significance of the phenomenon but have not examined it thoroughly. In his classic study of the Progressive era, *The Search for Order, 1877–1920*, for example, Robert Wiebe argues that the transformation from "a society of island communities"[22] characterized by a decentralized structure and local autonomy to an integrated, bureaucratic, centralized, hierarchical nation left many Americans at the turn of the century bewildered and confused. Failing to explain their suddenly transformed world by any familiar values, people seized upon size and amount as a criterion of value.

> What [Americans] saw about them were more tracks and more factories and more people, bigger farms and bigger corporations and bigger buildings; and in a time of confusion they responded with a quantitative ethic that became the hallmark of their crisis in values. It seemed that the age could only be comprehended in bulk. Men defined issues by how much, how many, how far. Greatness was determined by amount, with statistics invariably the triumphant proof that the United States stood first among nations. . . . For lack of anything that made better sense of their world, people everywhere weighed, counted, and measured it.[23]

Wiebe identifies a number of domains in which the "quantitative ethic" insinuated itself: the decisions of capitalists to expand and consolidate their businesses, architectural aesthetics, religious rhetoric, and naturalist fiction. While Wiebe's arguments are insightful, he underestimates the significance of the quantitative ethic in suggesting that it represented a temporary confusion of values. For one thing, the quantitative ethic maintained a hallowed place in the American pantheon of values throughout the twentieth century. For another, statistical ways of thinking were more integral to American and European cultural formation in the nineteenth century than Wiebe acknowledges.[24] Finally, the quantitative ethic in the Progressive era was not, as I hope to demonstrate throughout this book, simply a "confusion" of values: it represented a decisive *assertion* of values that found expression and coherence in disparate ideas, institutions, and practices, including economic structures, architecture, and naturalist fiction as well as anthropology, race science, medicine, political rhetoric, and imperialist and feminist discourses.[25] One sign of its pervasive influence and coherent formulation is the fact that it was actively contested by those who recognized it as a threat to their interests or to fundamental American principles.

Unlike previous explorations of the topic, then, this book examines Progressive-era attitudes toward size in relation to a variety of discourses, including both those that have been addressed elsewhere (such as architectural and economic discourses) and those that have received little previous attention (including discourses of race and gender). And, taking a somewhat different tack from previous studies, this work emphasizes the relationship between America's culture of expansion and representations of the body.[26]

My interest in the U.S. fascination with size and its effects on our notions of embodiment began with a concern about several contemporary phenomena, and in many ways (for better or worse) this concern has shaped the direction this book has taken. In the past twenty-five years sociologists have reported patterns of hiring and wage discrimination against short men and women in the United States, a preference among voters for taller political candidates, profound discrimination against people with dwarfism, a widespread desire among American men and women to be taller than they are, and a demand for high fashion models who are significantly above average height. Biomedical ethicists have addressed the continuing use of growth hormone on children and adolescents; in spite of criticisms of the ethics and effectiveness of such treatments, the U.S. Food and Drug Administration recently approved the drug for cosmetic purposes.[27] While these things may not be unique to the United States (sociologists have found evidence of height discrimination in other countries, for example),[28] they are necessarily connected to social and historical developments that are unique to the United States. As of yet, there has been scant attention to the history of attitudes toward physical stature despite a recent eruption of interest in the body.[29] While prejudices regarding size and height may cut across cultures and historical periods, they also vary both historically and regionally. Although this book studies attitudes toward stature in a particular moment in U.S. history, it has implications for other times and places. My work is intended as one part of a general history of the treatment of stature that remains to be written.

Because this book began with an interest in physical stature and the body as a whole, I have avoided addressing issues of size with regard to specific body parts. A discussion of cultural ideas about penis or breast size, for example, is beyond the scope of this text. I have also specifically chosen to ignore such issues because often scholarly attention to them has effectively foreclosed attention to stature (for a fuller discussion of this phenomenon, see the epilogue).

This project also, then, participates in a larger dialogue about the historical significance and signification of bodies. Impelled by the work of Michel Foucault and others, the burgeoning field of scholarship devoted to the body has yielded a number of key insights that are fundamental to this project. First is the notion that the body has a history; it has been invested with different meanings by different groups in different times and places. In the United States and Europe, the shift from the Enlightenment to the modern age (occurring roughly in the eighteenth century) coincided with a shift in the social treatment of the body, a "transformation of the way in which the body . . . [was] invested by power relations," according to Foucault.[30] In the modern era power has been directed at optimizing the body's capabilities and resources, and new forms of knowledge (the life sciences) have emerged with an understanding of the body as their central aim. It is in the modern era that the concept of the norm has acquired its power as a tool for regulating bodies and citizens and that new forms of discipline (medical techniques, Taylorism and Fordism, exercise movements, and the various disciplinary regimes of army barracks, schools, prisons, and hospitals, to name just a few) have been directed at the body.[31] "The new discourse[s] of the body" that emerged in the modern age, argue Gallagher and Laqueur in *The Making of the Modern Body,* "not only attributed a new set of social, political, and cultural meanings to bodies but also placed them at the very center of social, political, and cultural signification."[32]

The second key insight originating in recent writings on the body is the notion that the body is constructed by social and cultural discourses and is therefore expressive of social distributions of privilege, status, and power. To argue that the body is constructed by culture is neither to deny the materiality of the body nor to deny that social discourses, subjectivity, and cognitive structures are shaped by embodiment.[33] Neither is it to suggest that the body is a blank page awaiting inscription by culture and discourse; there is unquestionably an interdependence between body and culture, body and mind.[34] But it is to suggest, as Susan Bordo has done, that "the body we experience and conceptualize is always *mediated* by constructs, associations, images of a cultural nature."[35] The body, in other words, is neither a passive, inert material wholly constructed by social discourse nor is it knowable outside of discourse. This book adopts a strategic constructionist approach to the body as the best available means of addressing issues of representation and identifying the ways in which discourse attaches meaning to bodies.

The first of three sections in this book examines the treatment of physical stature in anthropology, medicine, and other branches of science. The shift toward modernity invested the sciences with unprecedented authority. Earlier theological metaphors persisted in scientific views of the body, however. As the evolutionary ladder supplanted the Great Chain of Being as an organizing metaphor of natural life, the underlying vertical scheme endured, and the figuratively vertical rhetoric of spiritual/evolutionary progress was superimposed literally onto human bodies. Small bodies became signs of evolutionary degeneration in the late nineteenth century, and the quest for an upward-tending, progressive body became the secularized, scientific version of America's age-old mission of ascent toward the city on the hill.

Chapter 1 examines the treatment of African pygmies in travel narratives, anthropological studies, and world's fairs. Small, black, and nonindustrial, the pygmies were conceived as antithetical to Americans. Pygmies were consigned to the bottom of the evolutionary ladder and regarded by many as the missing link between apes and humans. Simultaneously, encounters with the pygmies in the late nineteenth century induced American and European scientists to assign stature a central place in schemes of racial classification. Representations of pygmies reinforced assumptions about racial hierarchies, strengthened beliefs about the correspondence between physical and mental traits, and bolstered an American self-image that was predicated on growth. In the story of the pygmies, the histories of race and stature are inextricably entwined.

If representations of pygmies reassured Americans of their presumed physical and social supremacy, they were insufficient to wholly allay anxieties about the possibility of American degeneration. Fears of physical decay were particularly acute as the nation shifted from a rural agrarian society to an urban industrial one; record levels of immigration, which altered the ethnic composition of the country, exacerbated those fears. Chapter 2 situates the height and growth studies that proliferated in the United States at the turn of the twentieth century, a period in which scientific attention shifted from the periphery of empire to the center, in the context of these national concerns. It argues that the height and growth studies combated notions of American degeneration and attempted to derive an understanding of child growth so as to ensure a progressive nation by means of a progressive body. This chapter also situates Progressive-era assumptions about physical stature within a broader history of Euro-American study of height and growth, emphasizing in particular the adoption of racial paradigms in the late nineteenth century as explanations for human physical variation.

The first section also introduces a theme that is developed at various times throughout this book. The scientific endeavor to classify human groups according to an ascending evolutionary scale privileged visible, measurable differences (of height, skin color, skull capacity, etc.) and therefore sight over the other senses; in this respect, scientific discourse is one instance of the general primacy accorded to vision in modern and postmodern culture.[36] A complete discussion of the visual turn in the late nineteenth century is beyond the scope of the present work; however, at various times this book considers how the quest for a tall, Progressive citizenry found correlative expression in a quest for elevated vision. In chapter 1 I explore this idea through an analysis of the function of the Ferris wheel in the Chicago and St. Louis World's Fairs of 1893 and 1904. Chapter 3 examines the role of transcendent vision as a narrative device in naturalist fiction, and chapter 4 returns to the subject of the politics of vision with a discussion of debates circulating around skyscrapers.

If the first part of the book addresses the basic mythology of height and growth, including its scientific formations and its social effects, the second part deals with its more contested aspects, the ways in which America's culture of expansion was challenged and the semantic disorder that consequently arose over the meanings attached to large and small bodies.

Chapter 3 in this section addresses the ambivalent response to the growth of large-scale corporate capitalism in the late nineteenth and early twentieth centuries. It begins with a discussion of the three mythic figures that emerged during the national trust debates and that reckoned prominently in political and economic discourses of the day: big business's giant figure of the Incorporated Body, organized labor's equally gigantic figure of the Unionized Body, and the middle class's Little Man. These figures vivified economic theories as competing visions of a national body, and their presence suggests that by the late nineteenth century distinct subject positions had already emerged with regard to matters of size, positions that were as much determined by class as by anything. After characterizing the three figures, the chapter moves to a discussion of the ways they were deployed in popular naturalist fiction.

The writings of Louis Brandeis, Andrew Carnegie, Woodrow Wilson, and Theodore Roosevelt provide contextual background in this chapter for close readings of Frank Norris's *The Octopus* and Ernest Poole's *The Harbor*. Although Norris and Poole held very different opinions about the economic destiny of the nation, their works nevertheless attempted to accommodate middle-class Americans to the enlarged scale of modern life and modern institutions.

Chapter 4 in this section examines the skyscraper as an architectural rendering of the progressive, expanding, racially superior American body. While skyscrapers were widely regarded as quintessentially American, they also provoked a heated national debate, and this chapter explores the ambivalent response to skyscraper aesthetics in the writings of Henry James and the photography of Alvin Langdon Coburn. The chapter culminates with a discussion of the construction and reception of the Woolworth Building, which reigned as the world's tallest skyscraper from 1913 to 1930, offering an explanation of the building's remarkable and seemingly paradoxical success at a time when opposition to skyscrapers and the corporate culture they represented had reached its most fevered pitch.

Together, the two chapters in this section explore the connections between economic developments, shifting ideas about size, and the implications of both for conceptions of the body. This section wanders further from explicit discussions of the body in order to examine the historic backdrop that crucially informed changing conceptions of the body during the period. As a consequence, chapter 3 contains information on the economic and social developments that will seem familiar to readers conversant with the period but that crucially inform my arguments throughout this book. In economic discourses, bodily images served more often as metaphors and symbols than as explicit statements about the body (in contrast to representations of the pygmies). I hope to demonstrate in this section not only that economic discourses fundamentally affect(ed) ideas about the body but also that conceptions of the body play(ed) a significant role in shaping economic debates. In American capitalism, which places an extraordinary emphasis on growth and links expansion tightly to national progress, complex responses to that imperative inevitably follow—most especially at a time when its flaws are widely apparent, as they were at the turn of the century. That the responses to economic growth were so often embodied in the Progressive era suggests how viscerally they were experienced. That bodily metaphors were used so consistently in economic debates also suggests that people felt a need to render changes that often seemed abstract and bewildering in a comprehensible, grounded way. Rendering social change in bodily terms is one of the most direct ways of accomplishing that, since embodiment is one of the few universals in human experience. But the choice of bodily images, and the manner of their representation, is decidedly not universal. Images of the Corporate Giant, the Labor Giant, and the Little Man, for example, represented attempts to explain a changed world using familiar concepts. In the era of family-based or entrepreneurial capitalism, competitions among businesses could be understood as competitions among individuals; a business was conceived as an extension of its owner. In the era of corporate consolidation and unionization, businesses could no longer be easily conceived in the same way. Despite the talk of robber barons and the widely circulating images of giant and little men, businesses were increasingly collective bodies. Yet, until the mid-twentieth century, when a corporation was commonly referred to as "the organization," business imagery at the turn of the century continued to express an individualist ethic. In chapters 3 and 4, I am most interested in the things that economic discourses reveal about American attitudes toward physical stature, but I am also interested in more general discourses of size and what they reveal about American culture in broader terms.

The third section of the book continues to emphasize the anxieties created by the dramatic social and material changes of the Progressive era, this time as they related to gender ideologies. "In the popular imagination," writes Susan Brownmiller in her 1984 book *Femininity,* "masculinity always includes the concepts of powerful and large. . . . The equation of maleness with bigness persists as a dearly loved concept."[37] If attitudes toward size are bound up with notions of gender, as Brownmiller suggests, then any attempt to understand the history of American attitudes toward size must grapple with the gendered connotations of bigness and smallness.[38] This section focuses on images of growing women and shrinking men that abounded in literature, advertisements, political cartoons, and other texts at the turn of the twentieth century. As women swept into the labor force and clamored for equal education, equal economic opportunity, and the vote, they strained traditional notions of women's proper sphere. Meanwhile, normative notions of masculinity were under intense pressure not only from the social demands of women but also from changes in the economy, particularly the demise of independent business ownership as a practical ideal for the majority of men and the increasing presence of corporate hierarchies that placed the bulk of middle-class men in positions of subservience. In a period experiencing rapid shifts in gender ideologies, the body assumed a correlative instability of form. Images of shrinking men and growing women represented the simultaneous promise and threat of feminine enfranchisement and masculine disempowerment.

Chapter 5 in this section focuses on Mary Antin's immigrant autobiography *The Promised Land.* It examines the metaphor of growth in Antin's narrative in the context of debates surrounding the New Woman and American immigration policy. Contemporary feminists interpreted the reputed physical growth of modern American women as a sign of their social advancement, and Antin borrowed the trope of the growing woman to describe her own experience as an immigrant woman liberated from the patriarchal culture of Russian Jewry. Similarly, Antin adopted the figure of the growing Jew from contemporary Jewish anthropologists to argue for the restorative effects of American culture on oppressed Russian Jewish immigrants and to combat the arguments of immigration restrictionists, who portrayed the Jews' purportedly short stature as inimical to American racial progress. Antin's autobiography testifies to the ways in which physical size had become an expression of adaptation to modern American society and the condition of modernity; to qualify as fully "modern" and "American," in other words, women and Jews felt compelled to demonstrate a capacity for growth.

Chapter 6 in this section studies the images of shrinking men that proliferated in naturalist fiction, with an emphasis on Upton Sinclair's *The Jungle.* Shrinking male characters in naturalist literature reacted against hegemonic ideals of the era. Founded in part on national studies of Civil War soldiers (described in detail in chapter 2) and constructed in part as a defensive response to contemporary social changes, dominant notions of masculinity assumed that progressive male growth was a definitive American secular trend and a unique expression of U.S. exceptionalism. Deliberately challenging the progressive narrative of the growing male body, *The Jungle* offers the lurid tale of Jurgis Rudkus, a Lithuanian immigrant who shrinks rather than grows in the withering conditions of modern industrial labor. Depicting a world in which degeneration is the inevitable path for industrial-class masculinity, and yoking this narrative of lower-class degeneration to the middle-class image of the Little Man, Sinclair attempts to unite his (implicitly white) male readers across class lines in support of socialist change. Thus, as with many of the texts addressed in this book, *The Jungle* emphasizes threats to the autonomous individual created by the conditions of modernity, and size functions as the field on which anxieties about masculinity circulate and narratives of progress and degeneration battle.

In lieu of a more traditional conclusion, this book offers a brief coda to the third section that brings the discussion of the intersections between size and gender up to the 1950s, a period of equally vigorous material and economic expansion, with an analysis of the science fiction films *The Incredible Shrinking Man* and *Attack of the 50-Foot Woman*. The epilogue illustrates the continuing power of Progressive-era discourses of size as well as the ways such discourses were transformed in the middle of the twentieth century.

PART 1 • Stature and the Discourses of Race

CHAPTER 1 • Representing the "Pygmies"

In 1862, Paul Belloni Du Chaillu, a naturalized American citizen, set out on the second of two journeys into the interior of equatorial Africa. While his reports of gorillas and cannibals helped make the narrative of his first journey a financial success and a popular sensation, his earlier travels were also the subject of controversy. Inconsistencies in the chronology of his book *Explorations and Adventures in Equatorial Africa,* the absence of precise geographical measurements, and other oversights led scientific authorities to question the authenticity of his journey. In this second trip, he hoped to substantiate his earlier reports and further his investigations in natural history, including the search for the missing link between apes and humans that would help justify Darwinian theory.

The second trek ended disastrously—or so he believed at first. In 1865 he fled to the coast when one of his guides accidentally shot and killed a man, losing virtually all of his equipment along the way, including material that would be instrumental in validating his earlier journey. Before fleeing, however, he encountered a village of Obongos, a group of very small people whom he labeled "pygmies."[1] Although Du Chaillu devoted only nine pages out of five hundred to his encounter with the Obongos in the narrative of this second journey, his reports of pygmies immediately captured the popular and scientific imaginations, proving to be the major contribution of his second trip to Euro-American knowledge about Africa. In the ensuing years, additional reports of very small people living in the interior of Africa confirmed and supplemented Du Chaillu's reports. These reports merged with knowledge of the small Bushmen (or San) of southern Africa and increasing knowledge of small people in the Andaman Islands, New Guinea, the Philippines, and elsewhere to produce a growing conviction among Americans and Europeans that pygmies, regarded for centuries as mythical, did indeed exist.

Forty years after Du Chaillu's journeys, and a year after Du Chaillu died, Samuel Phillips Verner triumphantly returned from central Africa accompanied by several pygmies, including one man purchased from African slavers for a pound of salt and a bolt of cloth during the brutal Belgian occupation. Verner brought the young men to St. Louis, where, as the first pygmies to be seen directly by masses of Americans, they delighted fairgoers with their performances in the world's fair of 1904. At the same time, visitors to the fair had the opportunity to observe a functioning replica of a pygmy village of the Philippines, complete with authentic Aeta villagers. The exhibit was part of a larger representation of the various communities of the Philippines meant to inform fairgoers about the latest acquisition to the U.S. empire and to bolster the contemporary self-image of Americans as the culmination of social and evolutionary progress. Two years after the St. Louis World's Fair, one of the central African men, Ota Benga, appeared in the Bronx Zoo, where he performed in a cage with an orangutan in an exhibit designed to convince visitors of the close affinity between the two.

In the time intervening between Du Chaillu's encounter with the Obongos and Ota Benga's performances, anthropologists and ethnologists used the accounts of travelers like Du Chaillu to classify and hierarchize the existing races of man and to develop theories about the origin and evolution of humans. Stature became an increasingly important element in American and European racial classifications as awareness grew of populations of small people scattered throughout the world. Debates erupted over whether pygmies were degenerated versions of taller races or remnants of an early, primitive form of humanity. They ended with ethnologists and anthropologists agreeing unanimously that groups of small, dark-skinned peoples as disparate as west central Africa and the Philippines belonged to the same primitive branch of the family tree. Pygmies were consigned to the bottom of the evolutionary hierarchy, succeeded in a progressive history first by taller Negroes and then by the Mongolians and the Caucasians. As people "thrown into the side eddies of the great stream of evolution"[2] and weak contestants in the high-stakes struggle of the races, the pygmies were destined for extinction, claimed the scientific authorities.

As these first two chapters will argue, prevalent notions of race affected the acquisition and deployment of knowledge about physical stature at the end of the nineteenth century and beginning of the twentieth in profound ways. At the same time, myths and assumptions about stature affected the development of ideas about race. Influenced by travel writers, anthropologists used small bodies to bolster assumptions about the competition of races, the inevitable extinction of inferior races, and the origins of humanity; in this sense, physical characteristics were clues to the human past and the evolutionary future. World's fairs helped solidify an American national self-image predicated on progressive expansion and conducive to imperialism. All of these discourses shared a number of assumptions: that the small body was a sign of degeneration and the large body, within limits, was a sign of progress; that physical traits were signs of moral ones; and that evidence of the Darwinian struggle among the races was written on the body.

First Encounters: Du Chaillu and the Pygmies

In 1892, the American Geographic Society awarded Paul Belloni Du Chaillu a silver cup in honor of the twenty-fifth anniversary of his return from Africa and for discovering the gorilla, the equatorial forest, and the pygmies. While the honor recognized, in part, the social and scientific impact of Du Chaillu's travel narratives, *Explorations and Adventures in Equatorial Africa* (1861) and *A Journey to Ashango-Land* (1867), his widespread notoriety derived principally from the conversion of these narratives into lectures for American children and a series of five children's books, *Stories of the Gorilla Country* (1867), *Wild Life Under the Equator* (1868), *Lost in the Jungle* (1869), *My Apingi Kingdom* (1870), and *The Country of the Dwarfs* (1871). Through these works, Du Chaillu ushered in more than a century of fascination with the pygmies and helped shape narrative treatment of the group for decades to come.[3]

Du Chaillu wrote the first of his books, *Explorations and Adventures,* after traveling approximately eight thousand miles around the western coast of Africa between 1855 and 1859 with the support of the Boston and Philadelphia natural history societies. The narrative was an immediate success, selling over ten thousand copies in two years despite its large size and high price. Its success can be attributed in part to the fact that it was published shortly after Darwin's *The Origin of Species* and self-consciously participated in the raging debate over Darwin's view that humans descended from apes. Its popularity may also have been due to its wide appeal to a diverse audience. To the general public, *Explorations and Adventures* offered numerous enticements: it confirmed racist notions of the barbarity of Africans and the superiority of Europeans and Americans through its titillating accounts of customs such as cannibalism, the sale of women, and the execution of witches; it provided thrilling and exaggerated accounts of gorilla hunts; and it appealed to the virtues of Christian charity by addressing the possibilities of missionary work in Africa. For those with an entrepreneurial bent, it suggested ways of making money in Africa and bringing American industry to the continent. For ethnologists, it examined theories of the relationship between humans and gorillas, offering detailed comparisons between the skulls and skeletons of the two and confirming the work of the celebrated American craniologist Samuel G. Morton.

Throughout his book, Du Chaillu emphasizes the similarities between primates and humans, and we learn in the ethnological chapter near the end of the text that, like so many of his contemporaries, he had hoped to discover a connecting link between the two. Ultimately he admits his failure to find a link between Africans and gorillas in regions where the two live in close proximity; in spite of the stories he heard of African women being carried off by gorillas and of women giving birth to a variety of animals, Du Chaillu admits, "I found not a single being, young or old, who could show an intermediate link between man and the gorilla. . . . I suppose from these facts we must come to the conclusion that man belongs to a distinct family from that of the ape."[4]

Although Du Chaillu was reluctant to press the claim in his second book that the Obongos were the secret he had sought on his first expedition, *A Journey to Ashango-Land* nevertheless suggested to many readers that he had in fact found the much anticipated missing link.[5] As described in the book, his encounter with the Obongos was a relatively simple affair. Yet it is evident, given his increased emphasis on the similarities between the Obongos and apes, how his contemporaries may have come to such a conclusion. Du Chaillu describes his approach to the pygmies as a hunt, relying on his readers' familiarity with the frequent descriptions of gorilla hunts in *Explorations and Adventures* to enhance the resemblance between the Obongos and primates. "The Ashangos . . . told me . . . I had better take with me only a very small party, so that we might make as little noise as possible," he writes. "We approached with the greatest caution, in order not to alarm the wild inmates . . . but all our care was fruitless, for the men, at least, were gone when we came up."[6] The woodcut accompanying Du Chaillu's description of the Obongo village closely resembles a depiction of "gorillas surprised in the forest" from earlier in the text, a connection that is unlikely to be lost on a reader, especially since images of other Africans differ from both dramatically (see figs. 1 and 2). Du Chaillu depicts the Obongos, like the gorillas he had hunted, as extremely shy, the majority never remaining in the village long enough for interaction. When an old woman consents to speak to him, his first impulse is to measure her height and head, and he produces a measuring tape previously used only on apes. On a subsequent visit, he finds a woman mourning her recently deceased husband. Hoping to profit by collecting a pygmy skeleton, he asks his Ashango guides if they will inquire about where the Obongos bury their dead. The translators tactfully refuse. Du Chaillu makes several visits to the village and takes several additional measurements of its inhabitants, all of which he lists in the text of his narrative. He briefly records what little he knows of the Obongos' physical appearance, dietary customs, and language.

Du Chaillu made several significant changes to this episode in the children's book he published four years after the publication of *A Journey to Ashango-Land*. Capitalizing on popular interest in his reports about the pygmies, he titled his children's book *The Country of the*

Fig. 1. Paul Belloni Du Chaillu, "Approach to the Camp of the Obongo Dwarfs." The fleeing figures of the Obongos in the first visual representation of pygmies closely resembled illustrations of fleeing gorillas from earlier in Du Chaillu's travel narrative. (Reproduced from *A Journey to Ashango-Land* [1867].)

Dwarfs. Consistent with this shift in emphasis, he expanded the section on the pygmies; while the entire discussion occupied little more than nine pages of a chapter entitled "Ashango-Land" in *A Journey to Ashango-Land,* the passages on the pygmies expanded to approximately thirty-three pages in the children's book.[7] He fleshes out the encounter with more dialogue and repeats the stories of the pygmies told by Herodotus and Homer. References to such ancient authorities would become commonplace in later writings about pygmies, serving primarily to establish the ancient lineage of the group, to illustrate the lack of progressive development relative to Euro-American culture, and to add additional evidence to theories that pygmies were among the first races.

The most significant change, however, is the addition of an invented episode in which the entire Obongo village is present for a feast that Du Chaillu supplies. In this passage, Du Chaillu includes an imagined conversation with the Obongos to acquire their unwitting assent to three racial theories about the group. The first theory explained the short stature of the pygmies as a sign of degeneration. The second explained

Fig. 2. Paul Belloni Du Chaillu, "Gorillas Surprised in the Forest." (Reproduced from *A Journey to Ashango-Land* [1867].)

the residence of the pygmies in the recesses of the equatorial forest as a consequence of competition with superior races. The third categorized the pygmies in the hierarchy of races. Although the first theory would encounter some resistance before finally being rejected in the 1890s, the opposing theory would share many of the same premises. Du Chaillu's second and third theories would predominate as the explanatory myths of the pygmy peoples for the Western world.

As one might expect, theories explaining the height of pygmies immediately proliferated in the United States and Europe after Du Chaillu's reports were publicized.[8] Two explanations were most common. According to one argument, pygmies and other short races had degenerated from a more developed race. This was the view of Du Chaillu, who suggested in *A Journey to Ashango-Land* that inbreeding within the small, isolated communities of the Obongos was the cause of the "physical deterioration of their race."[9] In the fabricated conversation with the Obongos in *The Country of the Dwarfs,* Du Chaillu asks the villagers about their marriage customs, and they confirm his theory that "Generation after generation we have lived among ourselves, and married among ourselves."[10]

The second most common explanation for the shortness of pygmies, like the first, was based on a Darwinian model of progressive evolution. In *The Land of the Pygmies* (1898), Guy Burrows maintains that pygmies were not degenerate but were specimens of arrested evolutionary development. "They are a well-proportioned race, and, with the exception of their remarkably short stature, may be regarded as normal and well developed, not degenerate, as has often been stated, though socially inferior to other tribes."[11]

The debate over whether pygmies were a degenerate branch of ordinary Africans or a more primitive racial group was the most important controversy after the existence of the group became widely accepted. Both theories shared common premises: that height was a sign of intellectual and social development; that an increase in height reflected evolutionary progress and a decrease represented degeneration; and that groups of short people deserved special attention for the lessons that they might teach about the differential survival of human races. As an editorial in the *New York Times* of 1906 expressed it, "Whether they are held to be illustrations of arrested development, and really closer to the anthropoid apes than the other African savages, or whether they are viewed as the degenerate descendants of ordinary negroes, they are of equal interest to the student of ethnology, and can be studied with profit."[12]

Du Chaillu also used the contrived conversation with the Obongos in *The Country of the Dwarfs* to confirm a second theory explaining the nomadic lifestyle of the pygmies and their residence in the Congo forest. "If we had villages," the Obongos explain, "the strong and tall people who live in the country might come and make war upon us, kill us, and capture us."[13] The rain forest offered a kind of protective evolutionary cul-de-sac for a race that should have disappeared long ago. It was a theory that played an important role in an era of aggressive European and American imperialism. It naturalized warfare and expansionism, borrowing Darwinian theory to turn imperialist violence and colonialist oppression into biological law. "Racial extinction, even genocide, was a result of biology, not history"—this is how Nancy Stepan explains the view.[14] The theory also transformed the social process of imperialism into a biological one by rendering aggression not as one nation against another but as one race against another. While races were founded in blood and heredity, nations were contrived, mutable constructs; and while the imperialist success of a nation might be based on luck or circumstance, the success of a race revealed the superiority of a people bound by blood and a common descent.

At the end of his section on the pygmies in *A Country of the Dwarfs,* Du Chaillu suggests that the Obongos are related to the Bushmen of southern Africa, descending from the same original nation.[15] This, the third of Du Chaillu's theories on the pygmies, would play a significant role in later ethnological classifications. As Du Chaillu's reports of the pygmies were confirmed by later travelers like Schweinfurth of Germany and Stanley of England, and as more and more small, dark-skinned people came to the attention of American and European authorities on race, an attempt was made to fit the pygmies into existing racial and evolutionary hierarchies. Most authorities accepted Du Chaillu's suggestion that the Obongos and the Bushmen were related, and representations of both were increasingly informed by a unified set of codes and myths.

Despite the fact that later travelers vindicated Du Chaillu's reports of central Africa, the initial controversy surrounding his *Explorations and Adventures* lingered as a general public skepticism toward his findings. Until Henry Stanley confirmed Du Chaillu's tales of the pygmies, they persisted publicly as half-believed fantasies. The taint of humbuggery may have been augmented by Du Chaillu's decision to convert his narratives into children's books; at any rate, the misgivings kept his work in the public eye and added to the commercial success of Du Chaillu's children's books. Nevertheless, the association between pygmies and children that Du Chaillu and his publishers at Harpers created set a precedent that would remain for years to come. Books for children involving pygmies as main characters proliferated in later decades, including such works as *Toro of the Little People* (1926) and *Saranga: The Pygmy* (1939).

There were other reasons, of course, why pygmies would become associated with children and why publishers and authors would assume that books dealing with pygmies would appeal to children. Infantilization has long been a characteristic of the treatment of small people.[16] Additionally, while white Americans and Europeans regarded all blacks as childlike and in need of paternal (or imperial) guidance, the shortness of pygmies suggested that they were the most childlike of all. In evolutionary terms, many regarded pygmies as the first race—the children of humanity, so to speak—a notion that received support from ethnologists as well as scientific studies claiming that civilized races were taller than uncivilized ones.[17] Furthermore, childhood, like the pygmy race, is a vanishing state: just as the pygmies were destined for extinction, childhood is a fleeting and temporary state of being. Travel writers accentuated the similarities between children and pygmies, focusing on the pygmies' powers of imitation or mimicry, their lack of social organization and love of freedom, their capacity for education and improvement, their shyness and innocence. Because Du Chaillu and later authors like Henry Stanley described equatorial Africa as a place of dangers and wonders, furthermore, the lives of pygmies were assumed to be excellent subject matter for children's adventure novels. Like child heroes in juvenile literature, pygmies were faced with obstacles and enemies more powerful than they, demanding that they rely on wits and courage rather than superior strength. That the association between pygmies and children had a profound and widespread ideological resonance is acutely evident in the treatment of Ota Benga. When he was removed from his cage at the Bronx Zoo following protest by the Colored Baptist Ministers' Conference, the ministers thought it best to place him—a man in his mid-twenties—in an orphanage.

Du Chaillu's Descendants: Later Travel Narratives and the Pygmy Sensation

In 1904 William Allan Reed, author of a report on the Filipino pygmies for the U.S. Department of the Interior (part of a series of reports on the Philippines meant to assist the occupation and annexation of the islands), wrote that "Probably no group of primitive men has attracted more attention from the civilized world than the pygmy blacks."[18] Travel writers after Du Chaillu capitalized on the sensation of the pygmies and adopted many of the representational techniques of their predecessor. Later explorers often followed Du Chaillu's lead in placing the pygmies at or near the end of their written texts regardless of whether they encountered the pygmies at the end of their physical journeys, for example.[19] This formal device reinforced the underlying notion that pygmies were the terminus—or root—of human evolution, the furthest one could go and still remain human. The device also sets up the African travel narrative as a backward movement in time, a journey toward human antiquity and the evolutionary past. Vanden Bergh's suggestion in *On the Trail of the Pygmies* that African people grew progressively smaller as one approached the pygmies in the interior of the continent enhanced this narrative device of devolutionary progression.[20] Similarly, in an attempt to cash in on the phenomenon of the pygmies, the spine of Henry Morton Stanley's *In Darkest Africa* (1890) depicts an image of Stanley standing beside a pygmy. Stanley drapes his arm protectively over the man's shoulder, and below the pair is the phrase "Let there be light." The notion that Europeans are uniquely responsible for bringing light to a darkened Africa is rendered bodily by the sharp color contrasts in the image, with Stanley drawn in vivid gold and the pygmy in deep black. The use of a pygmy in this image ensured that it would convey the proper relationship between Europeans and Africans; the difference in height between Stanley and the pygmy guarantees that Africans will seem childlike and that Stanley's gesture will look paternalistic rather than comradely. Stanley's military dress, on the other hand, betrays the threat of violence underlying the outward show of benevolent guardianship. The double message in the image is appropriate considering Stanley's divided presentation of the pygmies in his narrative. He portrays them as quaint and delightful in their childlike innocence; meanwhile, Stanley's warlike caravan was severely harassed and demoralized by pygmy defenders who used deadly poisoned arrows against his entourage.

Stanley explored central Africa between 1870 and 1889 and did the most of any traveler to allay doubts about the existence of pygmies in the region.[21] Like Du Chaillu, Stanley used techniques that suggested to readers that the pygmies were the missing link between humans and apes—another irony, considering that Stanley was a vigorous anti-Darwinist who denied that a missing link existed. Just as Du Chaillu had used the language of a hunt to describe his approach to an Obongo village, Stanley only meets and converses with pygmies whom his soldier-porters succeed in "capturing." In the narrative of his last journey through central Africa, *In Darkest Africa,* Stanley describes a "splendid capture of pigmies," including four women and a boy.

> The monkey-eyed woman had a remarkable pair of mischievous orbs, protruding lips overhanging her chin, a prominent abdomen, narrow, flat chest, sloping shoulders, long arms, feet turned greatly inwards and very short lower legs, as being fitly characteristic of the link long sought between the average modern humanity and its Darwinian progenitors.[22]

Later Stanley would regret such descriptions since they provided ammunition for Darwinists. In an article written for *Scribner's Magazine* in 1891, the year after publication of *In Darkest Africa,* Stanley wrote:

> One of the most frequent questions put to me since my return from Africa is: "Is the pigmy a real human being?" Another is: "Is the pigmy capable of reasoning?" And another is: "Do you think he can argue rationally about what he sees; or, in other words, has he any mind at all?" And whenever I hear such ques-

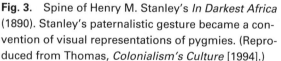

Fig. 3. Spine of Henry M. Stanley's *In Darkest Africa* (1890). Stanley's paternalistic gesture became a convention of visual representations of pygmies. (Reproduced from Thomas, *Colonialism's Culture* [1994].)

tions I mentally say: "Truly, I see no difference between the civilized man and the pigmy! For if the latter could but speak his thoughts in a dialect familiar to me, there is not the slightest doubt that he would have asked me, 'Can the civilized man reason like us men of the forest?'"

For the benefit of such of your readers as take an interest in pigmy humanity, I have taken the trouble to write this article, that they may have a little more considerateness for the under-sized creatures inhabiting the Great Forest of Equatorial Africa. They must relieve their minds of the Darwinian theory, avoid coupling man with the ape, and banish all thoughts of the fictitious small-brained progenitor supposed to be existing somewhere on land unsubmerged since the eocene period. For there is no positive evidence as yet that man was otherwise than he is to-day, viz., a biped endowed with mind.[23]

Like Du Chaillu, Stanley included a list of detailed measurements on the first mature pygmy man he encountered, including data on his height, head size, leg length, and so on—sixteen measurements in all.[24] It was an era of passion for bodily measurement, and travelers did their part to contribute to the great scientific endeavor, even when—as with Stanley—they questioned the theories informing the practice. It was the beginning of the reign of science over the body, the shift from a theological regard for the deviant body to the contemporary pathological or teratological view. According to Leslie Fiedler, who discusses this shift in *Freaks: Myths and Images of the Secret Self,* unusual bodies (the extremely small or large, the disabled, the hermaphroditic, the twinned, etc.) were once regarded as signs of divine vengeance or instruments of the devil in the Euro-American tradition. This view gave way to a racialist-imperialist one in the Victorian period. Deviant bodies were then considered lower stages on an evolutionary ladder, akin to the lower races (Africans, Asians, and others). Fiedler argues that the racialist-imperialist view spawned two myths: the myth of the missing link and the myth of devolution. The imperialist view gradually gave way to the teratological view that characterized the twentieth century. This is the current medical view that unusual bodies represent anomalies that can be corrected through science. Accomplishing this, as physicians and scientists at the turn of the century knew, would require first a notion of the limits of normality; studies were launched in the second half of the nineteenth century to gather millions of physical measurements on U.S. citizens. At the same time that Paul Du Chaillu was measuring the heights of pygmies in Africa, American Civil War physicians were using elaborate devices to measure every dimension of the soldier's body (see fig. 4). Citizens themselves were enlisted in the great crusade, encouraged by physicians to maintain records of their own and their children's physical growth.

Stanley supported the view that pygmies were fated to vanish, and he invented a complete history for the pygmies, suggesting that in prehistoric times, approximately twenty or thirty centuries before the Egyptians built their pyramids, the ancestors of the pygmies lived in comfortable circumstances. "There has been a degradation," he wrote, "from a former happier state." This degradation, simultaneously physical and social—or recognizably social through physical signs—occurred because superior nations or tribes dispossessed the pygmies. The result

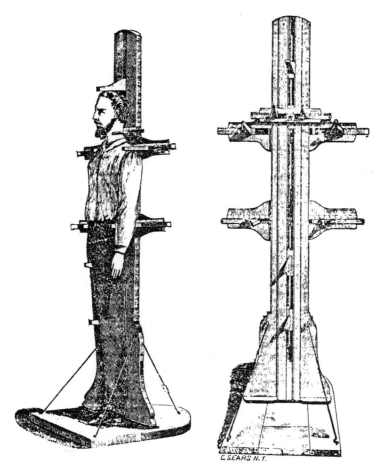

L. SEARS N.Y.

Fig. 4. B. A. Gould's Andrometer. Numerous devices were invented in the nineteenth century to measure American bodies for purposes of racial classification and comparison. Gould's was a particularly thorough one. (Reproduced from *Investigations* [1869].)

was that the pygmies were "obliged to retreat, . . . to take refuge in swamps or woods, to wander and seek a precarious subsistence in regions least likely to invite pursuers."[25] The banishment to inhospitable regions, along with inbreeding, accounted for the physical deterioration of the group. To Stanley, the pygmies were not the missing link but a lesson to opponents of imperialism: "where there is no progress, there must be decay."[26]

A series of turn-of-the-century travel narratives by American and English authors depicting pygmies followed Stanley's *In Darkest Africa*. Virtually all sought to capitalize on popular interest in the pygmies. They included *In Dwarf Land and Cannibal Country* by Reverend Albert

Lloyd (1900), *The Negritos of Zambales* by William Allan Reed (1904), *Tramps Round the Mountains of the Moon* by T. Broadwood Johnson (1908), *Pygmies and Papuans: The Stone Age Today* by the biologist A. F. R. Wollaston (1912), and *On the Trail of the Pigmies* by Father Leonard Vanden Bergh (1921). These narratives reinforced many of the ideas propagated by Du Chaillu and Stanley. The image on the spine of Stanley's *In Darkest Africa,* for example, exerted a powerful influence on later visual representations of pygmies; most authors followed the tradition with their own images of whites draping their arms paternalistically over pygmy shoulders (see fig. 5).

A somewhat different approach was taken in a photograph from the U.S. Department of the Interior's ethnological survey on the pygmies of the Philippines (Reed's *Negritos of Zambales*), reflecting the role that reports of pygmies played in U.S. imperialism (see fig. 6). Taken during vigorous Filipino resistance to American occupation of the Philippines, the photo, like the paternalistic illustration on Stanley's book spine, uses stature as a code for Euro-American evolutionary advancement. In his recent book *Bodies and Machines,* Mark Seltzer has suggested that the physical culture movements of the turn of the century presumed "not merely that the individual is something that can be made but that the male natural body and national geography are surrogate terms."[27] The photograph illustrates the link between the body and geography even more vividly. The print was part of a national self-image of progressive growth, explicitly physical and implicitly geographical; vigorous expansion of the nation's borders in the tradition of manifest destiny, the photo suggests, would find correlative expression in the bodies of the nation's citizens.

Like the image of Stanley embracing the pygmy, Reed's photo invokes an iconic tradition of benevolent paternalism. As Henry Louis Gates has suggested, a "central motif of nineteenth-century American art is a sculpted tall white male (often Lincoln) towering above a crouched or kneeling adult or adolescent slave, in the act of setting them free."[28] The photo in Reed's *Negritos of Zambales* reflects the more detached position that white Americans took regarding dependent races following Reconstruction. As John Haller explains, Spencer's notion of the survival of the fittest found support from European and American world travelers in Africa as well as scientific reports in the United States on the supposedly declining numbers of blacks in both continents, allowing many Americans to arrive at the conclusion (equally a wish) that blacks were doomed to perish. Political policies of "Segregation and disfranchisement . . . were not means of achieving eventual equality or for that matter, even complete separation; rather, they were first steps toward

Fig. 5. Leonard John Vanden Bergh, "Father, Mother and Godfather." Following in the iconographic tradition of Stanley's imperialist paternalism, Vanden Bergh embraces pygmies in this illustration from his travel narrative. (Reproduced from *On the Trail* [1921].)

preparing the Negro race for its extinction."[29] At the turn of the century, images like Reed's did not purport to resolve the great debate over whether benevolent paternalism would help uplift an inferior race or simply oversee its demise in a compassionate manner. Stature merely functioned as a token either of superiority or inferiority, progress or degeneration.

Fig. 6. William Allan Reed, "Plate Showing Relative Height of American, Mixed Blood, and Pure Negrito." This photo illustrates how the tall, progressive American man was shown to stand at the top of a racial hierarchy. Geographic, imperialist expansion was thereby linked to physical growth. (Reproduced from *Negritos of Zambales* [1904].)

Later travel narratives also endorsed Du Chaillu's view that pygmies were the missing link between human and ape, emphasizing the similarities between the pygmies and monkeys. "They live as close to the monkey as it is possible for human beings to do," wrote Vanden Bergh. The upper jaw of the pygmy, he claimed, "is almost apelike," the "face in profile [has] a monkeyish expression," and "to perfect the apish appearance their foreheads are low and slanting in the extreme." "Were it not for that splendidly formed miniature human body," he concluded, "one would imagine that their protoparent, at least, was allied to the monkey."[30] Reed emphasized the "abnormal length of the arm of the Negritos," suggesting that it was "an essentially simian characteristic." He also commented on the big toe that supposedly extended inward on some Aeta (the Filipino pygmies). "It may be caused by a constant practice of the tree climber—that of grasping a branch between the large toes and the other toes. I have seen Negrito boys who would use their feet in this respect as well as they used their hands."[31] First encounters with pygmies were commonly depicted as successful hunts. Like Stanley, Wollaston was not surprised when his Papuan guides chased and captured two pygmies; his only wonder was that the captives refused to escort him to their village.[32]

Like Stanley and Du Chaillu, later writers deferred to the myth that pygmies were an ancient race who had once flourished but had dwindled over time in the face of competition from superior races. This myth was eminently compatible with that of the missing link. Vanden Bergh, for example, wrote that the pygmy Mambuti of the Congo "claim to be the oldest race in the eastern part of the Congo. Originally they had a free hand in this country and roamed about as they pleased." Then, according to Vanden Bergh, the Wanyari, a race of larger people, moved in. The Mambuti still engage in guerilla warfare with the Wanyari, but "they dare not fight their foe in the open, where they know that they would not be the equal to the Wanyari."[33]

Both myths—that the pygmies were the missing link and that they were an ancient race doomed in a Darwinian struggle—explained the low stature of the pygmies as a racial phenomenon rather than an environmental one. Both depended on the assumption that the pygmies' small size was hereditary and had likely persisted for thousands of years. The existence of communities of people of very small size helped solidify arguments mounting in the middle and late nineteenth century that stature was primarily a racial and hereditary trait rather than an effect of nutrition and environment. Not everyone agreed with this view, and many travel writers contradicted themselves on this point, offering environmental explanations as well as hereditarian ones for the small size of the pygmies. Vanden Bergh, who had suggested that the Mambuti were the oldest race in the eastern Congo, also offered an explanation for the major preoccupation of U.S. readers: "Who shall dare to attempt to give . . . a reason for their undersized stature?" His answer: "Lack of sunlight and prowling about in a stooping position are the most forceful arguments."[34] Environmental theories, on the other hand, did not necessarily contradict racial ones; the conflict between monogenists and polygenists of the first decades of the nineteenth century had been resolved by a synthesis of environmentalist and racialist views. The various races had evolved from a single ancestor (the monogenist view), so the synthesis went, but as humans migrated around the globe they adapted to the various environments. What emerged were long-standing, relatively fixed races with varying physical appearances, intellectual capacities, and behavioral characteristics. Moreover, the races that developed later—that is, the white races—presented evolutionary advancements over the earlier races. The races could be arranged on a hierarchy as easily as they could if one assumed multiple origins (the polygenist view). Thus, the environment and heredity both played important and determining roles.[35] One can see indications of this synthesis in Henry Stanley's explanation for the short stature of pygmies. He too regarded them as an ancient race, yet they were also a "stock of ordinary humanity"— albeit a degenerated one. Both hereditary and environmental factors contributed to their small size, including three thousand years of isolation and inbreeding, a "precarious diet" lacking "gluten and saccharine," and the absence of sunshine.[36]

Ethnologists, Anthropologists, and the Pygmies

In his preface to Vanden Bergh's *On the Trail of the Pigmies,* the ethnologist Robert H. Lowie praises the author for filling a void in American books dealing with central Africa. He reminds readers that Vanden Bergh is not a professional anthropologist and therefore "he is merely pronouncing personal views such as may spontaneously suggest themselves to any traveler." The value of the work, he says, is that it provides firsthand accounts of African peoples and customs, particularly the Mambuti and two other groups who have not been the subject of previous writings. As a professional ethnologist, Lowie provides expert confirmation for Vanden Bergh's accounts: "some of the facts here described that may seem strangest to a lay reader are amply vouched for by independent authority."[37] Vanden Bergh himself expresses concerns in his introduction about the fact that audiences at lectures had been skeptical of his reports. Whether he or his publishers solicited the preface from Lowie is unclear from the text; what is certain is that Vanden Bergh himself went to the trouble of lugging photographic and motion picture equipment—"a scientifically certain register"[38]—along with him on his travels. He includes numerous photographs in *On the Trail of the Pigmies* to ensure that his reports will be believed, and the motion pictures of his travels evidently achieved some commercial success. Lowie predicts that the book will also be a popular success.

It was common for travel narratives to receive sanction from experts; American natural history societies financed Du Chaillu's initial journeys, and experts supported his controversial lectures, fending off attacks on their authenticity. But the relationship between travelers and ethnologists was fragile. Ethnologists often depended on travel writers for firsthand accounts of distant peoples. Travelers, however, were often untrained in the theories and practical techniques of ethnology. In addition, their reports often met with skepticism from readers, a phenomenon that was exacerbated by freak shows and sensationalized renderings of travel narratives whose basic themes resembled ethnological theories closely. Travelers, on the other hand, often depended on the endorsement of professionals for their written accounts when they faced criticisms from readers. Explorers did not necessarily have the time or leisure to acquaint themselves with the intricacies and contested theories of current academicians. If their writings failed to accord with current ethnological and anthropological theories, however, important scientific authorizations might be withheld. Moreover, the scientific community was often an important audience for the work of explorers; when Du Chaillu returned from his travels, for example, he lectured first to natural historians and other scientists.

By the end of the nineteenth century, ethnologists and anthropologists had usurped the authority of travel writers over the pygmies. Because few experts had firsthand acquaintance with any groups designated pygmies and therefore relied on information from explorers, however, the scientific and academic communities colluded with travel writers to reinforce the various assumptions, conjectures, myths, and theories about pygmies.

Encounters with groups of small people in several locations in the latter half of the nineteenth century prompted ethnologists to revise their system of racial classification. This was a process that had been under way for decades, as ethnologists turned from one physical characteristic to another in a vain effort to find a consistent criterion for racial comparison.[39] In addition to those groups encountered in Africa, including the Obongos, Akka, Wambutti, Batwa, and San, American and European travelers and scientists met communities of small people in the Andaman Islands, New Guinea, Malaysia, and the Philippines. These groups supposedly shared not just small stature but other physical traits, including hair texture and skin color. As a result of purported differences in height between these and other black communities, ethnologists divided the Negro race into two groups: the tall (or true) Negroes and the "pygmy blacks," or Negritos (sometimes called Negrillos). In addition to short stature, Negritos were generally thought to share characteristics that rendered them the most primitive of all people, including a hunting lifestyle rather than an agricultural one, an inability to manufacture metal implements, rudimentary languages, and small cranial capacity.[40] Despite their wide dispersal and lack of linguistic affinity, small black-skinned communities as far away as the Philippines and western Africa were thought to share a common origin. Ethnologists considered the Negritos "negroid to an intense degree,"[41] an exaggeration of the Negro type.

As stature became an important element in classifying "pygmy blacks," ethnologists and anthropologists increasingly relied on the physical characteristic as a criterion of race for other groups. "Among the various characters by which the different races of men are distinguished from one another, *size* is undoubtedly one of considerable importance," suggested Professor Flower, director of the Natural History Department of the British Museum, in a lecture titled "The Pygmy Races of Men" delivered at the Royal Institution in 1888 and reprinted in *Nature* the same year.[42] He divided all races into three groups, the tall (averaging 5'7" and above for men), medium, and short (whose men averaged below 4'11").[43] He argued that heredity rather than environment dictated the average stature of a race. "That the prevailing size of a race is a really deep-seated, inherited characteristic, and depends but little on outward conditions, as abundance of food, climate, &c., is proved by well-known facts," he asserted.[44] The British ethnologist Augustus H. Keane, vice president of the Anthropological Institute and author of the major works of ethnology in the English language during the second half of the nineteenth century, concurred. He included stature among his physical criteria of race, along with skin color, hair texture and color, skull shape, facial shape, appearance of the nose, eye color, and so on. In his book *Ethnology* (1895), Keane claims that stature is "more uniform amongst the lower than amongst the higher races," and he too segregated the races into three groups, including tall, middle-sized, and short races.[45] William Z. Ripley, author of *The Races of Europe* (1899), professor of sociology at Massachusetts Institute of Technology, and lecturer in anthropology at Columbia University, regarded stature as third in importance among the criteria used to distinguish European racial groups. He assigned first and second place to head form (measured by cephalic index) and pigmentation (or hair and eye color). He placed stature third because he believed environment did have an influence on the trait and a greater influence than it had on the other characteristics. Still, Ripley plotted average statures on a map of Europe and noted that stature tended to increase as one traveled northward from Italy to the British Isles and Scandinavia. This, he argued, "points indubitably to racial law." Ripley agreed with Keane that the influence of environment was greater among savages: "The advance out of barbarism is evidenced generally by a progressive increase in the stature of the population as an accompaniment of the amelioration of the lot of the masses."[46] As Ripley's remark suggests, even those who addressed the environmental influences on physical size were nevertheless subject to the increasingly racialized rhetoric surrounding physical characteristics at the turn of the century.

In addition to influencing ethnological and anthropological methods of classification, the existence of pygmies contributed significantly to debates over the cradle of humanity. With the discovery of the Java man, or *Pithecanthropus erectus,* in 1891 and the widespread acceptance of the fossilized being as the missing link, the notion of pygmies as the missing link gave way in anthropological discourse of the 1890s and later to a notion of pygmies as the earliest true human beings. The presence of small, dark-skinned peoples in Africa and scattered islands south of Asia suggested to late nineteenth-century anthropologists that they were remnants of a broadly dispersed race from a continent that had been submerged sometime in the geological past. Dr. Henry Schlichter, in his article "The Pygmy Tribes of Africa" in 1892, suggested that "various problems of history and anthropology would find an easy solution" if the theory of a land mass submerged below the Indian Ocean were proved conclusively.

> One of these problems is the origin of that peculiar branch of the human race which includes not only the Bushmen and the Hottentots, but also the Melanesians, Andamanese, and the now extinct aborigines of Tasmania. . . . Darwin's, Huxley's, and Haeckel's investigations about the origin of man point to the antiquity of these races, and although our information is at present too meagre and fragmentary to warrant us to compare the Negrillos and Negritos with the anthropoides, yet the diminutive size, and especially the development of the lanugo with many African pygmies, e.g., the Obongo, Wambutti, and Akka, are of the highest interest in this respect.[47]

Most anthropologists accepted the theory of the submerged continent and used it in defense of their placement of the Negritos at the bottom of the evolutionary tree. Professor Flower, after reviewing current knowledge about the pygmies, observes that the information

> opens a still larger question, and takes us back to the neighborhood of the south of India as the centre from which the whole of the great Negro race spread, east over the African continent, and west over the islands of the Pacific, and to our little Andamanese fellow subjects as probably the least modified descendants of the primitive members of the great branch of the human species characterized by their black skins and frizzly hair.[48]

Augustus Keane went further, constructing a complete evolutionary tree for Homo sapiens whose first branch is the "Generalised Negro," which Keane subdivided into the African Negro and two Negrito branches, the Indo-Oceanic and the African Negritos (see fig. 7). Although the illustration does not indicate it clearly, Keane believed that the Negritos preceded "the Negro proper," thus making them the earliest human beings: "the Negrito appears to represent the primitive stock, from which the Negro diverged later." The primeval home of all three sub-branches was "the Indo-Austral region now flooded by the Indian Ocean."[49] Prior to the flood, or concurrent with it, the Negroes and Negritos migrated to Africa, India, Malaysia, and Australia.

The views of Schlichter, Flower, and Keane are characteristic of a period under the sway of evolutionary theory, which supplanted the previous and more theological arrangement of living beings according to the Great Chain of Being. The similarities and differences between the two worldviews are evident when one compares nineteenth-century representations of pygmies with the most important treatment of pygmies in Europe prior to the nineteenth century. In 1699, Edward Tyson published the results of his anatomical research on a pygmy. Dr. Tyson's penchant for long-winded book titles was matched only by the grandiosity of his personal title. Tyson, according to the frontispiece of his book, was a "Fellow of the College of Physicians and the Royal Society, Physician to the Hospital of Bethlem, and Reader of Anatomy at Chirurgeons-Hall." One hardly needs to read further than the (slightly abridged) title of his book to understand his position on the subject of pygmies: *The Anatomy of a Pygmie Compared with that of a Monkey, an Ape, and a Man, to Which Is Added a Philological Essay Concerning the Pygmies . . . of the Ancients, Wherein it Will Appear That They Are . . . Either*

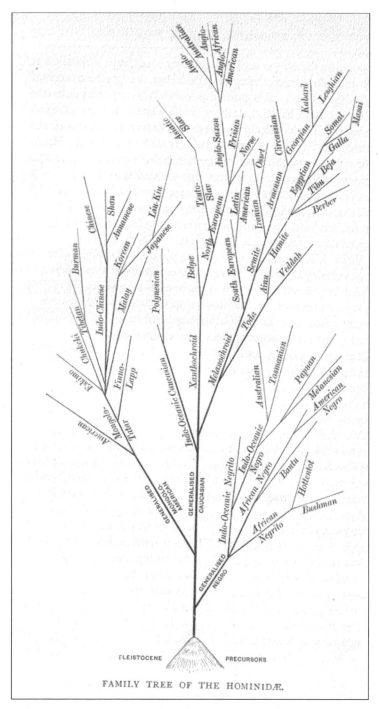

Fig. 7. Augustus H. Keane, "Family Tree of the Hominidae." Keane placed the pygmies, or "Negritos," at the bottom of his evolutionary tree. Anglo-Saxons occupied the top branch. (Reproduced from *Ethnology* [1909].)

Apes or Monkeys, and Not Men, as Formerly Pretended. Believing that all things, from minerals to plants to animals to humans to angels, existed in an orderly and hierarchical "Chain of Creation," Tyson regarded the pygmies as an "intermediate Link between an Ape and a Man," a place that Tyson called "the Nexus of the Animal and Rational."[50] His conclusions are less surprising when one knows the circumstances of his investigation. The honorable Dr. Tyson, as it turns out, was the hapless victim of a fraud; the body he dissected was actually that of a chimpanzee. At any rate, his error had lasting consequences, encouraging later scholars to view pygmies as less than human.[51]

When the shift from the belief in the Great Chain of Being to the theory of evolution occurred, an opportunity existed for a nonhierarchical worldview to develop throughout the scientific community as well as in American and European cultures generally. As it is understood today, evolution simply means change in a species over time, and Darwin's theory of evolution by natural selection, in today's parlance, means that the environment acts on the natural variation within a species, favoring those individuals better adapted and increasing the chances that they will pass on their genetic material to the next generation, resulting in a species better adapted to its environment. There is nothing inherently hierarchical or teleological about the concepts. Unless we believe that adaptation to one's environment is an especially valuable trait, a clam is equal to a person; if we wish to be judgmental, in fact, we might argue that clams, by virtue of having existed longer than humans, are probably better adapted to their environments and therefore more advanced than people. But the ideological inertia of the Great Chain of Being was difficult to overcome, and one of the consequences was that the vertical, hierarchical language persisted in the new worldview. This language affected attitudes toward animals as well as people, influenced as it was by racialist thinking in the nineteenth century. Thus, Darwin wrote both of "high animal species" and "low animal species" as well as "high races" and "low races" of humans.[52] The hierarchical worldview—implicitly judgmental, implicitly teleological and progressive—persisted through a metaphor of verticality. The vertical image of the evolutionary tree[53] (see fig. 7[54]) supplanted the previous vertical image of the Great Chain of Being, and the notion of progressive increments of upright posture among human ancestors produced images of human evolution, still common today, that depict gradual increases in height over time (see figs. 8 and 9). Similarly, the language of "uplift," used so often to describe the needs of African Americans, Native Americans, and other subjugated groups, shared in this vertical metaphor. The worldview underlying these images transferred readily to a belief that taller races were more advanced and superior to shorter ones, a belief that was bolstered by the fact that the shortest groups of people on earth were black. Every writer who addressed the pygmies regarded them as the earliest, most primitive, and most inferior humans, regardless of whether the writer accepted the submerged land mass theory that provided tenuous geographic corroboration for the view. A metaphor in science "does not directly present a preexisting nature but instead helps 'construct' that nature," explains Nancy Stepan. "Nature is seen via the metaphor and the metaphor becomes part of the logic of science itself."[55]

One scientist who rejected the submerged land mass theory was Armand de Quatrefages, professor of anthropology at the Paris Museum of Natural History and one of the most respected anthropologists of his time. His book *Les Pygmées,* published in 1887 and translated into English in 1895 after his death, was responsible more than any other work for legitimizing and popularizing the scientific study of the pygmies. De Quatrefages never accepted Darwin's theory of evolution; he was a committed monogenist, a believer in the unity of all people and their origin in a special act of divine creation. In *The Pygmies,* he argues against the prevalent notion of pygmies as the missing link. That the book was among de Quatrefages's last works suggests how important the defense of the pygmies as legitimate human beings was in the late 1880s

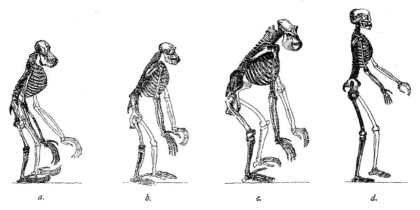

a.   *b.*   *c.*   *d.*

MAN'S PLACE IN NATURE (after Huxley).   *a. Orang; b. Chimpanzee; c. Gorilla; d. Man.*

Fig. 8. Augustus H. Keane, "Man's Place in Nature." Keane depicted the evolution of Homo sapiens as involving a progressive increase in height and upright posture over time. Note that this convention required significant manipulation of the facts: the height of the chimpanzee (fig. b) had to be exaggerated considerably to make it appear taller than the orangutan (fig. a). (Reproduced from *Ethnology* [1909].)

Fig. 9. An enduring legacy of nineteenth-century science is the depiction of human evolution as a progressive increase in height over time.

for those opposed to evolution; it also indicates how common by this time was the notion of pygmies as half human. "Almost unanimously," he writes, "the populations we have been considering have been regarded as very low in the scale of humanity. In regard to the Mincopies [the people of the Andaman Islands] particularly, some *savants,* of great merit otherwise, seem to have believed that here finally one had placed his hand upon the missing link between man and the ape. We have just seen that this is not so; . . . the Negritos show themselves true men in all things and for all things."[56] As evidence for his claim, de Quatrefages describes recent successes in educating pygmy children in a European manner. He describes the work of Dr. Brander of the Andaman Islands hospital, for example, as well as the case of two Akka children, Tebo and Chairallah, purchased by the Italian traveler Miani in central Africa and bequeathed to the Society of Italian Geography. Raised and educated by an Italian count, the two Akkas became the subjects of intense anthropological scrutiny. De Quatrefages reviews the numerous scientific treatises addressing their development. "In class they have shown themselves superior to their European schoolfellows of ten or twelve years old," he writes. Consistent with prevalent views about Africans being arrested in development at an earlier age than European children, however, he adds that "The general character of the two Akkas has remained sensitive, impulsive, and recalls that of our children." Still, the scholastic accomplishments of the two Akkas suffice to prove, "in spite of their little stature, their long arms, their pot-bellies, and their short legs, that the Akkas are indeed really men; and those who have thought to find in them half apes should by this time be fully disabused."[57]

De Quatrefages was among the first to unite the disparate communities of small, dark-skinned peoples under a common designation. Setting the precedent for later authorities, he divided the pygmies into two subgroups, the Negritos or Oriental pygmies (those who lived in the Philippines, New Guinea, the Andaman Islands, etc.) and the Negrillos or Occidental pygmies (those who lived in Africa). In justifying the unification of such scattered peoples, de Quatrefages opposed the submerged land mass theory. He contended that the pygmies migrated by boat from one island to the next. Anticipating and conceding to the objection that the pygmies would have found it impossible to populate areas already inhabited by larger, stronger races, de Quatrefages concludes that they must have been the first inhabitants. "In seeing these Negritos almost always confined to the mountains of the interior of islands of which other races occupy the plains and shores, it is difficult not to consider them as having been the first occupants."[58] In this belief particularly, one can see the limits of ethnological debates about the pygmies. Of all authorities, he came the closest to admitting the equality of the pygmies with Europeans, at least in terms of their common humanity.[59] Yet he shared numerous assumptions with his contemporaries. Among these was the assumption that the pygmies were an ancient race and the first inhabitants of many regions. This assumption had two effects: it justified the special racial classification invented by European and American anthropologists and imposed on disparate peoples without a common language and without a sense of their own unity; and it discredited the apparently common popular belief in the degeneracy of the pygmies.[60] De Quatrefages accepted the view that the pygmies "were formerly more numerous; that they formed populations denser and more continuous; that they have been crowded back, separated, divided, by superior races." Consequently, he also agreed that the pygmies were destined for extinction. "Wherever one meets with them to-day one sees them retreating, and often dying out."[61]

As the remarks of the eminent French scientist suggest, anthropologists and ethnologists perpetuated and contributed to the major themes of travel writers. They painted the pygmies as "living fossils."[62] "They are the least modified representatives of the people who were, as far as we know, the primitive inhabitants of a large portion of the earth's surface, but who are now verging on extinction," wrote Flower.[63] Anthropologists regarded the pygmies as everywhere displaced, hunted, and endangered. Like many of his colleagues, Flower represented this as a progressive natural process of racial competition. In the Andaman Islands, for example, the Negritos were now located only in the most inaccessible regions, according to Flower, exterminated and replaced by the Mongolian and Malay races to the east and the Aryans to the west, "exactly as, in the greater part of the Pacific Ocean, territory formerly occupied by the aboriginal dark, frizzly-haired Negroid Melanesians has been gradually and slowly invaded by the brown Polynesians, who in their turn, but by a much more rapid process, are being replaced by Europeans."[64] Ethnologists, like travel writers, emphasized the similarities between pygmies and primates. "Negritoes both in the western and eastern sections of the Negro domain, present more pronounced simian features than any other living human groups," wrote Augustus Keane. "Thus are found still persisting or till lately surviving . . . several groups, which approach nearest both to the higher simian and to the earliest known human types."[65] By the end of the nineteenth century, anthropologists were convinced that the pygmies were as distant in relation to white people as one could get and still remain human. "The typical white man differs enormously from the typical Negrito, so much so that they would have to be regarded as separate species but for the intermediate forms in actual existence," wrote Keane. "Here then we have in any case a range of evolution scarcely less than that which is covered by the transition from Gibbon to Orang to Chimpanzee."[66] Lurking quietly behind their remarks, of course, was an image not of pygmies but of whites.

Spectacles of Progress: Pygmies and the World's Fairs

Perhaps no other events contributed more spectacularly to the American national self-image than the world's fairs of 1893 and 1904. Attracting a combined total of more than 46 million people (Paul Du Chaillu was among the visitors at the 1893 Chicago fair), the Chicago World's Columbian Exposition and the St. Louis Louisiana Purchase Exposition were erected on a colossal scale. The Columbian Exposition boasted the world's largest edifice, the Manufactures and Liberal Arts Building. Roughly twice the area of the Great Pyramid, the Manufactures Building covered forty-four acres and housed both the world's largest telescope and the enormous Otis Elevator, capable of lifting sixty passengers 220 feet in one minute. Supplying power to the Chicago fairgrounds was the massive Allis two-thousand-horsepower engine, the largest of its kind in the world—until a three-thousand-horsepower generator at the same fair displaced it. Regarding the Allis engine as a sign of things to come, one souvenir guide to the World's Columbian Exposition predicted that "we must regard the whole electrical display at the Fair as only the seed of the mighty growth of the future, and we will look back with surprise upon the time when with reverence and awe we looked upon the huge bulk of the Allis Engine and thought that human ingenuity had here reached its limit."[67] The St. Louis World's Fair was itself the largest spectacle of its kind; commemorating the Louisiana Purchase, which more than doubled the size of the United States, the grounds covered approximately twelve hundred acres, almost twice the acreage of the Columbian Exposition. The fair was so large that medical professionals warned neurasthenic patients to avoid it or risk mental collapse.[68] The exposition exhibited the world's largest clock, 112 feet in diameter and twenty-five hundred pounds in weight; it measured the passage of time until the arrival of a promised American utopia, when a host of heavenly angels would descend to herald the new era accompanied by the deafening tones of the world's largest organ. For those who wondered at the apparent harmony maintained in arenas that encompassed so many of the nations and peoples of the world, both fairs quietly provided the answer. The Columbian Exposition housed the German-manufactured, 132-ton Krupp Gun, the largest cannon in the world. American engineers outdid the Germans in the Louisiana Purchase Exposition with their 141-ton cannon, the largest in its day.

The world's fairs of 1893 and 1904 were the most vivid articulation of a cult of size that gripped the United States at the turn of the century. As Phillips Verner Bradford and Harvey Blume have suggested, "The new sources of energy, the surge in technology, the infusion of population, the rapid pace of change in every area [of American life] led to an acute case of giantism."[69] Pygmies at the Louisiana Purchase Exposition stood in vivid contrast to all that represented American modernity and civilization. Small, black, nonindustrial, and expected to vanish, they were outcasts in a spectacle that celebrated the enormous utopian city of the future and its technological wonders. Like other nonwhite bodies displayed at turn-of-the-century world's fairs, the bodies of pygmies were deployed to elide class differences among fairgoers.[70] At a time of open class warfare in the United States, directors of the fair hoped to shift attention away from differences of class and to emphasize instead the gulf between white spectators and the nonwhite races on display. What the fairs said about racial differences—with an analogy to class differences that was implicit—was that they would eventually vanish in the march toward human and social perfection. Under the prudent management of dominant whites, those races fit for civilization would be brought into the congress of self-governing, progressive peoples; the unfit—and here is where the pygmies served an especially important function—would be left behind in the wagon train of human advancement.

Robert Rydell argues that world's fairs constituted "symbolic universes," affirming the visions of the dominant social and political powers and helping to shape widespread beliefs about the national destiny. The fairs at the turn of the century coincided with a national search for order precipitated by a rapidly expanding and diversifying American population with heavy immigration, cyclical industrial depressions, and bloody class conflicts. Increasing awareness of the world's diversity as a result of improvements in transportation and photography augmented anxieties about the place of Americans in the global community. "To alleviate the intense and widespread anxiety that pervaded the United States," writes Rydell, "the directors of the expositions offered millions of fairgoers an opportunity to reaffirm their collective national identity in an updated synthesis of progress and white supremacy that suffused the blueprints of future perfection offered by the fairs." The idea of progress endorsed by the expositions was rooted in the value of expansion, both economic and geographic, consolidating the power of the financial elite and endorsing a vision of the United States as a major imperial power. Celebrating the conquests of the Western powers, "World's fairs . . . put the nations and people of the world on display for comparative purposes," popularizing evolutionary ideas about race and progress.[71]

If the fairs reinforced the hegemony of ruling class interests, as Rydell argues, one of the things that the corporate and industrial sponsors of the fairs were especially eager to demonstrate was the economy of scale, a topic of considerable controversy at the turn of the century. As technology advanced rapidly, industrial production outstripped market demands. This was a major source of the cyclical depressions, mass unemployments, and bloody class conflicts to which Rydell refers. Captains of industry claimed that the elevated production was necessary and beneficial. In *The Gospel of Wealth,* for example, Andrew Carnegie argued that increases in production benefited consumers by lowering the costs of essential goods. "Cheapness is in proportion to the scale of production," he wrote in 1900. "Everywhere we look we see the inexorable law ever producing bigger and bigger things. . . . [The] overpowering, irresistible tendency toward aggregation of capital and increase of size in every branch of production cannot be arrested or even greatly impeded. . . . instead of attempting to restrict either, we should hail every increase as something gained."[72] If it could be shown that investment in massive structures like those at the world's fairs was not only essential to conveying the spirit of the times but also remunerative—if, in other words, the powerful appeal of an enormous spectacle could, in a sense, artificially induce market demands—then capitalists would have a powerful piece of evidence supporting their views on the economy of scale.

The revenues from the 1893 Chicago World's Fair did not sustain the capitalist position, unfortunately. The exposition plans continually outpaced the investments; what began as a $5 million project ended up costing approximately $22 million. The exposition company repaid its debts and recovered enough in ticket sales to pay off bondholders, but the revenues amounted to about a quarter of the total cost of the fair. The only real winners were local businesses in the host cities.[73] That did not prevent commentators from proclaiming the merits of large-scale enterprise, however. Lyman Gage, writing for *Cosmopolitan,* used familiar vertical metaphors to sanction the costs of the fair. "If we find financial sacrifice and loss to be the outcome," he wrote, "the wise man who sees far will find in the moral and social uplift thus obtained more than an abundant recompense." An authorized souvenir guide to the Chicago fair suggests how the exhibits at the exposition were designed to convince fairgoers of the economy of scale regardless of the financial balance sheets. Regarding the mammoth Allis engine, the guide explained that "the demand for current for lighting purposes and power" has been so great "that engines have had to be made larger and larger, to meet the growing need. It has been clearly demonstrated that there is economy in large engines."[74]

A second function of turn-of-the-century world's fairs, also suggested by Rydell, was to demonstrate that U.S. captains of industry could effectively manage an increasingly disordered and diverse world. If the United States was to be an international power, it would need to control and manipulate gigantic, complex forces. Science would have to cooperate with industry in the mastery of ever expanding and often unruly powers. Global multiplicity was managed and systematized in two ways at the fairs: through massive exhibits of industrial progress and through ethnological exhibits. Both arranged, classified, and reigned in new, refractory, and potentially threatening disorder. In the process, both conceived of the American nation and the American body as large and continuously expanding.

Fairgoers found evidence of the might of industrialists, among other places, in the electrical switchboard at Machinery Hall in the World's Columbian Exposition. The switchboard consisted of two parts: a "dynamo-board" that was twelve feet high and forty feet long and a "feeder-board" that was nine and a half feet high and seventy-one feet long. Together, the constituent boards controlled fifteen thousand horsepower of electricity. The entire board was elevated like a factory manager's platform, forcing fairgoers to look up to the structure. (The forced upward gaze was a common technique at the fairs, where objects were so huge.) Because the switchboard was too high for a single person to

Fig. 10. Switchboard in Machinery Hall, Chicago World's Fair (1893). The switchboard controlled the power at the exposition and was designed in a manner that harmonized with dominant aesthetics at the fair. (Reproduced from Shepp, *Shepp's World's Fair Photographed* [1893].)

manipulate effectively, designers added stairs to allow access to the upper tier. The height of the switchboard suggested that taller workers would be capable of operating the device most efficiently. As Andrew Carnegie wrote, "The bigger [industrial] system grows bigger men, and it is by the big men that the standard of the race is raised."[75] The height of the switchboard also enhanced the sense of hierarchy; it allowed several technicians to operate the device, who in turn were implicitly managed by higher, unseen authorities (see fig. 10, in which three workers are stationed at the switchboard). If the hierarchy was not plain enough, a single button pressed by President Cleveland initiated the flow of electrical power that signaled the opening of the World's Columbian Exposition at noon on May 1, 1893; clearly the switchboard and its operators could be subordinated to higher controls. Arched windows provided light above the switchboard, giving the room a cathedral-like aura and suggesting that the powers of industry served Christianity and its partner Civilization. (Machinery Hall was an odd but revealing combination of cathedral spires, Roman columns, and arched train station ceilings.) "It is wonderful," rhapsodized an authorized souvenir guide to the fair, "that Electricity, that great giant which in a single moment could destroy the earth and its entire population, can be controlled and held in the strictest discipline by such a machine."[76]

As Carnegie's remark about big men suggests, the debate over the industrial economy of scale impinged upon ideas of the body and reinforced racial hierarchies. Michel Foucault has argued that political and economic terrain is always mapped onto the body. "The body is . . . directly involved in a political field; power relations have an immediate hold upon it; they invest it, mark it, train it, torture it, force it to carry out tasks, to perform ceremonies, to emit signs. This political investment of the body is bound up . . . with its economic use; it is largely as a force of production that the body is invested with relations of power and domination." He adds that "power produces knowledge"; economic and political systems combine to determine "forms and possible domains of knowledge."[77] The world's fairs played a significant role in the political investment of the body and the shaping and public dissemination of knowledge about it.

Bodies were most thoroughly manipulated, measured, assessed, and classified by the Departments of Anthropology at the World's Columbian and Louisiana Purchase Expositions. Some of the most influential names in the field participated in the world's fairs: Franz Boas, Otis Mason, Thomas Wilson, Ales Hrdlicka, W. J. McGee, Frederick Starr, Frederic Ward Putnam, and others. The Department of Ethnology at the Chicago fair managed both the Anthropology Building and the Midway Plaisance. The general goals of the Department of Ethnology were to "show the physical and other characteristics of the principal races of men"[78] and to illustrate the progress of civilization. The mission was compatible with the main theme of the fair. According to G. Brown Goode, assistant secretary of the Smithsonian Institution and organizer for the fair, the World's Columbian Exposition would demonstrate "the steps of progress of civilization and its arts in successive centuries, and in all lands up to the present time."[79] In accord with this mission, the Anthropology Building contained an ethnological museum, archaeological exhibits, and an anthropometric laboratory. The laboratory displayed the methods and tools for the comparative study of the races. There intrepid fairgoers could submit to extensive bodily measurements, and they could use the results to compare themselves to statues of the ideal American male and female housed at the laboratory. The statues, dubbed Adam and Eve, measured 5'8" and 5'3" respectively. A writer describing them for *Scribner's Magazine* felt "reassured" that in height, weight, and strength the male statue "exceeds the average of any other nation, even England."[80] An essayist writing for *Camera Work* argued that the tall female figure approximated universal beauty ideals. "At certain periods of history, when a community is steadily growing in prosperity and power . . . , the average of women is by nature taller than at others. We in America have arrived at such a period. The ideal type of the American woman belongs to one of the most perfect expressions of beautiful womanhood."[81] The physician D. A. Sargent, who designed the statues from data on young men and women at elite colleges in the East, hoped that his research might be useful to factory superintendents, prison custodians, school officials, civil service examiners, and others who managed the physical regimes of dependent classes.[82] A founder of the physical education movement, Sargent believed that "better bodies" were necessary to "insure a higher development of the individual, and advance the conditions of the race." "Our neglect to apply the truths of modern science to the nurture of human beings as well as to the rearing of dumb animals is one of the most serious obstacles in the path of human progress," he wrote.[83]

If the Anthropology Building presented the highest types of humanity and encouraged fairgoers to attend to their own self-improvement, the Midway Plaisance displayed the spectrum of races beneath the highest types. A mixture of circus entertainment, concession stands, and global villages, the Midway contained representatives from numerous "savage" groups, including Samoans, Javanese, American Indians, and Dahomeyans of Africa, as well as national pavilions from Europe and elsewhere. Although the Midway was intended primarily as a revenue-generating facility, the Department of Anthropology claimed that the living exhibits had legitimate scientific value.[84] "On the Midway Plaisance," wrote Frederick Starr for *Popular Science Monthly,* "one may study ethnography practically."[85] Robert Rydell argues that the exhibits provided evidence of the evolution of man from the most primitive to the most civilized. He cites fairgoers who claimed that races in the Midway were arranged hierarchically, with the Teutonic and Celtic races closest to the White City, Asians and Middle Easterners in the center of the Midway, and the "savage" races, the Africans and North American Indians, at the far end.[86] "The best way of looking at these races," wrote the contemporary literary critic Denton Snider, "is to behold them in the ascending scale, in the progressive movement; thus we can march forward with them starting with the lowest specimens of humanity, and reaching continually upward to the highest stage."[87] More recently, Meg Armstrong has challenged this view, arguing that no clear sequence existed in the arrangement of nations. She agrees that the Midway complemented and reinforced the basic message of the ethnology exhibits (i.e., that races exist in a hierarchy topped by whites), but she suggests that the chaotic jumble of foreignness in the Midway served to steer visitors toward a modern cosmopolitan sensibility underwritten by racial stereotypes.[88] In any case, if the treatment of nonwhites at the fair prompted African American newspapers and leaders to protest the event,[89] it simultaneously encouraged white visitors to disregard their own class differences by imagining race as the fundamental criterion of human classification and progress. Shifting attention from class rifts was undoubtedly an important goal during one of the most serious financial panics in the nation's history and just a year after the Homestead Strike. The exposition company itself experienced these class tensions, negotiating over two hundred strikes during the construction of the fair.[90]

Anthropology held an even more esteemed position in the Louisiana Purchase Exposition of 1904. Fair directors decreed that the science would play an integral role in the organization of the exposition, and the Department of Anthropology was the most extensive of any world's fair.[91] F. J. V. Skiff, an organizer for the St. Louis fair, explained in his opening day speech that the exposition would indicate "the particular plans along which different races and different peoples may safely proceed, or in fact have begun to advance towards a still higher development." Science, he believed, could help create a "citizen capable of progress."[92] "The aim of the Department of Anthropology at the World's Fair," said the director of the department, W. J. McGee, "will be to represent human progress from the dark prime to the highest enlightenment, from savagery to civic organization."[93]

McGee ordered special agents to acquire races from around the world for display. In particular, he hoped to gather representatives from racial types least familiar to Americans. "The physical types first chosen for representation were those least removed from the subhuman or quadrumane form, beginning with the pygmy aborigines of Africa," he wrote. "In stature and proportions, in color and cranium, in form of face and function of limb, the little people of the African jungles are commonly considered to approach subhuman types more closely than any other variety of the genus *Homo*." McGee believed that Americans and pygmies occupied opposite ends of a social and evolutionary spectrum. Claiming that people were distributed among four planes of development—savagery, barbarism, civilization, and enlightenment—McGee wrote that "man reveals the stages of his own progress from a primal state to the condition of highest enlightenment—from the low level of . . . the African pygmies to the elevated plane of constitutional government."[94] All tests, whether social or physical, indicated that Americans occupied the highest plane. Physically and mentally, they were descended from select British, a race already "preeminent in perfection of body and brain." By the eighteenth century, Americans had surpassed their forebears; tested and improved by the fires of natural selection on the frontier, "American pioneers were, even before the Revolution, the strongest people of the world in body and brain." One piece of evidence for this preeminence was the alleged height of Americans: "in stature the American leads the world," claimed McGee.[95] "The rough-riding scion of enlightenment appals [sic] by his superior stature the puny soldier of unprogressive monarchism."[96] To those who questioned the "Law of Human Progress" at a time of tremendous class antagonism, political corruption, and imperialism in the United States, McGee responded that their worries would be unfounded "on the plane of enlightenment" toward which all classes and races were tending: "the peoples of the earth are steadily rising from plane to plane with the certainty of ultimate union on the highest of the series."[97]

McGee sent Samuel Phillips Verner, a former U.S. missionary, to gather eighteen pygmies from the interior of Africa. Newspapers heralded the journey as "one of the most difficult and dangerous of all World's Fairs assignments"; the pygmies, who stood "at the bottom of the [evolutionary] ladder," were in the inaccessible heart of an unhealthy and hostile continent.[98] Verner succeeded, returning amid much fanfare with five pygmies. Other groups represented at the Pike, the fair's amusement area, included Patagonian "giants," Ainus from Japan, and various Native American groups (both Geronimo and Chief Joseph were present). At a special reservation devoted to the newest acquisition of the U.S. empire, various ethnic groups from the Philippines were also represented, including the pygmies, or Negritos, of William Allan Reed's report for the U.S. Department of the Interior. The Negritos of the Philippines, according to McGee, were similar to the African pygmies in physical characteristics and evolutionary position.[99] According to most accounts, the pygmies—especially the African pygmies—were the most popular group at the fair. The world's fair prize committee awarded Verner their grand prize for bringing the African pygmies to the exposition, and fairgoers who were interviewed seventy-five years after the event said the Filipino and pygmy exhibits were among the most memorable.[100] Since few if any Americans had seen pygmies prior to the fair, the *St. Louis Post-Dispatch* issued a fact sheet about this group that was eliciting "the greatest interest of any race specimens shown."[101] The fact sheet reinforced the myths of travelers and anthropologists, including the ideas that the pygmies were an older race than the "true Negroes" and that they occupied a large part of Africa before the intrusion of the larger blacks.

Fig. 11. Pygmies at the St. Louis World's Fair (1904). Several small men from central Africa, including five Batwa pygmies, accompanied Samuel Verner to the 1904 Louisiana Purchase Exposition. (Reproduced from Bennitt and Stockbridge, *History of the Louisiana Purchase Exposition* [1905].)

A word about the Patagonian "giants" may be in order here. In Victorian Europe and the United States, the Patagonians were widely regarded as the tallest living people. McGee deliberately sought to juxtapose the Patagonians and the pygmies at the St. Louis fair to suggest that the entire spectrum of races was gathered at the spectacle. The label "giants," always applied to the Patagonians, derived from exaggerated physical descriptions of the group by European sailors (including Magellan and others) in the sixteenth, seventeenth, and eighteenth centuries. When Victorian travelers and anthropologists made the effort to measure selected Patagonians, they found that the Patagonians were not giants at all but simply relatively tall people. Charles Darwin, for example, claimed that the height of Patagonian men was about 6'0";[102] others suggested lower figures, such as 5'9" or 5'10". Reviewing the available data, a French author named Dastre, in an article translated from the *Revue des Deux Mondes* and reprinted in the *Smithsonian Annual Report* and the *Scientific American Supplement* in 1905, suggested that Patagonian men averaged about 1.78 meters—approximately 5'10". "There actually exists . . . no population or ethnic group of giants," concluded Dastre.[103] Giantism, he claimed, was a disease and not a racial condition.

European and American ethnologists, along with the general public, typically regarded the Patagonians, like the pygmies, as low on the scale of humanity, although to my knowledge they never suggested that the Patagonians were the elusive missing link. Representations of Patagonians usually included begrudging admiration of their physical qualities coupled with denigration of their social and intellectual characteristics—essentially the manner in which tall Africans were generally represented. It may seem contradictory that anthropological authorities, who typically regarded increased height as an effect of civilization, ranked Patagonians low on the evolutionary ladder. In fact, the position of anthropologists was contradictory. As Nancy Stepan explains, contradictions were not unusual in nineteenth-century science and reflected the power of metaphorical thinking (in this case, the power of vertical metaphors) in scientific theory formation. "Because a metaphor or analogy does not directly present a preexisting nature but instead helps 'construct' that nature, the metaphor generates data that conform to it, and accommodates data that are in apparent contradiction to it," she writes.[104] Those who claimed that increased height was an effect of civilization tended to ignore the evidence of savage peoples who were, according to the limited data available in the nineteenth century, relatively tall. This was true of William Z. Ripley, for example.[105] As discussed earlier, Ripley believed that the advance out of barbarism produced an increase in stature.[106] He ignored data indicating the tallest people on earth were Native Americans. Others regarded tall savages as exceptions to the general rule that placed Europeans and Euro-Americans at the top of the hierarchy of height. Herbert Spencer, for example, acknowledged the tremendous diversity in stature among primitive peoples reflected in the differences between Patagonians and pygmies. Nevertheless, he concluded that "the evidence taken in the mass implies some connexion between barbarism and inferiority of size."[107] J. H. Baxter, an army colonel and physician who compiled and interpreted statistics for the U.S. government on the physical measurements of Civil War soldiers, considered it an "ethnological axiom that blonde races are characterized by their superior statures." In *Statistics, Medical and Anthropological of the Provost-Marshal General's Bureau* (1875), Baxter included a table of the mean statures of various racial groups. First on the list were undifferentiated Indians living in the United States, followed by whites of the United States, the Norwegians, and the Scottish. "It is true that the list is headed by the aboriginal Indians," noted Baxter. He considered the possibility that the small number of available measurements indicated a biased selection of taller individuals on the part of researchers. More likely, he reasoned, the case of the American Indians "is really an exception"[108] to the general ethnological rule. S. Henry Dickson, a physician and instructor at the Jefferson Medical College in Philadelphia, agreed. As he explained in an 1866 article appearing in the *American Journal of the Medical Sciences* and presenting height and weight statistics for men and women in American schools, Dickson believed that moral and intellectual traits "have been found always closely if not indissolubly connected with physical form." "It is possible," he continued, "that some few exceptions may be pointed out, as in the Patagonians and some of the islanders of the Southern Seas; but these may be accounted for, when all the facts are known, by the efficient force of causes not yet appreciated."[109] While Victorians found circuitous ways to accommodate contradictions to their theories regarding the link between height and civilization, it was probably the inherent inconsistencies that prevented scientists from seizing upon stature as the single and definitive sign of the advancement of white people, just as every other physical trait (including head size and shape) was ultimately jettisoned in the fruitless search for a criterion of racial classification and hierarchization. And while the alleged height of the Patagonians and other American Indians undermined an axiom that ethnologists hoped to proclaim regarding the beneficial effects of civilization, the pygmies still served to illustrate that black-skinned races were at the bottom of the evolutionary hierarchy. This point may help to explain why the pygmies drew more attention at the St. Louis World's Fair than did the Patagonian "giants." The pygmies confirmed Euro-American prejudices; the Patagonians confounded them.

As with the World's Columbian Exposition, the Department of Anthropology at the Louisiana Purchase Exposition had its own building containing a museum and laboratory. Anthropologists at the laboratory measured the height, head size, strength, acuteness of vision and hearing, and other characteristics of willing fairgoers as well as the inferior races present at the exposition. They also conducted intelligence tests on the pygmies and other nonwhites. As always, anthropologists sought physical evidence of the superiority of whites. "African Pygmies," concluded the scientists administering the intelligence tests, "behaved a good deal in the same way as the mentally deficient person, making many stupid errors and taking an enormous amount of time."[110] Frederick Starr, translator of *The Pygmies* by de Quatrefages, offered lectures on the fairgrounds; students at the University of Chicago received academic credit for attending his sessions. The Department of Physical Culture offered its own lectures in the science of physical training, including such topics as "Muscular Movement and Human Evolution." While American and European athletes competed in the first Olympic

Games of the Western Hemisphere, the Department of Anthropology organized a segregated test of "interracial athletic records."[111] The "Anthropology Days" pitted the various savages against one another—and implicitly against the white athletes—in contests of archery, running, shot put, javelin throwing, and tug-of-war. An official history of the Louisiana Purchase Exposition expressed disappointment over the performance of the uncivilized contestants, including the pygmy who completed the one-hundred-yard dash in a time "that can be beaten by any twelve-year-old American school boy."[112]

The world's fairs reinforced prevalent views about the need for white oversight of nonwhite races. W. J. McGee believed that the dominant Caucasian race was expanding across the globe, eliminating unfit races and elevating those capable of adopting civilization and self-rule. "Perfected man is over-spreading the world," he said. "Human culture is becoming unified, not only through diffusion but through the extinction of the lower grades as their representatives rise into higher grades." As the paragon of physical and social development, Americans had a unique responsibility in the "White Man's burden."[113] "It is the self-taxed task of the white giant to lift darker fellows to liberty's plane rapidly as the duller eyes can be trained to bear the stronger light," he wrote.[114] At the fair, McGee intended to illustrate the management of nonwhites in the Model Indian School Building. "Indian school work," he said, is "America's best effort to elevate the lower races."[115]

If the directors of the Louisiana Purchase Exposition sought to demonstrate the path by which inferior races might be civilized, they also revealed how some races would inevitably be abandoned in the march toward utopia. Soon after the fair opened, a controversy arose over the ethnological exhibits in the Philippine Reservation. The reservation was divided into sections compatible with historical and evolutionary time lines. Some areas illustrated the former Spanish control of the islands; others showed the effects of the more recent U.S. occupation, comparing the advances of past imperial powers with those of the present. Specific areas of the reservation were devoted to exhibits of the progressive ethnic types in the Philippines: the Christianized Visayans, the Islamic Moros, the savage Bagobos and Igorots, and the "monkey-like" Negritos. While the entire reservation had the official approval of the U.S. government, early press reports about the nakedness of the Igorots and Negritos troubled the Roosevelt administration, which was in the midst of an election campaign against an anti-imperialist Democratic Party that would soon have a platform claiming the Filipinos were "inherently unfit to be members of the American body politic."[116] The Roosevelt administration, whose imperialist policy depended on the view that the Filipinos could be civilized, was concerned that the lack of clothing would "depreciate the popular estimate of the general civilization of the islands."[117] The administration urged the Philippine Exposition managers to dress the Igorots and Negritos in less objectionable clothing such as silk pants. The press publicized the affair, and a cartoonist for the *St. Louis Post-Dispatch* lampooned the administration's efforts with a drawing of William Howard Taft, the administration member most involved in the incident, chasing an Igorot with a pair of trousers. Eventually bowing to pressure from anthropologists like Frederick Starr and the exposition's Board of Lady Managers, who insisted that the value of the exhibit lay in genuine presentation of native culture and lifestyle, the administration relented. Meanwhile, the Philippine Exposition Board overcame the administration's dilemma by drawing sharp distinctions among the Filipino communities, claiming some were capable of adopting civilization and some were not. The Igorots, said an official souvenir guide, "are susceptible of a high stage of development, and, unlike the American Indian, will accept rather than defy the advance of American civilization."[118] The fair managers demonstrated the docility of the Igorots during a visit from President Roosevelt, when a class of Igorots in the reservation's mission school regaled him with a version of "My Country 'Tis of Thee." On the other hand, official guides claimed that the Negritos "will eventually become extinct,"[119] and images of a Negrito labeled "Missing Link" circulated in official fair documents. The episode may have been the clearest example of the way evolutionary and anthropological assumptions about pygmies contributed to U.S. imperialism.[120]

How did the pygmies respond to the fair? Unfortunately, written records from the perspective of the pygmies are scarce. Thanks to the excellent research of Phillips Verner Bradford and Harvey Blume, a great deal, relatively speaking, is known about Ota Benga. Although he remained in the United States after the St. Louis fair and learned English, none of Ota's written documents have survived. He and the other African pygmies did leave a record of parody at the fair, however. As the official history of the fair remarked, "the Pygmies were often very capricious and troublesome."[121] Reluctant to participate in Anthropology Days, for example, they made a mockery of several running events by going in every direction but toward the finish line. They participated enthusiastically only in the mud fight. They also parodied the passion for marching bands by forming their own chaotic and undisciplined marching team. And they attempted to play a practical joke on spectators by organizing a public dance that ended with a wild charge on the assembled crowds, complete with war whoops and brandished bows

Fig. 12. "Missing Link," St. Louis World's Fair (1904). This photograph of a Filipino pygmy, dubbed "The Missing Link" by fair organizers, was used to demonstrate the primitiveness of pygmies and to suggest that the group was doomed to extinction.

and arrows. The result was disastrous, however, as the alarmed fairgoers took them seriously and charged back, stopping only when blockaded by a state military regiment.[122]

If the Chicago and St. Louis World's Fairs encouraged fairgoers to regard themselves as participants in a physically immense, progressive, and vital national endeavor, the massive scale of the fairs also threatened to turn spectators into pygmies, to overawe and overwhelm them with the impersonal and intimidating forces of their surroundings. Describing the effect on the viewer of the assembled technology in Machinery Hall at the Chicago World's Fair, an authorized souvenir guide suggested that "man seems a weak being beside these forceful servants of his."[123] The immensity of the fairs threatened to make visitors feel insignificant amid the throngs and in relation to powers that were apparently beyond the control of any single individual, perhaps even of the mighty capitalists. As one visitor to the St. Louis fair reported, "the fatigue entailed in seeing the Exhibition was simply enormous." "The Fair is a succession of mental shocks," said another.[124]

Susan Stewart suggests some ways in which architects and exhibit designers might have negotiated the competing interests of the world's fairs. In her book *On Longing: Narratives of the Miniature, the Gigantic, the Souvenir, the Collection,* Stewart argues that the miniature is a metaphor for the subjectivity of the bourgeois individual and the gigantic is a metaphor for the authority of the state, technology, and corporate power.[125] Stewart connects the miniature to the cultural Other, and she claims that miniaturization is typically an act of domestication, transcendence, containment, control, and domination. "Although the miniature makes the body gigantic," she writes, "the gigantic transforms the body into miniature, especially pointing to the body's 'toylike' and 'insignificant' aspects." She suggests that miniatures like dollhouses, miniature books, and spectacles employing pygmies—all increasingly popular in the Victorian period—allow Western bourgeois subjects to internalize the transcendent, dominant perspective of the state. Gigantic structures that elevate people and afford a distant gaze offer a similar "illusion of mastery," granting subjects a semblance of power and authority. Structures like the Eiffel Tower (built for the 1889 world's fair in Paris and inspiring an abandoned plan for a similar structure, the Proctor Tower, at the Chicago fair) speak simultaneously "to an abstract transcendence above and beyond the viewer and the possibility that the viewer can . . . approach a transcendent view . . . himself or herself."[126] Stewart's remarks seem especially relevant to turn-of-the-century world's fairs when we consider that the nineteenth century was the heyday for monument building and that the viewing platform, a structure that confers upon visitors the transcendent gaze, is a characteristic of almost all large nineteenth-century monuments, especially those built in the last third of the century.[127] (The Statue of Liberty, built in 1886, is another noteworthy example of a colossal monument with a viewing platform.)

The carefully orchestrated juxtaposition of the miniature and the gigantic at turn-of-the-century world's fairs suggests that something like the techniques Stewart describes was utilized there. Machinery Hall at the World's Columbian Exposition, for example, contained not only seventeen acres of massive industrial machinery but also a tiny engine weighing half an ounce, built by a sixteen-year-old boy. In the same

Fig. 13. Ferris Wheel, Chicago World's Fair (1893). The world's first Ferris wheel offered fairgoers at the Columbian Exposition a panoramic view of the fairgrounds.

building, the Otis Elevator offered visitors a panoptic view of the whirling machinery below, helping them to apprehend an array of technology that would take days to view otherwise. One of the most popular attractions at the Chicago fair was the world's first Ferris wheel, designed and constructed by George Ferris of Pennsylvania. Ferris was a master of the techniques of miniaturization and gigantification, not only taking his beloved Ferris wheel to the St. Louis fair but also designing a scale model of Chicago's White City for display at later fairs. Like the scuttled Proctor Tower, the Ferris wheel was designed to outdo the Eiffel Tower of the Paris Exposition. Weighing over fifty-six tons, the axle alone was the largest single piece of steel ever cast in the United States, and the tallest derrick that had ever been built hoisted it into place. The Ferris wheel could carry more than a thousand passengers to a height of

250 feet. Significantly, the ride was located in the Midway Plaisance; in that location, it elevated patrons above the ethnological exhibits and offered them a comprehensive view of the lower races assembled below. Thus, the Ferris wheel complemented the efforts of the exposition directors to separate the spectators from the performers, providing the physical experience of elevation and mastery that corresponded to the anthropological placement of the white U.S. citizen at the apex of evolutionary and social development. It helped encourage white fairgoers to enter and participate in a social process of hierarchization and domination.

In an era of increasing corporate control in the United States, the new industrial powers depended on the willing participation of bodies for the rapidly increasing manufacture of goods; the urgent need for bodies is testified by the massive scale of immigration at the turn of the century. Perhaps the best way to achieve the complicity of the masses was to adopt a carrot-and-stick approach: to suggest, on the one hand, that those who refused or were unable to join the progressive march toward human perfection would be abandoned on the way and, on the other hand, that those who journeyed forward and upward would themselves be afforded a giant's gaze, the transcendent perspective of the corporation or state. Thus, fairgoers who remained at the base of the Ferris wheel were forced to look upward and feel themselves shrink in relation to the colossal inventions of a dawning era. For a price, spectators could enter the machinery, feel themselves lifted to a higher plane, and experience for themselves the panorama of invention and progress represented by the buildings and landscape of the world's fair.

CHAPTER 2 • The Height of Civilization
Science and the Management of Stature

As the previous chapter suggested, anthropological theories claiming that pygmies were the earliest human beings who preceded and then retreated from the larger races gained widespread acceptance at the turn of the century. Not surprisingly, anthropologists of the 1890s turned to Europe and the United States in a search for evidence of ancient pygmy inhabitants. The researches of two scholars in particular, Robert Grant Haliburton of Canada and Professor J. Kollmann of Switzerland, offered tantalizing evidence of ancient pygmy peoples in the West. Studies on the pygmies of Europe reinforced many of the messages in discourses surrounding the pygmies of Africa and Southeast Asia. In addition, these studies suggested that short stature in contemporary whites was potentially racial in origin, an atavistic sign of primitive ancestry. In this respect, the studies of Haliburton and Kollmann contributed to growing convictions in the second half of the nineteenth century that physical stature was determined by race rather than other factors previously regarded as paramount, including climate and wealth.

With stature assuming new importance in racial classification, and with suspicions aroused concerning the possible influence of an ancient pygmy race on contemporary white races, scientific authorities in the United States were anxious to determine the character and origin of the national body. The search for pygmies in Europe and the United States coincided with a shift in emphasis among Euro-American anthropologists from the periphery of empire to the metropolis.[1] This shift was reflected, for example, in attention to the classification of European races in the last decade of the nineteenth century. In 1899 William Ripley defied contemporary U.S. scientific dogma when he argued that whites were not all one race. "It may smack of heresy to assert, in face of the teaching of all our text-books on geography and history, that there is no single European or white race of men; and yet that is the plain truth of the matter," wrote Ripley in his influential book *The Races of Europe*.[2]

The inward-turning gaze of science at the turn of the century reflected growing concerns about urban problems in the United States. The U.S. Census of 1890 (the same year that witnessed an end to the major Indian wars) indicated that there was no longer any discernible line between very sparsely settled and completely unsettled land, a fact that was widely interpreted to mean that the frontier had officially closed. The U.S. Census of 1920 revealed that for the first time more

Americans lived in cities than in rural areas. As cities expanded, they also diversified. In 1910, after twelve years of record levels of immigration, one-seventh of the U.S. population was foreign-born; between 1870 and 1920 one out of three industrial workers was foreign-born.[3] When immigration restrictions during World War I reduced the flood of new arrivals, industrialists seeking new sources of cheap labor encouraged blacks to migrate from the rural South to the urban North. The disturbing (to many resident white Americans) diversification of American cities was compounded by national policies that grudgingly admitted American Indians and African Americans into the country's citizenry. Class divisions, as the next chapter explains, were simultaneously widening. Thus, the growing anxieties about urban problems were bound up with anxieties about the destiny and unity of the nation at a time of intense class conflict and racial-ethnic diversification.

Richard Slotkin has explained how the metaphors and rhetoric once applied to Indians and other "savages" shifted to urban groups at the turn of the century in the United States. As labor conflicts escalated into violence, and as violent conflicts with Indians on the frontier diminished, a "language of reversible metaphors"[4] developed in which characteristics once attributed to savages were shifted to the urban poor and racial categories were used to make sense of class conflicts. With the presumed closing of the frontier in 1890, moreover, the promise of open space to the West that had always been held out as a safety valve for urban discontent was believed to be eliminated. This problem was compounded by a prevalent view that current immigrants—primarily southern and eastern Europeans—were less hardy, both racially and because of the effects of industrial labor, than earlier colonists and so were unfit for life on the frontier. An era of "coercive paternalism" set in, according to Slotkin. Reigning ideologies suggested that the proletariat needed to be managed by "patrician intellectuals" and that there would be a permanent and rigid distinction between manager-owners and workers founded in differences of natural endowment. Since "dependent classes" could not be removed to the West, political authority in the metropolis had to be maintained by a "soldierly ruling class" based on the Civil War model of the regiment, the slave era model of the plantation, and the Indian wars model of the reservation. The view that there were hidden savages within white communities contributed to arguments opposing universal suffrage and led to the termination of Reconstruction and the Peace Policy in Indian country.[5]

More recently, Matthew Frye Jacobson has suggested that Slotkin's argument was more literally true than he realized. The description of the urban poor as savages, with all the attendant vices, was often meant in more than metaphoric and rhetorical terms. As scientists began to dissect the white race into a hierarchy of sub-races (such as Ripley's Teutonic, Mediterranean, and Alpine races), working-class immigrants began to be conceived as members of a distinct, separate race from native-born whites—a race whose fitness for the responsibilities and prerogatives of self-government was debatable.[6]

In this climate of shifting rhetoric and concerns, the techniques of racial classification developed by anthropologists for use on the peripheries of empire were increasingly used to address metropolitan problems. The methods of anthropometry—the detailed measurements of the human body used to classify and rank the races—were turned on urban communities, immigrants from Europe, and the men, women, and children of the Republic. Underlying the metropolitan uses of anthropometry were concerns about the hereditary transmission of physical, intellectual, and moral traits; the division of people into identifiable and manageable classes; and the destiny of the American people relative to other nation-races. (These were, of course, precisely the issues that had driven anthropometric investigations of distant or subjugated savage races.) Studies of human growth and the size of the human body—focusing on European-descended men, women, and especially children—proliferated dramatically in the final decades of the nineteenth century and the first decades of the twentieth. As the characteristics of savages were attributed to the urban poor, myths about the pygmies shifted to other groups who resembled the pygmies in physical size: women, reputedly small immigrants like Jews and southern Italians, the feeble-minded (who were found to be smaller on average than their peers), and children (particularly small children). These groups were increasingly regarded as more primitive, limited in their intellectual capacities, unfit for the complex modern world, and in need of special management by their superiors.

This chapter explores the treatment of physical stature within metropolitan scientific discourses at the turn of the century. It begins with a discussion of the search for traces of ancient pygmy races in Europe. Next it presents a brief history of Euro-American ideas about height. In the United States, two institutions were primarily responsible for investigating stature: the military, which investigated the heights of Civil War and World War I recruits, and the medical establishment, which investigated the growth of American children. I examine the first of these institutions next. I explore the earliest U.S. height studies—those derived from Civil War statistics—and the military-scientific tradition that these investigations spawned. I end with a detailed account of the major tradition of U.S. height studies: researches on the growth of children.

The Dwarf Era: Pygmies in Europe

Once anthropologists like de Quatrefages and Flower theorized that the pygmies represented vestiges of a once widely dispersed primitive race, it was not long before researchers began seeking evidence of this ancient race in Europe and the Americas. Robert Grant Haliburton and Professor J. Kollmann, who advanced the case for pygmies in these continents, argued that stature was a racial trait, that a race of small humans preceded the taller races, and that the extinction of the primitive pygmy race indicated a progressive history in which superior races continually displaced and eliminated inferior ones. The work of Haliburton in particular offered the tantalizing possibility that shortness among Anglo-Americans could be explained as a degenerate return to a pygmy ancestor who was, in fact, not white at all but a member of a distinct and inferior race.

Among scientists, Haliburton, a Canadian lawyer, was best known for his lectures and publications on the "dwarf races" of the Atlas Mountains of Morocco and the Pyrenees of Spain, where he traveled between 1887 and 1893. Based on scant information—testimonies from European colonists and travelers who claimed to have seen very small people, superstitions among Moors regarding a race of little people, and arcane linguistic coincidences—Haliburton theorized in 1891 that remnants still existed in Europe and North Africa of "a moribund race of dwarfs, who in the recesses of mountains are slowly going through the process of *dying out* through falling vitality just as many centuries ago their race must have died out on the plains of Europe and Asia."[7] Based on his research, Haliburton concluded that humanity began with a "Dwarf Era"[8] noted for "a migration of African dwarfs to the European countries bounding on the Mediterranean, and as far east at least as Moscow."[9]

To defend himself from critics who suggested that the individuals he had heard about were short for pathological, not racial, reasons, Haliburton argued that two types of "dwarfs" existed: "racial dwarfs" and dwarfs who were "stunted and deformed in infancy through disease."[10] Racial dwarfs, he argued, were an ancient group displaced by taller races. Extensive mating between racial dwarfs and taller peoples produced moderately short populations. Unusually short individuals were another sign of historic intermating, representing atavistic returns to dwarf ancestors: "We may safely put down to *atavism* cases of the Tom Thumb type hitherto looked on as 'freaks of nature,'" wrote Haliburton.[11]

> Atavism is very enduring and far-reaching; and generations, or rather centuries, are not able to efface the traces of racial, or even family traits, as can be seen in family portraits. The lead-

ing family in a district in Andalucia were surprised and
shocked at finding one of their number grow up, in all respects,
a typical Congo dwarf. No doubt they had inherited a remote
Nano strain [Haliburton's term for the ancient dwarf population
of Spain], which, though long forgotten, had at last asserted
itself.

Size, complexion, etc., point out the places where a dwarf
race must have once existed. The Black Forest is probably one of
these, for the manager of the German Dwarf Operatic Company
says he was able there to secure the services of several very
small dwarfs. Their relatives were generally of large stature. In
Sicily, and parts of Italy, Professor Sergi discovered and measured a surprisingly large number of dwarfs, many of which
were as small as Congo dwarfs.[12]

While Haliburton admitted that short stature could indicate the
effects of disease (neither he nor his critics considered that shortness
might represent normal variation in human stature), he nevertheless
argued that goiter and cretinism, conditions generally regarded as pathological, were really racial in origin for the individuals he classified as
racial dwarfs.

Despite the cordial reception of his ideas at the Orientalist Congress
of 1891, where he received a medal for his researches, and despite the
fact that eminent scientists like Karl Pearson eventually adopted his terminology of "racial dwarfs" and "pathological dwarfs,"[13] Haliburton's
theories were controversial. By the 1890s, few doubted the existence of
pygmies in Africa and Asia, but many remained skeptical that pygmy
races had ever existed in the heart of Europe. Haliburton's speculations,
however, received apparent vindication from the findings of Professor J.
Kollmann, an anatomist and anthropologist from Basel. In 1895 Kollmann reported on an archaeological dig in Switzerland that uncovered
two distinct sets of Neolithic human bones. One set of bones, Kollmann
claimed, was characteristic of "normal-sized persons of the usual European type"; four smaller skeletons resembled the bones of an Andaman
Islander housed at the Anthropological Museum of Florence. Kollmann
concluded that pygmies must have coexisted with a taller race at one
time in Switzerland.

In defending his claims, Kollmann, like Haliburton, cited the recent
work of the Roman anthropologist Sergi, who found pygmy skulls in
Sicily with a cranial capacity 400–500 cubic centimeters less than that
of taller Europeans. Sergi asserted that the hereditary influence of the
ancient pygmy populations could still be seen in present-day Sicily,

where small people made up 14 percent of the population, according to military enlistment records. Based on Sergi's researches and his own archaeological findings, Kollmann posited the following theory:

> To the normally tall varieties of man in Europe must be added smaller types which have their own special place in the anthropological system. These latter are not simply diminutive examples of the tall races, but represent a distinct species of mankind, which is found in several localities dispersed over the globe. We are led to believe that these smaller varieties have been the predecessors of the now predominant types of full-sized humanity.[14]

By this time, in 1895, Kollmann was simply restating the theories of prominent anthropologists like de Quatrefages and Flower, although he was also providing vital support for their views. But his and Sergi's suggestion that one could trace the racial history of a group by using data on body size resonated significantly with contemporaneous investigations among physicians and anthropologists on the heights of various national groups, both within the United States and abroad. Kollmann concluded his study with a call for more research: "I beg to direct the special attention of anatomists to these diminutive individuals wherever an opportunity may occur of examining any of them."[15] As discussed later in this chapter, physicians in the United States were happy to oblige Kollmann. But before turning to that subject, a brief history of the Euro-American treatment of stature will prove useful.

From Climate to Race: The Treatment of Stature in the Euro-American Tradition
Stature before the Nineteenth Century

Physical size had not always been racialized in the manner typical of the turn of the century. Before the second half of the nineteenth century, European scientific authorities were less likely to cite race or nationality as determinants of adult height than other factors, including climate, behavior, and diet. Virtually all authorities shared the view, however, that shortness represented a deficiency of some kind. Many theorists sought to identify factors that determined a person's height in order to offer programs for increasing the stature of children, a tradition that U.S. physicians in the late nineteenth and early twentieth centuries preserved.

Among the ancient Greek authorities, Hippocrates addressed growth and stature most directly. He suggested that the controlling factors in adult height were "the variability of the weather, the type of country and the sort of water which is drunk."[16] Aristotle added that premature sexual intercourse and excessive exercise could stunt human growth.[17] Aristotle was concerned about the proper growth of Athenian youth both for military reasons (he sought to devise a system of education that would make the young both strong and courageous)[18] and for philosophical reasons related to his notions of beauty. "Beauty implies a good-sized body," wrote Aristotle. "Little people may be neat and well-proportioned but cannot be beautiful."[19]

Two Roman scientists echoed Aristotle's views about the interference of sex with growth. The physician Soranus suggested that "men who remain chaste are stronger and bigger than others,"[20] and the historian Tacitus, who derided the moral degeneration of young Romans, argued that sexual promiscuity in Rome enfeebled and stunted the young of his day. Although he had no firsthand acquaintance with German culture, Tacitus contrasted the enervating luxury of Rome with the barbaric but vigorous civilization of Germany: "The Germans spend all their lives in hunting and war-like pursuits, and inure themselves from childhood to toil and hardship. Those who preserve their chastity longest are most highly commended by their friends; they think that continence makes young men taller, stronger, and more muscular."[21] J. M. Tanner, author of A History of the Study of Human Growth, suggests that Tacitus's views have had an enduring influence in Euro-American science and popular culture. The "Tacitan myth" (as Tanner names it) has three components: the notion that early sex will stunt growth; the idea that northern Europeans are especially tall and vigorous (a concept that played a key role in nineteenth-century views on the so-called Teutonic races and later in Nazi eugenic programs); and the belief that contemporary generations could be smaller than their ancestors as a result of immoral or degenerative practices (an idea that later resonated with biblical dogma suggesting that humans were gradually diminishing in height since the Creation[22]).

In the Middle Ages and the Renaissance, scientific authorities tended to view heat and moisture as determining factors in the growth of the body. Diet—both the kind and amount of food—was particularly important in promoting or inhibiting the body's natural heat and moisture. Scientists like Levinus Lemnius, Francis Bacon, and Hippolyt Guarinoni offered nutritional advice to readers who wished to increase the height of children. Lemnius criticized schoolmasters who fed their pupils insufficient or unwholesome food and drink, preventing them from attaining "personable stature" and suppressing "their natural moisture which requireth continuall cherishing and maintenance."[23] Bacon suggested that growth and stature could be increased "either from the Plenty of the Nourishment; or from the Nature of the Nourishment; or from the Quickning [sic] and Exciting of the Natural Heat."[24] Too much nourishment, Bacon argued, made children fat rather than tall; excessively dry foods diminished stature; and exercise promoted height by stoking the body's natural heat.

Scientists of the seventeenth and eighteenth centuries adapted earlier hypotheses (heat was still regarded as the fuel for growth, for example) while adding new ones of their own. These centuries also witnessed the beginning of the military tradition in height studies, in which scientists colluded with military authorities who favored tall soldiers and sought ways to enhance human stature for military purposes. Johann Stoeller, for example, investigated a variety of factors he considered potentially responsible for growth and stature, including sex, age, region, lifestyle, heredity, air, premature birth, illness, nutrition, circulation, and "the juices of the body and the condition of the bones."[25] Stoeller worked as a personal physician for a Prussian duke during the reign of Frederick-William I. Frederick-William was obsessed with giants, acquiring as many as he could (by kidnapping them when necessary) for his Grenadier Guards, whom he loved to parade for guests and state functions. Stoeller concluded that upbringing played a particularly important role in adult stature and that the effect of rearing was greater than heredity. "Amongst the things which hinder growth I think that an artificially soft treatment and regimen is the greatest," wrote Stoeller. "The more luxurious is the living and upbringing in youth, the more is the sickness and the smaller the growth. . . . Children must not be brought up over-tenderly."[26]

Perhaps the most important arguments concerning body size, with respect to U.S. height studies of the late nineteenth century, were those of George LeClerc, Comte de Buffon. Buffon was among the most influential European thinkers of the eighteenth century, one of the founders of anthropology, and perhaps the most respected naturalist of his day. As with most of his contemporaries, Buffon believed that climate (especially temperature and humidity) was the primary determinant of body size for animals. The quality and abundance of food (especially as they affected the body's natural heat and moisture) also played a role. Buffon believed that the animals and people of the American continents had descended from European forebears and that they had degenerated over time. To support this argument, Buffon suggested that animals common to America and Europe were smaller in America, that animals endemic to the New World were constructed on a smaller scale, that domesticated animals had diminished in size in America, and that the New World contained fewer animal species overall. Buffon attributed these supposed facts to the coldness and humidity of the American continent.[27]

Buffon did not spare the human inhabitants from charges of degeneration. The absence of evidence supporting the diminished height of Native Americans did not deter Buffon from connecting the reputed smallness of American animals to the degeneration of the American people. "Although the savage of the new world is about the same height as man in our world," he wrote, "this does not suffice for him to constitute an exception to the general fact that all living nature has become smaller on that continent." Buffon launched into a tortuous argument in which the diminished moral qualities, sexual organs, and population size all reflected the degeneration of American Indians. The reputedly sparse Indian population corresponded to the diminished size of American animals, he reasoned, and the small population in turn was caused by a diminished sexual capacity and an absence of human affection. "The savage is feeble, and has small organs of generation," wrote Buffon. Indian men "lack ardor for their females, and consequently have no love for their fellow men."[28]

As one might imagine, Buffon's assertions about American degeneracy were hardly pleasing to American intellectuals. Thomas Jefferson was a particularly tireless opponent of Buffon's claims. In *Notes on the State of Virginia* (1785), Jefferson presented detailed tables comparing the weights of quadrupeds in America and Europe. In a sense, Jefferson was the author of the first U.S. investigation of body size. Intended to discredit Buffon's four assertions regarding the size of New World animals, the tables demonstrate that animals in America and Europe are constructed on the same scale. Jefferson opposed not only the evidence Buffon used to support his claim but also Buffon's assumptions regarding the determining factors in body size. The various creatures of God's world, reasoned Jefferson, "received from their Maker certain laws of extension at the time of their formation. . . . Below these limits they cannot fall, nor rise above them. What intermediate station they shall take may depend on soil, on climate, on food, on a careful choice of breeders."[29] In the discussion that follows, Jefferson places particular emphasis on the quantity of food (rather than the type of food, as many of his contemporaries would have done) available to New World animals and people; thus, his arguments anticipated the class-based assertions of early nineteenth-century English and French humanitarians.

With regard to the supposed moral degeneration of Native Americans, Jefferson responded with praise for the character of Indians and a relatively sympathetic discussion of the conditions of their lives, including the famines that they routinely faced and, he said, suppressed their population. More important, he attacked the inconsistency in Buffon's arguments: "if cold and moisture be the agents of nature for diminishing the races of animals, how comes she all at once to suspend their operation as to the physical man of the new world, whom the Count acknowledges to be 'about the same size as the man of our hemisphere,' and to let loose their influence on his moral faculties?"[30] Thus, Jefferson questions the interchangeability of physical and moral qualities that Buffon relies on in his arguments. It was one of the few instances of such intrepid reasoning in the history of Euro-American height studies before 1930.

Jefferson's defense of Indian character was not wholly disinterested, on the other hand. He also contested the extension of Buffon's theories by the French writer and historian Abbé Raynal, who suggested that Europeans transplanted to America had also degenerated. Jefferson's desire to defend colonialism helps explain the energy with which he pursued the debate against the Comte de Buffon,[31] and ironically it may also explain the praise he offers for Native Americans. Like Buffon, Raynal relied on inner character (in this case, intellectual attainments) rather than physical characteristics for his arguments; he suggested that America's failure to produce any men of genius reflected the degeneration of American colonists.[32] Jefferson responded that since the United States had only existed a short time Raynal's accusation was unfair. He also enumerated the geniuses of the nation, including Washington, Franklin, and Rittenhouse.

Despite the intelligence and enthusiasm of Jefferson's rebuttal, he had little success in converting Buffon to his views. More important, both Buffon's assertion about American degeneration and the underlying assumption that declining physical size was a sign of moral decline would continue to haunt U.S. scientists. Typically, their tactics in responding to the allegation of American degeneracy remained the same as Jefferson's: Victorian and Progressive scientists amassed millions of statistics on the size of Americans, comparing these data with comparable information on European height and weight. Ultimately, these statistics would do more than reassure Americans that they were not degenerating; they would suggest that Americans were the vanguard of an advancing civilization.

In some respects, however, the tactics of Jefferson's descendants differed. Turn-of-the-century scientists and anthropologists almost never questioned the interchangeability of inner and outer characteristics. In fact, at a time when the place of African Americans, women, and the poor (especially poor immigrants) occupied much of the attention of policymakers, scientists did everything in their power to demonstrate the association between physical, mental, and moral traits. Thus, the debate between Jefferson and Buffon helped lay the foundations for many later U.S. height studies. It provided a motivation for assessing U.S. height; it offered a theoretical framework (the concept of degeneration) with compelling religious and evolutionary connotations; it had implications for debates on colonialism, which were often concerned with the effects (both physical and moral) of climate on a transplanted people; and it had relevance for the pressing social concerns of the United States at the turn of the century.

Stature and Class: The Early Nineteenth Century

In the early nineteenth century, French and English scientists offered a new theory on adult body size. Louis-René Villermé, Lambert Quetelet, and Edwin Chadwick were self-conscious champions of the poor who wished to expose the effects of poverty on the bodies of the disenfranchised. They argued that nutrition and the conditions associated with economic class affected the growth of the body. As humanitarians they hoped to reform social conditions for the underprivileged, and as scientists they sought evidence of the effects of impoverishment on the physical stature of the working poor.

One of the principal founders of the public health movement in France, Villermé demonstrated in 1828 that the poor had twice the rate of mortality as the rich, a notion that contradicted previous theories that the wealthy had higher death rates due to a lifestyle of luxury and excess.[33] In 1829, he examined the height of military recruits to determine laws of human growth. His study was part of a government investigation of the rejection of army recruits for physical reasons, including small stature; it was one of many that would follow in other countries in subsequent years.[34] In a famous and often quoted passage, Villermé asserted that poverty was more important than any other factor in determining human stature, including race and climate.

> Human height becomes greater and growth takes place more rapidly, other things being equal, in proportion as the country is richer, comfort more general, houses, clothes and nourishment better and labour, fatigue and privation during infancy and youth less; in other words, the circumstances which accompany poverty delay the age at which complete stature is reached and stunt adult height.[35]

Like Villermé, Quetelet played a major role in the French public health movement. He was among the founders of modern statistics and the first scientist to introduce the bell-shaped Normal curve into practical work. In *A Treatise on Man* (1835), Quetelet sought to determine the ideal of human beauty. Reacting against the aristocratic tendency of his day, he looked for perfection in *l'homme moyen,* the "average man."

> If the average man were completely determined, we might . . . consider him as the type of perfection; and every thing differing from his proportions or condition, would constitute deformity and disease; every thing found dissimilar, not only as regarded proportion and form, but as exceeding the observed limits, would constitute a monstrosity. . . . An individual who should comprise . . . in his own person . . . all the qualities of the average man, would . . . represent all which is grand, beautiful and excellent.[36]

Quetelet conducted the first cross-sectional survey of children ever, first of height in 1831 and then of height and weight in 1832. He was the first to show that human stature is distributed according to the "law of error," or the Normal curve.[37] His ideas were so influential that, following their publication, the term *stature* acquired its modern English denotation of relative rank or status; it was only after stature was used to exemplify the concepts of the mean and Normal curve, in other words, that the English language began to use the word as a synonym for rank.[38] Quetelet sought to advance Villermé's theories on the connection between class and stature. In *A Treatise on Man,* he compared the heights of city dwellers with rural inhabitants and found that the former were slightly taller. He also investigated the differences in stature between criminals and nonincarcerated citizens and found that the former were shorter. Quetelet accounted for both of these disparities by class: "Individuals who live in affluence generally exceed the average height: misery and hard labour, on the contrary, appear to be obstacles to growth."[39]

While Quetelet differed from late nineteenth-century Euro-American scientists in his emphasis on class, he shared some assumptions with them. He assumed that the laws governing the distribution of physical characteristics corresponded to similar laws in moral and intellectual qualities.[40] He also believed that the investigation of human stature and other physical characteristics could potentially reveal the progress of society. Quetelet argued that the limits of the Normal curve "narrow themselves through the influence of civilization, which affords, in my eyes the most convincing proof of human perfectibility."[41] While subsequent American studies agreed with Quetelet that height was indicative of progress, they deemphasized the notion that social advancement could be seen in a decrease in variability. Instead, post–Civil War American scientists were preoccupied with national averages, believing that a generally tall population indicated an advanced one. The American view was, in other words, a different notion of perfection: not a universal, divine average toward which all races and nationalities tended in a progressive system but separate racial averages existing in a hierarchy indicating superiority of the bigger and taller. The American view was hereditarian, not social.[42]

In England, investigation of the height and weight of children took place first in association with a series of child labor laws of the early nineteenth century designed to protect children from industrial exploitation. The British Parliament formed the Factory Commission to determine the effects of industrial labor on children "both with regard to their Morals and their bodily Health."[43] Edwin Chadwick, the author of the *Report of the Commissioners on the Employment of Children in Factories* (1833) and one of the major figures in the English public health reform movement, reported slight differences in height between factory and nonfactory children. The relative shortness of factory children was among the arguments that persuaded Parliament to pass the Factories Regulation Act of 1833, prohibiting children under the age of nine from working in certain types of factories and requiring rest and meal breaks for children aged nine to thirteen.[44]

By the middle to late nineteenth century, most scientists rejected the views of these humanitarians and social reformers in favor of racial explanations of height differences. Motivated simultaneously by nationalistic impulses and racist convictions, American and European scientific authorities began to use stature to define the people of their nations in opposition to other peoples of the world. When the English translation of Quetelet's *Treatise on Man* was published in 1842, the translator, Robert Knox, an anatomist at the University of Edinburgh, interrupted to dispute Quetelet and his mentor Villermé. In footnotes to the text, Knox remarks,

> The translator is firmly persuaded that Villermé and M. Quetelet, have failed to detect the real cause of difference of stature. . . . [I]t is a question purely of *race,* and not of feeding or locality. . . . The diminutive Bosjeman of Southern Africa, the athletic Caffre, reaching the full European stature, and the gigantic Boor, the descendant of the Saxon race, are as nearly alike in respect to food and climate as may be; the extraordinary

differences, therefore, which these men present, are ascribable to one cause alone—a difference of blood or origin; and the historic evidence derived from ancient Rome, and from the equally authentic figures depicted in the tombs of Egyptian Thebes, prove that these differences caused by blood or race are now neither greater nor less than they were at least 4000 years ago, thus, as it were, setting at defiance all minor causes, such as food, climate, localities, &c.[45]

Similarly, Dr. M. Boudin, a founder-member of the Society of Anthropology in France, argued in 1863 that selection during wartime, not poverty and famine as Villermé had contended, explained the reputed decrease in French stature in the early 1800s; the taller, "fitter" men had been sent to fight and die in wars while shorter men remained at home to propagate.[46] Boudin believed that race, altitude, and climate, as opposed to nutrition, were the most significant factors determining human stature. Paul Broca, the leading French physical anthropologist of the second half of the nineteenth century, believed like Knox that height was determined principally by race or ethnicity. "The height of Frenchmen," he wrote, "depends not on altitude, nor latitude, nor poverty or riches, neither on the nature of the soil nor on nutrition, nor on any of the other environmental conditions that can be invoked. After these have all been successfully eliminated, I have been brought to consider only one general influence, that of ethnic heredity."[47]

U.S. Height Studies: The Military Tradition

In an article appearing in the *Unitarian Review and Religious Magazine* of 1877, A. A. Livermore argued against the apparently widespread belief in American degeneration.

> There is a very general misgiving that the whole tenor of modern civilization is unfavorable to physical vigor and longevity, and bears within its bosom the seeds of its own dissolution. Especially the conviction extends that in the United States health and life are at a discount, and that a well developed and robust manhood is gradually succumbing to the difficulties of the climate and the wretched violations of the hygienic conditions and laws of life. Hardly a book is published on health which does not take us severely to task, as a people fast running down into national decay and decrepitude.[48]

Like many of his contemporaries, Livermore believed that degeneration was both a physical and a moral problem and that moral degeneration was evident in physical traits. He begins his essay with a catalog of the greatest and least peoples of the earth. Among the greatest he includes "the symmetrical Greek," "the iron-like Roman," and "the stalwart Anglo-Saxon"; among the least are "the stunted Esquimo," "the dwarfed Equatorial peoples," and "the pigmies of Africa." Livermore sets out to determine whether America will produce a superior race in the tradition of Greece, Rome, and England or "a weakling and a waif, destined, after a brief struggle with the powers leagued for his overthrow, to pass away and be forgotten."[49]

Physical stature figured prominently among Livermore's tests of American degeneration. For data on stature, Livermore turned to two recent military reports on Civil War soldiers. The government-sponsored studies of Benjamin A. Gould and J. H. Baxter reassured Americans that charges of degeneration were unfounded. They rendered data on average stature and other physical characteristics for the men of each state in the Union and compared these data with information on European conscripts in the Civil War as well as available data on European soldiers in Europe. The results tended to indicate that American men were, on average, slightly taller than European men. Livermore typified the public reaction to this news: "The North American type instead of being a degeneration is an improvement, physically, on its progenitor races."[50]

The post–Civil War American military studies participated in an international mania for information on the "average man" of each nation and race, a mania provoked in part by Quetelet's work as well as the ongoing quest for criteria of racial ranking. The military studies were enabled by a voluminous collection of statistics gathered by the United States Sanitary Commission, created in 1861 following the Union defeat at the first battle of Bull Run and authorized to conduct anthropometric studies of Civil War soldiers in order to offer recommendations for improving the efficiency of federal troops. Scientists regarded the data amassed by the Sanitary Commission as an unprecedented opportunity to determine the American racial "type," to compare this type with other nations around the world, and to determine whether colonial Europeans were indeed degenerating in the American climate.

In *Investigations in the Military and Anthropological Statistics of American Soldiers* (1869), Benjamin A. Gould, president of the American Association for the Advancement of Science, presented and compared the physical traits of more than 1 million men. The subjects included white men of various nationalities (including Americans,

English, Germans, Canadians, French, Scandinavians, and others who volunteered or were drafted for the Civil War), college students, Indians, and blacks. The data covered a host of physical characteristics besides stature that were thought to differentiate the races of men, such as head size, hip circumference, foot length, arm length, and facial angle (see fig. 4). The importance attached to the data on stature is indicated by the fact that Gould devoted roughly one-sixth of his book to their analysis and presentation. His finding that American men were slightly taller on average than men of other nations offered the first and seemingly definitive response to allegations of American degeneration.

When it came to identifying the principle factor determining stature, Gould was less dogmatic than most nineteenth-century scientists. Instead of proceeding from a priori assumptions, as did most of his contemporaries,[51] Gould set out to test the existing hypotheses. He considered four conventional views—climate, economic status, elevation, and nationality (a term he used interchangeably with race)—and rejected all of them. He rejected the views of Buffon on the influence of climate and temperature because he found no consistent association between these things and stature across the states. He also dismissed the views of Villermé on the influence of social class. Despite the fact that the Sanitary Commission had not been supplied with adequate funds to allow an investigation of the influence of class on adult male height, Gould nevertheless concluded that Villermé's theories were inapplicable to conditions in the United States because "excessive poverty," according to Gould, "hardly exists in the United States."[52] He rejected elevation as the chief agent in stature because men on the plains of Indiana and Illinois were among the tallest in the States. He rejected nationality, or race, because he found an unexpected difference in average stature between men who enlisted in their home states and those who enlisted in states other than where they were born. (He discovered, in other words, the migration effect; for some unknown reason, people who migrate across states are taller than those who remain in their native states. A similar phenomenon has been found in England.)[53] Local causes other than race, Gould reasoned, must play a role in adult height. With the exception of Franz Boas, subsequent American authorities would disregard Gould's comments on race.

Although he was unable to render a final verdict on the chief agent affecting stature, Gould used his finding on the migration effect to derive one rule that offered a biological incentive for the westward expansion of the United States. "Residence in the Western States, during the years of growth, tends to produce increase of stature," he wrote.[54] If the United States needed any further motivation for its imperialist policies, Gould's report provided it. His remark did not go unnoticed. Darwin referred to the finding in his *Descent of Man,* published two years after Gould's study. Walt Whitman was probably also aware of Gould's report. In *Specimen Days* he commented on the large size of western soldiers,[55] and he evidently believed the height of western men presaged a new, superior race in America's future: "To-day, ahead, though dimly yet, we see, in vistas, a copious, sane gigantic offspring."[56] In California, wrote Whitman, a "superber race" of men would arise; there they would be "hardy, sweet, gigantic"—they would "tower proportionate to Nature" and the enormous redwood trees of the Pacific Coast.[57]

As these examples suggest, Gould's *Investigations* found an immediate popular interest. His findings were cited in congressional speeches, magazine articles, and scientific studies. Reinforced by Baxter's study, Gould's *Investigations* played a decisive role in the formation of hegemonic notions of the American male body in the late nineteenth and early twentieth centuries. The image it conjured of a progressive American man (by which I mean progressively growing and advanced in social and evolutionary terms) quickly assumed a dominant position in the national ideology as the cultural climate increasingly favored bigness and growth in a variety of arenas. Gould's *Investigations* also forged a national unity by representing the Euro-American body, in spite of its diversity, as unique and distinct from European bodies. White American men were united in their physical superiority to the lands of their origin.

Gould's report did not end the controversy over stature. At the same time that Gould and the Sanitary Commission were analyzing the Civil War data, another government agency, the U.S. Provost-Marshal-General's Bureau, was also reviewing the information and formulating its own conclusions. The second study, published in 1875 under the direction of J. H. Baxter, a colonel and the chief medical purveyor in the U.S. Army, criticized the methods and reversed some of the claims of Gould's *Investigations.* Most important, Baxter's *Statistics, Medical and Anthropological, of the Provost-Marshal-General's Bureau* claimed that race was the dominant factor in adult height.

Baxter devotes considerable attention to the issue of stature in his massive report and regards it as the most important of the anthropometric measurements.[58] "There is probably no question connected with anthropology which has been more debated, and which has, notwithstanding, been left in a more unsatisfactory condition than that of the mean stature of the full-grown man," he wrote.[59] The comparative study of stature among the races and nations of the world, he explained, had been compromised by numerous problems. Too often scientists measured a select group of men (he never considered the neglect of women) such as convicts or college students and held that group as representative of the national average. Measurements of soldiers—a growing practice in Europe—had too often ignored the presence of minimum height limits for enlistment, thus inflating the results. Different studies measured men of different ages, regardless of whether they had attained their full adult stature. Methods of measurement differed: some scientists measured men with their shoes on, some without. In a table of the results obtained for various groups in previous studies, Baxter demonstrated that claims of average height for Irish men, for example, had differed by more than three inches, from 5'5.66" to 5'9.2". Baxter hoped to overcome some of these problems by using uniform methods of measurement, by comparing men of various races or nations at the same age, and so on.[60]

Baxter pointed out that Gould's contentions regarding American stature were unreliable due to poor data collection methods. "It is certain that, in the majority of cases, so great was the haste, and so unsystematic the recruiting, the [soldier's] own statement as to his height was held sufficient, or it was guessed by the officer; or, at best, that it was roughly measured against a wall or door-post, the shoes being seldom if ever removed from the feet."[61] Baxter recalculated the average stature of American men and other nationalities using more than half a million Civil War measurements selected (according to him) for their reliability. Again, Baxter found that men of the United States led the civilized world in stature.

Like Gould, Baxter also wished to identify the chief factor in human height. Unlike Gould, Baxter was content to proceed from a priori assumptions. He did not investigate the influence of class, and he dismissed the views of Villermé for the same reason that Gould had: "No one will suppose that the population of the United States suffers from want or misery to any general extent; it is probable that, with occasional exceptions in the large cities, lack of food is unknown."[62] Baxter concluded that race, not class, was the determining factor in male height. "The tables of this work, in most instances, confirm, and in no sense contravene, Boudin's well-known law that height is always an affair of race," he wrote.[63] Accordingly, Baxter presented tables and exhibits depicting stature for the various races, or nationalities, of men. He provided separate curves of height for white and colored U.S. soldiers showing that each followed Quetelet's laws of normal distribution. He argued that "blonde races are characterized by superior stature," although he acknowledged that American Indians appeared to represent an exception to the rule.[64]

Baxter's conclusions had become scientific dogma by 1920, when the U.S. Department of War issued its study of World War I recruits, *Defects Found in Drafted Men*. The report initiated a national panic over the condition of American men. It reported that roughly half of all men examined for the military demonstrated a physical defect of one kind or another and that roughly a third of the men called for duty had been rejected by military examiners. Along with reports of mental tests conducted on masses of recruits that proclaimed the average white American male had an IQ equivalent to a thirteen-year-old (or, in the contemporary psychological terminology, roughly half of American men were "morons"), the army reports suggested that something dire was occurring in the United States. Reviving anxieties over American degeneration, scientific authorities used these reports to suggest that the preservation of American exceptionalism demanded stringent measures.

Like Baxter, the authors of *Defects Found in Drafted Men* regarded stature as a racial trait that was unaffected by environmental conditions.[65] Because of its racial nature, the defect of short stature could only be managed through prudent immigration policies, according to authors Albert Love, a physician and major in the U.S. Army, and Charles Davenport, a leading U.S. eugenicist and erstwhile army major. In particular, Love and Davenport urged strict immigration restrictions against Polish Jews and southern Italians and more rigorous identification of "defectives" at immigration stations.[66]

Concerned less with the ranking of various nationalities and races by stature (this work had already been completed to the satisfaction of American scientists by 1920), *Defects Found in Drafted Men* perpetuated the concern with regional physical differences that also characterized the earlier military studies. Like Gould's report, it praised the physical character of western soldiers. Unlike Gould's study, which proclaimed a universal value in westward migration, the World War I study argued that there were important racial patterns in migration. The older generation of immigrants (primarily from England, Ireland, Germany, and Scandinavia) descended from superior races and had migrated west because they preferred rural conditions. Recent immigrants (primarily from Italy, Russia, and the Balkans) were from inferior races and remained on the eastern seaboard because they preferred urban conditions. Thus, the inadequate height that the report found to be more common in cities was "not due chiefly to repressing environmental conditions in urban districts, but to the fact that the short races prefer to live in cities."[67] Since the racial character of the early pioneers, rather than environmental conditions on the frontier, was the spark of progress, westward migration could no longer cure the ills of modern

America. The battle against American degeneration would have to be fought in the nation's cities. It would be a war of containment, not expansion.

By the end of the nineteenth century, American scientists had erected a new myth to replace Buffon's myth of degeneration. While the old myth resonated with Christian dogma about the fall of man and was probably the prevalent view in the United States throughout most of the nineteenth century, the new myth reflected the growing authority of science. Informed by evolutionary theory, this new myth identified progress as the trend of human history.[68] Increases in stature among the races of men, among other things, testified to this progress, and American superiority in stature reflected the nation's preeminence in evolutionary and social development. In spite of the new myth, anxieties about degeneration persisted. As nativist xenophobia took hold in the first decades of the twentieth century, these anxieties became more localized. *Defects Found in Drafted Men* reassured its readers that degeneration did not threaten the urban population as a whole—nor did it originate in America's sons and daughters who were migrating to the cities in increasing numbers. Rather, the nation was threatened by alien elements attracted to urban environments, like salmon to rivers, by racial instincts.

Ensuring a Progressive Nation: Turn-of-the-Century Child Growth Studies in the United States

In March 1905, a year after pygmies entertained crowds at the St. Louis World's Fair and ten years after Haliburton suggested a Dwarf Era had preceded the evolution and domination of taller human races, the Parents' Association of the University Elementary and High Schools in Chicago invited experts from the University of Chicago to address the physical growth of children and its relation to schoolwork. James Tufts, head of the Department of Philosophy at the university and the expert selected for the talk, discussed not only the recent discoveries of the new and burgeoning field of child development but also the questions that the discipline still promised to answer. His lecture is revealing for what it suggests about the assumptions guiding turn-of-the-century studies of child growth.

Tufts was influenced by recent developments in education theory, particularly the ideas of G. Stanley Hall. Hall was one of the most distinguished psychologists in the United States, a leader in child development theory, an advocate of school reform, and a committed eugenicist. Hall argued that human development could be divided into discrete stages. For children these stages included infancy, the juvenile period, and adolescence. Each had its own unique characteristics, but all differed from adulthood; children were not simply miniature adults, as traditional wisdom had it. In building his principles of child development, Hall was influenced by the naturalist Ernst Haeckel's popular theory of recapitulation, the notion that the growth of the individual replicates the evolution of the species. Believing that children were more like savages than modern adult men and women, Hall led the movement toward the *pedocentric* school, the institution arranged according to the developmental needs of the child, a system that replaced the historic *scholiocentric* school, which demanded that the child adapt to the institution.[69]

Tufts began his talk at the Parents' Association meeting with a chart illustrating standard growth curves for American children. Such charts had only become widely available in the final decade of the nineteenth century, when Franz Boas began compiling data from existing child growth studies to display the composite national growth curves at the Chicago World's Fair of 1893.[70] Flawed as they were, the growth curves had begun to exert a significant influence in education as well as pediatric and preventive medicine. Tuft's growth curves indicated the ages at which girls and boys began their respective adolescent growth spurts and the period of diminished growth that preceded this spurt. Tufts claimed that the period of slowed growth was a time of bodily and mental fatigue with important implications for education. Following Hall's lead, Tufts suggested that the period of slow growth was associated with a comparable period in evolutionary history—"a time of pigmy height."[71] Tufts recommended that parents be vigilant during this period, and he emphasized the need for schools to adjust their work expectations to the child.

The question that especially occupied Tufts's attention, however, was what to do with children during the adolescent growth spurt. Was this a period in which children were capable of sustained and vigorous work, or was it a period of fragility and weakness? More important, what were the implications for girls? Scientists had only recently discovered that girls began their growth spurt earlier than boys (as well as the fact that the growth of girls terminated sooner than that of boys), and this realization prompted a number of questions and concerns shaped by dominant social tensions, especially the demands of women for equal access to higher education. The fact that fewer women who attended high school and college graduated to marriage and childbearing than their less-educated sisters suggested to Tufts that school, as it operated at the time, had a dire effect on women. "There was an evil somewhere," he reasoned, so to be on the safe side, educators ought to assume that the burden of rapid growth during adolescence precluded severe mental work. "If the girl could not be taken into an entirely different environment, so that the strain under which she lived could be removed," he argued, "then the studies which taxed her the most should be diminished, and there should be much out-of-door life."[72]

Tufts's report at the Chicago Parents' Association meeting illustrates several of the characteristics of U.S. child growth studies and their application at the turn of the century. Like Native Americans educated and Christianized in reservation mission schools, and like African Americans educated in segregated, trade-oriented schools, the constitutionally weak demanded special treatment and careful scientific management. As the public education system in the United States expanded enormously to accommodate population growth and new compulsory school attendance laws, girls and boys were increasingly segregated into single-sex schools, the poor and immigrants were tracked into vocational schools, and the "feeble-minded" were institutionalized in schools for the mentally disabled. Even within schools, educators monitored children by intelligence tests and tracked them according to academic ability. Within coeducational schools, girls were directed toward single-sex disciplines like home economics. Thus, the revolutionary application of developmental theories to education at the turn of the century—in particular, the idea that education should be adapted to the individual needs of the child—was shaped by deterministic assumptions about the varying capabilities of different groups of people.[73]

Finally, Tufts's advocacy of the "out-of-door life" for adolescent girls and the increasing popularity of youth recreation and physical education programs suggest that educators hoped to combat the enervating conditions of urban life by approximating frontier conditions. Mark Seltzer has suggested that the presumed closing of the frontier generated "a three-fold relocation of the making of Americans" and a redefinition of the term *frontier* itself. Citizens would now be fashioned at "the surrogate frontier of the natural body" via the physical culture movement, the new national parks that preserved fragments of the old frontier, and the new overseas imperialist frontier.[74] But cities were also redefined as potential frontiers for the making of Americans. If the superior classes and races could no longer be invigorated by violent contact with inferior groups, life in the hinterlands would be recreated in the heart of metropolitan America. It was no accident that archery, horseback riding, swimming, and drills with Indian clubs were among the earliest exercises in American physical education. The first two decades of the twentieth century witnessed not just a proliferation of school gymnasia but also a proliferation of summer camps and the formation of the parks movement, the Boys' Clubs of America (1906), the Playground Association (1906), the Boy Scouts of America (1910), the Camp Fire Girls (1912), and the Girl Scouts (1912).

Tufts's lecture, however, doesn't tell the whole story. While some studies hoped to assist the efforts of educators in classifying children for special educational treatment, investigators had other motivations as well. As with the military reports, American child growth studies hoped to discredit Buffon's theory of degeneration. Believing that races might vary in growth rates just as they varied in other physical characteristics, researchers called for the creation of growth curves for each race. They imagined that this endeavor would enable them to determine the effects of various environments on those curves, thereby illustrating the consequences of colonialism and contributing to immigration legislation and programs for future imperialist efforts. They also hoped to develop national standards for growth. Precise growth standards would not only facilitate distinctions between individuals whose growth was "normal" and "abnormal," but it would allow scientists to track the national average over time, predict the adult height of individuals, and intervene with therapies that could enhance the collective public stature as well as the heights of individuals. When pituitary growth hormone was discovered in the early twentieth century, it was initially heralded, as one magazine expressed it, for its potential in "the elimination of the dwarf" and "the relief of the undersized."[75] Editorials suggested that an appropriate and beneficial use of the hormone would be to increase everyone's height.[76] The fanfare over growth hormone was, in other words, an exaggerated manifestation of more modest efforts that were already under way throughout the nation.[77]

Reinforcing the findings of the military reports and extending them to childhood, the early child growth studies sought to demonstrate that U.S. youth were taller than their European counterparts. Henry Bowditch and George Peckham, for example, amassed thousands of statistics on American youth. Bowditch, cofounder of the American Physiological Society and dean of Harvard Medical School, orchestrated the collection of height and weight measurements for 24,500 Boston schoolchildren and published his results in 1877. Peckham, a physician and high school biology teacher, arranged for the measurement of height and weight for 10,000 children in the schools of Milwaukee and published his findings four years later. Arranging their data according to nationality of the children's parents (they used the term *nationality* interchangeably with *race*), Bowditch and Peckham claimed that children of American parents exceeded children of Irish, German, and English parentage in physical size. (Although this is what they claimed, their data were not always so clear. In Peckham's study, for example, children of English parentage were taller than children of American parentage for half the ages recorded.) "It will thus be seen that the theory of the gradual physical degeneration of the Anglo-Saxon race in America derives no support from this investigation," concluded Bowditch. Comparing the data on Milwaukee children with Bowditch's Boston children, Peckham also reported that American youth in the West were taller than their eastern cousins, bolstering Gould's speculations about the advantages of westward migration for the national physique.

Bowditch suggested that his findings had implications for education policy. In particular, the differences in growth rates between the sexes "may . . . be regarded as an argument against the co-education of boys and girls, except during the earlier years of life in which rates of growth are practically the same; *i.e.,* up to ten or eleven years of age."[78] In a later study, he would repeat the claims of the German anthropologist Ranke, who suggested that the relatively greater length of the trunk in women relative to men was an indication of their lower embryological standing—meaning, in the language of recapitulation, a lower evolutionary position for women.[79] Bowditch proclaimed the importance of routine anthropometrical monitoring in American schools. Like most of his contemporaries, he believed that physical education could affect not only a child's weight and strength but his or her height as well. He hoped physical educators might use his standard height and weight tables to determine the progress of students in their classes.[80]

The award for the most outspoken advocate of national and individual height enhancement, however, belongs unquestionably to William Townsend Porter. Early in his career Porter worked as a professor of physiology at the St. Louis Medical College (later to become Washington University), where he gathered statistics on more than thirty-three thousand St. Louis public schoolchildren. Later he worked with Bowditch at Harvard, and together they founded the *American Journal of Physiology*. In a longitudinal study of child growth conducted roughly concurrently with the Department of War's study of World War I soldiers, Porter found that Boston schoolchildren were unlikely to deviate from their percentile rank in height and weight from year to year. "Small boys," in other words, "tend to remain small, unless they are rescued by a wise adviser," he wrote. Porter believed that with "intelligent care" the height of children could be increased; indeed, it was "parental and social incompetence" that produced "stunted children." "It is our duty to make our children reasonably tall," he declared in 1922, two years after the furor created by the Department of War's pronouncements on the degeneration of American men. "Those who have in charge the growth of children should aim first at making their wards taller than the average."[81] How much taller than the average? Porter suggested that the goal should be to bring managed children above the seventy-fifth percentile in both height and weight, since norms for each age included many children at the lower percentages who were "defective," thus artificially depressing the standards.[82] Although Porter never explained *how* advisers might "rescue" small children, in narrating the "happy success" of a hypothetical boy named John who rose in percentile rank relative to his peers, Porter suggested that family vacations involving horseback riding and fresh air played a significant role.[83]

Porter was particularly interested in the connection between intelligence and body size. Through his research on St. Louis children, he proposed to determine whether "mediocrity of mind [was] associated in the mean with mediocrity of physique."[84] In the public schools of St. Louis, children advanced in grades through academic achievement or the recommendations of their instructors (it is not clear which) rather than age. Children of the same age, in other words, could be found in different grades. Porter analyzed the distribution of children of the same age in separate grades and found that taller and heavier children tended to be found in the higher grades, while smaller children of the same age were more likely to be present in the lower grades. Assuming that "success in school life . . . is on the average a fair test of intelligence," Porter concluded that "Precocious [i.e., smart] children are taller as well as heavier than dull children."[85]

Most U.S. investigators ignored issues of class, even when they acknowledged the potential influence that economic status might have on child growth and final adult size. Porter was no exception. In the initial 1893 publication of his findings, he neglected to discuss the effect that class might have on the physical size and academic success of students, even though he was probably conscious of the fact, established by investigations of factory children in England, that children of the wealthy tended to be taller and heavier than children of the lower classes. Other researchers followed in his steps. Not only were few studies in the United States concerned with issues of class, but many of the child growth reports deliberately selected children of the middle and upper classes for national growth standards.[86]

Because successful students seemed to be larger than unsuccessful ones, Porter reasoned that "mental output is . . . directly related to the physical condition of the pupils."[87] Expecting dull students to meet the demands of precocious children meant placing an undue burden on the weak. Porter advocated immediate school reform that accounted for the different innate abilities of students; he called for "the regulation of mental labor from a physical standpoint."[88] "The connection between theory and practical affairs is here unusually short and clear," he explained. "[T]he evil effect of over study could be watched and intelligently combated, and systems of education, no longer exacting of all that which should be exacted only from the mean, could be rationally adapted to the special needs of the exceptionally weak and the exceptionally strong."[89] Porter argued that appointed school physicians should make routine anthropometric measurements on students. The physician would ensure that no child advanced beyond a grade suited to his or her constitution as determined by measurements of height and weight. Failure to protect a student from the evils of overstrain, Porter warned, meant a potential temporary deviation from normal growth and, worse yet, the possibility of depriving the child of his or her deserved adult size.[90]

Because several turn-of-the-century studies supported the belief that physical and intellectual characteristics were linked, growth experts argued that a student's physical constitution should be taken into account in grading, school advancement, college admissions, and college scholarships. Bird T. Baldwin, who earned his doctorate at Harvard when Porter and Bowditch were teaching there, suggested that "the smaller child should be treated as a younger person" by educators.[91] In his 1914 report for the U.S. Bureau of Education, *Physical Growth and School Progress,* Baldwin repeated the recommendations of Porter: "No child whose weight *or height* is below the average . . . for its age should be permitted to enter a school grade beyond the average of its age except after such a physical examination as shall make it probable that the child's strength is equal to the strain."[92] Educators, in other words, should consider the developmental (as determined by physical measurements) rather than the chronological age of a child when assigning him or her to a particular grade; tall children should be accelerated through school, while smaller ones should be help back.[93] Dudley A. Sargent, a physical education professor at Harvard, president of the College Physical Education Association, and creator of the models of the average American man and woman exhibited at the 1893 Chicago World's Fair, argued in 1908 that college admissions and eligibility for academic honors should include physical requirements based on minimum height, weight, and strength standards.[94]

One of the few researchers openly critical of Porter's findings was Franz Boas, an equally prominent child growth investigator and a leading American physical anthropologist. He issued an important objection that was consistent with current thinking on the development of children (and thus contributed to movements in educational theory) even though it conflicted with Porter's claims. Boas believed that developmental rates were distributed according to a probability curve and that children developed at different rates due to "accidental causes."[95] Some children reached puberty ahead of their peers, while others reached it later than the majority. Boas objected to Porter's wording, therefore, preferring the term *retarded* to Porter's *dull* (this was before the day when *retarded* became a euphemism for *dumb*) to signify that children who were less successful academically may simply be delayed in their development rather than innately dim-witted. "A retarded child," wrote Boas, "may develop and become quite bright."[96] Moreover, he challenged Porter's basic conclusion that there was a physical basis to intelligence. Porter, reasoned Boas, had only "shown that mental and physical growth are correlated, or depend upon common causes; not that mental development depends upon physical growth."[97] At the same time, Boas agreed with Porter that studies of human growth "are of fundamental importance for hygiene and education."[98] He believed that a fundamental question confronting anthropology was the supposed correlation between somatic and mental characters, and he called for a bureau dedicated to the collection and interpretation of child growth statistics.[99]

Despite the objections of Boas, and despite the fact that some subsequent studies found no correlation between physical size and school success,[100] Porter's study exerted tremendous influence because it affirmed contemporary assumptions about the correspondence between physical and mental traits. The author of a paper entitled "What Teachers Ought to Know About the Physical Growth of Children" delivered at the National Education Association meeting in 1918, for example, summarized current thinking when he insisted that "The stunted body will dwarf the mind."[101] It is difficult to say whether any schools followed Porter's recommendation that students be prevented from advancing in grades without a physician's approval, but many schools did incorporate routine physical measurements into their educational regimens. This trend accelerated rapidly after the government's reports on defects in World War I recruits, and it led to widespread misapplication and abuse of growth data in the 1920s. As Boas explains in an article published in *School and Society* in 1923, the tables of "normal" growth sent by the U.S. Department of Education to schools for the purpose of identifying ill and malnourished children often led educators and school physicians to misinterpret the results of their anthropometric tests. Too often, he said, health educators assumed that "all children under the normal stature and under the normal weight are undernourished."[102] Similarly, a 1930 editorial in *Health and the School* argued that the system of health education common in American schools after World War I, with its emphasis on routine weighing and measuring of children, should be reevaluated. Too often, the article explained, educators and physicians interpreted their data dogmatically. The editorial recommended that health educators abandon the concept of the average. "It is unscientific and unfair to regard average weight as the goal for all children or for an individual child," it said.[103]

Among the many who were impressed by Porter's findings was Henry H. Goddard, the eminent American eugenicist and director of research at New Jersey's Vineland Training School for Backward and Feeble-Minded Children. In his writings on the feeble-minded, Goddard argued for the segregation of the mentally deficient, claiming that institutions like his own Vineland were best suited to maintaining their comfort and preventing them from reproducing.[104] Goddard believed Porter had demonstrated conclusively that physical and mental traits corresponded. He began his 1912 report "The Height and Weight of Feeble-Minded Children in American Institutions" with a bow to Porter. "It has long been known that in man there is some connection between size of body and mentality. Even among normal people, on the average, size means efficiency,—as is shown by Porter's measurements of school children."[105] In his own study, Goddard sought to advance Porter's conclusions by comparing the growth curves of institutionalized "mental defectives" with "normal" children. Following contemporary fashion in psychology, Goddard divided his mental defectives into three groups: idiots (people without full speech), imbeciles, and morons (the elite of the defective underworld). Goddard found that mental defectives of either sex were generally shorter and lighter than normal individuals and that the lower-grade defectives deviated further than the higher grades from the normal. The differences were trivial—generally an inch and a pound or two until age fourteen (when the heights and weights of "normal" children were derived principally from the economically privileged, i.e., those still present in public schools). Despite the fact that his results may have indicated little more than class differences, Goddard concluded that "we have a remarkable correlation between physical growth and mental development." The fact that girls of the moron grade were actually taller and heavier than normal girls gave him some trouble. But he overcame the apparent contradiction by reasoning that institutional care provided an advantage to these borderline individuals in terms of nutrition, exercise, and sleep. He also suggested that "the absence of higher mental functions" might "allow a more perfect functioning of the purely physical,"[106] apparently without realizing that he was contradicting the very premise of his report: namely, that small body size was indicative of low intelligence.

Like Goddard, Linus W. Kline of Clark University also read and apparently admired Porter's studies on precocious and dull children. A disciple of G. Stanley Hall, Kline was an education reform advocate who believed that American schools should incorporate more exercise and less sedentary instruction since traditional education taxed the attention span of children. The unnatural demands of school, he argued, contributed to truancy and was creating a class of savages within the metropolis. Quoting the author of an 1896 study on juvenile crime in Great Britain, Kline wrote that "In very early life unadaptability to social surroundings usually shows itself in the shape of truancy, vagrancy, wandering habits, in short a disposition to revert to the nomadic stage of civilization. The greater the demand made by society on the child, such as the demand in the present century that he shall regularly attend an elementary school, the more clearly is the extent of the nomadic instinct brought to light."[107]

Kline set out to investigate the biological and physical roots of truancy, a behavior that he believed was homologous to the "migrating instinct" in primitive cultures. He published the results of his study in 1898 in *Pedagogical Seminary,* a journal edited and founded by G. Stanley Hall. Hall, in fact, assisted Kline in the study; together they collected anecdotal information about children who had run away and concluded that the behavior varied during three developmental periods in childhood. Between the ages of one and four, running away was common among all children and corresponded to an early phase in human evolution. During this phase, children were all more or less like very primitive savages. For most children, the next two phases of development—ages four through seven and eight through twelve—tended to counteract these early primitive tendencies. Attachments to parents, friends, and teachers "are all forces overcoming and destroying this powerful relic of primitive man."[108] Sometimes, however—either because of incompetent parenting or a powerful atavistic impulse—children never grew out of the early phase. Such individuals became permanent truants, out of sync with modern civilization, and, because they were "indifferent towards property," often ended up as criminals. The truant "has little sympathy with modern movements of society," wrote Kline, "and will not fuse with it, but stands out like an outcrop of an older formation, pointing the genetic psychologist back to the probable origin of the migrating instinct."[109]

After concocting his developmental theory of truancy, Kline conducted anthropometric tests to determine whether truants differed physically from "normal" children. He measured the height, weight, and chest girth for more than two hundred boys at Massachusetts truant schools. He compared these figures with measurements of more than six hundred boys at Worcester public schools. He found that truant boys were on average about an inch and five pounds smaller than public school boys between the ages of eight and fifteen. "The truant suffers from arrested development," announced Kline, using a concept scientists loved to apply to the pygmies and other primitive groups.[110]

Although Kline made no attempt to standardize for class between the two groups, he did set about to determine a posteriori whether "home conditions" had any effect on the observed differences. He found that roughly half of the truants came from homes of unskilled laborers, while only a third of the public school boys had parents of the same class. This fact was significant, Kline believed, in what it revealed about the child's nutrition and clothing. But he felt it did not wholly account for the small size of truants. He also noted that 65 percent of the truant boys had an absent father or mother (most were dead, some were imprisoned or alcoholic) and 43 percent were partial or complete orphans. These facts suggested to Kline that truant boys often had "degenerate" and "incompetent" parents. He concluded that five factors explained the small size of truants: poor food, insufficient clothing, incompetent parenting leading to improper hygiene, "a baneful heritage of a diseased and degenerate constitution," and a lack of exercise in school.[111] Thus, both heredity and environment contributed to the arrested development of truants.

Kline walked a precarious line between hereditarian and environmentalist positions because he wanted to show that there was some biological significance to truancy—it represented the reassertion of an atavistic behavior that could determine the child's fate for life—and simultaneously to convince educators that changes in pedagogical methods could achieve results. He therefore provided evidence that boys who were institutionalized in truant schools approximated more nearly the size of public school boys the longer they stayed in the institutions. Education in these schools included three hours of traditional sedentary instruction per day plus manual training and directed indoor and outdoor play. Kline believed that all schools should emulate this approach. American education, if it wished to prevent the arrest of development that created lifelong urban savages who would likely turn to crime, must include more physical activity and less traditional instruction. It must adapt to the developmental needs of children and recognize that all children at some ages and some children at all ages are more like primitive people than modern men and women. Thus, Kline synthesized hereditarian and environmentalist positions on the subject of body size to play on anxieties about degeneration while simultaneously offering a program for progressive education.

In spite of the massive investment of time and money in the normalization and surveillance of children's bodies, one should not assume that child growth studies proceeded without resistance. Just as the pygmies of Africa and elsewhere often refused to be measured,[112] many of the subjects of the American growth studies were apparently suspicious of the investigators' motivations. Considering that statistical methods efface the individual in the quest for averages, it is perhaps appropriate that such resistance was generally unspoken and collective. In particular, subjects of the growth studies were reluctant to answer questions regarding their ethnicity, suggesting that they were aware and distrustful of scientific notions of racial hierarchy, at least as they were applied to so-called white races. "In obtaining the nationality of the [children's] ancestors we encountered a great many difficulties," wrote George Peckham in his study of child growth for the Wisconsin State Board of Health. "Frequently it was necessary to send the blank back to the parents day after day before the questions were all answered. In some of the lowest grades the teachers sent in addition to the blanks, notes to the parents, asking their cooperation."[113] William Porter was particularly incensed by this unspoken hostility. "Some ignorant or prejudiced parents refused to answer the question in Form C [which asked about the birthplace of pupils' parents] and in such cases the answers were obtained as far as possible from the school registers."[114] Perhaps as a result of the interrogations they endured at processing stations like Ellis Island, immigrants who were the subjects of Franz Boas's 1911 study *Changes in Bodily Form of Descendants of Immigrants* put up particular resistance to his investigations. In his official report, Boas acknowledged the help he received from the Jewish, Italian, and Bohemian newspapers, which urged their readers to submit to being measured.[115]

Other resistance was more overt. Mary Antin, a Jewish immigrant from the Pale of Russia and, by her own admission, a very small woman who had often been teased as a child for her size,[116] wrote and lectured passionately in opposition to immigration restriction during the second decade of the twentieth century. She recognized the major role that scientific and anthropological studies of the bodies of immigrants played in debates surrounding immigration. In her major proimmigration tract, *They Who Knock At Our Gates: A Complete Gospel of Immigration* (1914), Antin urged her readers to disregard the copious scientific reports of the Dillingham Commission that warned of the eugenic and social dangers of open immigration.[117] The scientific studies, she argued, amounted to a grand red herring, appealing to racism to divert attention from questions that were properly moral, not scientific.

> Strip the alien down to his anatomy, you still find a *man,* a creature made in the image of God. . . . Where we have gone wrong is in applying the testimony of our experts to the moral side of the question. By all means register the cephalic index of the alien,—the anthropologist will make something of it at his leisure,—but do not let it determine his right to life, liberty, and the pursuit of happiness.[118]

The Jewish immigrant's small body is a repeated trope in Antin's writings, just as it is in the texts of race scientists and immigration restrictionists. In her short story "The Lie," published in 1913 in the *Atlantic Monthly,* Antin reversed the terms of contemporary science as well as arguments opposing immigration. The story's protagonists are a Jewish immigrant boy named David Rudinsky and his public school teacher, Miss Ralston. Considerably smaller than his peers in the sixth grade, David is nevertheless the brightest student in his class and Miss Ralston's favorite; the teacher often remains late to continue David's instruction after official school hours.

Because of his exceptional abilities, Ralston assigns David the part of George Washington in a school play. When David tries on his costume, the teacher discovers that the jacket is much too big for him. "Nothing of David was visible outside the jacket except two big eyes above and two blunt boot-toes below. The collar reached to his ears; the cuffs dangled below his knees. He resembled a scarecrow in the cornfield more than the Father of his Country."[119] Since the jacket was made for a twelve-year-old, Ralston asks him how old he is, "wondering for the hundredth time at his diminutive stature" (181). He responds that he is twelve, but his subsequent silence and listlessness cause the teacher to wonder what is troubling him. When he stays home from school the next day, suddenly taken ill, Ralston worries that he has succumbed to the pressures of school. "She attributed his sudden breakdown entirely to overwrought nerves, and remorsefully resolved not to subject him in the future to the strain of extra hours after school" (182). Deeply concerned about her prize student, however, Ralston eventually decides to visit his home. The doctor confirms her diagnosis; David is not sick, just overworked. "David is so weak and small," the doctor tells the family. "David studies too much altogether." "We push him too much when we ought to hold him back" (185), agrees Ralston, echoing the advice of medical authorities who warned against advancing small children too rapidly through school.

In a conversation between Ralston and David's father, however, we learn that David's emotional collapse has nothing whatsoever to do with school strain. To ensure that his son would get a free education in the public schools of America, David's father falsified his immigration records to indicate that David was twelve instead of fourteen.[120] (Thus, David is exceptionally small. As Ralston exclaims when she learns about the deception, "Why, he seems too little even for twelve!" [187].) David's emotional crisis was precipitated by his reluctance to tell Ralston the lie that his father imposed upon him. In his naïveté, David feels guilty about the contradiction between his own innocuous deceit and his role as George Washington, who, popular myth tells us, refused even to lie when it got him in trouble.

To put it another way, David's emotional crisis is precipitated by the contradiction between his Jewish heritage, symbolized by his small stature, and his adopted American identity, symbolized by the George Washington cloak. Rendered symbolically through the body, the contradiction is essentially ethical in nature. Jews in the Pale, oppressed by the Russian government, anti-Semitic laws, and predatory public officials, unconsciously adopted deceit as a tactic of self-preservation. "To many honest Jewish minds a lie was not a lie when told to an official" (188), Antin explains.[121] But the ethical code under which David's father (and formerly David himself) operates is no longer appropriate in his new home. "No ghost of a scruple had disturbed Mr. Rudinsky in his sense of triumph over circumstances, when he invented the lie that was to insure the education of his gifted child. With David, of course, the same philosophy had been valid. His father's plan for the protection of his future, hingeing [sic] on a too familiar sophistry, had dropped innocuous into his consciousness; until, in a moment of spiritual sensitiveness, it took on the visage of sin" (188). The lie had never troubled David until, in the role of the preternaturally honest George Washington, it acquired the character of a moral (or perhaps patriotic) transgression. Because physical and ethical contradictions are interchangeable in the story, David literally has difficulty embodying American identity; the cultural systems and the physical characteristics of Americans and Jewish immigrants are equally at odds. But unlike the contemporary physicians and anthropologists who claimed physical and mental traits were alike determined by race and heredity, Antin, by asserting that Jewish ethical attitudes were conditioned by the oppressive social and political environment of Russia, implies that the same may be true of physical characteristics. At the very least, she remains agnostic on the question of the basis of physical traits.

Again in opposition to the anti-immigrationists, Antin suggests that the ethical conflicts will ultimately vanish as immigrants become acculturated to the United States. In addition, Antin suggests that cultural incompatibilities between immigrants and their adopted home can be resolved by sympathetic Americans like Miss Ralston who are willing to traverse ethnic and cultural boundaries. Ralston's willingness to adapt American identity to the immigrant is apparent early in the story when she suggests that David's mother can adjust Washington's coat to suit David's dimensions. Later, she transgresses the boundaries of ethnic neighborhoods by visiting David's home. ("Half the children in the neighborhood escorted her to the door, attracted by the phenomenon of a Teacher loose on their streets" [185].) This symbolic defiance of ethnic boundaries is mirrored in her keen understanding of the conditions that have produced Jewish attitudes toward deception. Ralston praises Mr. Rudinsky's desire to educate his children at all costs, and she helps David overcome his prostration by convincing him that his father has conceived of "a *noble* lie" (189). In giving new value to Jewish ethics, Ralston helps David "weld . . . the scraps of his mixed inheritance, so that he saw his whole experience as an unbroken thing at last" (190). But, significantly, the cultural exchange goes both ways. David and his father show Ralston that Russian Jews have something to teach Americans about the value of education. "Why, you're a better American than some natives I know!" (186) she exclaims to Mr. Rudinsky. "In the hearts of men like your father," she tells David, "is the true America" (190). Far from threatening American values and racial character, argues Antin in "The Lie," immigrants will refashion and improve American identity.

Summary

While scientists regarded the small size of African and Southeast Asian pygmies as a sign of their antiquity and inferiority in a world characterized by racial struggle, both the writings on the pygmies of Europe and America and the turn-of-the-century American child growth studies treated the small body as an atavistic resurgence of primitive racial traits. Predicated on the view that heredity and race determined body size—stature in particular—these studies contributed to widespread anxieties about the presence of savages in the heart of the empire. Competition among the races might lead to the extinction of entire communities and nations, but it could not eliminate the reappearance of inferior traits in a mixed population like the United States. As the end of the nineteenth century drew near and with it the waning of bloody clashes on the vanishing American frontier, national vigilance was redirected toward urban problems and the battle against savage qualities in a progressive nation.

Before the nineteenth century, scientists and naturalists tended to assume that environmental factors and diet determined a person's growth and stature. French and English humanitarians in the first half of the nineteenth century argued that growth and size were determined by nutrition and social class. This view gave way to a widespread belief in the second half of the century that stature was an affair of race. The shift in attitudes was consistent with a general ideological shift in which environmentalist, monogenist positions on race gave way to hereditarian, polygenist ones.[122]

Despite these ideological shifts, tallness seems to have been a desirable trait throughout much of Western history. Early writers like Aristotle, Bacon, and Stoeller, for example, offered advice on how to make young people taller, a tradition that turn-of-the-century U.S. scientists revived. There are also indications from very early on that physical, mental, and moral traits were believed to be linked. The Tacitan myth, which proposed that immorality (i.e., early sex) could stunt growth, reflected ancient views on the relationship between body size and moral degeneration, for example. Buffon's version of the Tacitan myth—his suggestion that the climate of the Americas produced a physical degeneration reflected in the small size of animals and the deficient moral capacity of Native Americans—reflected an environmentalist view of degeneration.

Although they perpetuated the belief in the correspondence between physical, mental, and moral traits, turn-of-the-century U.S. scientists worked hard to refute allegations of American degeneration, continuing to use physical size as a gauge for national progress and decay. Post–Civil War military studies proclaimed the superiority of the American male relative to the man of Europe, affirmed the value of westward expansion as a force conducive to national progress, and rejected socioeconomic class as a determinant of stature. Despite the apparent success of U.S. scientists in refuting Buffon's allegations, the fear of American degeneration continued to haunt scientists and laypeople alike in an era when progress was both a cherished national goal and the supposedly defining characteristic of the Republic. Responding to the alarming social change produced by rapid urbanization and explosive immigration, U.S. military studies following World War I revived anxieties about degeneration (now conceived in racial terms), pointing to immigrants living in urban areas as the sources of American decay.

Anthropological and racial theories exerted a tremendous influence on turn-of-the-century child growth studies. This should not be surprising considering that the studies derived their methods—the weighing, measuring, and classifying of children—from physical anthropology. While the scientific investigators sometimes asserted more benign goals, such as the dispassionate derivation of the laws of human growth and the advancement of preventive medicine, the tools of their trade had a tainted legacy that was hard to overcome—and that virtually no authorities wished to overcome. Concerns about racial struggle and degeneration motivated virtually all American studies of child growth, which often compared small children, poor children, girls, immigrant children, and the "feeble-minded" to primitive people. Experts often argued against the coeducation of girls and boys on the basis of differential growth curves, and they recommended that small children of either sex be restricted in their school advancement. Belief in the value of segregation derived from the notion, developed at length by race theorists, that inner characteristics, like physical traits, were fixed. Scientists examined the correlation between physical size and intelligence and used their findings to bolster social hierarchies based on visible bodily signs. Despite calls for comparative studies of growth curves for different races, few resources and efforts were devoted to this research. Instead, most effort was directed toward regulating and increasing the stature of children of European descent. Medical authorities developed national height and weight standards in part as a tool for enhancing (Euro-)American stature, and they urged educators to use those standards to monitor the growth of children through routine measurements in schools. Evidence of the influence of racial theory on American growth studies can also be seen in the fact that most investigations ignored issues of class and that wealthy European-descended children were selected as the basis for national growth standards. When urbanization and the disappearance of the frontier seemed to threaten American progress by eliminating racial struggle and the promise of boundless resources, child growth experts and physical education advocates suggested that frontier conditions could be reproduced in the metropolis to revive the flagging American constitution. Attention to the child's body at the end of the nineteenth and beginning of the twentieth centuries represented, therefore, an attempt to maximize the potential of the nation's existing resources at a time when the United States could no longer depend on the seizure of distant lands. In the words of a physician who, in a lecture to the National Education Association in the early 1920s, advocated physical fitness and size standards for college admissions, "On all sides we meet testimony concerning the improved attitude and achievement resulting from bringing children . . . up to standards of normal health and strength. . . . The greatest satisfactions that arise in our work come from the effects that appear in the training for self-control when a child or young person has an opportunity to bear a part in working out his own program of welfare. He comes into the enjoyment of capital and resources beyond what he has known heretofore."[123] As American individuals acquired new and untapped resources, so too would the nation.

PART 2 • Size in the Marketplace

CHAPTER 3 • A Pygmy between Two Giants
The Economic Body in Popular Literature

In 1911, five years before he was appointed to the U.S. Supreme Court, Louis Brandeis was invited by Congress to testify to the merits of the La Follette-Stanley Bill, a federal antitrust bill that Brandeis helped to write and that would have limited the size of U.S. businesses had it passed. Before speaking, he sat for a day listening to the testimony of George Perkins, a partner in J. P. Morgan and Co. and representative of the formidable American steel industry. Perkins proclaimed the inevitability and beneficence of the trusts—the contemporary term for the enormous turn-of-the-century businesses that represented near monopolies in some sectors of American industry and that revolutionized the economy with their managerial hierarchies, mass production, mass distribution, and global activities. Brandeis disagreed vehemently with Perkins. After two and a half days of testimony in which he systematically refuted the claims of Perkins, Brandeis concluded, "There used to be a certain glamour about big things. Anything big, simply because it was big, seemed to be good and great. We are now coming to see that big things may be very bad and mean."[1]

The inherent danger of big things was a theme that Brandeis would espouse repeatedly over the coming years. In so doing, he was arguing against the growing consensus of his day. "Bigness in American industry and commerce," explained the *New York Times* in 1909, "is coming to be popularly associated with honest American progress."[2] As a way of challenging such orthodoxy-in-formation, Brandeis routinely destabilized the rhetoric of size in his writings. He labeled corporate consolidation the "curse of bigness"; a collection of his essays, legal opinions, and interviews published in 1934, in fact, would bear this phrase as its title. He celebrated the achievements of individual entrepreneurs, or the "big men" of the American economic scene, over big business, which he dubbed "little business" for its eagerness to take false credit for the development of American industry.[3] In a commencement day lecture in 1912, Brandeis told graduates of Brown University that big business would be truly "big"—that is, "great in service and grand in manner" rather than big "in bulk or power"—only when it acknowledged the rights of its workers. Only then would the term *big business,* he said, "lose its sinister meaning."[4]

Brandeis adopted his iconoclastic position during the rise of corporate capitalism, when the domination of big business that we take for granted as intrinsic to the U.S. economic landscape was still in the process of formation. From about the late 1870s to about 1920, the United States underwent profound social change; the influential economic historian Alfred Chandler has designated that period the Second Industrial Revolution. Debates over the virtues and dangers of simple bigness—debates that had significance beyond the economic register— were integral to the social response. The very meanings of *big* and *little* at this time were contested and in flux. Even as the significations of size extended into new realms such as the discourse of racial classification, the turn of the century paradoxically also presented an opportunity for a significant reconstitution of the meanings of size.

Carroll Smith-Rosenberg would describe this era as one of "semantic disorder"—a moment when vast social transformations were reflected in linguistic instability and competing symbolic systems. "During moments of social restructuring," she explains, "no one group will possess the power to impose its language, values, or behavior upon any other. . . . Dominant and marginal groups [will] construct elaborate symbolic systems which, like the rails of a train, cover the same territory, parallel to each other but never crossing."[5] In *Disorderly Conduct,* Smith-Rosenberg studies the distinctive symbolic systems that formed along the cleavages of gender in nineteenth-century America. Similar cleavages formed along class lines in response to transformations in the American economy. In political discourse, economic theory, labor images, and popular fiction, three "warring mythic figures," to borrow Smith-Rosenberg's phrase,[6] originated as three alternative visions of the economic future of the United States. The first of these images, the giant Incorporated Body, represented the dominant vision of the corporate elite and reflected its hierarchical worldview. Labor responded with its own image of the Unionized Body, a metaphor of democratic solidarity that turned the corporate image on its head. Both were images of giants that sanctioned the values of bigness, although the meanings they attached to large size were diametrically opposed. In a defensive move meant to forestall both the hierarchical and the socialist worldviews as well as the trend toward massive social institutions, the middle class offered its own mythic figure of the Little Man, the independent businessperson best suited to a competitive, Jeffersonian economy of small businesses. Although the corporate vision finally prevailed, remnants of the alternative ideologies remain in labor culture, folk mythology,[7] recent revivals of the economic debates on the merits of big business,[8] and the globalization debate.

In order to understand the various responses to the transformations wrought by the Second Industrial Revolution, it is important first to understand the institutional and social effects of those changes. Perhaps the most conspicuous change was a vast increase in the scale of American manufacturing. Gross domestic product in the United States expanded more than fivefold between 1870 and World War I.[9] Steel production alone increased more than sixty times between 1875 and 1914.[10] At the beginning of the twentieth century the Durham factories of American Tobacco stamped out 10 million Camel cigarettes in a day, more than five times the total daily world demand of the early 1880s.[11] Several factors enabled American manufacturing to expand so quickly, including innovations in industrial technology, permissive incorporation laws, a massive growth in population, innovations in communication and transportation that facilitated the development of a national market, and the economies of scale. Defenders of big business did their best to emphasize the latter factor and succeeded in persuading the public that this God-given economic "law," not to be resisted, was the chief cause of the industrial transformations. In fact, the supposed economies of scale were greatly overemphasized and assumed a mythologized status in turn-of-the-century economic debates.[12] Although large-scale production is significantly more efficient in industries like petroleum, steel, sugar, and tobacco, many labor-intensive industries like apparel, textiles, leather, lumber, furniture, printing, and publishing do not afford significantly greater efficiency with increases in size.[13] In many industries, furthermore, businesses increased to a size so great that the inefficiencies of their large bureaucracies outweighed the advantages of scale economies. Moreover, the economies of scale can only be exploited when there is sufficient demand. Despite the widespread obsession with increased productivity throughout American industry at the turn of the century, not all of the increases were needed. Production levels often exceeded consumer demand, contributing to the boom-bust cycles that were the hallmark of the era. One of the ways manufacturers responded to this dilemma was to rely on advertising to create demand for their products. Advertising firms took over the tasks that business proprietors had once performed themselves; the revenues of such firms tripled between 1900 and 1930. Changes in the nature of advertising hastened the development of mass production and helped to fashion the culture of consumption that would ensure high demand for manufactured goods.[14]

While production increased explosively, the number of businesses shrank as rapidly, shifting the nation's economy from one based on numerous small-scale family businesses and partnerships to an economy dominated by huge corporations. In part, this trend occurred as manufacturers sought additional ways to respond to the constraints of consumer demand while simultaneously exploiting the economies of scale; they succeeded by eliminating the number of producers and thereby regulating production levels more effectively. "In the realm of industry the big mill is absorbing the little mill; in the business world the big store is crushing out the little store; in the rural districts the great farm is absorbing the little farm," wrote John Williams, president of a Pittsburgh steelworkers' union, in 1912.[15] "The present organization of business was meant for the big fellows and was not meant for the little fellows," added Woodrow Wilson in the same year.[16] Between 1880 and 1905, three merger movements eliminated thousands of businesses and concentrated production in many industries among a few huge companies.[17] American Tobacco, for example, absorbed 162 separate firms during this time and eventually controlled 90 percent of the market in cigarettes.[18] The result of these changes was predictable, if revolutionary at the time: near monopolies and oligopolies dominated several major industries, American businesses developed bureaucracies with complex layers of management hierarchies, and the industrial wealth of the nation was concentrated in the hands of a few large corporations.

These profound changes in the nation's economy affected virtually every facet of life. Middle-class men learned that independent ownership of small businesses was less feasible than it had once been. "A greatly increased proportion of young men must expect to work on salaries in large organizations," advised Albert Shaw in a convocation address to the students of the University of Chicago in the first decade of the twentieth century.[19] As permanent salaried positions became the reigning ambition, business schools formed to train young middle-class men in the skills of middle management. A new vision of life emerged as a steady rise up a hierarchical ladder,[20] a vision that sanctioned the idea of hierarchies in other domains.

There were also notable changes in people's daily environment. Rural towns emptied and urban areas grew to accommodate the influxes of rural and immigrant workers serving the newly concentrated American industries. Railroad cars and terminals, public buildings such as libraries and courthouses, factories, and industrial machinery all grew in size. The skyscraper emerged as the dominant architectural symbol of corporate culture. With mass production came novel forms of mass distribution: the department store, the mail-order house, and the chain retail store. Magazine advertisements expanded from the double-column style typical of the 1870s to a quarter page in the early 1890s, a half page at the turn of the century, and a full or double page in the first decade of the twentieth century. They also grew in volume: between 1870 and 1890 ads in popular magazines like *Harper's Weekly* and *Peterson's Ladies National Magazine* multiplied from four to five pages with few illustrations to over one hundred lavishly illustrated pages per issue.[21] "Everything is being done on a large scale; everything is becoming colossal," observed F. B. Thurber, president of the United States Export Association, in a speech at the Chicago Conference on Trusts of 1899.[22]

The revolution in the economy also contributed to conflicts between labor and capital. With overproduction and the boom-bust economy came long periods of mass unemployment, depression, and labor unrest. Socialism experienced its greatest popularity at this time. During their best years before World War I, socialists captured twelve hundred state and local government positions, and the founder of the Socialist Party, Eugene Debs, garnered almost a million votes in each of his bids for president in 1912 and 1920.[23] Between 1881 and 1905, the nation witnessed thirty-seven thousand strikes involving 7 million workers.[24] The American Federation of Labor (AFL), the nation's largest union of the early twentieth century, expanded its membership from 278,000 in 1898 to 2 million in 1907.[25] As industrial labor grew to represent a larger proportion of the U.S. population than ever before or since—accounting, by some estimates, for almost 20 percent of the labor force in 1920[26]—and as inequalities in income distribution increased, reaching their peak in 1916,[27] these conflicts only accelerated. During the period of greatest labor activism in the nation's history, from 1915 to 1922, 1 million workers struck each year.[28] The need for organized labor was clearly evident. Industrial working conditions were frightful, and industry's mania for accelerated productivity and cost cutting endangered the lives of millions of workers. Each year between 1888 and 1908, an estimated thirty-five thousand industrial workers were killed and half a million injured on the job.[29] In the 1880s, about 40 percent of industrial laborers lived below the poverty line.[30] In 1912, the Associated Charities of Pittsburgh reported that an ordinary male steelworker with a wife and three children who worked 365 days a year for twelve hours a day would be unable to earn a subsistence wage. From the sweat of such laborers, the Steel Trust extracted dividends of 650 million dollars between 1902 and 1912.[31]

The increasing concentration of wealth and the increasing hierarchies in the workplace engendered concerns about the possibility of maintaining a political democracy in the presence of an industrial autocracy. "Can this contradiction—our grand political liberty and this industrial slavery—long coexist?" asked Louis Brandeis in 1912. "Either political liberty will be extinguished or industrial liberty must be restored," he warned.[32] The drumfire reports about government corruption and the writings of the muckrakers contributed to the sense that the moneyed powers, rather than the people, controlled the nation. From about 1870 to 1920, the great trust debates raged; in 1912 they were the single most important issue in the presidential campaign. Various proposals were offered, from the radical socialist solutions of public ownership of industry to the moderate ones of tariff reform, railroad rate controls, antitrust litigation, and federal incorporation certificates. Given the American distaste for radical economic reforms, predictably moderate pieces of legislation came out of the debates, including the Interstate Commerce Act of 1887, the Sherman Antitrust Act of 1890, and the Clayton and Federal Trade Commission Acts of 1914. All proved inadequate in preventing the domination of big business.

The increasing hierarchization and bureaucratization of the workplace also hastened the death of the American myth of individualism even as the myth was peddled more vigorously than ever in popular literature like Westerns. As Peter Conn explains in *The Divided Mind,* changes in the size of American businesses, cities, and industrial machinery, as well as the presumed loss of the frontier where the mythic American individual had supposedly been nurtured, "contributed to the actual and imaginative diminishment of the individual."[33] Evidence of this ideological transformation is apparent everywhere in the writings of the day. "There is a sense in which in our day the individual has been submerged," said presidential hopeful Woodrow Wilson in a campaign speech in 1912. "Men work for themselves, not as partners in the old way in which they used to work, but as employees—in a higher or lower grade—of great corporations. . . . Today, the everyday relationships of men are largely with great impersonal concerns, with organizations, not with other individual men."[34] John Hayes, general secretary of the Knights of Labor, expressed similar sentiments. "The great corporations, the trusts," he said in 1899, "with their capital, their machinery, special privileges, and other advantages, are overwhelming the individual, reducing him to the condition of a mere tool."[35] "The workingman loses his individuality as soon as he enters one of our modern industrial plants," added John Williams. "He becomes but an atom in the great aggregate of this industrial system, and his only hope of regaining his social and economic individuality is by uniting with his fellow workmen."[36]

Conn argues that a spirit of cooperation replaced the ideology of individualism in this era. Certainly one senses at times the egalitarian implications of that spirit in the writings of socialists and labor leaders of the day. The emerging corporate culture, on the other hand, infused the new spirit of cooperation with the principle of hierarchy, suggests Alan Trachtenberg in *The Incorporation of America;* corporate culture, he argues, valued "unity through subordination."[37] While these generalizations may be helpful, it is not always easy to disentangle those competing visions (egalitarian-socialist and hierarchical-corporate) in the thinking and writing of specific individuals. Consider Edward Bellamy's best-selling 1888 utopian novel *Looking Backward.* In describing an imagined transition from capitalism to socialism (or, in the term Bellamy preferred, Christian nationalism), Bellamy characterized his own era as "the age of individualism." The formation of large corporate businesses marked the turning point between his age and "the age of concert." "When the era of small concerns with small capital was succeeded by that of the great aggregations of capital, . . . the individual laborer, who had been relatively important to the small employer, was reduced to insignificance and powerlessness over against the great corporation. . . . Self-defense drove him to union with his fellows."[38] Like most socialists of his day, Bellamy believed that the trend toward large corporate institutions was a promising sign since it would ease the inevitable transition to a socialized economy. While the eventual achievement of an economy based on collective ownership of the means of production represents a shift toward socialist collectivism in his novel, it takes the form of a hierarchical state modeled on the army. Democratic collectivism and unity through subordination are both elements of Bellamy's vision of the future utopian state.

Often this social transformation—the loss of individualism, the appearance of massive institutions—was expressed simply as a fear of bigness in the presence of which human beings seemed to be shrinking; in this sense, the changes in social scale transformed attitudes about the human position in the world and sparked debates about inherent human capacities.[39] At the heart of the matter was the question, Will human beings keep pace with the social changes transforming the nation and world (will they grow?) or will they simply remain the same creatures in a terrifyingly new world (will they appear to shrink in a suddenly enlarged environment?)? Attention to the size of the human body, in other words, played a central role in these ideological shifts and debates. The upward, progressive evolution of Bellamy's socialist state, for example, is coupled with the upward growth of its citizenry. "From the moment men allowed themselves to believe that humanity after all had not been meant for a dwarf, that its squat stature was not the measure of its possible growth, but that it stood upon the verge of an avatar of limitless development, . . . every man stood up straight before God." Bellamy believed in the possibility of his utopian vision because he had faith in "the unbounded possibilities of human nature."[40] Others were less optimistic. Although he favored worker management of industry and applauded the cooperative movement as a step toward industrial democracy, Louis Brandeis rejected socialism because he believed it would lead, like unregulated corporate capitalism, to massive institutions uncontrollable by human beings with their inherent limitations. Unlike Bellamy, in other words, Brandeis did not believe that humans were likely to improve beyond their current capabilities, and like many of his contemporaries he used the language of stature as a signifier for human progress. It is essential, he believed, that we "adjust our institutions to the wee size of man." "If the Lord had intended things to be big," he wrote, "he would have made man bigger—in brains and character."[41] His opposition to institutional bigness was tested during the New Deal when Franklin Roosevelt proposed massive social programs that would greatly enlarge the powers and scope of the federal government while easing the rigors of the Depression. Brandeis remained consistent. "The federal government must not become too big just as corporations should not be permitted to become too big. You must remember that it is the littleness of man that limits the size of things we can undertake."[42] Brandeis liked to remind his readers of the German saying, "Care is taken that the trees do not scrape the skies."[43]

It may be apparent that the disagreement between Bellamy and Brandeis was not limited to the human capacity for growth. Their opinions on the dangers of big institutions also clashed. Dispute on this subject was widespread and became crucial in the presidential election of 1912. After years of confusion regarding the appropriate application of the Sherman Antitrust Act, which prohibited monopolies and any business combinations "in restraint of trade," the Supreme Court finally issued its Rule of Reason verdict in 1911. According to this ruling, the large size of a business was not in and of itself a legitimate motive for federal prosecution. Rather, it was unfair business practices made possible by economic power that merited punishment and the dissolution of a company.[44] Presidential hopeful Theodore Roosevelt supported the Court's decision. A firm believer in the value of big things and their necessity in the modern world, Roosevelt suggested that trusts could be divided into the good and the bad according to whether they used fair or unfair business practices. Size was irrelevant in this distinction. "We do not desire the abolition or destruction of big corporations, but, on the contrary, recognize them as being in many cases efficient economic instruments, the results of an inevitable process of economic evolution," said Roosevelt in 1903.[45] "I do not believe in making mere size of and by itself criminal."[46] "The line of demarcation we draw must always be on conduct, not upon wealth," he added. "Our objection to any given corporation must be, not that it is big, but that it behaves badly."[47] President Taft agreed with Roosevelt and the Supreme Court, as did the conservative and influential economist John Moody.[48]

Brandeis, not surprisingly, disagreed. "The proposition that mere bigness can not be an offense against society is false," he told the Senate Interstate Commerce Committee in 1911.[49]

> The statement that size is not a crime is entirely correct when you speak of it from the point of motive. But size may become such a danger in its results to the community that the community may have to set limits. . . . Concentration of power has been shown to be dangerous in a democracy, even though that power may be used beneficently. For instance, on our public highways we put a limit on the size of an autotruck, no matter how well it is run. It may have the most skillful and considerate driver, but its mere size may make it something which the community cannot tolerate.[50]

The Interstate Commerce Committee who listened to Brandeis— Senator Robert La Follette, the habitual presidential candidate William Jennings Bryan, and the respected economist John Bates Clark—lined up beside Brandeis.[51] All supported limits to the size of businesses. Woodrow Wilson, on the other hand, felt conflicted. He agreed with Roosevelt that "The development of business upon a great scale . . . is inevitable, and, let me add, is probably desirable." At the same time, he regretted the effect of giant corporations on small companies—"this crushing of the little man," as he called it. He was impressed by the ideas of Brandeis and relied on his economic advice during the election campaigns. Yet he did not share Brandeis's fundamental distrust of large economic institutions. "I am not jealous of the size of any business that has *grown* to that size," he said. "I am not jealous of any process of growth, no matter how huge the result, provided the result was indeed obtained by the processes of wholesome development, which are the processes of efficiency, of economy, of intelligence, and of invention." Through Brandeis's influence, Wilson became convinced that the trusts (which he distinguished from big businesses—"I am for big business, and I am against the trusts," he said) had not grown to their size through "processes of efficiency" but rather through predatory business practices. He vowed to prohibit such practices. He hoped that such measures would secure a place for the "little man" in an era of big business.[52] Ultimately there was little difference between Wilson and Roosevelt, and, as Martin Sklar has argued, "Wilson emerged as a foremost ideological and political leader of a social movement affirming industrial corporate capitalism."[53]

Fiction of the time reflected and contributed to this ideological ferment. In addition to Edward Bellamy, prominent writers such as

Theodore Dreiser, Jack London, Upton Sinclair, Frank Norris, and Ernest Poole all addressed the trust debates and the associated ideological disputes directly. It is probably no accident that the novel was the form most often chosen to examine these matters. As the most capacious literary genre, it was an appropriate medium in which to explore the contemporary trend toward bigness. Both Norris and Dreiser, in fact, went even further: each proposed a trilogy of novels (Norris's "Epic of the Wheat" and Dreiser's "Trilogy of Desire") to address the modern economic and social condition. The fact that one of the hallmarks of naturalist writing, moreover, is its length is indicative of the formative (and formal) relationship between naturalism and the large-scale, corporate economy.[54] Indirectly, virtually all of the period's literature reflected the nation's social transformations. While the emerging genre of the Western nostalgically glorified rugged, independent, self-sufficient heroes, for example, other genres expressed threats to the mythology of individualism as a rejection of the traditional hero. Naturalism characteristically proffered tragic or flawed heroes who succumbed to the implacable forces of nature (whether internal or external), while modernism would emphasize the antihero and challenge the notion of unified, stable subjectivity altogether.

The final section of this chapter examines two literary responses to the revolutionary changes in size and scale in Progressive America: Frank Norris's *The Octopus* (the first in his "Epic of the Wheat") and Ernest Poole's *The Harbor*. Like most writers of the day, Norris and Poole wrote to the Little Man of the middle class, attempting to accommodate their readers to the threatening scale of the modern corporate state. By privileging the middle-class response to social and institutional change, both writers helped solidify the ideological and political power of the group at a time when their numerical and economic power appeared to be jeopardized by an expanding lower class and a concentration of wealth among the industrial elite. While their sympathies differed (Poole was a socialist who shared labor's vision of a democratic, egalitarian gigantism; Norris expressed middle-class fatalism toward big business), both believed that large institutions were a distinctive and permanent part of the modern landscape.

The Giant Incorporated Body

American corporate laws played a key role in the development of big business and the trusts in the late nineteenth century. The device of incorporation was a legal form that allowed entrepreneurs to amass large amounts of capital from numerous individuals under a single business entity. Traditionally, the government conferred corporate status selectively upon businesses engaged in public service enterprises like water supply and transportation, and it generally restricted such businesses in size and scope. After the Civil War, when capital became scarce and the economy expanded rapidly, special government charters conferring corporate status gave way to less restrictive policies allowing virtually any business to incorporate. This facilitated capital formation and divorced the corporation from its public service responsibilities. The corporate form rapidly became the most popular business organization, especially among the large, capital-intensive industries.[55]

American corporation laws did more than facilitate the growth of big business, however; they also provided a new concept of personhood and embodiment with implications beyond merely the financial. According to key Supreme Court interpretations, a corporation had the legal status of a person; it could, for example, enter into contracts and hold property.[56] Virtually all later writings emphasized the animate quality of the corporation. The Incorporated Body was represented, especially by opponents of big business, as an octopus, a Frankenstein monster, a behemoth, a Goliath, a dinosaur, a Titan, and a giant. William Jennings Bryan offered a colorful expression of this common view at the Chicago Conference on Trusts of 1899.

> When God made man as the climax of creation he looked upon his work and said that it was good, and yet when God finished his work the tallest man was not much taller than the shortest, and the strongest man was not much stronger than the weakest. That was God's plan. We looked upon his work and said that it was not quite as good as it might be, and so we made a fictitious person called a corporation that is in some instances a hundred times—a thousand times—a million times stronger than the God-made man. Then we started this man-made giant out among the God-made men.[57]

As a person, however artificial, the corporation had specific properties that differed from other living beings as well as other economic organizations and that therefore made it appear more menacing. First, unlike business forms such as individual ownership and the partnership that were more common before the Civil War, this artificial being could outlive its founders. This potential immortality made the corporation, as a living creature, seem tremendously powerful and intimidating to contemporary observers. "When God made man," said Bryan, "he placed a limit to his existence, so that if he was a bad man he could not do harm long, but when we made our man-made man we raised the limit of his age. In some states a corporation is given perpetual life."[58] Second, it was indefinitely expansive; that is, it could have an unlimited number of members (or shareholders) and an unlimited amount of capital (not to mention an unlimited number of employees, unlimited profit, and apparently unlimited power). In *The Octopus,* Frank Norris represented this vast assimilative power of the corporation not as a potential symbol of democratic collectivism (the way unions would represent their unlimited membership) but as a limitless capacity and desire for destructive consumption. In bodily terms, this meant that the Pacific and Southwest Railroad, the villain of his novel, was a vast octopus, "gorged to bursting . . . a gigantic parasite fattening upon the life-blood of an entire commonwealth." The railroad's representatives, S. Behrman and Shelgrim, were large and fat; S. Behrman's "great stomach," wrote Norris, "protruded far in advance, enormous, aggressive," and Shelgrim was "a giant figure," an incomparably broad man, one "large, almost to massiveness."[59] In a scene of symbolic overconsumption, S. Behrman meets his poetic end when a flood of wheat in a grain elevator kills him. "The Wheat . . . covered the great protuberant stomach, it ran at last in rivulets into the distended, gasping mouth" (646). Third, the corporate form conferred limited legal liability upon its members; that is, shareholders could not be sued and would not be held liable for any debts the corporation incurred. Coupled with the fact that big companies often had large sums of money with which to fight legal battles, this suggested that the corporation, as an animated being, was unaccountable for its actions, potentially ruthless, unbound by conventions of morality—in a word, soulless. As Bryan put it, "When God made man he breathed into him a soul and warned him that in the next world he would be held accountable for the deeds done in the flesh, but when we made our man-made man we did not give him a soul, and if he can avoid punishment in this world he need not worry about the hereafter."[60] Its members, finally, were related in a hierarchical fashion: in exchange for limited liability, investors relinquished control over the organization to the board of directors or managers. Thus, as a living, composite creature, the corporation was nurtured in a climate of autocracy, a characteristic that suggested to opponents of big business like Brandeis that corporations threatened democracy.

> Ownership has been separated from control; and this separation
> has removed many of the checks which formerly operated to
> curb the misuse of wealth and power. And as ownership of the
> shares is becoming continually more dispersed, the power

which formerly accompanied ownership is becoming increasingly concentrated in the hands of a few. The changes thereby wrought in the lives of the workers, of the owners and of the general public, are so fundamental and far-reaching as to lead . . . scholars to compare the evolving "corporate system" with the feudal system; and to lead other men of insight and experience to assert that this "master institution of civilised life" is committing it to the rule of a plutocracy. . . . Such is the Frankenstein monster which States have created by their incorporation laws.[61]

One of the most conspicuous defenders of big business and laissez-faire economics was Andrew Carnegie. Carnegie owned and operated the most successful and largest single steel works in the country during the last two decades of the nineteenth century. Because he could manufacture high-quality steel more cheaply than any rival, Carnegie was a constant source of irritation to the massive Steel Trust. In 1900, the Steel Trust's owner, J. P. Morgan, finally succeeded in eliminating him as a competitor, paying an exorbitant sum for his company and making Carnegie the richest man in the nation. Although Carnegie's goal in such essays as "The Bugaboo of Trusts" (1889) and "Popular Illusions About Trusts" (1900) was to dispel the notion that giant corporations such as the Steel Trust threatened the nation by showing that efforts to monopolize an industry were ultimately doomed, his writings must have done little to assuage anxieties about the growth of big business. Like the corporate culture that sustained the trusts, Carnegie's vision of society was thoroughly hierarchical. In "The Gospel of Wealth" (1889), for example, he argued that great inequality of wealth was "not only beneficial but essential to the progress of the race" because it allowed "the highest type of man" to become a trustee for his "poorer brethren" and thereby administer his riches for the good of the community, bringing to the less fortunate his superior wisdom and experience and "doing for them better than they would or could do for themselves." Even more so than Edward Bellamy, Carnegie was, in his own words, an avowed "evolutionist, who sees nothing but certain and steady progress for the race." Consequently, he tended to assume that whatever social and economic developments occurred in his day were likely to bring good things. The trend toward bigness, which he helped to foster, was therefore advantageous. "The day of small concerns within the means of many able men seems to be over, never to return," he proclaimed. "The concentration of capital" permitted by economic organizations like the corporation, he said, is "an evolution . . . another step in the upward path of development."[62]

Like Bellamy and the evolutionary scientists of the day, Carnegie assumed that humans were constantly improving. Changes in the human body and character would mirror changes in the social fabric. "Dealing with petty affairs tends to make small men; dealing with larger affairs broadens and strengthens character," he wrote. "The small, petty master in his little store has given place to the bigger, much more important manager of a department, whose revenues generally exceed those of the petty owner he has supplanted. . . . This bigger system grows bigger men, and it is by the big men that the standard of the race is raised. The race of shopkeepers is bound to be improved."[63] In such utterances, Carnegie hoped to counteract the celebratory rhetoric of the independent store owner, or Jeffersonian Little Man. Both arguments, of course, rendered the social effects of corporate capitalism in terms of the male body; like the ideology of the separate spheres, they effectively banished women from the economic sphere, a subject I will return to in chapters 5 and 6. For the purposes of the present discussion, the key element of Carnegie's argument is his view that society is not constrained by the limitations of human beings because humans are constantly evolving.

There were many ironies in Carnegie's position. For one, he was an independent businessman yet owned one of the largest steel mills in the country. He never liked the corporate form, preferring to operate businesses as limited partnerships. The only corporation he willingly established was created for the purpose of dispensing his wealth to projects for the public good. He came to be associated with the robber barons, yet his company was not among the trusts. Despite his professed respect for labor, his company was responsible for one of the bloodiest labor battles in U.S. history, the Homestead Strike of 1892. His operation was profoundly hierarchical, yet it was more in line with family business than big business and undermined the power of the Steel Trust. As contemporary journalists loved to point out, Carnegie himself was a small man. Biographers have seized upon this fact to suggest that his ambitiousness was rooted in a Napoleon complex, so the very prejudices Carnegie relied upon have been routinely used against him.[64] Finally, Carnegie's business partners evidently lacked his faith in big business. When he heard of the company's expansion plans in 1897, Carnegie's partner, Henry Phipps, declared, "My breath was taken away. . . . By all means do let us go a little slower, my heart is often in my mouth when I read of their rushing way in *big* things."[65]

The Giant Unionized Body

The formation of large corporate trusts, said M. M. Garland, president of the Amalgamated Association of Iron and Steel Workers, in his speech at the Chicago Conference on Trusts, "was used as one of the exhorting features for organizing labor among the iron and steel workers . . . and now it works a most active development of organization among workingmen because of example from employer."[66] Certainly there were many factors contributing to the growth of unions in turn-of-the-century America—including brutal working conditions, the increasing distance between management and labor, the growing concentration of workers in large industrial plants, the presence of immigrants with backgrounds in European radicalism, and the diminishing possibility of escape from salaried labor in the form of independent ownership—but, as Garland says, the example of consolidations among employers no doubt played a role. Samuel Gompers, president of the AFL, argued that both the trusts and the unions were the "logical and inevitable accompaniment and development of our modern commercial and industrial system." Like Bellamy, Gompers believed the modern industrial system "obliterate[s] the individuality of the worker and thus force[s] him into an association . . . with his fellows," and he understood his own age as "the era of association as contrasted with individual effort."[67]

Their structural similarities reflect the influence of the corporate form on the union. Both were composite entities formed by a potentially unlimited number of individuals working in association. Both were capable of outliving their members—in the contemporary parlance, they had a life of their own. While there were obvious similarities, however, there were also important differences. As Alan Trachtenberg explains, "Corporations absolved their investors from liability should the joint enterprise fail. . . . But the predominant meaning of 'union' in these years lay in the motto of the Knights of Labor: 'An injury to one is the concern of all.' Rather than absolving members of liability, unions fostered a sense of mutual responsibility."[68] Equally important, unions were democratic in their aims, as opposed to the hierarchical character of trusts. Union leaders were elected, and decisions affecting the members were made collectively. Unions were driven not by the exploitative aim of profits but by a desire to defend the rights and needs of their members from exploitation. "*The trade union is not, and from its very nature can not be, a trust,*" Gompers exclaimed. "The trade union is the *voluntary association of the many for the benefit of all* the community. The trust is the voluntary association of the few for their own benefit. . . . The trade union ever seeks to distribute the benefits of modern methods of production among the many."[69] "The very word 'union,'" adds Trachtenberg, "echoed with the original principle of the nation itself—E Pluribus Unum—while 'incorporation' implied a unity based on unequal members."[70]

Gompers and other labor leaders felt compelled to distinguish unions from trusts in emphatic terms because the courts persistently failed to do so: in a bizarre perversion of the intent of the Sherman Antitrust Act and a clear indication of the judicial animosity toward labor unions, most early antimonopoly suits were leveled against unions rather than businesses.[71] The legal battles that unions faced for their mere survival drained their resources and hindered other activities. Union leaders, therefore, were justifiably suspicious of antitrust legislation, which was principally conceived and backed by middle-class businessmen. In 1899, Gompers concluded that efforts to curb the growth of big business were more likely to hurt ordinary workers than accomplish their intended goal.[72]

Like corporations, unions were also personified in popular literature and illustrations. The body imagined by socialists and labor activists, like the Incorporated Body, was that of a giant. The International Workers of the World (IWW), for example, rendered organized labor as a massive, muscled, often poorly clad industrial worker who towered above factory complexes (see fig. 14). The IWW's goal was the inverse of corporate goals: the unification of the world not through imperialist penetration of foreign markets and the quest for profit but through democratic inclusion of the world's workers within one organization and the destruction of capitalism and its attendant inequalities. Their slogan, appropriately, was "The One Big Union." Their giant figure of Labor reflected the IWW's democratic spirit. The figure's humble clothing, for example, suggested the austerity and unpretentiousness of the common industrial worker. In contrast to the humble dress of the giant Labor, the equally gigantic figure of Capital envisioned by the IWW and the socialists wore sparkling jewels and opulent coattails (see figs. 15 and 21). Often the giant Unionized Body was juxtaposed with a mass of indistinguishable, ordinary-sized workers moving together in one direction (see fig. 16). In such incarnations, the figure represented the egalitarian consolidation of workers in one integrated body. Because laborers needed to organize and develop a class consciousness before the ultimate aims of socialism could be realized, the giant figure of Labor was often depicted sleeping or blindfolded (see figs. 17–18). A blindfold, in fact, was the only garment worn by the "Giant Worker" in an illustration from the socialist periodical *The Masses*. His nakedness suggested the rebirth of man following a socialist revolution—a rebirth that would produce a larger, superior humanity, an idea reinforced by the illustration's label for the defenders of the status quo: "the pigmy retainers of Capitalism" (fig. 18).

The figure of the laboring giant replaced the image of the arm and

SOLIDARITY
TAKES THE WHOLE WORKS
JOIN THE
ONE BIG UNION

14. IWW, "Solidarity Takes the Whole Works" (ca. 1910). The giant Laboring Body in is IWW poster takes industry in hand. The oden shoe, a symbol of industrial sabotage French derivation, was a common element more militant labor imagery.

Fig. 15. *The Masses,* "Fe, Fi, Fo, Fan." Socialists rendered Capital as an obese, ostentatious giant putting the squeeze on Labor.

THREE THOUSAND HAVE JOINED THE I. W. W. IN THE LAST MONTH

Fig. 16. IWW, "Three Thousand Have Joined the I.W.W. in the Last Month." The giant Laboring Body was often depicted beside industrial masses to symbolize its collective, democratic consciousness. (Reproduced from *Industrial Worker,* June 15, 1911.)

WHEN WILL THE SLEEPER WAKE?

Fig. 17. IWW, "When Will the Sleeper Wake?" Socialists often depicted the Laboring Body as a sleeping giant waiting to rouse itself. (Reproduced from *Industrial Worker,* February 8, 1912.)

Fig. 19. *The Union,* Arm and Hammer. The arm and hammer was the dominant symbol of organized labor in the early nineteenth century. It was supplanted by the Labor Giant in the late nineteenth century.

Fig. 18. Philip Ward, "Taking Off the Bandage." " 'Do not take the bandage off your eyes!' shout the pigmy retainers of Capitalism to the Giant Worker," says the text below this illustration from *The Masses.* A common image in labor and socialist iconography was the giant Laboring Body exploited by the diminutive and small-minded institutions of capitalist society: the priesthood, the press, the judiciary, and the academy. (Reproduced from *The Masses,* August 1912.)

hammer as the dominant symbol of organized labor in the late nine-teenth century.[73] The image of the arm and hammer, conceived in the early nineteenth century, emphasized the simple virtue of hard, physical work. It sought to dignify manual labor at a time when independent artisans were threatened by new systems that eroded the value of their work (factory labor, the wage system, the putting-out system, and sweated labor) and when the traditional esteem for physical labor was being usurped by a growing middle-class admiration for white-collar employment.[74] By the late nineteenth century, when organized labor consisted primarily of factory workers performing repetitive, routinized, highly specialized tasks under fierce regimens of productivity—when the very bodies of workers were increasingly regulated, manipulated, and controlled by the labor they performed and the machines they worked with rather than the other way around—the image of the arm and hammer, which took for granted a worker's control over the tools and pace of labor, was increasingly outdated. Where the image of the arm and hammer offered a vision of bodily fragmentation, moreover, the figure of the giant imagined a bodily integrity that counteracted the frag-mentation inherent in the subdivision and specialization of labor under the scientific management regimes of the late nineteenth and early twen-tieth centuries. The figure of the giant represented a fantasy of empow-erment; as laborers were increasingly discomfited by the enormous scale of factories, machines, and corporate organizations, the Labor Giant offered an inverted vision of a powerful, muscular worker towering over vast industrial complexes.

If the musculature of the Unionized Body suggested latent power, his slenderness connoted a life of moderation that would enable a more equable distribution of wealth in a future socialist state. The giant Incor-porated Body, on the other hand, was (like Frank Norris's representa-tives of the Pacific and Southwest Railroad) powerful yet obese, enlarged from self-indulgence and the malevolent hoarding of wealth. Cultural historians have recently identified a major shift in attitudes toward weight that occurred at the turn of the century. A preference for corpulent bodies in Gilded Age America (as well as other eras prior to this one) gave way to a general disdain for fatness at the turn of the cen-tury, a trend that sharpened throughout the twentieth century.[75] Expla-nations for this phenomenon have emphasized economic developments but not economic debates. The shift to a culture of abundance aroused a general preoccupation with patterns of consumption, scholars have sug-gested.[76] The widespread promotion of dieting that began in this period, argues Peter Stearns, "was ideally suited to an American need for an implicit but vigorous moral counterweight to growing consumer indulgence."[77] Thus, thinness became a sign of responsible, measured consumption, while fatness implied a lack of self-discipline, a failure of individual control.

But if, as I argue in this book, America's turn-of-the-century culture of expansion had an effect on ideas about the body—if it encouraged Americans to extol tall bodies—how does one account for the simultaneous and seemingly contradictory denigration of fatness that began in this period? The labor illustrations provide one possible answer. The divided feelings about the nation's culture of expansion—particularly concerns about the growth of big business that were central to the trust debates—manifested themselves in a bifurcated attitude toward big bodies. The negative connotations of bigness—those connotations associated with unregulated corporate expansion—were attached to corpulent bodies, while the positive connotations of growth were attached to tall bodies. Tallness became a symbol of measured, responsible, regulated growth, in other words, while fatness became associated with the undisciplined, unrestrained, socially irresponsible growth typified by corporations. Labor illustrators used differences in body weight as a crucial visual code distinguishing the virtuous, socially conscious growth of unions from the pernicious expansion of corporations.

Labor iconography, then, helped foster the association between economic regulation and bodily self-regulation that was a central component of shifting attitudes toward weight. The near-universal representation of labor as white and male in labor iconography also did little to ease the prevalent neglect of nonwhite and female workers. Yet labor's image of the Unionized Body was a distinct improvement over images offered by the corporate elite, whose fears of the new urban immigrant workforce prevented it even from recognizing America's industrial laborers. The image of labor, for example, offered at the Chicago World's Fair of 1893, the showcase of recent corporate innovations, was that of a monumental agricultural worker (see fig. 20). Ironically, the statue's title was "Industry." Less than a year after the Homestead Strike and a year before the Pullman Strike, it was an ominous time to willfully ignore the industrial workforce.

Leftist groups were divided, however, in their views on the task facing the giant Unionized Body. For the radical IWW and the socialists of *The Masses,* organized labor would overthrow capitalism and install a socialist state in its place. They often represented this vision iconographically through an inversion of size. In a sketch from the *Industrial Worker* of 1909, for example, the present helplessness of labor relative to capital is rendered in the image of a small worker standing weary and befuddled beside a giant, scornful employer. Labor's future is repre-

Fig. 20. "Industry," Chicago World's Fair (1893). The corporate depiction of industrial labor at the Chicago World's Fair was, ironically, an agricultural figure. (Reproduced from Shepp, *Shepp's World Fair Photographed* [1893]).

sented in terms of physical growth and the reversal of size hierarchies: an organized workforce becoming a giant holding a shrunken employer in the palm of its hand (see fig. 21). As with Edward Bellamy, socialists had no reservations about large institutions. The only question was whether such institutions would represent or exploit the masses. The more moderate AFL also approved of big institutions, converting the corporate idea of consolidation to its own uses in the federation of separate unions within one organization. Yet the AFL envisioned Labor growing to giant proportions so that it might meet the giant Capital on equal terms. The AFL campaigned for higher wages, an eight-hour day, and improved working conditions rather than the socialization of industry. Because their mission was reformist rather than revolutionary, their giant never grew to quite the same proportions as the socialist giant—or perhaps it would be fairer to say that their opponent, organized capital, never shrank to the dimensions that the socialists hoped it would.

Just Now. | *Pretty Soon.*

DISORGANIZED, THE WORKERS ARE HELPLESS—INDUSTRIAL UNION IS A GIANT

Fig. 21. IWW, "Disorganized, the Workers are Helpless—Industrial Union is a Giant." For socialists, the future of labor pointed toward growth and empowerment, represented iconographically as a reversal in the relative sizes of the Laboring Body and the Corporate Body. (Reproduced from *Industrial Worker*, August 26, 1909.)

The Little Man

While the corporate elite and labor activists defended the merits of large institutions, staunch opposition came from the middle class. Owners of small businesses, wholesalers, traveling sales agents, and many farmers detested and feared big corporations because they eliminated small businesses, cut out middle distributors, retired legions of drummers, and dictated the prices of agricultural products by controlling shipping rates.[78] The middle class feared unions, on the other hand, because, to the middle-class mind, they threatened stability and the social order. "Cannot we join in rescuing our dear land and country from the curse of a corporate oligarchy of wealth upon the one hand or the horrors of a French Revolution upon the other?" asked M. L. Lockwood, president of the American Anti-Trust League, in 1899.[79] The bomb of Haymarket Square remained fixed in the middle-class consciousness as the symbol of radical causes, and all the major presidential candidates of 1912 (Roosevelt, Wilson, and Taft) exploited fears of violent revolution to fashion a consensus that would enable their political victory and the victory of capitalism over socialism.

It was not enough that many middle-class men were losing their jobs, seeing their incomes diminish, and assuming increasingly proletarianized positions as employees of large corporations. They also feared that their political and social power was being usurped by the large, powerful institutions representing the interests of the elite and the working classes, that is, corporations and unions. "Between organized labor, on the one hand, and organized capital on the other," wrote the *New Republic* in 1919, "the large class which lives by rendering services to both stands an excellent chance of being crushed as between the upper and nether millstones."[80] In *The Iron Heel* (1907), Jack London expressed the middle class's fear in even clearer terms of scale: "The middle class is a pygmy between two giants," he wrote.[81] As London's statement suggests, middle-class anxieties were often expressed as a belief that the group was shrinking and might ultimately vanish altogether; the myth of the pygmies as a doomed race functioned here as a warning about the middle class's fate. (For London, it was also an attempt to depict class warfare as a kind of race war.) If current economic trends continued, warned Henry Lloyd in his widely read tract *Wealth Against Commonwealth* (1894), the nation would witness "the wiping out of the middle classes."[82] This concern was unrealistic, of course, and little hindsight was required to recognize this.[83] While precise figures on the size of the middle class are hard to come by due to difficulties of classification,[84] most historians agree that it was growing even faster than the rate of the population at the turn of the century. Between 1870 and 1930, for example, the number of clerical workers increased almost fifty times. The number of store clerks increased sixfold.[85] One historian estimates that the middle class as a whole grew eightfold between 1870 and 1910.[86] Nevertheless, the association between size and power is strong. The possibility of a diminishment in the middle class's strength as a consequence of the formation of large institutions assumed the symbolic form of fears of shrinkage, even when the purported decrease in power was not coupled with a decrease in the size of the middle class.

As unions and corporations adopted the guise of giants, the middle class responded with its own mythology of the Little Man. The Little Man was little because he did not seek participation in something "larger" than himself: he cherished the independence and autonomy that supposedly came from ownership of a small business. The Little Man's small size also reflected the misguided belief that the middle class was on the defensive against larger, more powerful institutions; in fact, all the major political candidates and much of the popular literature of the day directed their appeals to the middle class, suggesting that the group had significant political and ideological authority. Woodrow Wilson emerged as the champion of the middle-class perspective. He talked of "setting the little men of America free,"[87] and he spoke of the "little men" as capable of defeating the inefficient, overcapitalized trusts. In his campaign speeches of 1912, Wilson combined the new myth of the pygmies with the older myths of Jack the Giant-Killer and David and Goliath to suggest that there were ways to view the Little Man that did not assume his demise was preordained. "Here we have a lot of giants [i.e., the trusts] staggering along under an almost intolerable weight of artificial burdens, and constantly looking about lest some little pigmy with a round stone in a sling may come out and slay them," Wilson said. "For my part, I want the pigmy to have a chance to come out. And I foresee a time when the pigmies will be so much more athletic, so much more astute, so much more active, than the giants, that it will be a case of Jack the Giant-Killer."[88] Wilson's pygmy with a sling offered a disempowered image of the middle class that tempered its fatalism with a vigorous spur to action. It evoked fears of extinction at the same time that it made action seem heroic in traditionally masculine terms—of little guys defeating giants and of individual action in a world of powerful agents and collective forces bent on the destruction of individualism.

Wilson believed that excessively large businesses were not the most efficient economic organization, and he contested the corporate view that the formation of larger and larger businesses was inevitable. "There is a point of bigness . . . where you pass the limit of efficiency and get into the region of clumsiness and unwieldiness," he said, parroting the arguments of Louis Brandeis. "The point of efficiency . . . has been overstepped many times in the artificial and deliberate formation of trusts."[89] At the same time, Wilson exploited the middle-class fear of revolution. "Don't you know that some man with eloquent tongue, without conscience, who did not care for the Nation, could put this whole country into a flame? . . . Society . . . stands ready to attempt nothing less than a radical reconstruction, which only frank and honest counsels and the forces of generous cooperation can hold back from becoming a revolution."[90] Emphasizing this latter fear, the historian Martin Sklar has argued that Wilson's appeals to the Little Man were nothing more than an attempt to secure middle-class assent to corporate capitalism.

> Wilson's position was not that of a representative of the "little man," or the "middle class," *against* "big business"; but that of one who, affirming the large corporate industrial capitalist sys-

tem, was concerned with establishing the legal and institutional environment most conducive to the system's stability and growth, while at the same time preserving some place within the system for the "little man." . . . Wilson refused to concede the irrelevance of the "little man"; but his refusal was not a matter of sentimentality: it stemmed from his fear that given a growing irrelevance of "little men" in the nation's economy, fewer and fewer people would retain a stake in the capitalist system, and more and more would lose hope for betterment under capitalism and turn toward socialism or other forms of radicalism.[91]

Sklar's position is compelling because Wilson was unequivocal in his opposition to socialism and radical reform, whereas he danced a clever two-step on the subject of big business, saying that large corporations were inevitable and beneficial but that excessively big, monopolistic trusts were inefficient and pernicious to the social order. Regardless of whether we accept Sklar's argument, however, Wilson's shuffle on the subject of large corporations is indicative of the divisions that were coming to characterize the middle class and suggests that Wilson felt compelled to appeal simultaneously to two major voting blocs. While small business owners and traveling sales agents opposed big business, a large new cadre of middle managers in corporations helped facilitate the development of corporate capitalism and fashion a middle-class ideology that was sympathetic to corporate values.[92] This group accepted big business and felt particularly threatened by the socialists' proposals for worker management of industry. Thus, Wilson's equivocation was emblematic of the middle class's own divided allegiances: there were those who, having a direct stake in the competition between large and small businesses, either opposed or cooperated with the growth of large corporations; and there was a smaller group who, having little stake in the outcome of this struggle, felt some combination of acceptance or resignation toward the dramatic changes occurring in the nation's economy.

The Economic Body in Popular Literature

Frank Norris's widely read novel *The Octopus* (1901) and Ernest Poole's best-selling *The Harbor* (1915) reflect the divided loyalties of the middle class at the turn of the century. Both books examine the fate of the Little Man in the modern industrial state, where immense, powerful entities beyond the control of individuals shape the lives of ordinary citizens. Both novelists accepted that the principles of independence and autonomy so long cherished by the Little Man were no longer tenable in an age dominated by massive institutions. Both believed the presence of large institutions was inevitable (although Norris, like much of the middle class, loathed this development).

"I have got a big idea, the biggest I ever had," Frank Norris reportedly told his friends before he began work on *The Octopus*.[93] His "big idea" was a trilogy of novels dealing with the three phases of the modern capitalist economy: production, distribution, and consumption. As the first of the projected three books (Norris would die before completing the third), *The Octopus* takes place in California and has as its historic backdrop the battle between the wheat growers of the San Joaquin Valley and the Southern Pacific Railroad trust, which culminated in the violence of the Mussell Slough Affair of 1880. The calamity began when farmers were lured to California by the promise of cheap land, ceded to the Southern Pacific Railroad by the government. When the time came several years later for the railroad to transfer ownership of the land to the farmers, the Southern Pacific priced the land according to its improved value (the value after agricultural development) rather than the unimproved rate it had originally promised the farmers. Simultaneously raising its shipping rates for wheat, the railroad ruined the wheat growers. Norris's depiction of the event in *The Octopus* was an immediate commercial success, and its sequel, *The Pit,* was third on the bestseller list of 1903.

Norris depicts the railroad trust as a living entity, massive beyond imagination, loathsome in its goals, and unopposable in its operations. Norris's excess of language mirrors the excesses of the trust's bulk and appetite: it is "a vast power, huge, terrible, flinging the echo of its thunder over all the reaches of the valley, leaving blood and destruction in its path; the leviathan, with tentacles of steel clutching into the soil, the soulless Force, the iron-hearted Power, the monster, the Colossus, the Octopus" (51). The Pacific and Southwest Railroad trust has all the characteristics of the modern corporation: it is apparently immortal, indefinitely expansive, unbound by conventional morality, and utterly tyrannical. It destroys every autonomous, middle-class individual populating the novel, whether by murdering them outright or driving them to insanity, prostitution, jail, or widowhood.

Although the middle-class farmers attempt to battle the railroad by uniting in a political action group called the League, they soon discover that their plan of mutual defense is completely ineffectual against the might of the Pacific and Southwest. Their scheme of setting shipping rates through state intervention dies when the railroad trust bribes the members of the state committee. In the end, the corporation destroys the farmers, ruins their families, and swallows their properties "as a whale would a minnow" (327).

As the impotence of the League suggests, there is no collective body capable of balancing the might of the railroad. Conspicuously absent from *The Octopus* is any conception of organized labor. Labor appears in two forms in the book: as the picturesque bodies of Portuguese field hands and Chinese house servants who silently populate the background of the novel like props on a stage; and as the figure of Caraher, saloon owner and anarchist. Caraher embodies the middle-class fear of revolution. Belonging to no apparent labor association, Caraher preaches the gospel of dynamite as he pushes rum on his disaffected clientele. It is true that most of Caraher's predictions about the duplicity and malevolence of the railroad come to pass, and it is also true that Presley, the character who perhaps most closely reflects the authorial voice in the novel, briefly entertains Caraher's socialist ideas as he helplessly watches the traumas of the wheat growers. Yet both Presley and the novel ultimately disavow socialism, which they equate with anarchistic violence, as well as the perspective of labor, which they equate with racialized Others (the Portuguese and Chinese). By failing to offer any viable alternative to corporate domination, and by representing such domination as an inevitable outcome of modern economic conditions, the book is, as Walter Benn Michaels has also argued, unintentionally complicitous with the corporate outlook, however much it assails the trusts.[94]

The book does offer its implicitly middle-class readers two palliatives that help temper the fatalism of its vision, however. Ironically, these palliatives are equally consistent with corporate ideology. First, the novel suggests that the trusts are not the first "unassailable . . . mighty world-force" (651) that humanity has known. Another force exists that, like the railroad trust, is an immaterial, disembodied amalgamation of material, embodied beings. This force is immortal, and it confers a kind of immortality on individuals through their participation in it. It is enormous, a "sprawling, primordial Titan" (60), and beside it individuals are like "Liliputians [*sic*], gnats in the sunshine" (448). It does not obey morality, although at times—as in the end of the novel, when it kills S. Behrman—it appears to do so. It is utterly unopposable, thoroughly autocratic in its operations. It simultaneously nourishes and destroys the human insects that depend upon it. In other words, it has all the characteristics of the modern corporation, but it is far older—we have been familiar with it from the dawn of time. This force is Nature itself.

Norris uses the same language to describe Nature that he uses to describe the railroad trust, even adopting industrial imagery (the imagery of engines and wheels and cogs) to depict it (just as, conversely, he applies naturalistic terms to the railroad).

> [Annie Derrick] recognised the colossal indifference of nature, not hostile, even kindly and friendly, so long as the human ant-swarm was submissive, working with it, hurrying along at its side in the mysterious march of centuries. Let, however, the insect rebel, strive to make head against the power of this nature, and at once it became relentless, a gigantic engine, a vast power, knowing no compunction, no forgiveness, no tolerance; crushing out the human atom with soundless calm, the agony of destruction sending never a jar, never the faintest tremour through all that prodigious mechanism of wheels and cogs. (180–81)

Nature is the only entity that Norris offers as a potential opponent to the Pacific and Southwest Railroad. But it is scarcely a friend to the middle class, the wheat growers of the San Joaquin; notwithstanding the poetic justice afforded in its destruction of S. Behrman, Nature is hardly a reliable agent of middle-class morality, and it does not intervene in the railroad's destruction of the farmers. Nature is not so much an opponent of the trusts as an incarnation of comparable forces. "The Wheat is one force, the Railroad, another," says Shelgrim at the end of the novel. "Men have only little to do in the whole business. Complications may arise, conditions that bear hard on the individual—crush him maybe—*but the Wheat will be carried to feed the people* as inevitably as it will grow. If you want to fasten the blame of the affair at Los Muertos on any one person, you will make a mistake. Blame conditions, not men" (576; emphasis in original). In likening giant corporations to Nature (a strategy reminiscent of the defenders of big business, who argued that the formation of large corporations was inevitable, a consequence of natural law),[95] Norris accommodates his middle-class readership to big business by suggesting they are already familiar with huge, implacable forces. In this respect, Norris's literary naturalism becomes a palliative to the baneful conditions of the modern corporate world.

A second anodyne *The Octopus* offers its readers is the transcendent perspective of the corporate state. Its tactics are a literary counterpart to those used by the architects at the turn-of-the-century world's fairs. Defenders of corporate capitalism routinely addressed the need for a larger, global vision in an era of expanding, international business.

"The market has grown world-wide," observed Sidney Sherwood, a professor at Johns Hopkins University, in 1900. This development, he said, has "placed a high premium on broad and deep intelligence in the *entrepreneur*. He must know the larger market. . . . He must possess also the ability to take broad views. . . . He must be . . . capable of forming large and far-reaching policies."[96] In *Drift and Mastery* (1914), Walter Lippmann spoke of a shift from "village culture" and "the limited vision of small competitors" to an era of "national and international thought" characterized by the rule of industrial "efficiency experts" with "enlarged vision."[97] *The Octopus* encourages its readers to view local, isolated events in relation to global developments; there is a repeated ascent and descent in the narrative perspective. (This is another reason for the length of naturalist texts like *The Octopus*. In an effort to draw connections between individual stories and general phenomena, naturalist novels shift between narrow and panoramic perspectives. Part of the rhetorical purpose is to persuade the reader that the author has an accurate panoramic perspective, and one way to accomplish that is to show a familiarity with as many and as wide-ranging social developments as possible. The naturalist narrator becomes an "expert" with "enlarged vision.") In the beginning of the novel, for instance, as the farmers plan their next crop, we are reminded that the San Joaquin wheat region, by the recent innovation of the stock market ticker, is connected to a global network including the major industrial cities of the world.

> The offices of the ranches were . . . connected by wire with San Francisco, and through that city with Minneapolis, Duluth, Chicago, New York, and at last, and most important of all, with Liverpool. Fluctuations in the price of the world's crop during and after the harvest thrilled straight to the office of Los Muertos, to that of the Quien Sabe, to Osterman's, and to Broderson's. During a flurry in the Chicago wheat pits [the setting of Norris's sequel to *The Octopus*] in the August of that year, which had affected even the San Francisco market, Harran and Magnus had sat up nearly half of one night watching the strip of white tape jerking unsteadily from the reel. At such moments they no longer felt their individuality. The ranch became merely the part of an enormous whole, a unit in the vast agglomeration of wheat land the whole world round, feeling the effects of causes thousands of miles distant—a drought on the prairies of Dakota, a rain on the plains of India, a frost on the Russian steppes, a hot wind on the llanos of the Argentine. (54)

We are constantly reminded of this connection between the wheat growers of the San Joaquin and the global market. In the end of the novel, for example, Norris offers us the reassurance that, however tragic and costly the battle between the California farmers and the Pacific and Southwest Railroad, one thing is certain: "*the* WHEAT *remained. . . .* Through the welter of blood at the irrigation ditch, through the sham charity and shallow philanthropy of famine relief committees, the great harvest of Los Muertos rolled like a flood from the Sierras to the Himalayas to feed thousands of starving scarecrows on the barren plains of India" (651; emphasis in original).

The novel inculcates its readers in this elevated, global, corporate perspective, just as one of its main characters, Presley, struggles to accept a "larger view" after witnessing the events in the San Joaquin Valley. Presley's final vision of the San Joaquin Valley, appropriately, is from an elevated position above Broderson's Creek. "The land of the ranches opened out forever and forever under the stimulus of that measureless range of vision," writes Norris. "The whole gigantic sweep of the San Joaquin expanded Titanic before the eye of the mind." From this transcendent position, a recognition of the Truth of events is visited upon him. "As Presley looked there came to him strong and true the sense and the significance of all the enigma of growth. . . . Men were nothings, mere animalculae, mere ephemerides that fluttered and fell and were forgotten between dawn and dusk. . . . FORCE only existed" (633–34). The Little Man, in Norris's conception, is, and always has been, nothing. In relation to colossal forces like Nature and the trusts—both intrinsic to the world as it is—the autonomous middle-class individual has no agency and little hope of salvation. But that same subject can find solace for local pains in a global (corporate) vision. As if expecting the resistance of his readers, Norris reinforces Presley's epiphany twice in the remaining few pages of the novel. First he repeats it in the observations of Vanamee, who instructs Presley to "Look at it all from the vast height of humanity . . . and you will find, if your view be large enough, that it is *not* evil, but good, that in the end remains" (636). And Norris repeats the lesson in the last sentences of the novel. "Greed, cruelty, selfishness, and inhumanity are short-lived; the individual suffers, but the race goes on. Annixter dies, but in a far distant corner of the world a thousand lives are saved. The larger view always and through all shams, all wickednesses, discovers the Truth that will, in the end, prevail, and all things, surely, inevitably, resistlessly work together for good" (651–52).

Ernest Poole would disagree sharply with Norris's outlook. Before Poole wrote *The Harbor,* he worked as a muckraking journalist in the impoverished immigrant communities of New York. In 1904, he covered the strikes in Chicago's stockyards for the *Outlook,* ultimately working as a spokesperson for the unions. Poole's experiences in Chicago were later instrumental in helping Upton Sinclair write his socialist novel *The Jungle.* Poole was an admirer of Brandeis, and in 1911 he wrote a profile of the lawyer for the *American Magazine* that was later reprinted as the foreword to a collection of Brandeis's essays on economics entitled *Business—A Profession* (1914). Although Poole's subsequent book *His Family* (1918) would earn the first Pulitzer prize for a novel, *The Harbor* remained his most influential work. Directed toward the middle class, it nevertheless had the socialist vision that characterized Poole's writing.

Unlike Norris, Poole regarded organized labor as a viable social and political institution. In *The Harbor,* two opposing forces vie for the sympathy of the novel's middle-class protagonist and narrator, Bill: corporate culture and labor culture. Bill is literally and figuratively, like his father before him, a Little Man—"I was middling small," he tells us.[98] He inherits from his father not only a small build but also a distinct social station and outlook. Bill is raised in a house overlooking his father's harbor and warehouses. He is not of the upper class; in relation to neighbors who have a mansion, coach, and butler, Bill feels "poor and small" (29). Yet, from the elevated position of his own home, he is taught to fear the lower classes who work the docks and sail the ships beneath him. Once, when a drunken man enters his family's yard, Bill's sister screams that a "giant" has erupted into their "garden." "Vaguely," Bill recalls, "I felt that he came from the harbor" (6). This image of the lower class as a giant becomes more significant later in the novel; for now, against all his teachings, Bill ventures down to the harbor and befriends an Irish boy named Sam. His experiences with Sam are revelatory. "I discovered that by making friends with the 'Micks' and 'Dockers' and the like, you find they are no fearful goblins, giants bursting savagely up among the flowers of your life, but people as human as yourself, or rather, much more human, because they live so . . . close to the deep rough tides of life" (15).

The two things Bill does not inherit from his father are money and a career. His father's business, a harbor that bustled during the era of clipper ships and the Jeffersonian economy that sustained it, is driven into bankruptcy by the corporate reorganization of the economy.

The very bigness of things, the era of big companies which at forty had thrilled [my father] by the first signs of its coming, now crushed down upon his old age. Vaguely he knew that the harbor had changed and that he was too old to change with it.

An era no longer of human adventures for young men but of financial adventures for mammoth corporations, great foreign shipping companies combining in agreements with the American railroads to freeze out all the little men and take to themselves the whole port of New York. My father was one of these little men. The huge company to which he was selling owned the docks and warehouses for over two miles, and this was only a part of their holdings. (106–7)

Bill's father is forced to accept a salaried position in his own warehouse from the company that bought him out. While Bill had once entertained notions of remaining independent as a writer of "fine" literature, his father's debts convince him that he must find some way to support himself and his family. Bill's position, in other words, reflects the dilemma of the middle class as a whole: with the cherished ideal of independence no longer tenable in an economy dominated by huge corporations, Poole suggests, the middle class is forced to choose between the ideologies of the corporate world and that of the proletariat into which many are being driven.

The appeals of corporate culture are numerous, of course, and Bill is at first thoroughly seduced by them. Through Eleanore Dillon, the daughter of an urban planner working for the big new harbor companies, Bill is welcomed into the heart of the corporate sanctuary, the secluded offices at the top of the Manhattan skyscrapers. Here Bill learns of the ambitious plans for the harbor, the goal of transforming New York into the world's greatest port. To prepare for the increased commerce furnished by the Panama Canal, Mr. Dillon tells Bill, "we've got to . . . organize this port as a whole, like the big industrial plant that it is" (185). Under corporate guidance and reconstruction, New York could be "a complicated industrial organ, the heart of a country's circulation" (186); until then, it would remain "a giant struggling to breathe" (184). Flushed with the heady plans of his corporate sponsors, Bill immediately begins working to translate their dreams and ambitions for the masses. "I set out to build my series of glory stories about it all, laying on the color thick to reach a million pigmy readers, grip them, pull them out of their holes, make them sit up and rub their eyes" (190). The popular periodicals reward him handsomely and urge him to write more. He quickly attains notoriety as a defender of corporate capitalism, and when he marries Eleanore Dillon he offers her the comfort and security of a middle-class home.

But corporate America offers Bill more than money, security, and the ideals of order and efficiency. It also offers him the vision that

Norris puts forth as the solace for the jarring changes shocking the middle class: namely, the transcendent perspective of the corporate state. In Mr. Dillon's penthouse apartment atop "the tower," Bill sees the entire New York port laid out clearly before him.

> Through Dillon's field glass I saw pictures of all I had seen before in my weary weeks of trudging down there in the haze and dust. Down there I had felt like a little worm, up here I felt among the gods. There all had been matter and chaos, here all was mind and a will to find a way out of confusion. The glass gave me the pictures in swift succession, in a moment I made a leap of ten miles, and as I listened on and on to the quiet voice at my elbow, the pictures all came sweeping together as parts of one colossal whole. The first social vision of my life I had through Dillon's field glass.
>
> "To see any harbor or city or state as a whole," [Dillon] said, "is what most Americans cannot do. And it's what they've got to learn to do." (184)

After descending from the tower, Bill's entire outlook changes. The "men of the tower, with their wide, deliberate views ahead" (187), the engineers and corporate planners, the "bigger men" (188), confer upon Bill a larger, more comprehensive vision. From them, he also acquires a measure of arrogance and callousness. "All the multitudes below seemed mere pigmies to me now," he explains. "How small they seemed, how petty their thoughts compared to mine, how blind their views of the harbor" (189). "From certain big men I had written about I had taken a spacious breadth of view that included a deep indulgence for all these skurrying [sic] pigmies" (222). If he briefly acknowledges that the corporate planners "would shift vast populations," disrupting the lives of millions, it is only to dismiss the fact as an inevitable consequence of "the inexorable harbor of to-day" (187–88).

But the value of this transcendent perspective and the complacency of Bill's secure life are soon unsettled by the appearance of Bill's college friend, Joe Kramer. Joe is a socialist and free thinker who travels the world as a muckraking journalist. Joe arrives in New York having spent several years as a stoker in the dank, deadly, superheated bowels of one of the era's modern ships. He has seen corporate capitalism at its ugliest and works to organize labor and overturn capitalism. Although Poole never states it openly, it is clear that Joe is a Wobbly, an IWW man, striving to organize the "un-organizable" (the immigrants and assorted races at the bottom of the economic ladder), attempting to unite labor across all industries, and preaching the general strike as a means to economic revolution. Joe contradicts Bill's aesthetic of height, which presumes that upward movement improves one's vision. He accuses the upper and middle classes of blindness. "You comfortable people . . . see nothing ahead but peace on earth and a nice smooth evolution—with a lot of steady little reforms," he says. "You're as blind as most folks were five years before the Civil War" (241).

In particular, those at the top of the social ladder are blind to the brutal reality of the lives of workers at the bottom, Joe suggests. To prove his point, he guides Bill through the levels of a modern ocean liner. It is a miniature model of the corporate state, complete with actual ladders leading upward and downward, and it was almost certainly meant to evoke the recent memory of the *Titanic,* whose sinking in 1912 led to the deaths of more than fifteen hundred passengers, predominantly those in the steerage and third-class compartments, many of whom were physically prevented from reaching the upper decks where lifeboats were offered preferentially to first-class passengers.

At the bottom of the ship, invisible to the wealthy passengers on the upper decks, live the stokers. "Most of them were undersized," observes Bill (244). They are small because their occupation exposes them to dangerous illnesses; we know this because Joe arrived in New York with typhus, from which Bill nursed him back to health. They have few possessions and little clothing. They live in foul, cramped quarters where no natural light infiltrates. They inhale coal dust as they shovel fuel into blazing furnaces. The food they receive is practically inedible. Some arrive as virtual slaves, sold to the shippers by "crimps"—modern-day press gangs. Death is common and comes in many guises: disease, being crushed under huge piles of coal that shift with the movements of the ship, and overwork. ("Heart failure is damn common here," says Joe [248].)

Bill cannot shake the effect of this tour. Interviewing a rich hotel owner afterward, Bill realizes that "the America he knew was like what I'd seen on the upper decks of the ship that had sailed a few hours before. . . . I kept thinking of what I had seen underneath" (252). Bill's experience on the ship transforms him, and he subsequently decides to shift his allegiance and cover the incipient labor strike at the docks. He immerses himself now in something opposing the corporate world and its bigness—the equally large labor culture of socialism. Bill becomes a part of the giant Unionized Body.

Back we would go into the crowd, and there in a twinkling we would be changed. Once more we were members of the whole and took on its huge personality. And again the vision came to me, the dream of a weary world set free, a world where poverty and pain and all the bitterness they bring might in the end be swept away by this awakening giant. . . . This to me was a miracle, the one great miracle of the strike. For years I had labored to train myself to concentrate on one man at a time, to shut out all else for weeks on end, to feel this man so vividly that his self came into mine. Now with the same intensity I found myself striving day and night to feel not one but thousands of men, a blurred bewildering multitude. And slowly in my striving I felt them fuse together into one great being. (321)

Through his experiences at the strike, Bill discovers a perspective that rivals the hierarchical, transcendent corporate one: it is the equally expansive, but horizontal, demotic perspective. Joe encourages him to perform the same functions in writing for the masses that he had performed for the corporate planners—to inculcate in his readers this large, democratic vision. But Bill's audience will now be the lower class, not the middle class (although implicitly Poole's book is an appeal to the middle class, suggesting that it too needs training in the socialist vision). "What's needed is so big," Joe tells Bill. The people "need a change . . . in their whole way of looking at things. They've got to learn that they are a crowd—and can't get anywhere at all until all pull together. . . . That's where you and me come in—we can help 'em get together faster than they would if left to themselves! You can help that way a lot—by writing to the tenements" (263). Thus, Poole rejects Frank Norris's ideological stance in three ways: he offers organized labor as a viable opponent to the corporations (even if labor fails to win the strike at the harbor); he suggests that the transcendent corporate perspective is faulty, ignoring the needs of labor and the plight of the impoverished; and he offers an antithetical vision that, while equally large, is more democratic than the corporate one.

In Poole's novel, moreover, the worldviews of corporate culture and labor culture are not merely opposed in the value they attach, respectively, to hierarchy and equality, represented in terms of vertical and horizontal vision. They also differ in their attitudes toward race. American corporate capitalism, Poole suggests, is fundamentally divisive. Oppressed races occupy the bottom rungs of the social ladder, and the various racial groups are routinely pitted against one another. Predictably, the harbor companies defeat the dockers' revolt by importing shiploads of black strikebreakers. Unions, on the other hand, are racially democratic, argues Poole. (Here, too, Poole represents the IWW as the voice of labor. Unlike the AFL, which did little to oppose racism in the workforce or within its own ranks, the Wobblies organized whites and blacks alike.) The voices of many races can be heard at the parliamentary meetings of the strikers, and on the docks all assemble in unity: "the sun . . . shone with radiant clearness upon eleven races of men, upon Italians, Germans, French, on English, Poles and Russians, on Negroes and Norwegians, Lascars, Malays, Coolies, on figures burly, figures puny, faces white and faces swarthy, yellow, brown and black" (323). While the throng presents a broad racial diversity, the assembled strikers are, significantly, described at one point as "a black tide of men" (309)—their blackness signifying that all are equally racialized (if not equally oppressed) by corporate America. When racism threatens to disrupt the first parliamentary meeting of the strikers, the fire is soon extinguished when an Italian denounces it. "Fellow workers," he shouts. "You call me Guinney, Dago, Wop—you call another man Coon, Nigger—you call another man a Sheeny! Stop calling names—call men fellow workers! We are on strike—let us not fight each other—let us have peace" (317). He offers instead his idea of festive excursions on a big boat to be owned and operated by the strikers, a ship that symbolically counters the hierarchical image of the corporate ship Bill and Joe toured earlier. "We stop all fighting," the Italian striker announces. "We take out this boat—all our comrades on board! No coons, no niggers, no sheenies, no wops! Fellow workers—I tell you the name of our boat! *The Internationale!*" The man's speech is "greeted with a sudden roar of applause," says Bill. "For the crowd had seen at once this danger of race hatred and was eager to put it down" (318).

Thus, Poole's narrative counters Frank Norris's twin visions of labor as a silent racialized underclass (the Portuguese and Chinese servants of the San Joaquin farmers) and the bomb-throwing anarchist (Poole represents labor leaders as deliberate, peaceful, thoughtful men). With regard to the former, in particular, Poole exposes and contests the racism inherent in the middle class's rejection and dread of the proletariat—their equation of lower-class status with a nonwhite, racialized identity. He suggests that the middle class must overcome its racism if it is to achieve a class consciousness compatible with the aims of socialism. Through the model of a Little Man who immerses himself in the "black tide" of labor, Poole attempts to train his readers in this egalitarian practice.

Conclusion

Throughout much of *The Harbor,* Bill's allegiance wavers between the two dominant institutions of his day, the giant corporations and the equally giant unions. These institutions possess two opposing visions of the nation's future—one hierarchical and racist, the other democratic and egalitarian. In comparison to these bodies, suggests Ernest Poole, middle-class men are suffering a crisis of vision. Should they identify with the proletariat in the new hierarchies of business, or should they collaborate with the elite? It is this tension that *The Harbor* explores. In choosing to narrate his novel through Bill's perspective, Poole is attempting to make socialism appealing to middle-class readers and to suggest that such individuals cannot continue to straddle the fence, that they must ultimately ally themselves with one institution or the other. As Joe tells Bill, "You've got to decide which side you're on" (197). Implicitly, then, Poole rejects the position of President Wilson, who declared three years earlier that the nation could secure a place for the Little Man in an era of corporate capitalism. Poole wishes us to believe that a middle position is untenable.

Norris held no such vision of the nation as divided between contending social institutions with opposing visions. For him, there was no body capable of matching the power of the trusts, unless it be some abstract entity, either Nature or God, that would ensure all social developments tended ultimately, and on balance, toward the good of humanity. Norris's position in *The Octopus* is a thoroughly fatalistic one, perhaps more in keeping with the noncorporate middle-class view of his day even if it did not adequately characterize the complexity of the political landscape and the contemporary struggle for power. Because it expresses economic fatalism, moreover, *The Octopus* is ultimately complicit with the hegemony of corporate capitalism. It represents corporate dominance as inevitable, and it inculcates its readers in the hierarchical, expansionist, racist vision of the corporate state.

What, then, does all of this mean in terms of the values attached to bigness and littleness at the turn of the century, to attitudes toward big bodies and small ones? Clearly, in Frank Norris's novel, we can draw no simple conclusion that bigger is better. If *The Octopus* is any indication of his personal convictions, Norris despised the trusts and depicted bigness as synonymous with rapaciousness, violence, and indifference to human suffering. Yet Norris's hatred of bigness in the economic realm did not extend fully to the corporeal realm; it was not incompatible, that is, with a preference for tall bodies.

Frank Norris's ambivalence toward big business, like the labor imagery of corporate and proletarian giants, finds expression in bodily metaphors. Norris bifurcates large bodies into heroic tall ones and vilified fat ones in the same way that he celebrates the transcendent gaze and criticizes predatory capitalists. Like labor iconography, Norris distinguishes between the large bodies of the representatives of the Pacific and Southwest (the obese S. Behrman and his massive liege Shelgrim) and the bodies of the San Joaquin wheat farmers. The middle-class bodies in *The Octopus* are characteristically tall and vigorous. Magnus Derrick, for example, is "all of six feet tall," and Norris uses his height to establish a sense of his natural aristocracy. Magnus is "a fine commanding figure, imposing an immediate respect . . . and a certain pride of race. . . . Instinctively other men looked to him as the leader" (63–64). Dyke, similarly, is "a veritable giant, built of great sinews, powerful, in the full tide of his manhood" (353). Not coincidentally, these characters resemble the heroes of Westerns, just as the novel, in its setting and plot devices, mirrors the genre. Norris anticipates the techniques of the Western because his novel, like most Westerns, is essentially nostalgic. *The Octopus* laments the disappearance of virtuous, independent, middle-class American individuals. The characteristics of rugged individualism, like the frontier that nurtured them, were vanishing, according to Norris. The book is intended as a poignant tragedy of the modern world; a significant component of that tragedy is that valiant, vigorous, wholesome men can be so utterly destroyed by the monstrous trusts.

For Norris, then, tallness is symbolic of the heroic virtues of the vanishing middle-class individual. The obesity of the agents of the Pacific and Southwest represents the new corporate value of heedless lateral expansion. This acquisitive bigness, the bigness of unappeasable consumption, is, in Norris's view, far from heroic—it is grotesque. (This is not to suggest that vertical bigness is not part of the corporate facade in Norris's novel. The book's first image of the Pacific and Southwest Railroad is an enormous advertisement that dominates the landscape from its elevated position on a water tower.[99] Also, as in Poole's *The Harbor,* the corporate perspective is represented as an elevated one. The instability in Norris's uses of bigness reflects the increasing instabilities in the term itself at the turn of the century.)

Poole's middle-class (male) bodies, on the other hand, are small. The littleness of Bill and his father reflects their desire for independence and isolation. They embody a bygone era, a Jeffersonian economy of Little Men and autonomous selves. The bodies of corporate and labor leaders, in contrast, are predominantly tall. Dillon and Joe Kramer, for example, are both long and lean. (Although Jim Marsh, the "arch-revolutionist," is "of middle size" [269], he strikes Bill as "big" [276].) Their tallness is consistent with their expansive vision. They represent the new American body, commensurate with the new America: progressive in its size, enlarged to meet the enlarged world, the modern American self extends beyond itself, whether through socialism or through modern corporate culture. While women play a separate, domestic role in this novel, they nevertheless share in this progressive bodily growth. Bill's sister Sue, with her radical ideas, her political activism, her support for suffrage, and her desire for a career, is predictably "tall and lithe." Like other women in the novel who participate in social causes (Bill's wife, Eleanore, and the stenographer Nora Ganey), Sue experiences a metaphoric growth that has physical manifestations.[100]

In both novels, then, tallness is valued, despite the fact that Norris challenges the value of bigness in certain registers. Tallness remains associated with heroism in *The Octopus,* even if it does not demonstrate the more current association with modernity. In *The Harbor,* on the other hand, tallness and bigness are both associated with modernity. "Was everything modern only big?" wonders Bill (88). Poole, it should be noted, attaches little inherent value to the adjectives *modern* and *big.* For Poole, bigness and modernity could be either good or bad, depending on whether they were consistent with or opposed to the more fundamental American values of democracy and equality.

For all the talk of giants and Little Men, few writers accepted the radical challenge to reexamine attitudes toward stature. Despite their ambivalence toward bigness, neither Norris nor Poole shared Brandeis's veneration for economic smallness. Why it was the case that the middle class's celebratory rhetoric of the Little Man failed to engender new attitudes toward smallness is a question that will be taken up again in the next chapter. For now, it is sufficient to point out that, in the history of this country, there have been as few proponents of the virtues of littleness as there have been opponents of corporate capitalism. The great turn-of-the-century trust debate, with its reexamination of assumptions about size, was a rare moment indeed.

CHAPTER 4 • The City of Dreadful Height
Skyscrapers and the Aesthetics of Growth

*The modern high building, whether it be ugly or beau-
tiful, whether it express pleasant or disagreeable traits
and truths, is distinctively of this day and this country.*
  —Lincoln Steffens, 1897[1]

*I see great forces at work; great movements; the large
buildings and the small buildings; the warring of the
great and the small.*
  —John Marin, 1913[2]

"The skyscraper has destroyed our sense of scale," wrote Lewis Mumford, the most influential architectural critic of his day, in 1924.[3] The
change of scale in U.S. cities at the turn of the century was nothing less
than revolutionary, and the skyscraper was perhaps the most conspicuous feature of the new metropolis. In the 1870s, buildings rarely
exceeded four stories, the maximum elevation a landlord could expect
tenants to climb day after day. The masonry construction of the period,
in fact, limited buildings to ten stories. By World War I, twenty-story
buildings, enabled by steel skeletons and made tolerable by elevators,
were common in places like New York and Chicago, and the tallest skyscrapers—a term invented in the 1890s—were higher than fifty stories.

Whatever else they thought about tall office buildings—and opinions varied tremendously—virtually every observer agreed that they
were distinctively American and uniquely modern. The editor of the
architectural magazine *Craftsman* summarized the views of skyscraper
enthusiasts in 1907 when she wrote, "The skyscraper is the first
absolutely genuine expression of an original American architecture. In
this tall, eccentric tower we have begun to feel our way toward national
buildings—buildings that suit our needs, our comfort, our landscape,
without regard to any other nation or civilization."[4] Even Mumford, who
believed skyscrapers represented an abhorrent feudalism, conceded that
"These modern colossi express our civilization." He found nothing
romantic in that fact, however. "Our slums express our civilization,
too," he added wryly.[5] The author of a 1908 article in *Putnam's* magazine captured the ambivalence that most people felt toward the skyscraper when he described the new architecture as simultaneously

"awful" and "awe-inspiring." The modern metropolis, he said, was a "city of dreadful height."[6]

There was good reason to regard the skyscraper as uniquely American. While building height restrictions in large U.S. cities in 1913 varied between 125 and 225 feet (in New York City there were no limits—the Woolworth Building, completed in 1913, was over 790 feet tall), height restrictions in Europe were much lower. London, Berlin, Paris, Rome, and Stockholm restricted their buildings to 65 to 80 feet in height.[7] Not surprisingly, European travelers and immigrants agreed with U.S. observers who saw skyscrapers as an expression of an original native architecture. "Americans have discovered a new type in architecture," observed the French novelist Paul Adam in 1906. "*And this art belongs to themselves exclusively!*"[8] Europeans simply did not share the American passion for bigness.

At a time when growth experts proclaimed the superiority of American stature, when ethnologists and pundits insisted that this represented American evolutionary and social progress, and when industrialists extolled the advantages of economic growth and consolidation, the skyscraper was a fitting national symbol. Despite the nationalist fervor that skyscrapers often aroused, however, they also provoked a heated debate that received a good deal of its fire from the trust controversy. The one arena in which the value of bigness was routinely questioned, the trust debate highlighted the ideological components of an architectural debate that (at least until the twenties) revolved primarily around aesthetics.[9] To put it simply, many observers at the turn of the century believed that tall buildings were analogous to trusts. Those who wrote about skyscrapers used the same rhetoric as those who wrote about big business: opponents of skyscrapers described them as "soulless agglomerations," "Frankenstein monsters," and "monstrous parasites." Skyscrapers and trusts created analogous problems. Tall buildings stole light and air from their smaller neighbors; thus, opponents of skyscrapers claimed they inhibited the liberty of their smaller peers and interfered with the survival and growth of the small businesses supposedly housed therein. Tall buildings afforded a striking physical experience of the diminishment of the individual in an era of corporate consolidation. (The language of pygmies surfaced often in the skyscraper debate, as in an article written by a skyscraper enthusiast for the *Craftsman* in 1913: "these buildings defy description. . . . At their base man walks as a pigmy."[10] Later in this chapter I will address the racialized nature of these metaphors more fully.) Comparable issues of public needs versus private greed were important to both controversies. The defenders of skyscrapers employed the same deterministic arguments to defend the proliferation of tall buildings: like the trusts, skyscrapers were a "natural," inevitable growth, they claimed, a product of architectural "evolution" designed to meet the peculiar needs of modern business. Opponents of skyscrapers adopted Louis Brandeis's arguments to contain the spread of high office buildings. They argued that there were certain height limits beyond which buildings were no longer profitable, just as Brandeis had argued that trusts in America exceeded the size at which businesses in their respective industries operated most efficiently.[11]

This chapter examines three major figures in the skyscraper debate. It begins with Henry James, whose book *The American Scene* presented the most famous and fully articulated opposition to the tall buildings. Alvin Langdon Coburn is the subject of the next section. One of the most respected photographers of his day, Coburn was among the first artists to picture the skyscraper in enthusiastic terms. More important, his series of photographs taken from the peaks of New York's tallest buildings in 1912 represented the first sustained attempt to adapt the aesthetics implicit in the new architecture to another art form.[12] The final section of this chapter addresses the Woolworth Building, the world's tallest skyscraper from 1913 to 1930. Praised even by opponents of skyscrapers and hailed by many observers as one of the most beautiful buildings in the world, the Woolworth Building temporarily silenced the skyscraper debate.[13] Paradoxically, the building was erected between 1910 and 1913, precisely the years when opposition to big business reached its most ferocious pitch. I analyze the success of the Woolworth Building in the light of this contradiction.

Of Bullies and Little Boys: Henry James and
The American Scene

After a twenty-year absence, Henry James returned to the United States in 1904 and traveled extensively throughout the nation. The literary product of these years was *The American Scene,* published serially between 1905 and 1906 and as a book in 1907. The travelogue is, among other things, a record of the dizzying changes the nation underwent at the end of the nineteenth century. The transformations that were most apparent to a visitor and that attracted most of James's scrutiny in *The American Scene* were the changes in ethnic composition and urban scale. Record-level turn-of-the-century immigration poured millions of Jews, Italians, and other minorities into New York City and other large urban areas. According to the U.S. Census of 1910, almost a quarter of the U.S. population was unable to speak English, up nearly 10 percent from 1900.[14] Everywhere James traveled—even in the supposed Anglo-Saxon sanctuary of New England—he discovered to his surprise and dismay that he was unable to converse with his fellow citizens in English. When James left the United States in the 1880s, furthermore, the tallest building in New York City, where he was born, was still Trinity Church, completed soon after James's birth in 1843. By 1904, more than a dozen skyscrapers overtopped Trinity. The sudden appearance of skyscrapers coincided with a period of enthusiasm for monumental civic and commercial architecture. Influenced by the aesthetics of the Chicago World's Fair, architects across the nation designed museums, government buildings, libraries, department stores, universities, hotels, and hospitals on a colossal scale.[15]

For James, the radically new appearance of American cities was an intensely disturbing sign of "the dreadful chill of change."[16] For skyscraper enthusiasts, on the other hand, the architectural changes were encouraging. The anonymous author of a 1913 *Craftsman* article suggested the New York skyline proclaimed to all foreigners that they had "reached the land of modernness and progress."[17] The futuristic illustrations in Moses King's popular tour guides of New York imagined upward growth as the city's destiny and reinforced this idea by combining densely packed super-skyscrapers with images of technological progress such as airships, elevated trains, and incandescent lighting (see fig. 22).

If skyscrapers epitomized modernity and progress for their advocates, to detractors like James these "monsters of the mere market" (63) represented crass commercialism and the increasing dominance of business values in American culture. The displacement of Trinity Church as New York's highest building, in particular, symbolized the sacrifice of "higher" values to the profane values of the marketplace. (It is worth pointing out here that both critics and advocates of skyscrapers agreed on the fundamental principle that height signified importance; the relative heights of religious and commercial buildings, in other words, supposedly indicated the relative importance to our culture of the values they represented.) James, however, was less concerned with the subordination of spiritualism than with the renunciation of aesthetics. In an effort to maximize on investments, commercial builders in New York at the time James visited often demanded that their architects reduce ornamentation to a bare minimum. The result was often unaccented stone cliffs pockmarked with innumerable windows. "Window upon window, at any cost," James observed, "is a condition never to be reconciled with any grace of building" (74). The contrast between these buildings and Trinity Church was unbearable to James. "Beauty indeed was the aim of

Fig. 22. Harry Pettit, "King's Dream of New York." Moses King, who commissioned this illustration for his tour guide of the city, predicted a future New York in which massed skyscrapers and teeming crowds would necessitate elevated walkways, airships, and elevated trains. The physical "uplift" of New York is complemented by an aerial perspective in the illustration. (Reproduced from King, *King's Views* [1908].)

the creator of the spire of Trinity Church, so cruelly overtopped and so barely distinguishable . . . in its abject helpless humility. . . . We commune with it, in tenderness and pity, through the encumbered air," he laments (61).

James's anxieties about the apparent repudiation of aesthetics in New York have clear significance for his own work, which was so meticulously crafted for discriminating readers. His eagerness to commune with the buildings "mercilessly deprived of their visibility" (61) by the skyscrapers reveals the extent to which he identified with those older structures. Returning to his first home, James is horrified to discover that his personal "view of the past" is blocked by a tall building erected on the plot of ground where his birthplace once stood. The effect on him "was of having been amputated of half my history" (70–71). He had imagined that some mural would have been erected on his birthplace to commemorate his career, but the presence of the tall building demonstrates the futility of such wishes. "Where, in fact, is the point of inserting a mural tablet, at any legible height," he wonders, "in a building certain to be destroyed to make room for a sky-scraper? . . . [T]he great city is . . . practically, a huge continuous fifty-floored conspiracy against the very idea of the ancient graces" (71).

Even more than commercialism, and even more perhaps than a conscious disavowal of aesthetics, skyscrapers represent to James a callous disregard for the past—or, what was perhaps worse, a conscious repudiation of the past that had sinister implications for his own posthumous literary career. Because skyscrapers were seemingly built for temporary purposes (their lack of ornamentation and the haste of their construction suggesting they were not meant to last) and because so many buildings of historical significance were simply razed to make room for them, the tall buildings represented principally a thoughtless obsession with change and provisionalism to James—a kind of architectural adaptation of the principle of endless consumption upon which capitalism rests. "Crowned not only with no history, but with no credible possibility of time for history, and consecrated by no uses save the commercial at any cost," he wrote, "they are simply the most piercing notes in that concert of the expensively provisional into which your supreme sense of New York resolves itself" (60–61).

James's fear is that the rejection of the past, like the destruction of his birthplace, may imply an immanent chucking of his own literary accomplishments; he is anxious, to use the words of one recent critic, about "the impending extinction of his literary identity in his native land."[18] *The American Scene* was among the products of James's late phase of writing, in which his preoccupation with form diminished his popularity and exposed him to criticism on stylistic grounds. Even his brother William chided him for his abstruse, tangled writing manner and urged him to abandon it. "Why won't you, just to please Brother, sit down and write a new book . . . with absolute straightness in the style?" wrote William in a letter of 1905. "In this crowded and hurried reading age," he added in a letter after reading *The American Scene* two years later, "pages that require such close attention remain unread and neglected."[19]

Perhaps more to the point here, New York's skyscrapers repeatedly impress James with a sense of his own age and obsolescence. He remarks that he has witnessed in the latter half of the nineteenth century the shift from one historic era to another. Seeing the era of his youth represented in the "shabby, shrunken, barely discernible" Castle Garden Concert Hall produces for James "a horrible, hateful sense of personal antiquity" (63). The apparently shrunken, menaced presence of so many landmarks of his past (Trinity Church, Castle Garden, City Hall, and the Boston Athenaeum) encourages James to apply metaphors of childhood—when physical size is unstable, when change is immanent, and when one developmental period inevitably succumbs to a more permanent one—to the architecture of skyscrapers. The tall buildings of Wall Street, which "make one feel one's age," crush the old landmarks "quite as violent children stamp on snails and caterpillars" (63). The image of skyscrapers surrounding the Boston Athenaeum is a vision of "a pair of school-bullies who hustle and pummel some studious little boy" (173). Everywhere the shift in scale encourages him to identify with smaller things. In Boston, for instance, James feels trapped in "the bigger, braver, louder" city and stares as if through "bars of a grating" at "'my' small homogeneous Boston of the more interesting time" (172).

James's misgivings about his literary legacy are compounded by his sense that the culture he writes to and from may be undergoing a slow death—or at the very least a radical reconstitution such that the product, if it ever reaches a settled state, may be unrecognizable from a late nineteenth-century perspective. Immediately after paying witness to "the extinction of Trinity" (65), James describes his visit to Ellis Island, where he records feeling shaken "to the depths of his being." He compares the sight of so many "inconceivable aliens" entering his home to the vision of "a ghost in his supposedly safe old house" (66). The scale of assimilation is for James perhaps the greatest testament to the American embrace of transience and change, of "*the will to grow* . . . at no matter what or whose expense" (43; emphasis in original). On one hand, James goes on to ponder in the following pages, immigration is proceeding at such a scale that it must challenge the forces of American assimilation. "You recognize in [the immigrants]," he says, "those elements that are not elements of swift convertibility, and you lose yourself in the wonder of what becomes, as it were, of the obstinate, the unconverted residuum" (95). Later he describes the difficulties facing the "man of letters" who must write to a reading public that is changing so swiftly and irrevocably. He describes the cafés on New York's East Side, susurrant with the Yiddish accents of recent immigrants, as "torture-rooms of the living idiom." Here he believes he catches hints of the "Accent of the Future," which, he reasons, "may be destined to become the most beautiful [language] on the globe and the very music of humanity . . . ; but whatever we shall know it for, certainly, we shall not know it for English—in any sense for which there is an existing literary measure" (105–6). Thus, immigration is one element of the cult of impermanence that contributes to the demise of the American man of letters.

It is no accident that the chapters on New York in *The American Scene* are dominated by discussions of skyscrapers and immigrants: the two become inextricably linked in James's mind. (This was true for other writers as well. One of the characters in Willa Cather's "Behind the Singer Tower" describes that skyscraper as a "Jewy-looking thing," and skyscrapers become, accordingly, symbols of materialism in her story.)[20] Both appeared as direct results of the American "will to grow" at any cost, and both represented an embrace of change for its own sake—change at the expense of tradition and history. Some even claimed, erroneously, that skyscrapers were erected to accommodate the enormous population growth stemming from recent immigration.[21] Thus, both symbolized everything James detested. But only the skyscraper mounted a particular aesthetic to which James could respond with his own counteraesthetic. *The American Scene,* then, can be read as a carefully crafted response to the aesthetic of the skyscraper.

The formal contrasts between *The American Scene* and turn-of-the-century metropolitan commercial architecture are especially striking. Skyscrapers reflected the haste of modern American commercial life: they were built as hurriedly as possible to reduce building expenses and to minimize the length of time when the real estate was not paying dividends; their occupants, James noted, seemed to move as if harried by a lash; and they owed their existence to the elevator, that "intolerable symbol," for James, "of the herded and driven state" (140). James's writing style in *The American Scene,* in contrast, is slow, plodding, and meticulous—those not inclined to be gracious might even say torturous. The book expects, or attempts to impose, a measure of leisure that few were privileged enough to possess, as William James recognized. The stylistic complexity of the writing opposed the spare functionalism of the typical skyscraper at the time James visited New York. The lengthy, often convoluted syntax of the sentences in *The American Scene* requires for comprehension that the reader move constantly backward and forward, mirroring James's search for a national and personal past in his journeys—a search that was frustrated by the presence of skyscrapers. We enact in our reading the experience that he failed to have, in other words: a constant deciphering of the connections between what has come before and what we see directly in front of us.

Those who wrote about skyscrapers invariably noted that the view from the top made pedestrians look tiny and insignificant. "If you are a philosopher you can do this thing," wrote O. Henry in 1910 in a short story entitled "Psyche and the Pskyscraper." "You can go to the top of a high building, look down on your fellow men 300 feet below, and despise them as insects. . . . Man, . . . to the housetopped philosopher, appears to be but a creeping, contemptible beetle."[22] Sightseers flocked to the observation decks of New York's tallest buildings to experience for themselves the unprecedented and thoroughly modern perspective that skyscrapers afforded of the city and its inhabitants.[23] In *The Harbor* (1915), Ernest Poole would argue that the corporate mentality expressed in the view from a skyscraper summit was consistent with the contempt big business executives felt for the masses and with the way they callously disrupted people's lives. Unlike most of his literary contemporaries, James for the most part refuses to enter New York's tall buildings and rarely offers elevated perspectives. Pedestrian views dominate *The American Scene*. He dislikes skyscrapers in part because they indoctrinate us in their elevated, distant vision; they make "our eyes, however unwillingly, at home in strange vertiginous upper atmospheres" (61).[24] As a kind of literary analogue to his pedestrian vantage point, the authorial position of the book remains rigidly first person. James rejects the omniscient perspective that might correspond to the transcendent vision from skyscraper peaks. However exasperating it may be at times, we remain confined within James's own consciousness; he consistently resists the impulse to imagine how others might view and think about the subjects that preoccupy him throughout his narrative.

The skyscraper represented, among other things, America's "insistence on gregarious ways," according to James (140). Often capable of housing as many occupants as a moderate-sized city, skyscrapers at the turn of the century created new patterns of urban congestion (particularly before and after the typical workday) and reflected the reality, as one recent historian explained, that "daily life was lived more and more in the mass . . . under conditions of mass production, mass transit, mass education, and mass culture."[25] As an anodyne to modernity and an alternative to mass entertainment, *The American Scene* deliberately opposed not only the frenzied pace of modern life but also its congestion. James's travelogue is the antithesis of crowded; virtually no one exists in the book but James. If one did not know that James toured the United States as a celebrity, dining with figures as prominent as President Theodore Roosevelt, Secretary of State John Hay, and Mark Twain, one might picture him wandering America's streets like a friendless old derelict. The only voices other than his own in the book are those of buildings—and since buildings do not generally speak, we can only assume that James multiplied his own voice in a clumsy form of literary ventriloquism.[26]

The eerie magnification of the self in *The American Scene* is a deliberate response to the diminishment of the individual in America's corporate culture. The book's excessive individualism defies not only the feeling of diminishment one has in the presence of skyscrapers—it also restores the individualism that many believed was threatened by corporate culture, mass production, enormous factories, and the urban concentration that these things demanded. In addition, it offers an experience directly antithetical to that of riding an elevator in a skyscraper, which for James is symbolic of "the gregarious spell" of modern cities, "the abject collective consciousness of being pushed and pressed in" (140).

The relentless introspection of the book opposes the skyscraper's emphasis on surfaces and exteriors, furthermore. Despite the lack of ornamentation on many tall commercial buildings, photographs, illustrations, and written descriptions of skyscrapers in popular magazines, books, art exhibits, and postcards unfailingly pictured the buildings from outside in order to emphasize their defining characteristic: height. Lewis Mumford sarcastically criticized the skyscraper on the grounds that it "has no accommodating grace or perfection in its interior furnishing, beyond its excellent lavatories."[27] James's inward retreat in *The American Scene* represents his desire for seclusion, isolation, and privacy, which he finds everywhere thwarted in American buildings and American culture generally. American architecture conspires against the very notion of a room, James believes. From homes to public institutions (but presumably excluding elevators), James observes "the enlargement of every opening, the exaggeration of every passage, the substitution of gaping arches and far perspectives and resounding voids for enclosing walls, for practicable doors, for controllable windows, for all the rest of the essence of the room-character." The result is a "diffused vagueness of separation between apartments, between hall and room, between one room and another, between the one you are in and the one you are not in, between place of passage and place of privacy." This "suppression of almost every outward exclusory arrangement" (125–26) is the democratic principle rendered architecturally, and it is repugnant to James. He applauds the introduction of the country club, which, to quote one astute critic, "both insured privacy and promoted leisure" for the "white, largely Protestant upper class" who sought to "withdraw into their own enclaves and to sharpen the lines between themselves and other classes and ethnic groups."[28] Similarly, James praises the erection of the spiked iron fence and heavy sealed gates around Harvard Yard. Here his architectural aesthetics and immigration politics converge: James believes an open door policy is unwholesome in both realms. "The open door . . . may make a magnificent place," he writes, "but it makes poor places" (49).

In the preface to *The American Scene,* James admits that his book deviates from the documentary tradition—the tradition of newspapers, government reports, surveys, and censuses, with their emphasis on statistics and generalizations. The often trying singularity of his voice reflects his strict adherence to a limited, idiosyncratic vision as opposed to the comprehensive, totalizing one that is characteristic both of the documentary tradition and the elevated perspective. He creates an aesthetic equivalent of the architecture that he believes is missing in the United States—a literary space of intimacy, leisure, seclusion, and exclusion. It is a space that is compatible with his preference for small, private places as opposed to the expansive, inclusive ones that so many of his contemporaries in the United States seemed to favor. Rather than inviting us to the observation decks of skyscrapers, James beckons us (some of us, that is) to join him in the leisure and seclusion of his quiet literary drawing room.

An Art That Must Live in Skyscrapers: Alvin Langdon Coburn and Urban Photography

Virtually the only occasion in *The American Scene* when James offers an elevated perspective is in his description of Trinity Church. "Our eyes, made, however unwillingly, at home in strange vertiginous upper atmospheres," he writes, "look down on [Trinity Church] as on a poor ineffectual thing, an architectural object addressed . . . to the patient pedestrian sense and permitting thereby a relation of intimacy" (61). He uses an elevated vantage point here to garner sympathy for the outmoded architectural style of the cathedral, to represent the injuries caused by the new commercial architecture, and to emphasize the effects of modern buildings on our consciousness.

It is likely that Alvin Langdon Coburn attempted to render James's vision photographically in "Trinity Church from Above" (fig. 23), one of five pictures taken in 1912 and exhibited in London the following year under the title "New York from Its Pinnacles." Although James was not alone in his ruminations on the visual displacement of Trinity Church by New York's skyscrapers,[29] Coburn was accustomed to following James's photographic instructions. Between 1906 and 1907—the same years he was also working on *The American Scene*—James was involved in editing his collected works for the authoritative New York Edition. He

Fig. 23. Alvin Langdon Coburn, "Trinity Church from Above" (1912). Coburn's photograph of Trinity Church offers an elevated perspective of the building from a nearby skyscraper. Many New Yorkers at the turn of the century criticized the construction of commercial structures that towered above the city's churches. (Courtesy George Eastman House.)

took the unusual step of collaborating with a photographer—Alvin Langdon Coburn—for illustrations accompanying his works.[30] James provided Coburn with detailed instructions for the photographs he wished, and Coburn, by all accounts, carried out his orders to James's great satisfaction.[31]

But Coburn was no mere photographic lackey. He was a celebrity in his own right by the time he began working with James. A member of Alfred Stieglitz's inner circle and inducted into the coveted Photo-Secession and Linked Ring before the age of twenty-one, Coburn was regarded by many as a prodigy and one of the most talented American photographers of his day. Not only was he inundated with requests from popular U.S. magazines like *Harper's, Everybody's, Cosmopolitan, Century,* and *Literary Digest* during the first decade of the twentieth century, but he also photographed two U.S. presidents (Roosevelt and Taft) and numerous famous artists (George Bernard Shaw, William Butler Yeats, Auguste Rodin, Mark Twain, H. G. Wells, Gertrude Stein, Henri Matisse, Max Weber, and Ezra Pound, to name a few) between 1904 and 1916.

Coburn labored at a time when aesthetic conventions were shifting. While the late nineteenth century was dominated by the picturesque (one critic has suggested that *The American Scene* was "the last important work in the picturesque tradition"),[32] the early twentieth century witnessed a shift toward modernism. Early images of skyscrapers (circa 1875–1910) in magazines, photographs, and artist's renderings tended to employ picturesque devices.[33] Typically this reflected the ambivalence that many felt toward the skyscraper; through the use of picturesque techniques, artists sought to create images "which accorded with traditional notions of taste," in the words of one architectural historian, and which deemphasized the commercialism of urban architecture.[34] Picturesque compositions, according to another historian, also tended to "diminish or obscure" the verticality and height of the skyscraper.[35] Unlike modernism, "The picturesque aesthetic . . . was not one that could appreciate verticality unto itself."[36] In this regard, the picturesque mode was compatible with early skyscraper design (circa 1875–1900), which sought to divide tall buildings into separate stylistic components, thereby drawing attention away from the building's height and emphasizing its horizontal elements. It was not until the architect Louis Sullivan made his famous pronouncement in 1896 that designers began accentuating the verticality of their creations.

What is the chief characteristic of the tall office building? . . . At once we must answer, it is lofty. This loftiness is to the artist-nature its thrilling aspect. It is the very open organ-tone in its appeal. . . . It must be tall, every inch of it. The force and power of altitude must be in it, the glory and pride of exaltation must be in it. It must be every inch a proud and soaring thing, rising in sheer exultation that from bottom to top it is a unit without dissenting line.[37]

One can see the transition toward modernism embodied in Coburn's photographs in "New York from Its Pinnacles." "The Woolworth Building" (fig. 24) and "The Municipal Building" (fig. 25) employ picturesque conventions. Both utilize atmospheric effects (smoke rising from chimneys, hazy backgrounds) to add motion and complexity to the images and to convey a sense that the skyscrapers exist within a natural environment. The photograph of the Municipal Building frames its subject on all sides, populating the foreground, middle ground, background, and side screens in a manner consistent with picturesque aesthetics.

Fig. 24. Alvin Langdon Coburn, "The Woolworth Building" (1912). Coburn's photograph of the Woolworth Building (still under construction at the time) is in the picturesque tradition. (Courtesy George Eastman House.)

Fig. 25. Alvin Langdon Coburn, "New York from Its Pinnacles" (1912). Like his image of the Woolworth Building, Coburn's photo of the Municipal Building used common picturesque devices. (Courtesy George Eastman House.)

The photograph of the Woolworth Building combines the smoke in the foreground with the fog or smog in the background to diminish the size of the skyscraper. Coburn's choice of the Woolworth's side view rather than its frontal view, furthermore, makes the horizontal and vertical lines of the building equally important.

But these photos, it should be noted, differed from typical picturesque renderings of skyscrapers in one important respect: they use an elevated vantage point rather than a street-level perspective. "Trinity Church from Above," "The Octopus," and "The House of a Thousand Windows" (figs. 23, 26, and 27) all utilize the elevated perspective more self-consciously. They are among the first modernist photographs; in all likelihood, they represent the first sustained attempt to render the aesthetics of skyscraper height artistically. Like subsequent modernist photographs, they employ unusual, disorienting angles and emphasize pattern and shape rather than lighting and other naturalistic effects. Concerned with the aesthetics of height, they do more than depict the verticality of modern cities: they look down on the city, using the skyscraper not simply as a symbol of growth and progress but as a vehicle for new possibilities of vision.

Fig. 26. Alvin Langdon Coburn, "The Octopus" (1912). One of five photographs selected for Coburn's "New York from Its Pinnacles" exhibit, "The Octopus" offers an aerial perspective of Madison Square Park. (Courtesy George Eastman House.)

Fig. 27. Alvin Langdon Coburn, "The House of a Thousand Windows" (1912). Coburn's photograph offers a heady aerial perspective of one of New York's turn-of-the-century skyscrapers. (Courtesy George Eastman House.)

The fact that the skyscraper enabled a new kind of vision in urban environments suggests that it was analogous to the camera, which also provided new ways of seeing. Cameras, as numerous historians have pointed out, produced unprecedented views of the world and altered our understanding of reality in fundamental ways. The fact that a single object or event in time could be photographed simultaneously from different angles, for example, contributed to the belief that reality was multiplicitous, that individual perspective and consciousness dictated one's experience of the world. Coburn, in fact, regarded skyscrapers and photography as correlative. "Photography born of this age of steel," wrote

Coburn, "seems to have naturally adapted itself to the necessarily unusual requirements of an art that must live in skyscrapers, and it is because she has become so much at home in these gigantic structures that the Americans undoubtedly are the recognized leaders in the world movement of pictorial photography."[38] Coburn's "House of a Thousand Windows," in fact, can be read as a metaphor for photography. Not only is the picture itself taken from an unusual angle, suggesting the way photography afforded new views of the world, but the numerous windows of the skyscraper (exaggerated in number by Coburn's title) suggest the way photography offers the possibility of multiple perspectives on reality. Like the skyscraper, which housed many individuals within a single structure and afforded each a different view, reality could no longer be said to be monolithic. The imagery in the photo's title—Coburn's description of the tall building as a "house"—substitutes the typical turn-of-the-century commercial associations of skyscrapers with domestic ones, suggesting that the buildings function as more than corporate symbols; like photography, they enable new places of mental residence, new forms of consciousness.

Coburn was not alone in his belief that skyscrapers and photography were related. Many writers observed that New York's skyscrapers and skyline were best viewed from a distance; appreciation of the city's architecture was effectively foreclosed to the common pedestrian. "Not one in a hundred of its citizens has ever seen New York. It is too near," wrote John Van Dyke, a skyscraper enthusiast, in his popular 1909 tour guide to the city. "There is no perspective, no proper focus. Even our painter people are a little bewildered by its 'bigness.' . . . The material is here and . . . needs only the properly-adjusted eyes to see its beauty."[39] Lewis Mumford took up this point in 1924, arguing that skyscrapers depended on photography to make their aesthetic characteristics accessible and appealing to the public.

> What our critics have learned to admire in our great buildings is their photographs. . . . In an article chiefly devoted to praise of the skyscraper, in a number of The Arts, the majority of the illustrations were taken from a point that the man in the street never reaches. In short, it is an architecture, not for men, but for angels and aviators! If buildings are to be experienced directly, and not through the vicarious agency of the photograph, the skyscraper defeats its own ends.[40]

Coburn tacitly agreed with both critics. "How romantic, how exhilarating it is in these altitudes, few of the denizens of [New York] realise," observed Coburn in a written statement accompanying his "New York from Its Pinnacles" exhibition. "They crawl about in the abyss intent upon their own small concerns."[41] (Note that Coburn, unlike Mumford, places the blame for this failure of vision on New York's residents, who are "intent upon their small concerns," rather than the architecture itself.)

Responding to critics who claimed that he worked too quickly in his craft, Coburn also argued that haste was constitutive of photography—another respect in which his art was at home in skyscrapers.

> To me New York is a vision that rises out of the sea as I come up the harbor on my Atlantic liner, and which glimmers for a while in the sun for the first of my stay amidst its pinnacles; but which vanishes, but for fragmentary glimpses, as I become one of the grey creatures that crawl about like ants, at the bottom of its gloomy caverns. My apparently unseemly hurry has for its object my burning desire to record, translate, create, if you like, these visions of mine before they fade.[42]

Coburn's statements suggest that his view of the role of the artist in the modern metropolis is compatible with a hierarchical, corporate conception of society. The artist, like the corporate executive, is a person of exceptional vision, responsible for instructing his contemporaries, who rarely if ever attain comparable heights. Photographs serve to "uplift" their viewers, to elevate them above their sordid daily world to a realm of romance, beauty, and order. "Photography helps us . . . to see afresh, and to cultivate the capacity to see with more clarity, and this is of great value in the ability to lead a fuller and richer life," wrote Coburn in his autobiography.[43] "Reality . . . is an ascending ladder," he added, "with earthly beauty at its lowest rung and Divine Beauty as its Crowning Glory, and in between them a sequence of ascent in perfect symmetry and order."[44] The best perception, the best vantage point for seeing the city, Coburn assumes, is the elevated one at the top of a skyscraper (or the distant one from the harbor). There is no sense here, as in Poole's novel *The Harbor,* that this vantage point blinds one to certain facts or that the view from the bottom (of the city, of society) is valuable in any way.

The relationship between skyscrapers and photography was symbiotic: skyscraper builders did not merely depend on photographers to render their creations accessible to the public; photography also had a substantial effect on urban architectural design. Architects tacitly acknowledged the influence of photography—or at least the technological developments of which photography was a part—on the construction of skyscrapers following about 1910. After Louis Sullivan's solution to the initial "problem" of the skyscraper—how to represent its height appropriately—the second "problem" of the skyscraper was what to do with its crown.[45] Early skyscrapers tended to be built on the principle of an upended rectangular box. The roof was flat, often with a heavy overhanging cornice, and the top was invisible to pedestrians in the street (see, for example, fig. 28). Roofs were, as a consequence, often loaded with unsightly apparatuses: water tanks on stilts, penthouses for elevator motors, chimneys, steam vents, and exposed pipes.[46] The design assumed that the buildings would be viewed from the street. As aerial perspectives of the city became more common—in part through photography but also because of the proliferation of skyscrapers with observation decks and the advent of airplanes, balloons, and dirigibles—architects increased their attention to the skyscraper's crown. The result was the skyscraper tower, or setback design, introduced by the Woolworth Building in 1913 and reproduced by later skyscrapers such as the art deco buildings of the thirties.

If skyscraper builders depended on photography to disseminate

Fig. 28. Louis Sullivan, Guaranty Building (1896). With its flat roof, Sullivan's Guaranty Building was typical of skyscrapers built before the Woolworth Building. (Courtesy Buffalo and Erie County Historical Society.)

images of their structures to a public that had little access to the proper vantage point from which to appreciate their buildings, then photographers were in a sense advertisers. They bore the responsibility for conveying to the public the ideological and aesthetic freight articulated in skyscraper designs. Although Coburn did not work directly for any corporation or builder, his photos did tell his contemporaries something about these corporate symbols. But what exactly did they say?

Of Coburn's five photographs in his "New York from Its Pinnacles" exhibition, "The Octopus" and "The House of a Thousand Windows" might best help us answer that question. They are not images of particular, well-known buildings. Rather than honoring specific structures, they meditate self-consciously on the effects of New York's vertical growth on one's sense of reality, one's vision and consciousness. Perhaps for this very reason they have been prized the most highly by critics and historians of photography; they are certainly the most unconventional of the five and elicited the strongest responses.

"The House of a Thousand Windows" and "The Octopus" both emphasize abstract shapes. "The House of a Thousand Windows" draws attention to the repetitious squares in the principle building's windows and contrasts these shapes with various triangular structures, such as the peaks of the building's uprights, the isosceles triangle of which the building and the street form two sides, and the rooftop at the bottom left of the principle building. "The Octopus" contrasts the circular, curved footpaths of Madison Square with the straight lines of the street, sidewalk, and buildings. In both, the attention to pattern offers visions of urban order at a time when people were increasingly preoccupied with the apparent disorder of America's cities.

The use of naturalistic imagery in "The Octopus" places that photograph in the tradition to which Frank Norris belonged. The title is an almost certain reference to Norris's novel of the same title. (The image of the octopus was synonymous with the corporate trust by this time; whether Norris's *The Octopus* of 1901 produced this association or whether his work popularized terminology already in circulation is unclear to me.) The choice of title might suggest, as Norris does in his novel, that the disturbing and seemingly unfamiliar perspective engendered by modern architectural and commercial developments is an extension of familiar facts. The natural resides even within the most thoroughly manufactured, the photo seems to suggest. This idea is reminiscent of the arguments of corporate apologists, who claimed that both the skyscraper and the trust were inevitable products of "natural" or "social evolution." It is also characteristic of literary naturalism and its tendency to blur the distinctions between nature and technology.[47]

In both photos—in fact, in most of Coburn's skyscraper images[48]—people are either absent or extraneous. In this sense, his photographs represent the diminishment of the individual that accompanied corporate growth. One might argue that this was unavoidable in photographs taken from the tops of New York's skyscrapers; it was not in fact inevitable, although it was common. In an essay about skyscrapers published in *Everybody's Magazine* in 1908, for example, Ernest Poole and the photographers who collaborated with him focused their attention on the laborers who built the city's tall buildings (see fig. 29). In his essay, Poole emphasized the ethnic heterogeneity, the class and ideological divisions, and the carnival disorder apparent in the city from such a height.

> Looking straight down through the brisk little puffs of smoke and steam, the whole mighty tangle of Manhattan Island drew close into one vivid picture: Fifth Avenue crowded with carriages, motors, and cabs, was apparently only a few yards away from the tenement roofs, which were dotted with clothes out to dry. Police courts, churches, schools, sober old convents hedged close round with strips of green, the Tenderloin district, the Wall Street region, the Ghetto, the teeming Italian hive, lay all in a merry squeeze below.[49]

Poole's deliberate juxtaposition of images of wealth and poverty (Fifth Avenue and the tenements), order and chaos (police courts, churches, schools, and the ghetto), was unusual in descriptions of the city from skyscrapers. Most writers focused on the maplike quality that the sight conveyed. They pointed out that the metropolis looked more harmonious and orderly; "from that height," said the *New York Times* in 1912, the city looked "small and white and clean."[50] People, observers noted, became indistinguishable, equally "full of soap-bubble loves and hates, of ephemeral cares and joys."[51] Differences of race, ethnicity, class, and gender that seemed so important in everyday routines dwindled to nothing.

There are contrasts in Coburn's photographs, to be sure—contrasts of light and dark, of shapes, of nature and civilization; but the photos do not attempt to render the social heterogeneity of New York in the way Poole's essay does. People play a role only in giving scale to the city. In this sense also Coburn's photographs are idealized visions of order and human uniformity.

The omission of people in Coburn's urban photography, and his preoccupation with pattern that substitutes for an interest in human sub-

Fig. 29. Hewitt and Clarke, "With Only a Glance Now and Then Down Into the Tangle of Civilization." The photographs accompanying Ernest Poole's essay "Cowboys of the Skies" honor the men who built New York's turn-of-the-century skyscrapers. These photos may have been a model for Lewis Hine's later and better-known homage to the men who built the Empire State Building. (Reproduced from *Everybody's Magazine,* 1908.)

jects, is striking—even troubling—in his pictures of industrial Pittsburgh, taken in 1910 (see fig. 30). Pittsburgh was notorious for its steel mills, and, as one of the biggest of the large-scale industries in the country, U.S. steel was synonymous with trust. As the home of American steel production, moreover, Pittsburgh was notorious for its antilabor stance; the violent suppression of the nearby Homestead Strike in the 1890s crushed unionization efforts among steelworkers. It was no accident, therefore, that Pittsburgh was the site chosen in 1907 for one of the major Progressive studies of working conditions in the United States, the Pittsburgh Survey. Lasting a year and a half and resulting in a six-volume report, the comprehensive study investigated labor conditions, family life, education, ethnic composition, housing conditions, and other matters with the aim of promoting liberal reform.

The leaders of the study hired the documentary photographer Lewis Hine. Members of the Photo-Secession, such as Coburn, deliberately sought to distance their work from the documentary tradition, which used straight photographic techniques in the service of unambiguous realism and practical social reform. Unlike Coburn's pictures, which

Fig. 30. Alvin Langdon Coburn, "Station Roofs, Pittsburgh" (1910). Coburn's Pittsburgh photos omit people and ignore the dramatic social strife that characterized the city in the Progressive era. Like his pictures of skyscrapers, his industrial images emphasize abstract shapes and contrasts of light and darkness. (Courtesy George Eastman House.)

emphasize the patterns of industrial buildings, Hine's photos of Pittsburgh capture maimed steelworkers, ramshackle tenements, impoverished families, and child laborers (see fig. 31). Hine also shot numerous isolated portraits of immigrant laborers to emphasize the individuality of the steelworkers. While Coburn omitted individuals, for Hine "The individual is the big thing after all."[52]

If the contrasts between Hine's and Coburn's Pittsburgh photos appear to provide compelling evidence of Coburn's collaboration with the new corporate vision, there are aspects of Coburn's photographs, not

Fig. 31. Lewis Hine, "Accident Case in Steel Mills" (1908–9). Hine's photographs of Pittsburgh drew attention to the effects of industrial working conditions on the poor. (Courtesy George Eastman House.)

easily dismissed, that challenge that view. For all their abstraction, there is a lurking sense of menace in "The Octopus" and "The House of a Thousand Windows." The steep angles of both photos create an uncomfortable sense of vertigo, as if we are falling into the picture—or onto the pavement—from a great height. This deliberate evocation of vertigo could be meant to convey a warning about the perilous, breakneck speed of changes in America or the risk that rapid industrial growth poses for the individual. Both photos employ an off-center focus, disrupting the complete order and symmetry of the compositions. The narrow, darkened streets of "The House of a Thousand Windows" seem to reinforce the arguments of skyscraper detractors, who claimed that tall buildings cut off light and air to pedestrians. The looming shadow of the skyscraper in "The Octopus" enhances the ominous mood in that picture, and the title itself may be meant to evoke not the mundane, harmless variety of octopus but rather those gigantic and terrifying creatures that rise up out of the murky oceanic depths like mutant forces of nature in the novel that was so popular at the turn of the century, Jules Verne's *20,000 Leagues Under the Sea.* In both photos, furthermore, the view of the city is limited and fragmentary rather than comprehensive and maplike. Thus, Coburn resists the panoramic, totalizing view that Michel Foucault and other writers have suggested is indicative of a desire for social domination.[53] There is, then, an undeniable ambiguity in these pictures.

Alan Trachtenberg would argue that this very ambiguity in modernist photography, like the absence of people, signifies a retreat from material, social relations into aesthetics. He has made this argument, in fact, when comparing Alfred Stieglitz's skyscraper photographs from 1932 (which were clearly influenced by Coburn's earlier work) with Lewis Hine's *Men at Work* (also published in 1932), a photographic essay celebrating the laborers who erected the Empire State Building. Unlike Hine's photos, whose social messages are relatively unambiguous ("cities do not build themselves"), Stieglitz's photographs are "indeterminate, spectacles of ambiguity," according to Trachtenberg; they are images of skyscrapers detached from concrete social matters, and they invite a similarly detached, aestheticized analysis of their contrasts and possible meanings.[54]

While this is a compelling argument, especially in light of the dissimilarities between Coburn's and Hine's Pittsburgh photographs, I would not like to dismiss out of hand the possible value of ambiguous art, nor would I care to discount the possibility of a politically engaged ambiguous art. On the other hand, it seems clear that Coburn's work was not politically engaged in the manner of Hine's. The ambiguities in

Coburn's "The Octopus" and "The House of a Thousand Windows" most likely reflect Coburn's awareness of the tensions in contemporary views of the skyscraper. Coburn could not have been ignorant of the controversy surrounding urban architecture. While his photos served to represent, probably even to celebrate, the new modes of vision and consciousness such architecture enabled (the attention to urban shape and order skyscrapers invited, the diminished view of the individual they imposed), he also sought to make his work appealing to a sharply divided audience. Extending the appeal of his art was the most effective means of accomplishing his primary agenda: promoting photography's status as a genuine art form, also the goal of the Photo-Secession movement generally. The ambiguity in his modernist photos, therefore, represents his self-conscious intervention between opponents and enthusiasts of the skyscraper.

In spite of the ambiguity in "The Octopus" and "The House of a Thousand Windows," then, it seems clear that these images represented a photographic adaptation of the new corporate vision. They helped disseminate this vision, familiarizing the public with its ambitions and effects. Coburn's modernist photography was heir to much that was gained and much that was lost in the shift to corporate capitalism: the spectacular and expansive new forms of vision and the dreams of order that this shift enabled, as well as a disengagement from the needs and desires of individuals and the traditional values of liberal humanism.

The Woolworth Building: A Monument to Small Things

At any time, the praise heaped upon the creators of the Woolworth Building would have marked this corporate icon as a remarkable success—both as an advertising device and as an architectural invention. At a time when both the skyscraper and big business were intensely embattled, the popular and critical reception of the Woolworth Building was nothing less than astonishing. The *New York World* hailed it as the "American architectural masterpiece of the twentieth century."[55] An editorial in the *New York Times* compared it to the world's greatest architectural wonders: the Taj Mahal, the Pyramids, and the Roman Coliseum.[56] Montgomery Schuyler, the dominant voice in skyscraper criticism of the 1890s and 1900s, flew into virtual paroxysms of rapture. "How it cleaves the empyrean and makes the welkin ring as it glitters in the sunshine of high noon," he rhapsodized. "Its inherent right to its dominant position there is none to dispute."[57] Even Claude Bragdon, a Louis Sullivan disciple who, along with Sullivan and Mumford, vehemently disapproved of "feudalistic" architecture (the Woolworth Building, with its Gothic ornament, would fall into this camp), offered grudging admiration for the skyscraper. "The Woolworth Building . . . remains today in many respects the finest embodiment of the skyscraper idea," he wrote in 1932. "It so stimulated the architects throughout the country to emulation and to imitation that Gilbert's must be reckoned the next important influence after Sullivan's on skyscraper design."[58]

But even those most thoroughly devoted to the building saw reason to wonder at President Woodrow Wilson's participation in the opening ceremonies of April 1913.[59] As the eight hundred distinguished guests of Woolworth's sumptuous banquet gathered on the building's twenty-seventh floor, the lights in the hall dimmed and a telegraph was sent to Wilson in Washington. Wilson pressed a button, initiating the dynamos in the skyscraper's basement and setting eighty thousand electric lights ablaze throughout the building.

Wilson's participation in the unveiling of the Woolworth Building suggested a startling government endorsement of a specific U.S. business. There was some precedent for Wilson's action, perhaps, in the public appearances of Presidents Grover Cleveland and Theodore Roosevelt, who, respectively, inaugurated the World's Columbian Exposition and Louisiana Purchase Exposition by turning "golden keys" that initiated the lights and fountains of those fairs. Yet those earlier appearances were associated with ostensibly public rather than private events. As if it were not bad enough that Wilson appeared to be endorsing a particular company, he had campaigned the previous year on a platform opposing the trusts. As the largest retail business in the United States, the Woolworth Company was a corporation that exhibited many of the features of a trust. It achieved its dominance through an aggressive program of mergers; between 1904 and 1912, Frank Woolworth gathered 313 independent stores into his national chain of five-and-dimes. Woolworth was able to offer unusually low prices for his goods, furthermore, by keeping his employees' wages low (especially those of his female employees),[60] aggressively stomping out unionization attempts, securing special shipping rates with the railroads, eliminating middlemen by buying directly from manufacturers, and using scale economies to his advantage[61]—all favorite devices of the trusts (the first three were also commonly censured by politicians and the public). Woolworth even used a business practice that Wilson specifically linked with trusts and expressly condemned in his campaign speeches: deliberately accepting losses on goods in a single store (offset by profits in other locations) in order to put a rival small store out of business.[62]

The speeches delivered at the opening banquet provide some

insight into Wilson's possible reasons for participating in the ceremony. The speeches are riddled with anxiety about the recent attacks on the robber barons and big business. "The attacks on our rich men are constant," observed F. Hopkinson Smith, a novelist and painter who acted as the dinner's toastmaster. "The criticisms are various, reflecting . . . particularly on the fact that [wealthy capitalists] crush out the smaller men."[63] The engineer who constructed the building, Louis Horowitz, spoke of "the recent senseless persecution of big business."[64] W. U. Hensel, a dignitary from Lancaster, Pennsylvania, where Woolworth established his first successful store, spoke of the "agitation for the altruistic in business" and "those mighty questions of the relation of capital to labor . . . which seem to disturb and confuse and perplex and complicate our legislators and the critics of our social system."[65]

The speakers attempted to dissociate Woolworth and his company from the robber barons and their trusts. "What competitor complains that this man, who has organized hundreds of stores, has enforced against the public an odious trust?" asked Hensel.[66] They emphasized Frank Woolworth's rags-to-riches story. He spent the first twenty-one years of his life on a farm, they noted, and for his first paid job he worked as a three-dollar-a-week errand boy. He established his retail empire, in addition, without the aid of significant startup capital: he opened his first five-and-dime with just three hundred dollars of borrowed cash. And, of course, he built his empire on the nickels and dimes amassed from the small purchasers who constituted the nation's lower-class consumers. Thus, in the minds of many, Woolworth was already aligned with the little guy.

The speakers attributed his success, furthermore, to traditional virtues that predated the corporate era: diligence, thrift, prudence, and most especially an antipathy toward debt and capitalization. Cass Gilbert, the building's architect, emphasized Woolworth's unprecedented decision to pay cash for his multimillion-dollar skyscraper. "This structure is unique in New York, and perhaps in the whole history of great buildings in this country, in that it stands without a mortgage and without a dollar of indebtedness." Gilbert concluded that Frank Woolworth's life "shows that this is the land of equal opportunity, and that under our laws and under this government a man may start in life with nothing of this world's goods, and, single-handed, achieve success; that this opportunity is open to all and that it is not through agitation and unrest our people will prosper, but by the good old-fashioned virtues of honesty, clean dealing, industry and thrift."[67] Thus, Woolworth's Horatio Alger–like social rise testified to the continued vibrance of American capitalism in an era when many questioned its soundness and future.

Frank Woolworth, in other words, functioned effectively as a poster boy for Woodrow Wilson, who had campaigned on the principle that the nation could still secure a place for the Little Man in an economy dominated by big business. If Woolworth used Wilson's involvement for advertising purposes, Wilson, like the speakers at the opening dinner, used Woolworth's example to restore public faith in capitalism and to reinforce the primary myth sustaining it: the myth of upward mobility. The speeches suppressed the characteristics of Woolworth's business that resembled the trusts and fashioned a mythic Frank Woolworth who set out on the road to fortune as a Little Man and ended up "one of America's greatest merchant kings."[68]

If the dominant theme of the Woolworth Building's inauguration was the upward mobility of the Little Man, the design of the Woolworth Building itself was expressive of upward mobility. Gilbert said he wanted his skyscraper to convey "the greatest degree of aspiration,"[69] a "soaring sense of uplift."[70] He achieved it through the pioneering use of the setback design. By means of tapering steplike recessions, the building appears to ascend indefinitely; in the words of one architectural historian, it presents an "illusion of infinite climbing."[71] The rocketlike form is reinforced by an emphasis on vertical elements. Darkened and recessed transoms and spandrels accentuate the prominent white piers and mullions. The piers extend through the setback divisions, moreover, creating a unified upward sweep and suppressing the building's horizontal lines. In place of heavy cornices, the skyscraper features delicate, arrowlike filigree, which also subdues the horizontal elements. Every critic of the day agreed that Gilbert had achieved his aims. "How it flatters and satisfies the eye," wrote Montgomery Schuyler. "What an 'uplift' there is in that sudden, rocket-like shooting of the white and channeled shaft."[72]

The Woolworth Building was more than a steel and terra cotta representation of upward mobility; it was also, and more particularly, an architectural rendering of the Little Man's rise. Contemporary observers noted that the delicate Gothic tracery of the building was evocative of fairytales, and Montgomery Schuyler struck a chord when he compared the skyscraper to Jack's beanstalk.[73] The skyscraper's promoters capitalized on the symbolism of "Jack and the Beanstalk" in a cover illustration for the official pamphlet distributed to the skyscraper's visitors; the drawing depicts the building's peak rising through the clouds in a manner suggestive of the cloud castle in that fairytale (fig. 33; Coburn may

Fig. 32. Woolworth Building (1918). The Woolworth Building was the first skyscraper to utilize the setback design, which transformed skyscrapers from intimidating, looming structures to ones that suggested uplift and drew viewers' eyes ever upward. (Reproduced from Bragdon, *Architecture and Democracy* [1926].)

have had the same thing in mind in his photograph of the Woolworth Building, which rises majestically out of New York's haze). As an early narrative of upward mobility, a tale that uses a skyward physical ascent as a metaphor for economic rise, and a fable whose hero is quite literally a little man (that is to say, a boy), the story of "Jack and the Beanstalk" is an ideal summation of the symbolic portent of the Woolworth Building and Frank Woolworth's life. It is no wonder that one writer described the world's tallest skyscraper as "a monument to small things."[74] Schuyler believed the Woolworth Building testified to the fact, as

Fig. 33. Woolworth Building from the cover of *Above the Clouds and Old New York* by H. Addington Bruce. This illustration of the Woolworth Building from an official souvenir pamphlet is evocative of the cloud castle in the story "Jack and the Beanstalk." (Reproduced from Bruce, *Above the Clouds* [1913].)

Tennyson put it, that "men may rise on stepping stones . . . to higher things."[75]

In his poem "Virginia" from *The Bridge* (1930), Hart Crane would deftly play on the fairytale associations of the Woolworth Building, satirizing its promoters' facile visions of upward mobility.

VIRGINIA

> O rain at seven,
> Pay-check at eleven—
> Keep smiling the boss away,
> Mary (what are you going to do?)
> Gone seven—gone eleven,
> And I'm still waiting you—

> O blue-eyed Mary with the claret scarf,
> Saturday Mary, mine!

It's high carillon
From the popcorn bells!
Pigeons by the million—
And Spring in Prince Street
Where green figs gleam
By oyster shells!

O Mary, leaning from the high wheat tower,
Let down your golden hair!

High in the noon of May
On cornices of daffodils
The slender violets stray.
Crap-shooting gangs in Bleecker reign,
Peonies with pony manes—
Forget-me-nots at windowpanes:

Out of the way-up nickel-dime tower shine,
Cathedral Mary,
shine!—[76]

In the poem, Crane replaces the myth of Jack and the beanstalk with the story of Rapunzel ("O Mary, leaning from the high wheat tower, / Let down your golden hair!"). In place of a magical ladder to fairy castles and giants' gold we get an image of Woolworth's "nickel-dime tower" as a limbo of isolation ("I'm still waiting you"), a tool of entrapment rather than economic freedom (recall that the tower in "Rapunzel" has no entrance and no stairs) where its workers (its numberless "Marys" who made up the backbone of Woolworth's labor force) live from paycheck to paycheck dreaming of rescue by princes ("Spring in Prince Street" where *spring* has the double meaning of the spring season and to spring from jail) while, even if they do succeed in "smiling the boss away" (that is, not letting down their hair in deference to their boss's sexual coercions), they nevertheless will let down their golden hair in service to the "witch" (Woolworth), who will use their devalued labor to ascend (indeed, build) his own tower of wealth. Appropriately, images of gambling weave throughout the poem: the "Crap-shooting gangs in Bleecker" Street; the repeated references to seven and eleven, the key numbers in the game of craps; the "green figs" and "shells" that one critic has interpreted as monetary allusions (green standing for money, figs for figures, shells for "shell out");[77] and the repetition of "shine" (which according to the *Dictionary of American Slang* can refer to any mirrorlike surface that a card shark uses to see opponents' hands).[78] These images emphasize not the rewards Woolworth and his publicists promised as the dividends of hard work and thrift but the "creed of the lucky break" (as one critic astutely describes it)[79] that keeps menial workers in a capitalist system complacent with dreams of striking it rich. Thus, underneath the poem's blithe exuberance, its emphasis on pop music melodies (the poem was self-consciously modeled on the popular song "What Do You Do Sunday, Mary?" from the 1923 musical comedy *Poppy*), kitsch icons ("forget-me-nots at windowpanes," the jingles of popcorn vendors), and tourist attractions (Woolworth's "Cathedral of Commerce"), we get an image of the masses as "Pigeons by the million," individuals made small and obedient by the soaring forces above them and doomed to live on the crumbs of capitalist wealth (the word *pigeon* having at least three meanings here—a scavenging bird, a dupe, and a young woman—and perhaps also meaning a professional gambler, as the *Dictionary of American Slang* suggests).

For its builders, on the other hand, the Woolworth Building was more than a static icon of the upward mobility available to the Little Man. It encouraged viewers to participate in that rise. Whereas the heavy cornice and rectangular form of the earlier flat-roofed skyscraper yielded buildings that loomed imposingly over pedestrians, the setback form encouraged a viewer's eyes to continue moving upward past the building's pinnacle, performing a kind of visual "uplift" that was consistent with the Woolworth Building's function as a public observatory. The erection of the observation deck, moreover, ensured that the building's peak would not just be looked *at* but also looked *from*. The Woolworth Building constituted a new rendering of height, in other words— a deployment of tremendous scale that was less intimidating to the street-bound viewer. For the viewer the building is both an expression of elevation and a means to elevation.

Kenneth Gibbs has argued that commercial architecture adopted overtly philanthropic imagery as criticisms of the business world escalated during the Progressive era. "The Woolworth Tower may be considered the culmination of the philanthropic image," suggests Gibbs.[80] Buildings like the Woolworth used many of the devices of civic institutions (e.g., untenanted space and stylistic references to historic monuments) to present a benevolent image to the public. Such devices weakened the distinction between corporate and public architecture and portrayed "public and private interests as synonymous"[81]—a strategy that the business community widely adopted in the 1920s to shore up allegiance to capitalism. Gail Fenske has explained how Frank Woolworth attempted simultaneously to serve public interests, maximize on the visibility of his giant billboard, and emphasize the civic character of his skyscraper by selecting a location that connected his building with the public transit lines and placed it in close proximity to New York's municipal government buildings.[82] The location of the Woolworth Building, one might add, also helped render the remarkable height of the structure more benevolently. Because the skyscraper was relatively isolated, it did not loom over other buildings and steal their light and air. (The setback design contributed to this function.) Thus, in selecting the site for the building, Woolworth responded simultaneously to a criticism that was applied with equal frequency to skyscrapers and big businesses.

If the Woolworth Building depicted height and upward mobility in a way that contemporaries found particularly appealing, one should note that part of the force of its appeal lay in its use of accepted ideas about height. The vertical features of the skyscraper—the piers and mullions—were radiantly white, while the horizontal elements were all colored in darker hues. There were undeniable racial undertones here. In its use of color, the Woolworth Building helped solidify the association between whiteness and upward progress; in doing so, it perpetuated a convention established at the 1893 Chicago World's Fair (appropriately labeled the White City), where stark white was used in all monumental architecture to depict the evolutionary and social progress of the "civilized" white nations. Thus, the public observatory at the top of the Woolworth Building functioned like the Ferris wheels at the Columbian and Louisiana Purchase Expositions. It lifted visitors above the darkened streets and afforded distant views of the "pygmy" pedestrians below. It encouraged visitors to identify American business development with racial progress.

In *The American Scene*, Henry James described American culture as "a huge white-washing brush" that sought to impose a universal homogeneity on the nation (97, 225–26). He pondered whether it would be capable ultimately of destroying the unique and diverse "colour" of the various immigrant groups and replacing that color with a bland uniformity (97–99). As if to resolve James's puzzle, at least one of the promoters of the Woolworth Building asserted that the skyscraper's message would be particularly important for immigrants. The Woolworth Building, said W. U. Hensel, "will be a lesson, an instructor, . . . to the millions not only of our own countrymen, but to all immigrants from all lands."[83] This was not the first time skyscrapers were used in the service of assimilating and regulating immigrants. Metropolitan Life Insurance officials invited future social workers from women's colleges like Vassar and Bryn Mawr to the top of their Metropolitan Tower (built in 1909 and the tallest skyscraper prior to the Woolworth), where they could look down at the tenements and obtain a comprehensive view of the task facing them.[84] Woolworth himself reputedly tracked immigration figures in order to get some sense of the future of his business, which catered especially to those of small means—immigrants, blacks, and the poor generally.[85] The Woolworth Building, in other words, was an object lesson in the American dream not only for Little Men generally but for newly arrived citizens in particular. To the growing number of Americans who regarded immigrants as a threat to the stability of capitalism and the nation's racial progress, the Woolworth Building functioned as a reassuring bulwark of national values.

To say all of this another way, the Woolworth Building diverted attacks on big business during the Progressive era by emphasizing the company's example and service to the myth of upward mobility. Virtually every aspect of the building—from the public speeches emphasizing Frank Woolworth's rags-to-riches story, to the tower's architectural design, to its function as a sightseeing device, to its role as an object lesson for immigrants—contributed to the building's cultural function as a purveyor of the American dream. Woolworth's skyscraper and career contributed to the defenses that Woodrow Wilson and other supporters of capitalism relied on to restore faith in capitalism and stave off socialism. The Woolworth Building made economic imperialism and its aesthetic of growth palatable to the public by disguising them behind the myth of individual upward mobility. As a monument to the Little Man, moreover, the Woolworth Building helps explain why even those who trumpeted the cause of the Little Man (e.g., Woodrow Wilson) failed to engender a new attitude toward small size. The skyscraper encapsulates the contradictions in the middle class's embrace of littleness. The virtue of the Little Man (and an economy that allowed his existence) was not his littleness per se but his capacity for spectacular growth. The Little Man, in other words, was noble insofar as he demonstrated an aptitude for growth that was compatible with the dominant spirit of the age. The Little Man was little only in comparison to the gigantic trusts and unions; he was small only because he was an individual in a world of collectivity. His aspirations remained big, his successes remained great, and his destiny was large.

Conclusion

Several scholars have recently identified a mutual influence between urban architecture, or urban design and planning, and ideas about the body.[86] "Master images of 'the body,'" writes Richard Sennett, "have frequently been used . . . to define what a building or an entire city should look like."[87] In *Flesh and Stone,* Sennett examines particular cities at specific moments in history and compares their architecture and design to contemporaneous notions of the body. He argues that the design and architecture of Athens, for example, corresponded in important ways to the naked body; that Roman architecture was influenced by a belief in the geometry of the body; and that eighteenth-century European cities were influenced by an image of the body as a circulating system.

The skyscraper, a structure so peculiar to turn-of-the-century America, was clearly a case in point. It originated at a time when the dominant conception of the American body was shifting, when scientists and social pundits were declaring the preeminent height of the American male. Tall office buildings were commensurate with the height of this progressive, expanding, racially superior American body. Contributing to the aesthetic of growth informing both urban architecture and notions of the body were several important sociopolitical developments: the unparalleled economic expansion and consolidation of American businesses and the extension of U.S. imperialism beyond North America onto a global stage.

The Woolworth Building added a new spin to the image of the progressive American body: that body was a modern Jack of fairytale fame, a figure of obscure origins and financial insignificance who could nevertheless rise spectacularly in a competitive world of giants and trusts. This rise was available to all, Woolworth and his publicists insisted: one could experience it vicariously by visiting the world's tallest building and viewing the city from its public observation deck, and one could achieve it personally through the traditional values of nineteenth-century America: hard work, prudence, and thrift.

Henry James recognized the dubiousness of that argument. Such spectacular growth was not open to all. If James regarded the Jewish and Italian immigrants of New York with apprehension and disdain,[88] he nevertheless understood clearly their precarious position in the new corporate economy. Individuals in the ghetto, he wrote in *The American Scene,*

> shrink and dwindle under the icy breath of Trusts and the weight of the new monopolies that operate as no madnesses of ancient personal power thrilling us on the historic page ever operated; the living unit's property in himself [is] becoming more and more merely such a property as may consist with a relation to properties overwhelmingly greater and that allow the asking of no questions and the making, for co-existence with them, of no conditions. . . . There is such a thing, in the United

States, it is hence to be inferred, as freedom to grow up to be blighted, and it may be the only freedom in store for the smaller fry of future generations. (104)

James saw nothing advantageous about the new body symbolized by the skyscraper and much that was abandoned in America's heedless rush to attain it. For James, skyscrapers were analogous to schoolyard bullies, who intimidated their more studious, refined peers and rode roughshod over the values of Culture and Civilization. The dominance of skyscrapers in the New York landscape suggested that it was these bullies, grown up and wearing business suits, who had come to dominate American culture at the expense of a more refined, cultivated class. His work was an attempt to imagine an alternative to this schoolyard bully, the progressive American body. In *The American Scene,* James sought to reinstate the discarded virtues of leisure, seclusion, and tradition—virtues that belonged to an era of village culture rather than the modern global economy. What he apparently did not recognize (or was unconcerned about) was how these values allowed for the same kind of hierarchical, stratified society that the new capitalist era imposed. The cultural dominance of mannered, well-bred Boston Brahmins was in some ways as exclusive and divisive as the dominance of robber barons.

Alvin Langdon Coburn, on the other hand, embraced the skyscraper and its implicit aesthetic of the new American body. For Coburn, the highest skyscrapers were like the "Men of Mark" he photographed and compiled in an album of that name. They distinguished themselves in unique ways, rising above common men and offering their exceptional vision to the rest of us. Just as the world's fairs did, Coburn sought to accustom the American public to the visual capacities of that new body. His photographs from elevated perspectives sought order and pattern in a city that was increasingly regarded as disordered and chaotic. Significantly, his photos ignore people. To acquire the transcendent vision, as Poole would soon warn in *The Harbor,* was to lose sight of individuals and their needs. The progressive American body with its transcendent vision was thoroughly dehumanized in Coburn's photographs. His most thoroughly modernist pictures were as abstract as the insistent calls for material growth at any cost: no principles of justice informed them, and no visions of social improvement for the majority guided them.

PART 3 • Growing Women, Shrinking Men

CHAPTER 5 • The Growing Woman and the Growing Jew
Mary Antin, the New Woman, and the
Immigration Debate

*Have we not all observed the change even in size of
the modern woman . . . ? The Gibson Girl and the
Duchess of Towers,—these are the new women; and
they represent a noble type, indeed.*
—Charlotte Perkins Gilman, 1898[1]

*For children of our immigrants to outgrow their par-
ents, not only intellectually, but physically as well, is a
common phenomenon. Perhaps it is due to their being
fed far better than their parents were in their childhood and youth. . . . The American children of the
Ghetto are American not only in their language, tastes,
and ambitions, but in outward appearance as well.*
—Abraham Cahan, 1917[2]

The image of America that greeted most immigrants at the turn of the
century, the greatest period of immigration in the history of the United
States up to that time, was that of a gigantic woman holding a book—the
"Mother of Exiles" according to the poem by Emma Lazarus inscribed on
its pedestal. Although Mary Antin, who disembarked in Boston after
emigrating from the Russian town of Polotzk in 1894 at the age of thirteen, included no description of the Statue of Liberty in her autobiography *The Promised Land,* the powerful cultural resonance of the image
was certainly not lost on her when she published her best-seller in 1912;
a drawing of the statue adorned the cover of her book. As a passionate
advocate of open immigration during a period of increasing nativism, as
a New Woman who celebrated the opportunities education afforded
women in the United States, and as a Jew—a community often described
as the "People of the Book"—Antin cherished everything that the image
of Liberty symbolized.

In many ways, Antin's self-representation mirrors the image that
America adopted as its own in the years following the erection of Liberty
in 1886. In the free atmosphere of America, where Antin acquires an
education that was denied her in Russia, she experiences a metaphoric
growth that far exceeds her bodily growth. Physically, Antin was a small
woman, a point she reinforces several times in her autobiography. "I was

small myself, and constantly reminded of it by a variety of nicknames, lovingly or vengefully invented by my friends and enemies. I was called Mouse and Crumb and Poppy Seed. Should I live to be called, in my old age, Mashke the Short?"[3] In Russia, her physical size was symbolic of the constricted social position of Jews in the oppressive Russian Pale and of women within the patriarchal Jewish community. Exposure to education, the scale of modern life in America, greater opportunity for women, and the novel ideas of modern science, especially Darwinism, allow Antin to expand in proportion to her new environment. As she put it, she experienced an "enlargement" when she "exchanged Polotzk for America" (258). "I grew all the faster [in America] because I was so cramped before" (151). In the last paragraph of her autobiography, she describes the feeling of emerging from the past of medieval life in Polotzk to a modern life in America, a feeling that washes upon her at the steps of the Boston Public Library. It is an upward journey and a tale of personal growth.

> In that moment I had a vision of myself . . . emerging from the dim places where the torch of history has never been, creeping slowly into the light of civilized existence, pushing more steadily forward to the broad plateau of modern life, and leaping, at last, strong and glad, to the intellectual summit of the latest century. . . . My spirit is not tied to the monumental past. . . . The past was only my cradle, and now it cannot hold me, because I am grown too big. (285–86)

On the day of her graduation from grammar school, as she delivers the valedictorian address, Antin seizes the opportunity to speak on behalf of the cause of immigration. In the process, she is transformed into a kind of statue herself. "I stepped up on the stage to read my composition. . . . I did not know where my body began or ended. . . . My wonderful dress, in which I had taken so much satisfaction, gave me the most trouble. I was suddenly paralyzed by a conviction that it was too short, and it seemed to me I stood on absurdly long legs. And ten thousand people were looking up at me" (220).

In using the metaphoric language of growth, Antin was allying herself with the cult of New Womanhood as well as with turn-of-the-century Jewish race scientists. In contemporary illustrations and the popular imagination, the New Woman of the 1890s and 1900s was unmistakably tall, a fact that drew considerable attention and discussion. Her height was symbolic of the opportunities supposedly available to women at the turn of the century in the most advanced of all nations. The reputed shortness of Jews, on the other hand, was a central piece of evidence in eugenic arguments opposing open immigration; for non-Jewish race scientists, the Jews' shortness was emblematic of their racial degeneration. Jewish American scientists like Franz Boas and Maurice Fishberg, on the other hand, studied the stature of Jews in order to defend immigration from accusations that the physical degeneracy of Jews threatened American racial progress and superiority. As in the social and scientific discourses, the metaphor of growth in Antin's work is a metaphor of progress, inseparably racial and gendered.

While existing critical discussion of Antin's *The Promised Land* has emphasized Antin's resistance or lack of resistance to dominant ideologies,[4] most critics have underestimated the extent to which the text participated in specific turn-of-the-century debates on the roles of women and Jews in the United States. The autobiography was a sophisticated piece of rhetoric produced in a complex, highly charged social context. My investigation of the tropes of the growing woman and the growing Jew suggests that the sharp divisions in the critical response to Antin's work are predictable consequences of a rhetorical strategy that depended on subterfuge, mimicry, and calculated evasion.

Antin and the New Woman

When Theodore Roosevelt published the fifth installment of his autobiography in the *Outlook* in 1913, he attributed his allegiance to women's suffrage to his association with activists and New Women like Jane Addams, Frances Kellor, and Mary Antin.[5] It was an ironic admission, since just a year earlier Antin claimed she was not a suffragist in an essay supporting Roosevelt's presidential candidacy.[6] Given the stormy political debate surrounding suffrage, it is almost certain that Antin was lying in her essay of 1912 as a means of attracting voters opposed to or ambivalent about suffrage to the liberal Progressive Party. Calculated deception was a tactic that Antin often resorted to in order to secure her political aims and was a skill, according to her, that Jews in the oppressive Pale of Russia developed, by necessity, to a fine art. Her support for women's suffrage, her belief in the value of education for women, her fight for workingwomen's causes,[7] and her use of her maiden name in her writings all clearly mark Antin as a New Woman.

If Antin was a New Woman, however, it was certainly not because of her physical appearance. Images of the New Woman produced between Antin's arrival in the United States and the publication of her autobiography were invariably tall. In fact, everyone seemed to be commenting on the growth of American women at the turn of the century. "Were there ever in another age so many tall girls?" asked one observer.[8]

The icon of New Womanhood and the reigning beauty ideal between 1890 and 1912 was the Gibson Girl (see fig. 34).[9] She was created by Charles Dana Gibson, the highest-paid and best-known illustrator during the golden age of illustration, when technological innovations in printing enabling rapid and cheap reproductions of black-and-white drawings fueled a tremendous growth of illustrations in magazines, books, and advertisements. Tall, slim, and athletic, the Gibson Girl was immensely popular, and her image soon appeared everywhere: in framed copies of Gibson's illustrations hanging in living rooms across the nation; in Gibson albums on parlor tables; as a design adorning everything from ashtrays, teacups, and saucers to tiles, wallpapers, pillow covers, and matchboxes; as a reference in popular songs, dances, and theater productions; and as a favorite marketing device for corsets, shirtwaists, shoes, hats, and other products.[10] During her reign she dramatically influenced artistic tastes as well as popular fashion ideals. Artists deliberately sought tall female models for their work, and Gibson's imitators, artists like Howard Chandler Christy, James Montgomery Flagg, and Albert Beck Wenzell, churned out images of tall women.[11]

Feminists and nonfeminists alike saw the Gibson Girl as a prototype of the New Woman. While feminists such as Charlotte Perkins Gilman regarded her height and athleticism as an augury of women's advancement and used her image to promote women's emancipation, the Gibson Girl as conceived by Charles Dana Gibson was at best an ambiguous figure.[12] She engaged in activities considered venturesome for women of her day—bicycling and golf, for example—and she wore the daring attire of modern outdoor sports, the revealing new swimsuits and short golfing skirts. Yet she could hardly be accused of radicalism. She disdained the bloomer and remained tightly corseted wherever she ventured. Her activism remained confined to the tennis court and the beach. She did not campaign for the vote, and she was rarely depicted as a college or working woman. She remained primarily a manikin for the latest fashions, leading several recent critics to dismiss her image, however popular it may have been among contemporaneous women's rights advocates, as a safety valve for women's discontent. "Gibson Girl images," writes one critic, "embodied the values necessary to sustain a consumer-based economy—discernment, purchasing power, and insatiable demand—thereby harnessing and transforming the 'New Woman's' desire for social and political change into a desire for new goods."[13]

Young Widow: HOW LONG SHOULD I WEAR MOURNING?
"I'M UNABLE TO SAY. I WASN'T ACQUAINTED WITH YOUR HUSBAND."

Fig. 34. Charles Dana Gibson, "The Young Widow" (ca. 1900). As this illustration attests, the Gibson Girl was frequently taller than the men around her.

Next to the ubiquitous Gibson Girl, Charles Dana Gibson's best-known character was Mr. Pipp, the beleaguered father of two statuesque and profligate Gibson Girls who had the thankless task of sustaining his daughters and their spending habits prior to their marriage (see fig. 35).

The Gibson Girl's widespread appeal was complemented in sculpture by a proliferation of colossal female figures, many of which were compared to the Gibson Girl by contemporary observers.[14] Such figures included the Statue of Liberty, the figure of Columbia at the Chicago World's Fair of 1893, and the sixty-five-foot statue of the Republic, also

Fig. 35. Charles Dana Gibson, "The Overworked American Father. His Day Off in August" (ca. 1899). Two Gibson Girls tower above the hapless Mr. Pipp. Saddled with expensive daughters, Mr. Pipp dreamed of the day when they were married and their support would fall on their husbands' shoulders.

built for Chicago's White City and the largest statue ever erected in the United States to that date.[15] In these incarnations, the gigantic Gibson Girl became not only a beauty ideal and icon of women's emancipation but a symbol of America itself. Through their size and attitude, colossal images of women represented the dominant, implicitly masculine ideals of the turn of the century: materialism, nationalism, militarism, and imperialism. Through their sex, they represented an attempt to reconcile the separate spheres and introduce the moral virtue of women into public arenas and national endeavors.[16]

The preference for tall women, moreover, was distinctly a turn-of-the-century phenomenon. The Gibson Girl supplanted both the small, frail, and submissive "steel-engraving lady" and the heavier, curvaceous "voluptuous woman," the beauty standards of the antebellum and post–Civil War years, respectively.[17] The Gibson Girl and her counterparts in public statuary also represented a new incarnation of feminine moral virtue. Before the Civil War, argues Martha Banta, two characters from Harriet Beecher Stowe's *Uncle Tom's Cabin* personified feminine purity: Little Eva and the tiny Mrs. Bird. "Diminutive mothers and physically frail children of great moral strength," writes Banta, "were replaced as champions of the helpless. Gigantic female forms now expressed the sense of national destiny; they redefined the nature of the protective zeal that went with the new moral and territorial imperialism."[18] Like the popularity of skyscrapers, the Gibson Girl was also, evidently, a distinctly American phenomenon.[19] She was the imagined companion to the tall, progressive American man revealed by the military studies on Civil War soldiers.

Scientists sought to confirm the popular impression that the social, economic, and political advances of American women were reflected in physical changes. Clelia Duel Mosher was one such scientist. Trained as a physician, she advocated physical education for women, dress reform, and other feminist causes and held a position as associate professor of personal hygiene and medical adviser of women at Stanford University. In a series of articles on the height of college women, Mosher reported that students at Stanford, Vassar, and Smith College had increased more than an inch in height between 1890 and 1921. She found no evidence supporting racial explanations or a biased selection of westerners for the study—the factors most often cited in the tallness of American men. (Like earlier studies on men and children, and unlike Antin, Mosher ignored issues of class.) Instead, she announced that "exercise and more hygienic clothing are among the causal factors in the development of this finer physical type of woman." "This splendid modern woman, grown taller and more vigorous because, freed from restricting fashions of dress, she exercises more and consequently eats more, has become better fitted to be the mother of finer sons and daughters, the promise of a stronger race," declared Mosher.[20]

Mosher's promise that the modern woman would be a fitter mother of a superior race, along with her contention that changes in fashion and exercise were bringing about important physical changes for women, typified the arguments of mainstream feminist writers. In *Women and Economics* (1898), for example, Charlotte Perkins Gilman argued that women's emancipation would ensure American racial progress. Evidence of the physical effects of social improvements for women in recent decades could be seen, she said, in the reputed growth of the New Woman. "Have we not all observed the change even in size of the modern woman . . . ? Women are growing honester, braver, stronger, more healthful and skilful and able and free, more human in all ways."[21] The failure to continue improving conditions for women was a sure path to racial decay, since evolutionary progress depends on both sexes, she reasoned. Accepting both the language of science and the masculinist view that largeness indicated progress, Gilman warned that "Small, weak, soft, ill-proportioned women do not tend to produce large, strong, sturdy, well-made men or women. When Frederic the Great wanted grenadiers of great size, he married big men to big women,—not to little ones."[22] The dire effects of social oppression on the bodies of the oppressed could be observed not only in the smallness of women but in the Jews of Russian ghettos, she suggested—evidence that physical size was not biologically determined but a product of social conditions.[23] In Gilman's feminist utopia, the differences in size between the sexes vanished.[24]

In their insistence that racial progress depended on the social advancement of women, Mosher and Gilman were simultaneously writing from within the masculinist scientific discourses and subverting the more conservative views on women that dominated medicine and the sciences. They were attempting, as Carroll Smith-Rosenberg argues, "to use male myths to repudiate male power—to turn the male world upside down."[25] Following the Civil War, influential physicians like S. Weir Mitchell and Edward Clarke warned about the dire effects on the bodies of women and the subsequent racial deterioration that would result from equal education. They claimed that the body was a closed energy system; diverting necessary resources from the development of a woman's reproductive organs to her brain functions would produce—in fact, had already produced in too many cases—a stunted, deficient mother, prone to hysteria and neurasthenia.[26] The child growth studies conducted by Henry Bowditch between 1877 and 1891 were motivated in part by a desire to investigate this "alleged inferiority of the physique of American women." Bowditch wondered why the female sex had been "strangely neglected" from anthropometric studies when clearly "in all questions relating to the growth and development of the race, its importance is at least equal to that of the male sex."[27] Evolutionary and race scientists, moreover, contended that women, like the pygmies, were arrested in their development and represented a conservative element in racial evolution, a view that was supported by the reports of travel writers who claimed that the two sexes were more nearly alike in size among primitive people. Since height had become one of the measures of racial hierarchy, and since women were smaller on average than men, the relative size of women suggested to turn-of-the-century scientists that Euro-American women were inferior to Euro-American men and were, in evolutionary terms, similar to savage races. Both Gilman and the renowned sexologist Havelock Ellis accepted as axiomatic that women were arrested in development and that the sexes were at one time more nearly equal physically, diverging as a result of the division of labor accompanying civilization. The two iconoclasts disagreed with those who claimed that the supposed narrowing of the size gap between men and women constituted devolution to a more primitive state[28] by arguing that the increasing equality in size and strength between men and women associated with the erosion of sex role distinctions was a sign of advancement to a higher social-evolutionary state.[29]

As the arguments of the conservative male physicians suggest, the New Woman was simultaneously celebrated and vilified, and her purportedly enhanced size was alternately encouraging and threatening. Her demands for greater economic opportunity, education, political power, social autonomy, and sexual freedom challenged the existing social order. "To male physicians, politicians, and even modernist writers," explains Smith-Rosenberg, "the New Woman . . . symbolized disorder in a world gone mad."[30] Scientists and social observers foisted numerous epithets upon her; the image of the "manly woman" or "Mannish Lesbian" most fully reflected widespread fears about the reversal of traditional gender roles.[31] They criticized her for committing race suicide and eagerly disseminated statistics indicating that college-educated women were the least likely to marry and produced the fewest children once married.[32] Antifeminist male and conservative female writers ridiculed her in fiction, inventing dire punishments for female characters who defied marriage, social convention, and traditional femininity.[33] The size of the New Woman was used alternately as a symbol of her progress and a warning about the reversal of male-female hierarchies. Sharing the spotlight with the image of the healthful, athletic, capable Gibson Girl—and often created by the same artists—was an image of the Amazonian Woman, who was intimidating, aggressive, presumptuous, and emasculating (see figs. 35–36). At times, this image could be appropriated for nationalistic purposes (see fig. 37), but more often it was used to represent the erosion of male power and the inversion of heterosexual courting rituals (see fig. 38).

As Patricia Marks has pointed out, the imagined "masculinization of women entailed the feminization of men."[34] Because smallness and largeness are so often gendered,[35] images of shrinking men went hand in hand with images of growing women. Marks explores this phenomenon in cartoons satirizing the New Woman. "The recurrent fear of masculine effacement," she says, "reappears as a motif in many bicycling cartoons [bicycling was the favorite pastime of the New Woman] in which diminutive men seek to teach their buxom wives and sweethearts how to ride."[36] In response to the tall women of Gilman's utopian *Herland*, the male narrator remarks that he and his comrades often "felt like small

Fig. 36. "Sarah Grand and 'Mere Man.'" This illustration accompanied a review of a lecture by Sarah Grand, an English feminist and humorist who toured the United States at the turn of the century. Its Amazonian female figure was a more menacing one than the towering Gibson Girl. (Reproduced from *Harper's Weekly*, November 2, 1901.)

Fig. 37. Charles Dana Gibson, "Come, Let Us Forgive and Forget" (1898). At times the statuesque Gibson Girl served as a symbol of America, as in this illustration representing Spain and the United States after the Spanish-American War.

Fig. 38. Charles Dana Gibson, "The Weaker Sex—II" (1903). A man shrinks under the scrutiny of gigantic Gibson Girls.

boys, very small boys."[37] An editorialist alarmed by the height of the Gibson Girl criticized Gibson for fashioning women who tower over ordinary men and for creating a national obsession with tallness.[38] Turn-of-the-century marketers capitalized on (and contributed to) men's increasing anxiety about their size by introducing the elevator shoe and advertising the "Cartilage System." One man claimed to have increased his height by several inches through an unidentified surgical procedure.[39] Bodybuilding and athletic programs, increasingly popular at the turn of the century, promised the rewards of a transformed body. The 1870s witnessed the beginning of exhibitions of strong men like Eugen Sandow, and Charles Atlas claimed to be the "world's most perfectly developed male" in one of the physical culture magazines that became increasingly popular during the first two decades of the twentieth century.[40] The aesthetics of male bigness were supported by popular physical culture movements like Muscular Christianity and the YMCA; they were also bolstered by the increasing militarism and imperialism of the period, fears of urban degeneration, the doctrine of social Darwinism,

Fig. 39. Cartilage Company, "Every Woman Admires a Tall Man" (1904). The Cartilage Company promised to increase men's height through an undisclosed "scientific and physiological method of expanding the cartilage." The company's advertisements featured tall, Gibson-like women and often appeared in *Life* magazine, whose pages were frequented by the Gibson Girl.

and scientific studies that showed a connection between size and intelligence.

"In the popular imagination," writes Susan Brownmiller in *Femininity,* "masculinity always includes the concepts of powerful and large. . . . The equation of maleness with bigness persists as a dearly loved concept."[41] From a contemporary perspective, Brownmiller's assertion seems irrefutable, but recent historical studies have suggested that the association between masculinity and large size has historical ties to the turn of the century.[42] Lois Banner, for example, argues that small men set the standard for male attractiveness in the first third of the nineteenth century as a result of influential figures like Lord Byron, Napoleon, and Prince Albert. Images of men accompanying the "steel-engraving lady" were typically as small and slight as she was.[43] Whether or not the association between size and masculinity transcends history, ethnicity, and class, it is certainly the case that the subservient social and domestic role of women is often rendered symbolically by their smaller size or by their position beneath a man. The expectation that husbands be taller than their wives (a phenomenon labeled "sexual heightism" by one recent writer) represents such a combination of sexism and stature prejudices and reflects our desire to impose social hierarchies on domestic relations.[44]

Considering that the supposed growth of the New Woman appeared to jeopardize heterosexual relations, it is hardly surprising that the threat she posed was characteristically dispelled by domesticating her. Popular female novelists who employed the image of the New Woman in positive ways showed her challenging traditional sex roles up to the point of marriage; "once she had taken on her 'real' role as wife and mother," explains Patricia Raub, "she cast aside all pretense of insurrection and settled down to a life of domesticity."[45] Feminist writers such as Gilman and Mosher defended the New Woman from charges of race suicide by assuring their readers that she was not only taller, healthier, and more vigorous but also "the mother of finer sons and daughters, the promise of a stronger race."[46] Images of colossal women in the second and third decades of the twentieth century increasingly represented women's domestic virtues—their feminine capacity for nurture and selfless care (see fig. 40).

Further complicating the position of the New Woman at the turn of the century was her relationship with marginalized communities and women. The Gibson Girl, as well as most dominant incarnations of the New Woman, was white and unmistakably middle- or upper-class. Martha Banta has suggested that the towering New Woman of Progressive-era public statuary represented not only military power, moral

The
GREATEST MOTHER
in the WORLD

Fig. 40. A. E. Foringer, "The Greatest Mother in the World" (1918). Gigantic images of women were domesticated in the late Progressive era through traditionally feminine roles, as in this wartime poster for the Red Cross.

virtue, and materialism but also racial purity—an argument supported by Gilman's and Mosher's rhetoric of race suicide.[47] Minority women were excluded from the progress represented by the New Woman. When minority authors such as Sui Sin Far and Pauline Hopkins deployed images of the New Woman, argues Martha Patterson, they often did so with ambivalence. Sometimes the New Woman represented an icon of assimilation into Anglo-American culture; less often she was a means of protest or rejection of that culture.[48]

It is clear from Antin's autobiography that she tapped into contemporaneous debates about the position of women in the United States. Aside from borrowing a major trope of New Womanhood, the image of the growing woman, Antin emphasized the patriarchal nature of Russian Jewish culture and contrasted it with the modern condition of women in America. In particular, she railed against women's exclusion from education in Polotzk. The most privileged social position in the small Russian Jewish community was that of Torah scholar or rabbi, she explains. Women were barred from such pursuits.

> It was not much to be a girl, you see. . . . For a girl it was enough if she could read her prayers in Hebrew, and follow the meaning by the Yiddish translation at the bottom of the page. It did not take long to learn this much, . . . and after that she was done with books. A girl's real schoolroom was her mother's kitchen. There . . . her mother instructed her in the laws regulating a pious Jewish household and in the conduct proper for a Jewish wife; for, of course, every girl hoped to be a wife. A girl was born for no other purpose. . . . While men . . . might busy themselves with the study of the Law, woman's only work was motherhood. (29–30)

Antin is careful not to denigrate the value of parenthood; "To rear a family of children was to serve God" (30), she explains, rendering arguments against race suicide as a modern version of Mosaic Law. But she questions the right of men to be both fathers and scholars when women are allowed to be mothers only. Later she offers a striking comparison between the lamentable, monotonous condition of a treadmill horse and the condition of women in Polotzk (77–78). In contrast, she claims, the United States offers women free and equal education and more career opportunities (her own writing career being the major example).

Her celebration of conditions for women in America is understandable, considering the somewhat different position of women in Polotzk, but critics have nevertheless chastised Antin for failing to apply the same skepticism to New World conditions that she applies to Old World culture.[49] Mary Dearborn has gone so far as to suggest that Antin "thoroughly internalized the dominant culture's vision. . . . More interesting as a text of American patriotism and as revealing of American values and typologies, *The Promised Land* seems to lack any alternative, protesting voice."[50] More recent critics have questioned Dearborn's assumption, arguing that the book is more complicated than initial assessments suggested. While there are things that Antin surprisingly ignores—including the condition of blacks in America and the role of American education as an evangelical, Christianizing force for Jewish immigrants—it is fairer to claim, as Magdalena Zaborowska does, that *The Promised Land* contains a submerged voice of protest.[51]

Antin was particularly attentive to class divisions in the United States and the ways in which poverty prevented many women and immigrants from achieving the American promise of equality. In *They Who Knock at Our Gates*, Antin argues that the social problems wrought by American capitalism are often blamed on immigrants. "Not the immigrant is ruining our country," she writes, "but the venal politicians who try to make the immigrant the scapegoat for all the sins of untrammeled capitalism."[52] In narrating the day her father triumphantly escorted her to school in *The Promised Land*, a day that was "the apex of my civic pride and personal contentment" (157), Antin dwells at length on her sister Fetchke, who was required by economic necessity to forego school and become a dressmaker. At the end of her meditation on the sad differences in their fates, Antin includes a subtle reminder that life for poor women in America may not be so different from life in Russia after all: she says that Fetchke's feet "were bound in the treadmill of daily toil" (159), quietly recalling the image of the treadmill horse from earlier in her book. Perhaps more important, Antin describes her own metaphoric growth in the United States as halting. As her family's fortunes deteriorate and the Antins move to poorer and poorer neighborhoods in the tenements of Boston, Mary Antin's personal growth is increasingly jeopardized. When they finally take up residence on Dover Street, a place so impoverished, overcrowded, and depressing that Antin uses metaphors from Russia to describe it (she says it is a "prison" and a "battlefield" [224], the same terms she used to describe the Russian Jewish ghettos), she explains that "I did not grow much" (231). Food, she says, was scarce in the Antin household at this time. The "City Fathers" themselves seemed to be conspiring with poverty to inhibit the growth of slum children. Borrowing from contemporary scientific claims about the association between the mind, body, and spirit, as well as physical culture arguments about the need for parks and playgrounds in urban areas, Antin writes:

> The City Fathers provide . . . excellent schools, kindergartens, and branch libraries. And there they stop: at the curb-stone of the people's life. They cleanse and discipline the children's minds, but their bodies they pitch into the gutter. For there are no parks and playgrounds in the Harrison Avenue district. . . . we have not learned the lesson of modern science, which teaches, among other things, that the body is the nursery of the soul; the instrument of our moral development. . . . we try to make a hero out of a boy by such foreign appliances as grammar and algebra, while utterly despising the fittest instrument for his uplifting—the boy's own body. (225)

When Antin leaves Dover Street to speak with the principal of the prestigious Boston Latin School for Girls, the institution she will ultimately attend, she claims that "I grew an inch taller and broader between the corner of Cedar Street and Mr. Tetlow's house, such was the charm of the clean, green suburb on a cramped waif from the slums" (230). In the Dover Street passages, Antin's growth increasingly requires an effort of transcendence; it is less physical and more spiritual than in other passages.

Furthermore, Antin was more attentive to issues of class than many of her New Woman compatriots, suggesting that she openly resisted the bourgeois elements in the ideology of New Womanhood. Her family's temporary residence on Wheeler Street, she says, was "not a place where a refined young lady would care to find herself alone, even in the cheery daylight. If she came at all, she would be attended by a trusty escort" (207). To emphasize her own transformation in later years, she explains that she returned to Wheeler Street "attended by a trusty escort" (209): she has by the time of writing attained the privileged position of the conventional New Woman. But she is also aware of the differences that her class consciousness has imposed upon her. The "refined young lady," she writes, "would not get too close to people on the doorsteps, and she would shrink away in disgust and fear from a blear-eyed creature careering down the sidewalk on many-jointed legs. The delicate damsel would hasten home to wash and purify and perfume herself till the foul contact of Wheeler Street was utterly eradicated, and her wonted purity restored" (207). In this damning picture of the privileged New Woman, Antin highlights the ideological practices so common to Progressive-era reform efforts: the demonization of the poor that accompanied criticisms of social injustices. Antin responds effectively to this logic. "I only wish," she writes, "that [the 'delicate damsel'] would bring a little soap and water and perfumery into Wheeler Street next time she comes; for some people there may be smothering in the filth which they abhor as much as she, but from which they cannot, like her, run away" (209). Rather than denigrating the people of Wheeler Street, Antin says she enjoyed the neighborhood and its residents when she lived there. In defiance of the "refined young lady" and her disgust at public intoxication, Antin delights in depicting a drunken man ejected from a bar. "The fellow would whine so comically, and cling to the doorpost so like a damp leaf to a twig, and blubber so like a red-faced baby, that it was really funny to see him" (209–10). Antin criticizes "right-minded students of sociology" who are "too hasty to run and teach The Poor." Turning the rhetoric of social reform on its head, she suggests that "The Poor may have something to teach you" (217, 219); her book, with its lessons in the psychology of the immigrant, is the primary example of this principle.

Another indication that Antin resisted the conventions of New Womanhood lies in the fact that she concealed the circumstances of her own life in the ending of the book. In 1901, she married the paleontologist Amadeus Grabau and moved to New York, where he taught at Columbia University. Antin never graduated from the Boston Latin School, and so she could only take special classes at Columbia Teachers College and Barnard College. In the end of her autobiography, she mentions neither her marriage nor the birth of her daughter in 1907 nor the fact that she never acquired a college degree; on the contrary, she intimates that her academic successes continued and helped her attain a position of financial independence and comfort. The veiled ending of the book suggests that Antin refused to capitulate to the imperatives of marriage and domesticity that so often characterized the ending of New Woman texts. To do so would have been to undermine the very premise of her social critique and her narrative of women's progress through education. It would suggest, indeed, that "every girl hoped to be a wife. A girl was born for no other purpose" (29).

Antin and the Immigration Debate

Antin had more than the ordinary reasons for employing the image of the growing woman. The physical size of Jews, both men and women, attracted a great deal of scientific attention at the turn of the century and played a central role in debates about the relative effects of environment and race on body type. From this debate emerged the figure of the growing Jew, a counterpart to the image of the growing woman, a being who also benefited from the freer, less oppressive atmosphere in America.

The image of the growing Jew emerged in response to dominant attitudes toward immigrant Jews and was seldom officially recognized by those opposed to open immigration. The dominant view of the Jews originated in the anthropological and ethnological discourse. In this discourse, the Jew emerged as a distinctively small individual who, in addition, possessed an unusual resistance to certain diseases such as consumption, lived longer than other race types, was drawn to urban areas, and preferred careers that supposedly demanded little physical exertion such as tailoring. In many ways, the Jew was the antithesis of America's favorite son or daughter, the pioneer, who reveled in outdoor labor and preferred the rigors of virgin land to the stultifying, class-ridden culture of the city. Consequently, the Jew, like the New Woman, was a lightning rod for many of the fears of turn-of-the-century Americans, especially fears of the city and urban degeneration. (Asians, although also characterized as short and stigmatized on that basis within ethnological and popular discourses, were less worrisome to most Americans, at least outside of California, since the Chinese Exclusion Act of 1882 ensured that relatively few Asian immigrants made it to the United States at the turn of the century.)

The belief that short stature was among the distinguishing characteristics of the Jew was universal. Among those who contributed to the belief was William Z. Ripley, the influential author of *The Races of Europe* and an opponent of open immigration. "Jews are one of the most stunted peoples in Europe," he wrote. To him it was evidence of their "physical degeneracy" and the fact that they were a "defective type." "How far this is the result of centuries of oppression, and in what degree it is an inherent ethnic trait, we need not stop to consider," he wrote. "It is an undisputably proved fact." Ripley did, in fact, give evidence for both racial and environmental views on the stature of Jews (he did not unequivocally support either position), but the resolution of the sticky question did not ultimately make much difference to him in practical matters like immigration policy. "This great [Polish Jewish] swamp of miserable human beings, terrific in its proportions, threatens to drain itself off into our country . . . unless we restrict its ingress," he warned.[53] Madison Grant, trustee of the American Museum of Natural History and author of the popular Aryan-supremacist tract *The Passing of the Great Race* (1916), agreed. He warned that the "dwarf stature, peculiar mentality, and ruthless . . . self-interest" of the Polish Jew "are being engrafted upon the stock of the nation."[54] Prescott Hall, founder of the Immigration Restriction League in 1894, believed that "The physical degeneration of the Jew in New York and Philadelphia has been accompanied to some extent by a moral and political degeneration."[55] Edward Ross, professor of sociology at the University of Wisconsin and author of the widely read anti-immigration tract *The Old World in the New* (1913), argued that

> Hebrews are the polar opposite of our pioneer breed. Not only are they undersized and weak-muscled, but they shun bodily activity and are exceedingly sensitive to pain. Says a settlement worker: 'You can't make boy scouts out of the Jews. There's not a troop of them in all New York.'. . . Natural selection, frontier life, and the example of the red man produced in America a type of great physical self-control, gritty, uncomplaining, merciless to the body through fear of becoming 'soft.' To this roaming, hunting, exploring, adventurous breed what greater contrast is there than the denizens of the Ghetto?[56]

Following Frederick Jackson Turner's well-known thesis that the frontier was essential to American character and national development, innumerable authorities chimed in with claims that the quality of recent immigrants was deteriorating. The supposedly decreasing stature of immigrants, although there were no data from earlier immigration on which to base any comparison, was regarded as one sign of this reputed deterioration. Between 1830 and 1860, suggested Francis A. Walker, superintendent of the U.S. Census and opponent of immigration, "the standard of height, of weight, and of chest measurement was steadily rising, with the result that, of the men of all nationalities in the giant army formed to suppress the slaveholders' rebellion, the . . . American bore off the palm in respect to physical stature. The decline of this rate of increase among Americans began at the very time when foreign immigration first assumed considerable proportions." Walker believed that recent immigrants were "beaten men from beaten races."[57] Predominantly derived from eastern and southern Europe, the new immigrants were made up of "peoples which have got no great good for themselves out of the race wars of centuries"; they were "the worst defeats in the struggle for existence."[58] Prescott Hall predicted a national deterioration in stature, coupled with a darkening of skin color and an alteration in skull shape, if immigration continued in its present form.[59]

Along with their consensus that the stature of the Jews was a sign of their degeneration, that Jews were among the losers in a harsh Darwinian racial contest, and that the group represented a threat to American racial progress, the immigration restrictionists were also, not surprisingly, committed hereditarians. In opposition to those who maintained a "pathetic and fatuous belief in the efficacy of American institutions to obliterate immemorial hereditary tendencies," to borrow the words of Madison Grant,[60] the restrictionists believed that environment, particularly education, was ineffectual in overcoming the effects of heredity. "Recent discoveries in biology show that in the long run heredity is far more important than environment or education," wrote Prescott Hall. "Education, imitation of others, will do much to produce outward conformity, but racial characteristics will withstand the influence of centuries."[61] Madison Grant was as firm in his view that heredity and not environment determined stature[62] as he was in the belief that racial traits determined the rise and fall of nations. The hereditarian stance of the restrictionists was essential in supporting their position that certain races, including the Jews, were unassimilable and threatened American racial superiority. In this context, it is hardly surprising that Antin emphasized the power of education in fashioning immigrants into American citizens. In doing so, she undermined hereditarian arguments claiming education was insufficient to make Americans out of "the scum of Europe," to use the contemporary phrasing.

The popularity of eugenics and obsessions over the body ensured not only that the restrictionists would ultimately triumph in the early 1920s with a set of anti-immigration bills designed to reduce the numbers of southern and eastern Europeans arriving in the United States; they also contributed to new inspection policies at immigration stations like Ellis Island. Beginning in 1890, immigrants were forced to submit to medical inspections for contagious diseases, physical deformities, and mental defects. Short stature was among the "minor defects" that could be cause for deportation if other evidence could be produced indicating the immigrant might become a public charge.[63] Many restrictionists favored tougher laws regarding the deportation of immigrants on the basis of physical tests, and several government reports argued that "poor physique" should be grounds for automatic rejection.[64]

These developments did not occur without active resistance, of course. A group of Jewish scientists, including the Americans Franz Boas and Maurice Fishberg and the Englishman Joseph Jacobs, conducted their own anthropometric studies on Jews and used them to emphasize the Jews' potential for assimilation. As professional anthropologists, they accepted mainstream scientific views on race, but they also adhered to Enlightenment principles of the brotherhood of man. Their views were, therefore, a complex mix of environmentalism and hereditarianism; but, often adopting a neo-Lamarckian position, they stressed the power of the environment far more than their non-Jewish scientific contemporaries. They also firmly resisted the idea of racial hierarchies based on comparative physical anthropology.[65] Their researches offered a counternarrative to the image of the Jew as degenerate and racially inferior. They argued that poverty and anti-Semitism had inhibited the development of the race. In the conditions of modern America and England, they argued, Jews would shed their racial peculiarities, including short stature. The physical growth of the Jews would be a sign of their racial progress and the mark of their successful assimilation.

An Australian immigrant to England, Joseph Jacobs responded to the growing anti-Semitism in that country following the wave of persecution and emigration beginning in 1881 that brought millions of Russian Jews westward. Like Fishberg and Boas in the United States, Jacobs hoped to show that Jews could assimilate successfully into English society. He acquiesced to the dominant scientific view that Jews were among the shortest Europeans,[66] but he insisted that environment, not race, was the cause. "I have found it necessary," he wrote in a paper he read before the British Anthropological Institute in 1885, "to scrutinise somewhat closely many Jewish qualities and habits that have hitherto been regarded as peculiarly the results of race. Most of these, however, have been found to be due to social causes, and cannot therefore be regarded as primarily racial."[67] Among these was stature. Comparing the heights of Jews in the East End of London, a ghetto of impoverished immigrants, with that of West End Jews, a wealthier and native-born group, Jacobs found differences in stature between the groups. He also found that the height of West Enders was comparable to that of non-Jews in England.[68] He concluded that environment played a significant role in physical traits, and his study was frequently cited as evidence of the effect of economic conditions on Jewish height.

A German Jewish immigrant, Boas did his major work on American Jews for Congress's Dillingham Commission, which investigated the social and economic effects of immigration in the United States. Stacked with restrictionists like Senator Dillingham and Henry Cabot Lodge, the commission produced a forty-seven-volume report in 1911 that warned of the dangers various "undesirable" races, notably eastern and southern Europeans, posed to the nation. Boas's portion of that report, *Changes in Bodily Form of Descendents of Immigrants,* opposed the major slant of the commission's recommendations. In a study of several thousand immigrants including but not limited to Jews, Boas found that American-born children of immigrants differed from foreign-born children of the same immigrants in several physical characteristics, including stature and head form. The stature of American-born immigrant children, he showed, was on average greater than the stature of their foreign-born siblings. His findings simultaneously undermined dominant beliefs in the racial determination of stature and threatened one of the central tenets of contemporary race theory: the permanence of racial traits. "While heretofore we had the right to assume that human types are stable," wrote Boas, "all the evidence is now in favor of a great plasticity of human types, and permanence of types in new surroundings appears rather as the exception than as the rule."[69] Boas's claims sent shock waves through the scientific community, which immediately attacked his findings; the debate continued unabated until 1928, when he published the complete raw data of his study in *Materials for the Study of Inheritance in Man.* In opposing the commission's xenophobia, moreover, Boas emphasized that immigrants changed physically after residing in the United States and that this physical change reflected mental changes. "We are compelled to conclude that when [the most permanent] features of the body change, the whole bodily and mental make-up of the immigrant may change."[70]

Maurice Fishberg was acquainted with both Boas and Jacobs; the two men read and revised his manuscripts. In the same year that Boas published his findings on immigrants, Fishberg published the most authoritative turn-of-the-century anthropological treatise on the Jews, titled *The Jews: A Study of Race and Environment.* In it, Fishberg also responded to charges that the Jews were unassimilable. Like Jacobs, Fishberg accepted that many of the characteristics attributed to the Jews had some basis in fact, but he also insisted that Jewish traits were the product of environmental conditions. "The fact that the differences between Jews and Christians are not everywhere racial, due to anatomical or physiological peculiarities, but are solely the result of the social and political environment, explains our optimism as regards the ultimate obliteration of all distinctions between Jews and Christians in Europe and America."[71] Fishberg was able to measure almost three thousand Jews in New York through his position as medical examiner for the United Hebrew Charities. Based on his measurements of this impoverished group of immigrants, he generalized that Jews were a race of small people. But he maintained that the height of Jews was everywhere comparable to the height of non-Jews among whom they lived and that ghetto conditions artificially suppressed Jewish stature. The influence of poverty, he believed, was reflected in the increase in stature of first-generation American Jews (he assumed that children of immigrants were better off economically than their parents).[72] While Boas offered no explanations for the increase in stature among American-born immigrant children, Fishberg asserted that it was due, in addition to

improved economic conditions, to the effects of modern public school-
ing and outdoor recreation.

> We have good reasons for the superior stature of the native
> American Jews. Here, during the period of most active growth,
> the Jewish child attends a modern public school instead of the
> insanitary *cheder* (Jewish school) in eastern Europe. . . . Besides
> this, the native Jewish youth in the East side in New York City
> enjoys quite freely open-air recreation, games, bicycle riding,
> etc., all of which are conducive to healthy growth and develop-
> ment of the body. The superior stature of the native American
> Jews is thus seen to be a result of superior social conditions and
> environment.[73]

Like the educated, athletic New Woman whose growth was fueled
by school, physical education, and outdoor activities such as bicycling,
the Jew in America would develop rapidly into the wholesome, assimilated subject of the modern state, argued Fishberg. His remarks were
wholly consistent with Antin's claims in *The Promised Land,* and it is
hard not to suspect that Antin was familiar with Fishberg's work, published only a year before her autobiography.[74]

Reviewers of Antin's book were quick to point out the similarities
between Antin's story and recent anthropological findings. "Facts showing change in the physical characteristics of races subjected to an American environment have been forthcoming from anthropologists for some
years past," begins a review in the *Christian Science Monitor.* "Here is a
book 'The Promised Land,' . . . which tells of the mental and spiritual
changes that come with residence in the United States, transformations
so radical that the author speaks of 're-birth,' of being 'made over,' of
having 'lost physical continuity with an earlier self.' "[75] In her autobiography, Antin quite consciously adopted the language of science, using it
at times to explain her growth in America. The theory of recapitulation,
for example, which posited a connection between the growth of an individual and the evolutionary development of a species or race, appealed
to Antin as a metaphor for her own rapid entrance into the modern
world: "I have to recapitulate in my own experience all the slow steps of
the progress of the race," she wrote (108). Even further, education in science and evolutionary theory, she suggested, was an engine for her
metaphoric growth equal in power to her immigration to America.

> More and more, as the seasons rolled by, and page after page of
> the book of nature was turned before my eager eyes, did I feel

the wonder and thrill of the revelations of science, till all my thoughts became colored with the tints of infinite truths. . . . By asking questions, by listening when my wise friends talked, by reading, by pondering and dreaming, I slowly gathered together the kaleidoscopic bits of the stupendous panorama which is painted in the literature of Darwinism. . . . Vastly as my mind had stretched to embrace the idea of a great country, when I exchanged Polotzk for America, it was no such enlargement as I now experienced. (258–59)

Nature study provoked the "second transformation of my life" (251), she writes, and learning the laws of Darwinian evolution through her participation in the Natural History Club at the Hale Settlement House afforded her a second glimpse of the "peaks of the promised land"—in this case not the promised land of America but "the promised land of evolution" (262).

Just as scientific learning contributed to her own "enlargement," instruction in science is one sign that Jews have collectively grown, that they have abandoned their medieval past and entered the modern world. "History shows that in all countries where Jews have equal rights . . . they lose their fear of secular science, and learn how to take their ancient religion with them from century to awakening century, dropping nothing by the way but what their growing spirit has outgrown" (90). Darwinism, furthermore, comforted Antin by allowing her to think "in aeons and in races, instead of in years and individuals" (261). It was perhaps this substitution of races for individuals and of centuries for years that allowed her to view her own personal history as a collective history. "Although I have written a genuine personal memoir," she explains, "I believe that its chief interest lies in the fact that it is illustrative of scores of unwritten lives" (2). "Should I be sitting here, chattering of my infantile adventures, if I did not know that I was speaking for thousands?" (72).

We might regard her metaphor of the growing body as evidence of the influence of anthropology and race science on her thinking. But if Darwinism appealed to her, Antin manipulated it to her own ends, just as the Jewish anthropologists did in defending immigration. Like them, she could not ignore the authority of science, acquiescing to many of the prevalent stereotypes of Jews reinforced by the anthropological discourse. Like them, Antin insisted that physical and cultural traits were products of environmental conditions, not heredity, and that education was effective in eliminating negative traits. In emphasizing her own small size in Russia and using her autobiography as a story of Jewish communal experience, she implicitly agreed, for example, that Jews in Russia were physically small; but her rapid growth in America demonstrates, like the anthropometric studies of Jews in the United States and England, that this diminishment was a product of oppressive conditions and could be ameliorated by residence in the liberated environment of the West. Like Boas, Antin used her physical growth as a sign of mental growth; and like Fishberg, Antin used the growth of the Jew as a metaphor for racial progress in a restorative atmosphere. Moreover, poverty in the New World, as discussed previously, inhibited her growth just as oppression in Russia inhibited her growth there; in this, she went further than the Jewish American anthropologists by admitting that ghetto conditions in the United States were injurious as well. Like Fishberg, and in opposition to the restrictionists, she suggested that education and exercise could help remedy the debilitating effects of poverty. Similarly, for Antin cultural traits are products of environmental conditions. To those who claimed that Jews were miserly and deceitful in business dealings, Antin surprisingly agreed. She argued that it was a consequence of the oppressive laws governing Jews in the Pale. "People who want to defend the Jews ought never to deny this," she wrote. "Yes, I say, we cheated the Gentiles whenever we dared, because it was the only thing to do. . . . What his shield is to the soldier in battle, that was the ruble to the Jew in the Pale" (21–23).

In rejecting hereditarian dogma, Antin was discrediting the essential principle of racial hierarchy. Wherever hierarchies did exist, she insisted, they were products of social tyranny, not natural law. Antin also questions the applicability of Darwinian laws to human communities. Russia, she implies, is a good test of social Darwinist theory, since the savage conditions of ghetto life there virtually transformed people into unreasoning animals. "A glance over the statutes of the Pale leaves you wondering that the Russian Jews have not lost all semblance to humanity," she writes (23). The czar "had us cooped up, thousands of us where only hundreds could live. . . . When there are too many wolves in the prairie, they begin to prey upon each other. We starving captives of the Pale—we did as do the hungry brutes" (21–23). But Darwinian laws fail in the presence of Jewish solidarity. Rather than turning on each other, the beleaguered Jews of the ghetto directed their animosity toward their Gentile neighbors, according to Antin. "Whenever we could, we spared our own kind, directing against our racial foes the cunning wiles which our bitter need invented" (21–23).

Cooperation rather than competition typifies Antin's experiences throughout her autobiography. Getting the entire family to America demanded the assistance of the United Hebrew Charities, a major catalyst in bringing Russian Jews to the United States. Once in America, both her immediate family and Jewish neighbors like the grocer Rosenblum continuously sacrificed to keep Antin in school. Communal responsibility in the Jewish ghetto went both ways, according to Antin: "A characteristic thing about the aspiring immigrant is the fact that he is not content to progress alone" (279). She finds that this community of support exists outside the ghetto; the social activists in the settlement houses assisted her in getting into college and encouraged her in her writing. She acknowledges the influence of non-Jewish mentors and sponsors like (the ironically named) Miss Dillingham and Edward Everett Hale repeatedly in her autobiography, a fact that Mary Dearborn regards as testament to the excessively "mediated" nature of the autobiography, the way in which Antin was in part compelled and in part allowed herself to adopt completely the perspective of the dominant culture in order to translate her experiences to an alien and sometimes hostile readership.[76] But another way of looking at her openly acknowledged debt to more privileged, liberal native-born Americans is as a sign of her commitment to communitarian values. Once she had attained some measure of success and fame from the sale of her autobiography, Antin immediately began campaigning on behalf of the disenfranchised, writing and lecturing for open immigration and workingwomen's causes.[77] Antin's adherence to communal uplift opposed social-Darwinist laws of competition as well as the American dream of individual success.

One way to view Antin's use of the growing body is as a symbol of racial uplift conceived in anatomical, Darwinian terms. Kevin Gaines has argued that the deployment of scientific ideologies of racial uplift among turn-of-the-century African American writers like Pauline Hopkins "constituted a measure of collusion with discriminatory ideologies and practices" because it bolstered Darwinian notions of racial hierarchy and imperialist notions of the "civilizing mission." As such, the language of racial uplift "restricted the possibilities for resistance" and contributed to overseas imperialism and domestic oppression of minorities; it was in some measure self-defeating, in other words.[78] Like those African American writers, Antin accepted (at least for rhetorical purposes) that race development could be conceived of in evolutionary terms; but her understanding of evolution was more complicated than Gaines's analysis suggests. Like the Jewish scientists of her day, Antin emphasized the role of environment rather than heredity in evolution and rejected ideas of racial hierarchy. By emphasizing the environmentalist strain in the science of race, Antin suggested that racial progress was immediately attainable through economic and material improvements in the conditions of peoples' lives, a position consistent with calls for economic reform and open immigration that constituted Jewish American resistance to two of the major forms of oppression in their lives (i.e., poverty and the anti-immigration movement). It is doubtful, therefore, that Antin's adoption of evolutionary language interfered with Jewish American resistance to discrimination. Also like Hopkins and the black American writers who used the trope of racial uplift, Antin appeared to accept the idea that white, industrial, bourgeois, Christian America was the standard of progress by which other races and nations might be measured; but, again, Antin conceived of that progress in material, social, and political terms, not racial-hereditary terms. In Russia, Jews "had no chance to progress" because they were denied secular education and other forms of political equality (25). If Antin's language of racial uplift indirectly contributed to discriminatory ideologies and practices that sustained imperialism, she was nevertheless aware of American imperialism and resisted it. In her essay "A Confession of Faith," published in the Boston *Jewish Advocate* in 1917, Antin endorses pluralism and observes that "the war god of modern history is the conqueror seeking to impose his own brand of civilization on the conquered people." Characteristically, she advocates international cooperation and respect for differences. "It is where cooperation on equal terms is denied that despotism sets in. . . . Cultural tolerance is the gateway into the new world."[79] Finally, we might say, following the lead of Kevin Gaines, that by adopting the language of evolution and superimposing its vertical metaphor of racial progress on the body, Antin reinforced in her autobiography the belief that a bigger body was a sign of racial progress and that cultural and mental growth could be read through the physical growth of the body. Antin's adoption of science and her use of the image of the growing body, however, were ambivalent and sometimes contradictory. As I suggested in my analysis of her short story "The Lie" in chapter 2, Antin rejected the idea that physical size and intellectual ability corresponded. In that story, the central figure is a small Jewish boy who does not grow at all, and Antin suggests that American identity, represented by the oversized Washington cloak, should be tailored to suit his dimensions, not the other way around. In *They Who Knock at Our Gates,* Antin urged the American public to disregard the voluminous scientific reports of the Dillingham Commission, arguing that the apparently irrefutable "facts" of science simply muddled an issue that was properly moral in nature. Thus, Antin adopted different tactics at different times while her goals remained the same: to ensure that the millions of Jews devastated by civil war and anti-Semitic oppression in eastern Europe would be brought west safely.[80] Perhaps the worst we could say is that Antin's use of the language of racial uplift and the conventions of valorized large size made her autobiography an unwitting endorsement of the attitudes she fought against at other times.

All of these things suggest that there may be other ways to read Antin's figure of the growing Jew. The bodily expansion in her work may be a deliberate performance, a calculated depiction of physical transformation used to secure a place for Jews in a restrictive cultural environment that associated growth with progress.

Let me be clear here: I do not mean to imply that Antin's use of the growing body is performative in the sense conceived by Judith Butler, although there are certain parallels and my argument is informed by Butler's theories. Butler defines the performative as a set of reiterated practices that take on the status of natural fact; it is a "persistent impersonation that passes as the real."[81] The subject, according to her theory, is constituted in and through such performative rituals. In her primary example, Butler argues that gender is performative because it is a set of habituated ways of being, a "corporeal style,"[82] that is so familiar and ingrained as to conceal its genesis and that simultaneously serves as the precondition for subjectivity. Butler carefully distinguishes performativity from performance. Where performance implies a temporary and conscious adoption of a role, performativity is inherent in all that we do and is the necessary condition for subject formation; where performance suggests an act that calls attention to itself *as* an act, performativity "functions to produce that which it declares"[83] (in the case of gender performativity, it produces a subject defined as male or female—that is, a subject with a sex); where performance connotes no sense of danger to the performer, performativity occurs under constraint, that is, under the social threats of discipline, punishment, and even death.[84]

Certainly Antin's staged enactment of bodily growth occurred under a variety of cultural constraints. One might even argue that Antin's metaphor of growth threatens to become more than a self-conscious act (although I will question that supposition later in this chapter). But it is difficult to be certain that the notion of growth as progress was so thoroughly accepted at the turn of the twentieth century that it constituted a discursive formation similar to that of gender, one that would represent a persistent, reiterative "corporeal style" and a necessary condition for subject formation. One can more easily conceive of a writer at the turn of the century rejecting the idea that growth equals progress (however rare it was in fact), for example, than one can conceive of a writer rejecting the idea that a fictional character need be designated by the terms *he* or *she*. (Unfortunately, Butler does not attempt to define what performativity might look like for something other than gender and sexuality.) Additionally, Butler's concept assumes the subject's immersion in a unified set of regulatory norms. As an immigrant and, one has to assume, a late-comer to the peculiarly American notion of growth as progress, Antin was not thoroughly acculturated within a climate in which notions of identity were bound up with progressive ideas of growth. This points to one of the limitations of Butler's theories, which assume that subject formation occurs within a relatively stable, monolithic sociohistorical environment. One wonders how gender might come to seem natural for an individual acculturated under conflicting or multiple gender norms (and, to a greater or lesser extent, aren't we all?).

Butler's theories do seem particularly relevant to Antin's autobiography, however, in their notion of subversion. Subversion of hegemonic norms that compel certain forms of performativity becomes possible, according to Butler, when those norms are cited and disrupted through parodic repetition. Parody is evident in part as a playful and exaggerated repetition of norms; thus drag becomes a key illustration for Butler of gender subversion.[85] In the half-serious, half-farcical scenes describing her childhood poem about George Washington in *The Promised Land,* Antin parodies both the conversion of immigrants into Americans and the notion of the progressively growing Jewish body. Using herself as the heroine of the tale, Antin undergoes exaggerated bodily transformations more similar to the experiences of Alice in Wonderland than the Jew in America. When she recites her poem at school on the day of the Washington celebration, she acknowledges that "I was not a heroic figure" (180). Thin and pale, with bulging eyes and hollow cheeks, Antin looks consumptive, an effect only enhanced by a plaid dress that "had a ghastly effect on my complexion" (180). Her poem is overblown, repetitious, and strains to rhyme; few of her classmates understand the "hail of big words" (181) that descend upon them. Claiming that Washington wrote the U.S. Constitution, the poem itself is a parody of official American history as understood by immigrants. In spite of all this, she is applauded and lionized by students and teachers alike. Encouraged by her father and the praises of her teachers, Antin sets out to publish the poem in a local newspaper. In the urban press of downtown Boston and the noisy offices of Newspaper Row, Antin alternately grows and shrinks, rises and falls. She climbs and descends tall buildings. A "tall newsboy had to stoop to me" (184). The first newspaper editor she met "made me feel about eleven inches high" (185); after meeting with another, "I had regained my full stature and something over, . . . and when I stepped out into the street . . . I swelled out of all proportion" (186). The second editor accepts her poem, and when it is afterward published in the *Herald* her father buys every copy he can find and dispenses them liberally, giving copies to many people who cannot read.

Antin believes she has become an instant celebrity and lords it over her classmates; she takes every opportunity to be interviewed by distinguished classroom visitors and to hold "public audience with the great" (189). Her experiences with the Washington poem testify to Antin's belief, repeated again in *They Who Knock at Our Gates,* that America does not simply adopt immigrants—they "take possession of America" (162). The idea was clearly displeasing to some native-born Americans; in 1917 Harvard professor Barrett Wendell observed that Antin "has developed an irritating habit of describing herself and her people as Americans, in distinction from such folks as Edith [Wendell's wife] and me, who have been here for three hundred years."[86]

If the scenes surrounding the Washington poem comically exaggerate the ritual of Americanization and the reputed transformation of the Jewish body in America, we should be careful to note that parody does not always have a subversive effect. "Parody by itself is not subversive," argues Butler, "and there must be a way to understand what makes certain kinds of parodic repetitions effectively disruptive, truly troubling, and which repetitions become domesticated and recirculated as instruments of cultural hegemony."[87] Context and reception crucially determine whether parody becomes subversive, Butler concludes. That Antin anticipated multiple responses to her work seems implicit in her recognition that her Washington poem had a different meaning for her Jewish classmates than it had for others. "There ran a special note through my poem—a thought that only Israel Rubinstein or Beckie Aronovitch could have fully understood, besides myself" (183).

What exactly was this thought? Was it a subtle undercurrent that questioned the poem's dominant narrative of faith in America? That seems unlikely. Still, for those willing to look, there are indications throughout her autobiography that Antin opposed its official narrative of progress and faith in America. Antin's awareness of Fetchke's fate, her recognition that later generations of Jewish Americans might regret the cultural losses that their parents were compelled to endure (198), and her acknowledgment that, in later years, her father discovered "a new-born pessimism" engendered "by his perception that in America, too, some things needed mending" (171) are all strongly suggestive of a suppressed critical eye. Perhaps a stronger indication that Antin did not wholly subscribe to the view that America was the promised land—that is, that the promise of American freedom and equality had not yet been fully realized—can be seen in the sequence of chapter titles in her autobiography, which reverse the official biblical story of exodus and redemption that the book title endorses. (The title of the autobiography,

by the way, was suggested to her by an editor; it was not the one she originally chose.)[88] The chapter entitled "The Promised Land" occurs in the
middle of the book after the chapters "The Tree of Knowledge" and "The
Exodus." Up to this point the biblical progression holds up. But later
chapters are titled "Manna," bringing us back to the story of the Jews'
wanderings in the desert, and "The Burning Bush," which returns us to
the biblical story of the Jews' slavery in Egypt. The implication here is
that Antin only initially imagined that America was the promised land;
once in the United States, her estimations of the country changed considerably. Within the book, in fact, the idea of the promised land is often
invoked as an abstract, future ideal rather than a present reality.

Conclusion

One of the curious things about existing criticism on Antin's work is the
absence of attention to the rhetorical elements in her writing. Antin, it
seems to me, was first and foremost a clever rhetorician, yet most scholars seem to take her writing at face value. Mary Dearborn is shocked at
what she considers Antin's shameless patriotism, for example. "*The
Promised Land* actually contains the phrase 'Three cheers for the Red,
White, and Blue!'" Dearborn notes, as if surprised by that fact.[89] But it is
precisely when Antin is being most patriotic that one has to be most suspicious of her writing. The theme of lying, after all, suffuses her work.
She confesses in *The Promised Land* that she lied constantly as a child:
"my childhood was spent in a maze of lies and dreams" (108). While
scholars of the genre have noted that this is a common theme in autobiographies,[90] Antin suggests that there were specific cultural explanations for the phenomenon. She explains that Jews in the Russian Pale
were compelled to lie and cheat as a survival skill. "I knew how to dodge
and cringe and dissemble before I knew the names of the seasons," she
informs us (23). She offers a powerful example of that compulsion in the
story of the mock patriotism demanded of Russian Jews. Every Jewish
home, she explains, contained a portrait of the tyrannical and anti-
Semitic Czar Alexander III in order to impress the predatory local police
and government officials. When these same officials announced that
every home was required to display a Russian flag, the desperate and
impoverished Jews of the Pale scurried to pawn their valuables and buy
"lengths of cloth, red, and blue, and white" (17). One wonders, after
reading these passages, whether her "Three cheers for the Red, White,
and Blue!" and her lengthy passage about the poem honoring George
Washington are sincere or sham displays of patriotism; the fact that

Werner Sollors was unable to find Antin's poem on Washington in the *Herald,* where she claims it was published, only reinforces my distrust of her glib patriotism.[91]

Her short story "The Lie," moreover, is a meditation on the continuing effects of cultural traits, in this case deceit, that originated in a climate of oppression and may no longer be appropriate for individuals who have been freed from tyranny. Considering that Antin concealed the circumstances of her own life at the end of her autobiography and lied about her personal beliefs when supporting Roosevelt's candidacy, it seems she was quite capable of dissembling as an adult in the United States. Her belief in the potential value of strategic deception, in fact, is reflected in a brief passage in her autobiography. When Antin's family had lost its financial stability in Russia (her father had emigrated to seek better opportunities in America while her mother struggled to support three daughters following a period of poor health), Mary helped by delivering tea to her mother's customers. On one occasion a shopkeeper told her that the tea she delivered was of an inferior quality. Tactlessly, Antin informed the shopkeeper she was wrong. "I understood . . . that I had spoken like a fool, had lost my mother a customer. I had only spoken the truth, but I had not expressed it diplomatically. That was no way to make business" (117). Antin learned early, and out of dire necessity, the need for careful diplomacy and rhetorical sophistication. The story suggests Antin believed that subterfuge was sometimes useful in accomplishing important goals; in the case of the tea sale, a benign lie (e.g., a diplomatic agreement with the shopkeeper) would have retained her mother's customer and provided money for her family when they were desperately poor. In the more important case of American immigration legislation, Antin's autobiography would serve a vital function in testifying to the Jews' potential for assimilation at a time when eastern European Jewry was being devastated by pogroms and civil war. Who can say how much of her autobiography is sincere? And who can blame her for telling her readers what they wanted to hear?

More to the point of my argument in this chapter, Antin clearly recognized that physical size could be used as a rhetorical tool. As a child, she traveled on two occasions from the small town of Polotzk to the larger city of Vitebsk; these journeys are symbolic precursors of her emigration to America. On one occasion she travels by train with her Cousin Rachel, who conceives a plan to save money by deceiving the ticket agent about Antin's age. Antin is old enough at the time to pay half fare, but she is so small that she can pass as a younger child and thus travel for free. Rachel tells her how to accentuate her smallness. "When we approached the ticket office she whispered to me to stoop a little, and I stooped. . . . In the car she bade me curl up in the seat, and I curled up. . . . I heard the conductor collect the tickets. I knew when he was looking at me. I heard him ask my age and I heard Cousin Rachel lie about it" (120). Antin believes her cousin was perfectly justified in resorting to this trickery.

> I was fond of my cousin, and I smiled at her in perfect understanding and admiration of her cleverness in beating the railroad company. I knew then, as I know now, beyond a doubt, that my Uncle David's daughter was an honorable woman. With the righteous she dealt squarely; with the unjust, as best she could. She was in duty bound to make all the money she could, for money was her only protection in the midst of the enemy. Every kopeck she earned or saved was a scale in her coat of armor. We learned this code early in life, in Polotzk; so I was pleased with the success of our ruse on this occasion, though I should have been horrified if I had seen Cousin Rachel cheat a Jew. (120)

The story testifies to the way in which the oppressive climate of Russia "reduced" or "diminished" the Jews: on a literal level, it encouraged Antin to stoop (just as in scientific terms it supposedly reduced the stature of Jews in the Pale); on a metaphoric level, it compelled honorable Jews like Cousin Rachel to lie and cheat. But the story also suggests that Jews often turned this "diminishment" on its head; Mary and Rachel used trickery and a faked smallness to combat their oppression. (The anecdote's subtle reference to the story of David and Goliath, accomplished in part by Antin's substitution of "my Uncle David's daughter" for Rachel's name, reinforces both the theme of communal resistance and the idea of size as a strategic device.) Because Antin's anecdote about her diminishment at the Russian train station directly opposes her narrative of growth in the United States, the element of deception in this early episode suggests that trickery may play an equal role in her subsequent narrative. One wonders, in other words, whether the same rhetorical flourish isn't at work in Antin's use of the figures of the growing woman and the growing Jew in America as in her use of the shrinking Jew at the train station in Vitebsk.

I am suggesting that it is difficult to form final judgments on Antin's work because of its self-consciously rhetorical nature. How much of what she wrote did she believe? How much was deliberate, calculated posturing? One way to answer this question might be to examine how Antin's use of popular tropes differed from those of her contemporaries, as I did earlier in this chapter. I suggested that Antin defied conventions of the discourse on New Womanhood even as she borrowed its trope of the growing woman. She rejected the bourgeois elements in the ideology as she sympathized with the impoverished and envisioned her growth as halting, inhibited by the poverty of American ghettoes. She rejected the racist elements as she positioned herself, a Jew, in the role of the New Woman. The ending of Antin's book demonstrates neither the fatalism of Edna Pontellier's tragic demise in *The Awakening* nor the more common capitulation to marriage and domesticity in popular New Woman novels. In comparison, the differences between her autobiography and the writings of Jewish anthropologists are less pronounced. She adapted the language of evolutionary theory and the figure of the growing Jew to describe her own development in the United States. Like her scientific compatriots who defended Jews against mainstream scientific racism and the attacks of anti-immigrationists, Antin rejected racial hierarchies and hereditarian dogma, emphasizing the environmental and social roots of human culture and anatomy. Opposing prevalent notions of racial competition, furthermore, Antin endorsed cooperation and communal values.

Whether or not we are finally able to disentangle Antin's personal beliefs on science and the ideology of New Womanhood, however, her use of the figures of the growing woman and the growing Jew attests to the powerful cultural appeal of those images and Antin's willingness to use whatever tools came to hand to aid the Jewish people. Moreover, her book suggests that disenfranchised groups felt obligated at the turn of the century to demonstrate a history of or capacity for growth in order to claim entitlement to full participation in American social and political life. In this light, the rhetoric of "uplift" that suffuses so many discourses at the turn of the century, particularly writings on the so-called Negro question, is understandable not only as a deployment of America's central myth of vertical movement—the myth of upward class mobility—but also as a peculiarly embodied ideal. For groups whose very bodies seemed to demand "uplift"—for women and Jews—physical growth was expected to accompany or foreshadow the economic, moral, and political growth that attended social advancement.

CHAPTER 6 • The Incredible Industrial Shrinking Man
Upton Sinclair's Challenge to
Hegemonic Masculinity

Tiny heroes like Tom Thumb, shrinking figures like the heroine of Lewis Carroll's *Alice in Wonderland,* and miniature worlds like the one in Mary Norton's *The Borrowers* (1953) have been staples of children's tales for centuries, and several writers have addressed the appeal and significance of miniaturization in these and related cultural productions such as dollhouses, miniature paintings, and model trains.[1] But as Caroline Hunt suggests in a fascinating essay on the theme of miniaturization in children's literature, most writers have focused on one type of miniature and dealt with the concept as a single idea, ignoring "the rich variety of metaphors of the miniature."[2] She identifies three types of miniatures in children's literature and examines the distinct functions of each. The small hero, she suggests, is typically used to address discrimination and dehumanization. Miniature society books characteristically present idealized portraits of timeless communities, reassuring readers in moments of historical crisis of the existence of a world that can be controlled. Stories of shrinking people address the vulnerability associated with death and the inevitability of change.

Hunt's observations on the last of these types, the shrinking protagonist, are especially intriguing for a discussion of masculinity in the Progressive era. At a time when the male body seemed unusually unstable, images of shrinking men abounded. We have seen several examples in the previous chapter. The New Woman's spectacular growth—a perceived change in height that mirrored the expansion of her social opportunities—threatened men with comparative shrinkage. In Charles Dana Gibson's drawings, in political cartoons, in Charlotte Perkins Gilman's utopian fiction, in newspaper editorials, and in advertisements the male body was in danger of a dwindling displacement. But perhaps nowhere, with the possible exception of Gibson's drawings, does the shrinking man appear so often as in naturalist fiction. The economic trajectories of characters in Dreiser's *Sister Carrie* (1900), for example, are mapped literally onto their bodies. Hurstwood experiences a "marked physical deterioration" as his fortunes dwindle. His downfall has physical, financial, social, and psychological components, and Dreiser makes it clear that he considers these realms correlative: "A man's fortune or material progress," Dreiser postulates, "is very much the same as his bodily growth."[3] In keeping with the novel's interest in the culture of consumption—of desires and appetites—Hurstwood's diminishment is rendered primarily in terms of bulk and the fit and quality of his clothing.

> No more weakly looking object ever strolled out into the spring sunshine [from Bellevue Hospital] than the once hale, lusty manager. All his corpulency had fled. His face was thin and pale, his hands white, his body flabby. Clothes and all, he weighed but one hundred and thirty-five pounds. Some old garments had been given him—a cheap brown coat and misfit pair of trousers.[4]

In other naturalist texts, male shrinkage is signified through musculature and stature. Jack London's *The Sea Wolf* (1904) depicts the gradual dissolution of the magnificent captain Wolf Larsen, a Nietzschean superman whose philosophy boils down to a belief that "the big eat the little that they may continue to move, the strong eat the weak that they may retain their strength." By the end of the book Larsen has lost his strength—in his paralysis he has become, in fact, "disembodied"—and the regenerated Humphrey Van Weyden taunts him with the knowledge that Larsen has experienced "a diminishing." "You are no longer the biggest bit of the ferment," Hump chides. "You were, once, and able to eat me, as you were pleased to phrase it; but there has been a diminishing, and I am able to eat you."[5] Likewise, the protagonist of Upton Sinclair's *The Jungle* (1906), the principal subject of most of this chapter, systematically shrinks both in stature and musculature throughout the novel as the meatpacking industry steadily extracts the labor capacity of his body.

Caroline Hunt believes the shrinking protagonist in children's literature expresses "universal uncertainties"[6]—psychological fears of bodily control and eventual nonexistence. In the context of children's literature she may be right, although one would want to test that theory with historical or cross-cultural analysis. In the previous chapter, on the other hand, I pointed out that the turn-of-the-century U.S. image of the shrinking man was linked with the figure of the growing New Woman, suggesting that the trope of male shrinkage represented anxieties about changing gender roles and threats to patriarchal privileges stemming from women's social demands. Certainly men had reason to be anxious. Women continued to insist on the vote, equal education, and access to professions traditionally denied them, and they steadily achieved victory in these arenas. They also left the home and farm in ever greater percentages; one historian estimates that the number of women in the labor force doubled between 1880 and 1900 and increased by another 50 percent between 1900 and 1910.[7] Some positions, such as clerical work, in which women made up an estimated 3 percent of the workforce in 1870 and 35 percent in 1910,[8] were increasingly feminized, threatening men in those occupations and forcing both sexes to revise their assumptions about men's and women's proper spheres. Anxieties about feminization were so great at the time that some were prompted to denounce the entire age as feminized. As Basil Ransome in Henry James's *The Bostonians* (1885) famously fumes, "The whole generation is womanised; the masculine tone is passing out of the world; it's a feminine, a nervous, hysterical, chattering, canting age, an age of hollow phrases and false delicacy and exaggerated solicitudes and coddled sensibilities."[9]

Dreiser's *Sister Carrie* is a perfect example of the use of the paired growing woman and shrinking man to represent anxieties about changing gender roles. Like Hurstwood's descent, Carrie's rise has physical manifestations, and these are consistent with New Woman iconography. When Drouet briefly reappears in the end of the novel he compliments Carrie on her appearance. "Well, you do look great," he says. "I never saw anybody improve so. You're taller, aren't you?"[10] Carrie confirms his speculation. In the latter half of the novel, when Hurstwood loses his job and becomes dependent on Carrie and her acting income, his masculinity quickly evaporates. But his emasculation, like his bodily transformation, includes a role reversal; Hurstwood steadily assumes the feminized positions of Carrie and his former wife. He takes over the domestic chores of cooking, shopping, and cleaning, for example; he reluctantly appeals to Carrie for household expenses; he stifles objections when Carrie comes home late for dinner and leaves peremptorily for evening entertainment with Lola Osborne; he spends more time occupied by Carrie's favorite activity—rocking listlessly and dreaming. As Hurstwood's fortunes go from bad to worse, he suffers repeated humiliations from women. Acting as a scab on a transit line, he ignores the pleas of striking male workers to "be a man" and walk away from his work. Withstanding several aborted attacks, Hurstwood is finally driven from his work by a woman—"a mere girl in appearance"[11]—who tries to strike him with a club. An even younger girl taunts him as he limps home after the incident. By the end of the novel, when Hurstwood sustains himself by begging, he makes one last attempt to appeal to Carrie for money. Pushed away by an attendant outside Carrie's theater, Hurstwood slips in the snow and falls. From high above in their penthouse apartment, Lola and Carrie look down (presumably) at him. Lola laughs. "How sheepish men look when they fall," she says (650). It is a scene of tremendous narrative economy. In this brief vision of a man's fall observed by two downward-gazing women, we recognize Hurstwood's bottomed-out social mobility, his loss of male dignity and respect, his loss of masculine sexual appeal, his subordinated social status, and a reversal of gender hierarchies. Thus Hurstwood's fall and Carrie's ascent are not simply coincidental, the clever conjoining of a singular personal tragedy and an equally singular success story that makes for an intriguingly balanced novel. Hurstwood's fall and Carrie's rise have, in more ways than one, an intimate relation, and they bespeak a cultural anxiety that was not unique to Theodore Dreiser.

But it would be an oversimplification to say that the image of the shrinking man at the turn of the century was strictly a response to women's social demands and shifts in gender roles. The shrinking man expressed concerns about masculine disempowerment that stemmed from a host of historical changes. The most important of these was economic. The increasing dominance of big business and the associated fading of independent small businesses meant that middle-class men increasingly occupied subservient positions within large corporate hierarchies, a loss of independence and autonomy that obstructed traditional routes to masculine identity formation.[12] Bankruptcies, unusually common during the recurring economic depressions between 1873 and 1896, also threatened masses of men with economic failure and thereby challenged the financial success that was and remains a central component of masculinity.[13] And while bankruptcy did not strike every man, the fear of it was a constant companion of middle-class men. In 1902 William James claimed that "the prevalent fear of poverty among the educated classes is the worst moral disease from which our civilization suffers."[14] The widespread middle-class fear of failure that stemmed from the long depression and the frequency of bankruptcies was both an emasculation fear and a fear of proletarianization, an anxiety about slipping into a demonized caste that often served as a fearful reverse image of middle-class morality and stability.

While historians have suggested that many of the worries surrounding masculinity at the turn of the twentieth century were most prevalent within the middle class,[15] the fear of losing one's masculinity was hardly confined to that group. A variety of technological and structural changes posed particularly acute threats to lower-class masculine identity. Ava Baron's fascinating study of the printing industry at the turn of the century, for example, reveals that a host of changes jeopardized traditional avenues by which printers secured their sense of manhood, including the erosion of the apprenticeship system, the turn to skill specialization, the casual employment system, the shift of operational control from workers to management, and threats to job security and the family wage.[16] James Barrett's study of labor conditions in the meatpacking industry indicates that similar changes were occurring there.[17] Social critics, furthermore, claimed that modern industrial labor, with its emphasis on specialization and repetitive routinized labor, was inherently destructive to masculinity. Anthony Ludovici, for example, spoke of the "steady degeneration of men" caused by "working at tasks which every woman knows she could easily undertake."[18] Cities themselves, to which men increasingly migrated in search of jobs, were perilous for masculinity. Jack London believed that "mind and body are sapped by the undermining influences ceaselessly at work" in modern cities. "Moral and physical stamina are broken, and the good workman, fresh from the soil, becomes in the first city generation a poor workman; and by the second city generation . . . actually unable physically to perform the labor his father did." Pursuing his analysis through an investigation of conditions in the impoverished East End of London, he warned that urban life was capable of creating "a new and different race of people, short of stature, and of wretched or beer-sodden appearance." Among the "short and stunted people," the "city savages," of the East End, wrote London, "The men became caricatures of what physical men ought to be."[19]

Other crucial historical changes contributed to men's sense of confusion and anxiety. These included, for example, the increased economic competition that native-born white men in particular faced not just from women but from foreigners immigrating in record numbers to the States and blacks migrating in increasing numbers to northern industrial centers. They also included the threats to the ideology of individualism that, as one historian has pointed out, were specifically threats to masculinity, since "from the start, individualism was a gendered issue,"[20] a privilege arrogated to masculine identity.

But what I wish to emphasize here is that the distillation of these social conditions in the figure of the shrinking man suggests how important physical stature and size were to dominant notions of masculinity. As the authors of a recent book on the relationship between masculinity and body size have argued, stature in particular continues to be a key component of male identity. These researchers found that tall men and men of average height are regarded as significantly more masculine than short men, who, according to respondents of questionnaires, are assumed to possess traditionally feminine characteristics such as passivity, submissiveness, and timidity. "A male's sense of self and masculinity is, to a large degree, interwoven with the concept of bigness," the researchers conclude. "Research solidly demonstrates that greater height is positively related to greater social power and perceived social status."[21] Perhaps McTeague, in Frank Norris's 1899 book of the same name, expresses it most directly. Whenever he feels threatened, he defends his masculinity by reaffirming his tremendous size: "You can't make small of me" he intones throughout the book.[22]

Given the relationship between masculinity, body size, and social power, it may come as no surprise that men at the turn of the century sought to defend their masculine privilege—or assuage their sense of dispossession—by embarking on a mission of bodily regeneration. As if to ward off the threat of male shrinkage, a well-documented "physical imperative" emerged seemingly everywhere in the late nineteenth century.[23] The physical culture movement, for example, promised the rewards of bodily regeneration, particularly for those men trapped in the proliferating sedentary urban occupations. In 1912 the mouthpiece for the movement, *Physical Culture* magazine, expanded its regular interest in bodybuilding and other exercise programs with a special issue on the subject of making the body taller.[24] In the late 1880s, the YMCA adopted physical culture as a major mission for the development of young men. Numerous boys' clubs with similar goals appeared shortly thereafter, including the Boys Brigades, the Boone and Crocket Club, the Knights of King Arthur, the Woodcraft Indians, and the Men of Tomorrow. None was as popular, however, as the Boy Scouts of America, incorporated in 1910, which vowed to "make big men of little boys" and issued calls for adult scoutmasters who were "REAL, live men—red-blooded and right-hearted men—BIG men."[25] Hunting and boxing experienced revivals, and vigorous, masculine spectator sports such as football, rodeos, and Wild West shows were born in the late nineteenth century. The Muscular Christianity movement participated in this "cult of the body"; it sought to infuse traditional morality with masculine invigoration.[26] The program of overseas imperialism launched in the 1890s reflected and reinforced the new martial spirit pervading the nation, and those who advocated imperialist expansion, like Teddy Roosevelt, yoked masculine revitalization to racial dominance. Similarly, narratives of masculine regeneration became staples of boys' adventure fiction and the Western; the latter solidified as a genre and attained market dominance during this period. Like the cowboy-protagonists of Westerns, heroes of magazine articles in the 1890s suddenly grew to larger-than-life proportions. While popular magazine authors of the early Republic tended to ignore the body and emphasized instead the intellectual traits and personal character of their protagonists, turn-of-the-century authors dwelled extensively on bodily descriptions. The typical hero at the time, according to one study, was "in every way a large man—large in build, in mind, in nature. He is nearly six feet high, and with a kind of stately bulk which turns the scales at something like 250 pounds."[27]

Numerous tales of personal growth and masculine recuperation testify to the fact that these ambitions did not remain merely fictional and
cultural ideals. In 1909, for example, Charles Atlas had the experience
that would motivate his transformation to the "world's most perfectly
developed male" and serve as the famous narrative hook in advertisements for his book on the Dynamic Tension method: a tall, muscular
lifeguard kicked sand in his face as he was sitting on the beach at Coney
Island with a girlfriend.[28] In his autobiography, Teddy Roosevelt
recounts the transformation he experienced from an asthmatic "sickly
boy . . . nervous and timid" to a vigorous paragon of masculine forti-
tude.[29] What is far more significant than the methods he adopted for this
self-transformation (he dedicated himself to a program of boxing and
wrestling) was the particular nature of the transformation. When Roosevelt initially learned to box, he prided himself on an award he won in
a lightweight contest; it made him feel solidarity, he wrote, with another
"little man" he had read about. By the time Roosevelt served as New
York's governor, he routinely wrestled with a "champion middleweight
wrestler."[30] Throughout his career, Roosevelt asserted that personal
growth through the strenuous life would serve national interests and
duplicate national processes. Thus, Roosevelt's bodily rhetoric was tied
to the political agenda that he pursued throughout his career and reiterated in his autobiography. His physical transformation from lightweight
to middleweight served as an allegory of the Little Man's ascension in
political terms, his rise to the role of independent, rational middling
figure who could recognize and negotiate the nation's common good and
stand between the "battered, undersized foreigners" and the "big men"
of corporations and local machine governments.[31]

The image of the shrinking man proliferated, then, just as "the male
body moved to the center of men's gender concerns" (in the words of
one recent historian)[32] and as images of masculine growth began to
express dominant ideals. Both the image of the growing man and the
obverse image of the shrinking man reflected pervasive anxieties about
the state of masculinity at the turn of the century. It may not be, as some
historians and critics have argued, that masculinity was undergoing a
"crisis." Certainly the insights of Abigail Solomon-Godeau and Tania
Modleski are relevant here—namely, that "masculinity . . . is, like capitalism, *always* in crisis" and that "male power is actually consolidated
through cycles of crisis and resolution."[33] The evidence does suggest,
however, that rapid changes in the social fabric propelled equally rapid
and dramatic adjustments in gender ideologies, and the figures of the
dwindling and expanding man were used to negotiate the tensions and
anxieties inherent in these transformations.[34]

In his muckraking novel *The Jungle,* Upton Sinclair participated in the general preoccupation with the state of masculinity at the turn of the century. Deliberately challenging the progressive narrative of the growing male body, Sinclair adopted the figure of the shrinking man as a rhetorical tool for exposing the impersonal and mechanistic brutality of U.S. industrial capitalism at the turn of the century. The book revealed the threat to lower-class masculinity inherent in modern industrial methods, and in the process it demonstrated the ways in which modern industrialism was sustained by conventional middle-class notions of masculinity such as competitive individualism as well as the extent to which hegemonic ideals of masculinity excluded large classes of men. But the book went beyond exposing the destructiveness of laissez-faire capitalism; it also suggested that the system was inimical to Democratic ideals and national progress. A healthy, recuperated masculinity was thereby linked to national interests, and the ideal of healthy masculinity imagined by the novel is in part defined by white men's protection of women and containment of black men. The novel can be read, in other words, as an attempt to unify white men across class lines in order to inculcate widespread support among voters for socialism. This attempt at unification can be seen clearly in the figure of Jurgis Rudkus, the book's main character, who unites the middle-class image of the shrinking man (or Little Man) with the lower-class figure of the Labor Giant.

A Shrinking Man in a Human Jungle

When Jurgis Rudkus arrives in Packingtown from Lithuania, he is an energetic "giant"[35] fully confident in his ability to support a family and a believer in an economic system that condemns the "puny fellows," the "unfit," to destitution (20, 58). The bosses of the Chicago stockyards immediately reinforce his self-confidence and social-Darwinian worldview, selecting him for a job among a crowd of men because they "noticed his form towering above the rest" (30). But Jurgis's body and his faith in the system are quickly shattered. As the narrative progresses, Jurgis suffers an endless series of disappointments, defeats, and outright disasters, and identical scenes of selection plot the downward course of his fortunes and map that downward mobility onto his body. "He was no longer the finest-looking man in the throng" we learn in the first such episode following his slow recovery from a work-related injury, "and the bosses no longer made for him" (123). It is not simply, evidently, that he no longer "towers above the rest." By this time "he was thin and haggard," his cheeks were "sunken in," his muscles were "wasting away, and what were left were soft and flabby" (119, 123). Jurgis's body continues to dwindle as he steadily loses everything of value, and inevitably he comes to feel like the other workers he had once scorned and displaced, one of a multitude of "worn-out parts of the great merciless packing machine" (124).

In many respects the novel—particularly the first half that traces Jurgis's experiences in Packingtown—is designed on the principle of an extended analogy, and Jurgis's shrinkage is a literalization—an incarnation, one might say—of that analogy. Immediately after Jurgis arrives in Packingtown and secures a job, he and his family are taken on a tour of a Durham meatpacking plant. Sinclair inserts this scene deliberately, knowing that most visitors and residents of Chicago are exposed to this portion only of the meatpacking industry and do not see beyond the impressive and overwhelming facade of mass production, which took place in some of the largest factories in the United States at the time.[36] (As the architect Louis Sullivan would write in his autobiography in 1924, "all distinguished strangers, upon arrival in [Chicago], [are] at once taken to the Stock Yards, not to be slaughtered, it is true, but to view with salutary wonder the prodigious goings on, and to be crammed with statistics concerning how Chicago feeds the world.")[37] Sinclair duplicates this process, cramming his readers with statistics and exposing us to the astounding industrial system, not forgetting to remind us of its intended effect.

> It seemed impossible to [Jurgis and his family] that anything so stupendous could have been devised by mortal man. . . . It was a thing as tremendous as the universe—the laws and ways of its working no more than the universe to be questioned or understood. All that a mere man could do, it seemed to Jurgis, was to take a thing like this as he found it, and do as he was told. . . . Jurgis was even glad that he had not seen the place before [acquiring a job], for he felt that the size of it would have overwhelmed him. But now he had been admitted—he was a part of it all! He had the feeling that this whole huge establishment had taken him under its protection, and had become responsible for his welfare. (40–41)

Jurgis will come to see the naïveté of his initial faith in the immense system—a major purpose of the remainder of the novel is to demolish the myths that these carefully orchestrated tours create—but in this initial episode Jurgis can only feel relieved that he is not one of the animals whose destiny is to arrive in Packingtown. "*Dieve*—but I'm glad I'm not a hog!" he mutters (36).

At the Durham factory, Jurgis and his family watch as a stream of hogs climbs a chute to the top of a tall building. At the end of this climb the hogs are jerked aloft by a chain and their throats are slit. From there the hogs' journey is progressively downward, and as they travel their bodies are systematically cut and shaved and scoured until no part remains. First they are dropped into a vat and boiled. Descending to the next floor their bristles are pruned by a machine. Next their heads and entrails are removed and dropped through holes in the floor. A level down the chilled carcasses are cut up. And so the process goes until the hogs reach the bottom floor where any remaining parts are converted to fertilizer.

Jurgis himself will undergo an analogous descent in Packingtown, even to the point of becoming a "fertilizer man" in his final job. Like the hogs, he and his family will initially be deceived into rising "by the power of their own legs" (33). Fresh from the country, they will find jobs immediately and enter willingly into the trap of buying a house and furniture that they will never be able to own outright. Like the pigs whose "weight carried them back through all the processes necessary to make them into pork" (33), their own momentum will carry them downward through an ineluctable process of destruction. On several occasions Jurgis's fears of ruin manifest as a vertiginous feeling like what the hogs must feel before they are killed, when they are jerked aloft and the ground beneath them suddenly vanishes. "It was like seeing the world fall away from underneath his feet; like plunging down into a bottomless abyss, into yawning caverns of despair. . . . It might be true that, strive as he would, toil as he would, he might fail, and go down and be destroyed!" (115–16). Jurgis, like the hogs, will physically shrink during his descent, and his family will undergo an analogous reduction: their numbers will dwindle as first Antanas, then Kristofaras, and finally Ona and little Antanas will die. Even the children will shrink—Vilimas, Kotrina, and Kristofaras, "like most children of the poor," will be "undersized" for their age (125, 131, 202–3). For the sake of Jurgis and any readers who may have missed the allegorical implications of the initial scene in the factory, the socialist tailor Ostrinski (a "little tailor" [314] almost certainly meant to recall the brave little tailor who defeats giants in children's fairytales) explains at the end of the novel that, as far as the packers were concerned, "a hog was just what [Jurgis] had been" (316).

Critics and readers have complained about the novel's lack of credibility, the way for example that bad things keep happening relentlessly to Jurgis. But the book is set up as an analogy, and its failures are from another perspective the accomplishments of analogization: Jurgis experiences the efficiency of destruction in a narrative sense that the hogs experience in an industrial sense—he enters the slaughtering machine as surely as the hogs. The perceived failures of the book are also, as critics have pointed out, more generally the presumed failures of naturalism as a literary style. Where realists had invested individuals with agency and moral responsibility, naturalists, writing in a mode more compatible with an industrial, bureaucratic corporate world than an economy of self-made men, created characters more often controlled by forces beyond themselves.[38] Thus naturalist characters, in the revealing words of one critic, are "troublingly diminished beings."[39] To another critic, the "fundamental crisis of selfhood" implicit in naturalism's deterministic worldview "is reflected in images of bodily disintegration," of "persistent depictions of men in various stages of fragmentation."[40] Recurring images of shrinking men, therefore, participate in naturalism's attempts to subvert individualism and decenter the subject.

The shrinking man narrative might also be viewed as one mode or element of the "plot of decline" regarded by several recent critics as a hallmark of naturalism.[41] For June Howard, the naturalist plot of decline reflected middle-class fears of proletarianization, and it grew out of the middle class's vulnerable position at the turn of the century between a large and increasingly visible urban proletariat and the newly formed giant corporations.[42] Certainly Sinclair's own background—his childhood of impoverished southern gentility—places him squarely in the company of many naturalist writers haunted by downward drift from the middle class,[43] and the seven weeks he spent in the Chicago stockyards gathering material for *The Jungle* as a reporter for the socialist *Appeal to Reason* might accurately be described as an even more vivid "confrontation with proletarianization."[44] Socialist writers like Sinclair and Jack London, influenced by Marxist theory, took this anxiety one step further, imagining an eventual extinction of the middle class. "All over the world two classes were forming, with an unbridged chasm between them—the capitalist class, with its enormous fortunes, and the proletariat, bound into slavery by unseen chains," writes Sinclair in *The Jungle* (313). Jurgis's shrinkage and downward mobility, then, unquestionably play on middle-class anxieties, and in this sense Jurgis typifies the middle class's own Little Man, an embattled individual hoping to preserve some autonomy and middle-class respectability (home ownership, a family wage, a wife's domesticity) while being squeezed between mobs of the unemployed and enormous, belching factories.

But Howard also argues that the plot of decline, while it evokes and reflects middle-class readers' anxieties, acts to contain the threat of proletarianization. It typically accomplishes this, she argues, by distancing readers from the lower-class Other, the "brute," who, as in the classic example of Norris's *McTeague,* is so often the protagonist of naturalist novels.[45] While her argument is compelling for many naturalist works, especially the novels of Frank Norris, it is less convincing with respect to *The Jungle.* Howard herself appears to recognize this and modifies her argument accordingly. "The plot of decline is defeated" in *The Jungle,* she acknowledges, and Jurgis is rescued from "the sordid life and narrow horizons of the brute."[46] Yet Howard ultimately concludes that a substantial chasm nevertheless separates the reader and protagonist in a way that is consistent with other naturalist texts, suggesting that Sinclair had difficulty extricating himself from a technique that translated class divisions into narrative schisms between the audience and the fictional characters. "There is no pretense in *The Jungle,*" Howard asserts, "that the group Sinclair is writing *about* is the same or even has much in common with the group he is writing *for.* . . . The worlds of the observer and the participant . . . remain polarized, joined only by the narrator's pity and good intentions."[47]

On many occasions *The Jungle*'s implied reader does seem to be middle class as Howard claims, but on other occasions the implied reader is more ambiguous. Consider, for example, Sinclair's claim in *The Jungle* that the *Appeal to Reason,* which first serialized his novel, was published for the "American working mule" (327);[48] or the fact that the socialist speaker at the end of the novel appeals directly to "workingmen" (302–4); or that a garment workers' union leader claimed that Sinclair's "writings had tremendous impact on working people."[49] Consider also that, if Sinclair truly believed the Marxist theory that society was divided (or dividing) into capitalists and proletariat—that is, if he was not simply parroting this argument for rhetorical effect—then any presumed separation between Jurgis and the reader (whether middle or lower class) would be void. If so, we might regard Jurgis's initial feeling of separation from the hogs in the Durham meatpacking plant as a mirror for middle-class readers' reflexive desire to distance themselves from Jurgis and the proletariat. The novel ideally works to undermine that separation just as Jurgis's experiences undermine his feelings of separation from the hogs.

Whether or not Sinclair succeeded in writing simultaneously to a lower-class and a middle-class audience (the repeated criticisms he has received on this score suggest that he did not[50]—a fact we may take as an indication either of Sinclair's literary failings or of the inherent difficulty of such a task), there are other respects in which the novel more successfully erodes divisions between the classes. The most significant is through its figure of the shrinking man. The story of Jurgis unites the plot of decline—a script that Howard rightly identifies as peculiarly middle class and distinctly expressive of its fears—with a working-class hero. *The Jungle,* in fact, was unique among naturalist texts in its proletarian perspective; it has been called the first proletarian novel in the United States, and it inspired later socialist works in that genre.[51] More significant, depictions of Jurgis are fundamentally divided, shifting between an emphasis on his shrinkage and his inherent gigantic proportions. Jurgis is a "prisoned giant" (117) ready to "tear off his shackles, to rise up and fight" (212). He is compared to "Prometheus bound" (115), "the victim of ravenous vultures that had torn into his vitals and devoured him" (177). Descriptions of Jurgis as a giant bear an increasing resemblance to contemporaneous socialist graphics (see especially figs. 17 and 18), and in the socialist speaker's oration at the end of the novel we find the culminating expression of this image of "Labor" as "a mighty giant, lying prostrate—mountainous, colossal, but blinded, bound, and ignorant of his strength" (307). Thus Jurgis unites the middle class's figure of the Little Man—a person conceived as shrinking in relation to the giant figures of Labor and Capital—with the proletarian image of the shackled giant.

Sinclair's synthesis of the images of the Little Man and the Labor Giant suggests that he was hoping to negotiate class conflict in order to fashion broad consensus on socialist change. But by invoking major tropes of the trust debates, Sinclair was directing his arguments primarily to white male readers. As the historian Robyn Muncy has pointed out, the trust debate was "a race and gender specific issue," limited "almost exclusively [to] the community of white men."[52] Black men were relatively unaffected by the shift toward corporate capitalism and were more concerned with lynching, disenfranchisement, and discrimination of various kinds. White women were more preoccupied with securing the vote, achieving equal education, and breaking into the professions; if anything, the corporate revolution improved their condition, offering them new white-collar employment opportunities as secretaries and clerks. The interests of black women overlapped those of black men and white women both.[53] The images of the Little Man, the Labor Giant, and the shrinking man were all specifically images of white men,[54] and the attacks on big business, among which *The Jungle* takes its place, were in large part concerned with "the shape that white manhood should take in the twentieth-century United States," according to Muncy.[55]

Sinclair's attempts to dismantle class divisions were more specifically efforts to unify white men of the middle and lower classes— the major voting public whose support Sinclair counted on to usher in a socialist revolution through the ballot.[56] In addition to integrating key middle-class and lower-class symbolic systems in the figure of the shrinking giant, Sinclair copied the labor movement's emphasis on the family wage, a strategy that sought to expose industrial capitalism's threat to national values and to unify white men in the defense of hegemonic gender ideals.

Jurgis's degeneration has numerous dimensions, and the erosion of his domestic values is even more conspicuous than his physical shrinkage. The road to dissolution for Jurgis begins when conditions force him to abandon the view that "He would not have Ona working—he was not that sort of a man . . . and she was not that sort of a woman" (43). From there he readily assents to having the children work, and it is not long before conditions test his capacity for family affection altogether; Ona wonders "if he cared for her as much as ever, if all this misery was not wearing out his love" (122). Predictably, circumstances deteriorate further; Jurgis begins to beat Stanislovas when the boy refuses to leave for work, he takes to spending the family's income on alcohol, and on one occasion he even resorts to stealing money from the children to support his drinking habit. But worse than all of these things is Jurgis's impotence in the face of threats to Ona. His inability to protect her from the sexual advances of her boss and the "womb trouble" that besets her after Antanas's birth becomes the ultimate symbol of industrial capitalism's threat to masculinity. Conditions in Packingtown make male support (in all its senses) of a family impossible, and Sinclair repeatedly emphasizes that "no workingman ought to marry" (140). In a dark reversal of prevalent attitudes, *The Jungle* renders the principle of competitive individualism as an attack on the American family. "This was no world for women and children, and the sooner they got out of it the better for them. . . . [Jurgis] was going to think of himself, he was going to fight for himself" (212–13). The novel construes domesticity and industrial labor as fundamentally incompatible, which is another way of saying that the text exposes how dominant gender norms (particularly the ideals of the male breadwinner and female domesticity) exclude men and women of the lower classes and that industrial capitalism, as Sinclair describes it, is inherently pernicious to lower-class manhood and femininity.

As in *The Jungle,* where economic constraints prevent Jurgis from defending Ona, narrative tests of men's capacity to protect women are common in naturalism. Humphrey Van Weyden's successful defense of Maud Brewster in *The Sea Wolf,* for example, is crucial to his attainment of masculinity. "What of my new-found love, I was a giant. . . . I felt myself masculine, the protector of the weak, the fighting male," says Van Weyden.[57] Norris's *The Octopus* renders an implicit warning about the dangers of the destruction of manly independence through the fates of Mrs. Hooven and her daughter Minna: Mrs. Hooven starves to death on the streets of San Francisco, and Minna is forced into prostitution after the Pacific and Southwestern Railroad destroys Mr. Hooven. The menace of prostitution or white slavery, in fact, haunts all three texts as the price for masculine failure to protect women. Perhaps it should come as no surprise that the white slavery crusade, which reached a frenzied pitch by the time Sinclair published *The Jungle,* would subtly haunt the interstices of literature at the turn of the century.[58] If, in the words of one historian, "The campaigns against white slavery . . . were attempts to define the boundaries of the traditional social order [and] . . . to restore the old gender order: his sphere and especially hers,"[59] then the threat of white slavery in naturalist texts represented a corresponding effort to link the ideology of the separate spheres (i.e., male support of women through the family wage) with the sexual safety of women.[60]

Sinclair repeatedly hammers on the sexual dangers industrial labor creates for women. With her family dependent on the income from her job, and with her boss pressuring her into sex, Ona is forced to choose between prostitution and destitution. Like Ona, but without her self-loathing, Marija ultimately accepts prostitution as the only available means of sustaining her family after she loses her place in the meat-packing factories. Even the young Kotrina narrowly evades a rape on her way home from work one night. Scenes from the packers' union strike reveal in microcosm the industry's wholesale indifference to women's safety and compound white slavery anxieties with miscegenation and racial fears. When striking workers are replaced with scabs, the meat packers heedlessly house men and women together; the result, rendered in the extravagant language of Victorian melodrama, is "a saturnalia of debauchery—scenes as had never before been witnessed in America." On the streets one encounters the horror of "young white girls from the country rubbing elbows with big buck Negroes with daggers in their boots." Sleeping quarters are breeding grounds for "the nameless diseases of vice," passed from "the dregs from the brothels of Chicago" to "ignorant country Negroes" and thence distributed via the processed meat to "every corner of the civilized world" (274–75).

One can see in this episode how industrial capitalism's endangerment of workers poses a national risk, a threat to the "civilized world" that depends in part on capitalists' willful failure to protect white women and supervise black men. It is not simply, as the book also repeatedly emphasizes, that the workings of capitalism pervert the notions of freedom and jeopardize national ideals of democratic citizenship (Jurgis eagerly sells his vote for desperately needed money), honest labor (he flirts with crime to sustain himself), and national security (the novel raises the specter of violent revolution as a possible consequence of the nation's economic course). In the strike scene we see in exaggerated form how the meat packers knowingly create an island of savagery, a "jungle," within the heart of civilization—an island of degeneration that is literally infectious to the rest of the nation.

Throughout *The Jungle,* Sinclair depicts socialism as antithetical to industrial capitalism. Where capitalism thwarts American values and democracy, union membership offers Jurgis his only lessons in democracy and constitutes his first genuine steps toward Americanization. Joining the union inspires Jurgis to learn English, to attend night school, to take an interest in national issues; participation in the Socialist Party, an organization "controlled absolutely by its own membership" (314), acquaints Jurgis with an authentic democratic process. Where Packingtown destroyed Jurgis's family, socialism provides him with a surrogate family of "comrades and brothers" (310) who replace his original family as an incentive for sobriety and industry (323). And where the meatpacking industry decimated Jurgis's masculinity, the socialist speaker resuscitates it with visions of newfound freedom, power, and self-determination. "He knew that in the mighty upheaval that had taken place in his soul, a new man had been born," writes Sinclair. "The whole world had changed for him—he was free, he was free! . . . He would no longer be the sport of circumstances, he would be a man, with a will and a purpose. . . . He would dwell in the sight of justice, and walk arm in arm with power" (309).

Thus *The Jungle* attempts to unite white men across class lines in part by posing the protection and support of women and the containment of blacks as a fundamental (white) masculine and national need. While it holds out tantalizing visions of a restored democracy, a rehabilitated family (curiously minus women and children), and a revived (white) manhood as the reward for economic revolution, the novel is utterly silent on the subject of what socialism can do to end racism and almost equally mute on the subject of what it can do for women, except vaguely to imply that it will hasten female sexual sovereignty.[61] In many ways, then, Sinclair's narrative of the shrinking man does not argue explicitly with hegemonic codes of masculinity—particularly the white man's burden as a manager of dependent classes—so much as it reveals the exclusivity of those narratives. *The Jungle* calls for a reformation of capitalist society primarily in order to secure the good of progressive civilization for all white men, lower-class and middle-class alike.

Conclusion

As critics have suggested elsewhere, many narratives that defy dominant codes of masculinity nevertheless fail to offer a radical critique of
patriarchy and may, at times, even bolster it (or—which often amounts
to the same thing—undermine feminist ambitions).[62] I have suggested in
this chapter that *The Jungle* is no exception. By deliberately inverting
the dominant script of masculine growth, in fact, the novel works to
keep that ideal constantly in mind. Its program for social change, however radical in other arenas, is implicitly one that will restore masculinity to its rightful course—a goal, one suspects, that can only mean a
reconsolidation of patriarchal power.

There are other ways of reading the novel's discourse on masculinity, however. One reading in particular, which I find less compelling,
nevertheless has some value for the other arguments in this book.
Instead of attempting to refashion the world in a way that makes conventional masculinity accessible to more men, the novel may be refash-
ioning masculinity to make it compatible with a social movement perceived as irreconcilable with some of the conventional notions of
manhood. Socialism emphasizes cooperation and collectivity over competitive individualism. Earlier I pointed out that individualism was
tightly linked with masculinity in the Victorian era. This suggests that a
collective ethos might have been associated with femininity. While it is
difficult to say how widespread and consistent such an association
might have been (undoubtedly one could find many exceptions to the
rule), it is suggestive that the novel introduces socialism through a
female character, Grandmother Majauszkiene (66); that Jurgis's first
experience at a socialist meeting is crucially mediated by an unnamed
female character who calls him comrade and encourages him to listen to
the orator (300); and that Jurgis's conversion to socialism is described in
terms resembling a religious conversion in a novel in which religion is
explicitly associated with women ("Jurgis had always been a member of
the church, because it was the right thing to be, but the church had never
touched him, he left all that for the women. Here, however, was a new
religion" [90]).[63]

If it was necessary for Sinclair to redefine masculinity because of its
tight link with individualism, it may also have been necessary to recon-
struct masculinity because emphasizing men's lack of autonomy and
self-sufficiency, as the novel does in charting the fate of Jurgis, aligns
them with the weaker classes (e.g., women and children), creating a
paradox for a writer who wishes to represent the strength of socialism
and the potential (masculine) vitality of its adherents. (This tension

between the need to represent individual weakness and collective strength, incidentally, might explain equally well the simultaneous deployment of the shrinking man and Labor Giant figures.)

One can see this reformulation of masculinity at work in the episode describing Jurgis's reaction to initial attempts by the butcher helpers' union to enlist him. A representative from the union explains that some workers cannot keep up with the constant speeding up of production and the union is hoping to halt this practice. Jurgis rejects the argument (and union membership), believing that anyone who can't keep pace with the work deserves to be replaced. Yet, Sinclair tells us, like many "philosophers and plain men" who subscribe to the principles of laissez-faire, Malthusian economics, Jurgis is nonetheless committed to caring for his father, who has worked hard and honestly all his life yet cannot find work in Packingtown because he is perceived as too old. "There was a crack in the fine structure of Jurgis' faith," Sinclair explains (58)—a crack, intriguingly, that is exposed not by the need for the protection of women and children but by a hard-working, honest, sober man's ultimate need for support. Significantly, Jurgis flees Chicago and adopts an autonomous tramp's life immediately after his son dies—his son who looks like him and is named after his dead father. In other words, it is only after the symbolic deaths of Jurgis's youthful and aged selves (the parts of him that are dependent, that need support from others—the parts represented by his father and son) that he is able to wholly embrace autonomy. In this, male autonomy is shown not only to be harmful to women (Jurgis leaves Elzbieta, Marija, and the others to fend for themselves) but to repress the fact that men themselves are not permanently capable of it. The rest of the novel, of course, will hammer this point home even more forcefully by showing how Jurgis's independence is fragile and short-lived; he repeatedly needs the help of others to survive.

Thus, one could argue that Sinclair reconstructs masculinity in *The Jungle* in collective terms as a way of making masculinity compatible with socialism. The collectivity of socialism is depicted as an updated and expanded form of traditional masculine prerogatives: protection and support of the weak or defenseless (which can, at times, include men themselves). Sinclair's expanded, more inclusive conception of masculinity is in sync with the times; it is consistent with an age committed to growth and expansion in a host of domains. The masculine power that socialism restores to Jurgis ("he would be a man . . . and walk arm in arm with power" [309]) is a power that comes from joining something larger than the self.

In fact, collectivism is presented as the only recourse open to men in the modern world, a world governed by corporate plutocracy, political machines, and other big institutions. Jurgis faces appeals from a host of groups in the course of the narrative. First the beef trust promises to support him; despite its seeming permanence, solidity, and institutional power, it turns out to be untrustworthy, both as an institution and as a dependable piece of the social landscape. (Even if the packing corporations harbored any loyalty to their workers, Sinclair reminds us, antitrust laws, founded on principles of competition, require that they "try to ruin each other under penalty of fine and imprisonment" [41]. It should be pointed out that Sinclair is also attempting to persuade his readers that corporations are a form of collectivism in spite of the widespread belief, reflected in the Sherman Antitrust Act, that they preserve a competitive ethos. Sinclair seeks to dismantle the association between capitalism and individualism in order to make a collectivist masculinity compatible with both.)[64] Unions attempt to enlist him, but Jurgis learns that unions can be infiltrated and subverted by corporations. A crime syndicate and Scully's political machine sustain Jurgis temporarily until his second attack on Connor banishes him from those organizations. Socialism is the last of the institutions presented by the novel, and while it offers an alternative to the other forms of combination, it shares with them a foundation in collectivism. One of the socialist agitators makes this similarity clear when he explains that a "process of economic evolution" inevitably leads toward combination. Like animals competing in a Darwinian natural world, workers have "no choice but to unite or be exterminated" (326).

The novel does not leave us wondering, finally, whether Jurgis should join something big. Jurgis's attempts to evade groups larger than the family—or to deny that such groups he does join are forms of collectivity—repeatedly and dismally fail. On their own, the novel suggests, men are simply grist for the mill. The only pertinent question for Jurgis—and for readers of his story—is which large thing one is going to submit to. In the story of one individual who experiences a wide range of collectives, the novel illustrates the various dynamics by which the individual acquires power—and, in fact, survives—by abandoning the doomed effort in autonomy and becoming part of something bigger.

EPILOGUE • Shrinking Men and Growing Women (Reprise)

Fifty years after Upton Sinclair published *The Jungle,* America's culture of expansion was in full swing again. The U.S. economy experienced unparalleled growth. The nation's gross national product expanded by more than two times between the end of World War II and 1960, and per capita disposable income grew more than three times during the same period.[1]

The nation was now unapologetically corporate. Salaried white-collar workers outnumbered blue-collar workers for the first time in U.S. history.[2] Perhaps more telling is the fact that salaried and wage workers together outnumbered independent entrepreneurs by a factor of four to one.[3] According to observers at the time, the Jeffersonian-Wilsonian ideology of the Little Man with its attendant fears of bigness was finally and irrevocably dead. Independent entrepreneurs, wrote C. Wright Mills in 1951, were no longer "models of aspiration for the population at large."[4] College seniors, William Whyte observed in 1956, no longer aspired to own businesses of their own, preferring instead to work for big corporations.[5] In college students of the 1950s, Whyte found a significant measure of the changes that had transformed the nation in recent decades.

> Far more than their predecessors they understand bigness. My contemporaries, fearful of anonymity, used to talk of "being lost" in a big corporation. This did not prevent us from joining corporations, to be sure, but verbally, at least, it was fashionable to view the organization way with misgivings. Today this would show a want of sophistication. With many of the liberals who fifteen years ago helped stimulate the undergraduate distrust of bigness now busy writing tracts in praise of bigness, the ideological underpinnings for the debate have crumbled.[6]

Corporate ads during the fifties promised that "A Man Can Grow and Keep on Growing with Owens-Illinois Glass Co."; that "An Equitable Life Insurance Man is 'A Man on His Way Up'"; and that "The Sky Is Our World."[7] Corporate culture could now be painted as a vehicle for individual growth rather than an impediment to it.

After a twenty-year disaffection with the skyscraper brought on by depression and war (the Empire State Building, completed in 1931 and displacing the Woolworth Building as the world's tallest skyscraper, was ridiculed for years as the Empty State Building because it couldn't find commercial tenants), Americans rediscovered their passion for tall buildings, and skyscraper construction experienced a revival in the booming postwar economy.[8]

Like urban architecture, consumer products after the war relied on an aesthetic of size and power. Although home appliances like refrigerators, washers, and dryers tended equally toward the monumental,[9] the fifties' aesthetic reached its supreme expression in automobile designs. The expansive chassis, protuberant tail fins, and baroque chrome grilles of cars in the period required the internal support of V-8 engines and a new host of automotive innovations whose names were so expressive of the era's dominant aesthetic: power brakes, power steering, and power transmissions. The 1951 Kaiser-Frazer sedan was typical of the dilating cars of the fifties. In an expansive two-page ad with broad, modish text, Kaiser's marketers announced the company's latest design concept: "Anatomic Design," which meant "the principle of engineering the anatomy of the car, every feature of the body and chassis, to suit the needs of human anatomy" (see fig. 41). In their emphasis on size and power, automobiles and other consumer products of the fifties fashioned an image of Americans as physically large, offering a kind of biological

The newest car in America!

The 1951 Kaiser

Triumph of Anatomic Design ✳

One glance and you know it's the newest car in America!

One mile behind the wheel and you'll want to own it!

Built to Better the Best on the Road!

✳ *Anatomic Design*...(Ana-TOM-ic)...is the newest, most advanced step in motor car making. It is the principle of engineering the anatomy of the car, every feature of the body and chassis, to suit the needs of human anatomy in a way never before achieved. It results in a car that is easier to control, more comfortable, safer for you and your family to ride in.

Fig. 41. Kaiser-Frazer's 1951 Sedan. Kaiser-Frazer's anatomic design principle implied that the auto manufacturer had determined the correct specifications for the American anatomy. Like the immense car, the American body was enormous, powerful, and prosperous. (Reproduced from *Time,* May 22, 1950.)

corollary to America's newfound global power and authority following World War II.

Industrial engineers and consumer designers were hardly unique in touting an enlarged conception of the American body in the postwar period. In 1945, the physician Robert Latou Dickinson and the sculptor Abram Belskie, encouraged by the American Museum of Natural History, the YWCA, the Cleveland Health Museum, and other health and educational organizations, collaborated in the construction of models of the average American man and woman. Like their predecessors at the turn of the century, Dickinson and Belskie hoped to determine the national type through the methods of physical anthropology, and like their predecessors they relied on measurements of thousands of Americans gathered during war, on college campuses, and at world's fairs. After Dickinson and Belskie completed their models, officially dubbed Norm and Norma, scientists hastily exhumed Sargent's statues of Adam and Eve from the 1893 Chicago World's Fair for comparison. Although it seems unlikely that Norm and Norma were actually taller than Adam and Eve, this did not prevent Harry Shapiro, curator of physical anthropology at the American Museum of Natural History, from announcing, in phrases echoing turn-of-the-century scientists, that "the people of the United States . . . are undergoing [an] expansion in height" that represented the "progress . . . of the American type."[10] As with the turn of the century, however, this conceived progress was reserved for European Americans alone. Norm and Norma, as marble-white as Adam and Eve, were constructed from measurements taken exclusively from whites. Blacks and other minorities continued to be exempted from the progress embodied by the average American man and woman just as the politics of segregation (only reluctantly abandoned during the decade) continued to exclude them from full participation in American civil life.

Belief in the distinctive superiority of Euro-American stature was bolstered by popular racial theories about the nation's enemy, Japan, that circulated widely during World War II. Preoccupied with the reputed shortness of Japanese soldiers, the American press painted Japan as a nation suffering from excessive pride; the contrast between the presumed heights of Japan's and America's soldiers gave biological legitimacy to U.S. hopes for victory and helped create the conditions for a postwar aesthetic in which size functioned as a token of national character and international ascendancy.[11]

Fueled by the baby boom and advances in medicine, the nation's population grew from 150 to 180 million—a remarkable 20 percent increase—between 1950 and 1960, the biggest gain in a single decade in the nation's history.[12] As with the turn of the century, leisure establishments and public institutions expanded in scale to keep pace with the rapid population growth. Large public schools sprouted in the suburban enclaves to which middle-class white Americans migrated in droves. In 1945 there were eight shopping malls in the United States; by 1960 the nation boasted 3,834.[13] The 1950s witnessed both the opening of California's enormous Disneyland and the introduction of huge movie blockbusters on suddenly enlarged superscreens with evocative names like VistaVision and Cinerama.[14]

The cinematic innovations of the fifties were dramatic materializations of a more expansive vision that paralleled America's new global authority and reflected the expansionist ethic that was an integral component of the nation's cold war containment policies. To put this another way, U.S. foreign policy participated in and contributed to the same cultural impulse that one sees in a variety of domains in the fifties: the containment of communism within a limited sphere of influence was merely the inverse expression of a policy geared toward expanding the U.S. sphere of influence around the globe.[15]

But if these developments—the remarkable economic growth; the triumph of corporate culture; the revival of an indigenous urban architecture; the expansions in consumer products, population, and material culture; the reputed physical improvements in the nation's citizenry; and the elevation of the country to new heights of international power and prestige—were cause for celebration, they contained, as with social developments at the turn of the century, the seeds of anxiety.

Perhaps most pressing was the fact that the United States had been propelled to the position of international superpower by the invention of the atomic bomb. "The atomic age held out a double-edged sword to the American public," writes the film critic Cyndy Hendershot. "Atomic energy was portrayed as the force which could lead postwar society to a utopian existence, even as the atomic bomb threatened to plunge the world into a horrific dystopia." Because "postwar America inherited from Victorian social theory," she continues, "the Darwinian opposition between evolving and devolving," nuclear energy held out the divergent possibilities of dramatic social evolution and sudden and catastrophic devolution.[16] Containment, therefore, describes the nation's nuclear policy in the fifties as well as its foreign policy; the gigantic destructive power of the bomb and radiation's massive potential for environmental contamination would have to be carefully and rigorously contained in order to ensure that nuclear energy served the nation rather than destroyed it.[17]

If the prospect of total annihilation made average American men and women feel insignificant and helpless in the face of powers that they could not control and that did not discriminate on the individual level, the triumph of corporate culture only exacerbated this feeling. "On every hand," wrote C. Wright Mills in a passage reminiscent of Progressive-era declarations, "the individual is confronted with seemingly remote organizations; he feels dwarfed and helpless before the managerial cadres and their manipulated and manipulative minions."[18] Conformity became the catchword of the day; social critics worried (yet again) about the death of individualism in the faceless corporate culture that seemed to encourage blind obedience, and it did not help matters that the great masses of white-collar workers went home from their hivelike offices to the new homogeneous suburbs with their cookie-cutter homes. William Whyte described the United States in the middle of the twentieth century as an "organization society," and he spoke of the need for "individualism *within* organization life," of the "premise that individualism is as possible in our times as in others," as if his readers needed to be persuaded that such was the case.[19]

If such ruminations harked back to Progressive-era debates, so too did concerns about white-collar proletarianization. In his widely read treatise on the new middle classes, C. Wright Mills argued that salaried employees "have become increasingly subject to wage-worker conditions."[20] White-collar employees, he argued, were more and more affected by the boom-bust cycles of the economy, the threat of unemployment, the specter of technological death, and rationalization of the workplace.[21] They were alienated from the products of their labor, and, because their work increasingly demanded the interpersonal skills of people management and calculated self-presentation, they were alienated even from themselves.[22] Their incomes were drifting toward the wage-worker level, he added, the majority of white-collar workers entertained little hope of significant upward mobility and they were increasingly prone to organize themselves into unions.[23]

As with the turn of the twentieth century, rapid changes in American society at midcentury strained dominant gender ideologies. During World War II two hundred thousand women served in the military,[24] and of those who remained at home millions entered the paid labor force to replace men recruited to fight. This trend increased during the 1950s; by the end of the decade, 40 percent of women held jobs outside the home, compared to 25 percent in 1940.[25] During the same time, the percentage of working wives doubled,[26] a shift that coincided with a dramatic change in prevailing attitudes: in 1942 only 13 percent of Americans objected to wives working, down from 80 percent during the Depression.[27] By 1960 one in four women between the ages of eighteen and twenty-one was enrolled in college, up from one in ten in 1930 and one in thirty-five in 1900.[28]

Women's gains were seen by many as men's losses. In 1958 *Look* magazine published a series of articles titled "The Decline of the American Male" in which it pointed to economic and demographic data indicative of women's "domination" of men. Not only were women increasing in numbers in the paid labor force, the magazine fretted, but American women also owned the majority of stock in AT&T, DuPont, and General Electric; they controlled consumer expenditures; and female voters outnumbered male voters by more than 3 million.[29] The workplace was increasingly feminized as well, the editors of *Fortune* magazine argued a few years earlier, and men within it were increasingly feminized by the middle management imperative of submission to superiors, the fifties' emphasis on conformity in the office, and the workplace demands of personnel relations.[30] Submission in the office was paralleled by a new domestication of men in the home, social observers added. *Life* magazine declared 1954 the year of "the domestication of the American man," a time when men were spending more and more leisure hours in the home with their wives and children.[31] Such trends suggested to the editors of *Playboy* magazine in 1958 that the whole nation was suffering from "womanization" and American men in particular were undergoing an "emasculation."[32]

Concerns about threats to American masculinity were augmented by the apparent fragility of the male body. As with World War I, studies of

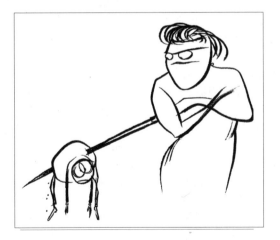

Fig. 42. Robert Osborn, "Untitled." Osborn's illustrations in *Look* magazine's special issue "The Decline of the American Male" featured gigantic menacing women and diminutive hapless men. (Reproduced from *Decline of the American Male* [1958].)

military recruits in World War II revealed a host of physical defects among American men.[33] Later, as veterans returned from the war, concerns about their lingering physical and emotional wounds were compounded by widely publicized evidence of the physical dangers to men posed by job stress, including high blood pressure, ulcers, depression, and heart disease.[34] The rapid changes in gender roles, the defensive reaction on the part of many outspoken men of the era, and concerns about the male body have suggested to at least one critic that the fifties, like the turn of the century, experienced a "masculinity crisis."[35]

Given the similarities between the postwar and Progressive eras, it should come as no surprise that the fifties witnessed its own spate of shrinking men and growing women.[36] None of these was more famous (or infamous) than Scott Carey in Jack Arnold's 1957 film *The Incredible Shrinking Man* and Nancy Archer in Nathan Juran's film of the following year, *Attack of the 50-Foot Woman*. In these remarkable cultural artifacts one can discern elements of all the era's preoccupations fused into the powerful metaphors of masculine shrinkage and feminine growth, and both films attest to the persistence of Progressive-era concerns well into the twentieth century.

The Incredible Shrinking Man opens in a scene of human isolation. Scott Carey (Grant Williams) and his wife, Louise Carey (Randy Stuart), are sunbathing on a boat in a vast expanse of unoccupied ocean. As the camera descends we witness the two having a lighthearted argument: he asks her to get him a beer, she tells him to get it himself, and they bicker until he finally agrees to make dinner in exchange for the favor. As Louise goes belowdecks to get Scott his beer ("To the galley, wench," he jokes before she descends), a mist appears on the horizon and approaches quickly, showering Scott with a glimmering dust. Inspired by the Bikini atoll nuclear tests of 1954 in which a Japanese fishing boat was blanketed with radioactive fallout,[37] the mist turns out to be far more noxious than the glitter it suspiciously resembles—it is, in fact, a radioactive cloud that, in part, triggers Scott's inexorable shrinkage. In addition to resonating with contemporary nuclear fears, the opening scene of the film foreshadows the isolation that will come to Scott later in the narrative and establishes gender conflict as a central concern of the movie.

Several scenes that take us quickly forward in time demonstrate that Scott is shrinking, and we soon learn that the cause is not simply radiation poisoning: the radioactive ash altered an insecticide to which Scott had also been exposed to create what doctors describe as a "degenerative process." The term proves prophetic—Scott's shrinkage will culminate in a primitivist adventure that will transform him into a latter-day savage in the heart of modern America—but the cause of his shrinkage is equally significant: the fact that Scott Carey's life will eventually be threatened by a spider because he has been exposed to a spray meant to kill such creatures is among the many ironies of this film.

Early scenes in the movie identify Scott Carey as a white-collar employee of an advertising firm owned by his brother. In many respects, Scott is an exaggeration of C. Wright Mills's "new little man." Mills argued in 1951 that "the new little people," the white-collar workers who made up the middle class, offered the key to understanding modern American society because they lived the "characteristic . . . twentieth-century existence."[38] The New Little Man, Mills contended, differed from the Little Man of nineteenth-century mythology in several important ways: he lacked independence; he yearned for upward mobility but typically failed to accomplish it (and in many respects, Mills intimated, his movement was downward); he was "pushed by forces beyond his control";[39] he harbored traditionally proletarian concerns, including fears of unemployment, technological death, and the problems of self-alienation; he led an isolated existence; and his success and failure at work depended on a "fetishism of appearance."[40] Like Mills's New Little Man, Scott Carey worked for someone else (even the boat he and Louise rode in the opening scene was provided by his brother) and eventually lost his job because of a degenerative condition over which he had no control—a condition that fundamentally altered his appearance, isolated him from others, and threatened him with an extravagant form of technological death. The novel by Richard Matheson upon which the film was based (*The Shrinking Man* of 1956; Matheson also wrote the screenplay for Arnold's film) puts even greater emphasis on Carey's quest for economic security and the ways in which his shrinkage undermines his ability to work with others in the office and causes him to feel alienated from himself.[41] If we view Carey's shrinkage as a science fiction dramatization of Mills's downwardly mobile New Little Man, then Scott's observation at the end of the film that he may be "the man of the future" makes a peculiar kind of sense.

While Carey's plight may literalize the experience of the American middle class as described by Mills in much the same way that turn-of-the-century narratives of shrinking men played on middle-class fears of downward mobility, his shrinkage, like Progressive-era stories of shrinking men, also represents a specifically masculine nightmare.[42] Despite the fact that women were entering the paid labor force in increasing numbers in the fifties, dominant masculine ideals continued to insist that men serve as family breadwinners. In Matheson's novel Scott repeatedly refuses to hear of Louise's working in spite of the mounting hospital bills, the loss of his job, and the rejection of his application for a GI loan, and he projects his own anxieties about making his family financially secure onto Louise, chiding her as a "security bug" more concerned about their finances than his health.[43] Similarly, the film is quite explicit about the ways in which Scott's diminution magnifies his demands for authority and provokes concerns about the reversal of conventional gender hierarchies. "Every day a little smaller. And every day I became more tyrannical, more monstrous in my domination of Louise," he confesses. Thus, the story belongs squarely in a tradition of narratives about shrinking men who lose their masculinity with their height. (The name Carey, coincidentally, may be an oblique reference to Dreiser's novel *Sister Carrie*, which bears several striking similarities to Matheson's story. It too recounts the tale of a shrinking man plagued by emasculation, financial worries, depression, and fears of dependence on his wife—a man ultimately separated from the wife [that is, Carrie] he had increasingly depended upon and faced with a harsh struggle for survival on his own.)

Like Hurstwood's experiences, Carey's shrinkage entails a growing social isolation, and one of the intentions of the film (and the book) is to ponder the meaning of personhood—the story will ask us to determine what it is about Carey that makes him a human being even at the size of an insect. Starting as a typical middle-class suburban white male—that proverbial figure of the fifties, the man in the gray flannel suit—Carey occupies an ever more marginal position. After he begins shrinking he loses his job, becomes estranged from his wife, applies for an unlisted phone number, and becomes a virtual prisoner of his home, hounded by the media and curiosity seekers. His isolation becomes complete when Louise accidentally lets the cat into the house and Scott, now the size of a mouse, is chased into the basement; imagining her husband has been eaten by the cat, the distraught Louise packs her things and moves out.

Midway through the movie, however—and midway along Scott's descent, when he is about the size of an average three-year-old—he wanders into a carnival freak show and forms a friendship with a circus performer and little person who helps him to overcome his feelings of self-loathing and to recognize his innate worth—a boost in self-esteem that lasts only as long as he remains taller than her.[44] The episode is significant not only for what it reveals about Scott's mental state. With its historical role as a vehicle for exploring the boundaries of humanity, and with its ties to racial constructions,[45] the freak show represents a key threshold in Scott's journey away from society and serves as the first indication of the film's underlying motif of racial degeneration. As with the pygmies at the turn of the century, a little person acts in the movie as a kind of gatekeeper to the realm beyond civilized life.

The motif of racial degeneration is developed more fully in the basement sequences. Here Scott's clothing increasingly resembles the primitive garb worn by "savages" in Hollywood films of the era, and Scott takes up residence in an empty matchbox with the label "Firechief" clearly visible on the outside (an inventive alteration of the original story, in which Carey finds a home on a cloth-wrapped sponge). Subtle references to the story of Robinson Crusoe also abound—as, for example, when Carey compares his existence in the cellar to that of a "desert island castaway"—and the book describes his hardships in the basement as a "jungle life."[46] For those inclined to view the basement sequence as a reaction against the domestication of American men and an attempt at recuperating masculinity in a modern bureaucratic age, it would be easy to point to similarities with turn-of-the-century notions of restored masculinity, which demanded similar brushes with savagery.[47]

Among such viewers is Margaret Tarratt, who, although she does not address issues of race, nevertheless regards Carey's adventures in the basement as a drama of recuperated masculinity. For Tarratt, the overriding theme of the film is "fear of castration by the female." In Tarratt's view the cellar represents Carey's subconscious, the spider he battles there is a symbol of femininity, the pin he uses to impale the monster is a recovered phallus in the grand Freudian tradition ("With these bits of metal, I was a man again," Carey says, hefting his pin-sword), and his defeat of the spider is a fantasy of freedom from female domination and a repudiation of castration anxieties.[48] Tania Modleski adds a further twist to this reading, pointing out that the pin Carey uses to destroy the feminine-associated spider comes from Louise's sewing kit. In this respect, Modleski argues, the movie belongs to a tradition of Hollywood films in which male characters appropriate femininity even as their narratives advance misogynist agendas.[49]

I have several reservations about this interpretation, but it is worth pointing out first that this reading of the film is compelling for a number of reasons. Certainly the spider is a feminine symbol—even more so in the book, where it is a black widow rather than a tarantula. "Black widow. Men called it that because the female destroyed and ate the male, if she got the chance, after the mating act," Matheson writes.[50] The hourglass shape on the belly of the black widow is, additionally, a clear sign of the female body—a shape that fifties' fashions for women, the restrictive boned girdles and "Merry Widows," notoriously exaggerated.[51] And the spider is indeed associated with Louise in many ways. In the book Louise will be a widow when Scott dies (an occurrence that he anticipates endlessly but that never arrives), and in the movie the "cake threaded with spider web" (a wonderful symbol of feminine guile) that Scott hopes will sustain him in the cellar was left by Louise while she was sewing. It is also significant that the basement is represented as a feminine space in the film. The first shot of the cellar is a scene of Louise altering a dress; when Scott falls into the basement he lands in Louise's sewing box; and Louise's sewing equipment—her pins and thread—are essential to his survival there.[52] Scott's desire for domination in this subterranean realm ("I resolve," he says, "that as man had dominated the world of the sun, so I would dominate my world") is a desire for a return to masculine dominance that has been subverted by his shrinkage.

One of my concerns about this interpretation, on the other hand, stems from reservations about interpreting narratives of shrinking men in Freudian terms. Such analyses reveal limitations in existing critical investigations of masculinity, which have focused almost exclusively on two aspects of the male body. Influenced by psychoanalytic theories and attuned to the relationships between identity formation, social power, and the body, many critics have devoted their attention to the male genitalia—the penis-as-phallus.[53] Others, interested in the explicit manufacturing of masculinity, have focused on muscularity and the built body.[54] Some critics have addressed both. Exclusive attention to these undeniably important subjects has meant that other key elements in the edifice of masculinity have been ignored, including stature.[55] Brief anecdotal remarks suggest that scholars are aware of the importance of height in dominant constructions of masculinity, but as yet the subject has received virtually no sustained attention.[56] When it has been addressed, the limitations of the critical focus become evident quickly. Peter Lehman's chapter on Fritz Lang's film *Scarlet Street* in *Running Scared,* for example, offers some important insights on the significance of stature in Hollywood cinema. Yet Lehman's discussion is subsumed within a book preoccupied with phallic symbolism and informed by psychoanalytic theory. Although he recognizes the limitations of his preferred analytical method, Lehman is inclined to read the discourse on height in *Scarlet Street* (and other texts such as Jim Thompson's 1953 novel *Savage Night*) as a metaphor for sexual anxieties.[57] Thus the movie "displace[s] its fears about male sexual adequacy to other sites of the body,"[58] namely stature. Tall and short male bodies in his analysis become synonyms for long and short penises and connote the presence or absence of phallic power. It is as if body height can only be understood theoretically in Freudian terms such as castration anxiety. In such an environment, a metaphor like bodily shrinkage is too often read in predictable ways; critics resist seeing it as specifically conveying anxieties about social positioning related to height prejudices.[59]

To ignore physical size and all it signifies is to ignore not only the discrimination that short people suffer in the United States and elsewhere but also a basic fact of embodied sexual difference: that men are, on average, taller and bigger than women. To regard the tall male body primarily as a phallic image is to suppress the fact that tall bodies themselves are symbols of power and dominance, a representational system that can be analyzed without recourse to theories of phallicism. Images of male shrinkage may represent castration anxieties or fears of sexual impotence, but I would insist that they are more than this and sometimes other than this. They may, for example, relate to fears of death, change, or bodily control, as Caroline Hunt suggests (see chap. 6). They may represent infantilization fears, degeneration anxieties, feminization phobias, or the dread of downward economic mobility. And they may represent specifically what they are: fears of being small, of being positioned at the bottom of a bodily hierarchy that is rarely acknowledged but nevertheless operative in diffuse social relations and constant mental practice. "Stature taps psychological conditioning felt by all and directly acknowledged by almost none," argue Martel and Biller in *Stature and Stigma*.[60] Yet, as they clearly demonstrate, stature is nevertheless a key component of dominant conceptions of masculinity.

While there are many compelling reasons to interpret *The Incredible Shrinking Man* as a fantasy of masculine redemption predicated upon a conquest and destruction of femininity, moreover, such readings ignore the self-conscious irony that pervades the film. The representation of the cellar as a feminine space is one minor example—in the fifties, cellars were typically constructed as male refuges.[61] (This is but one of many ironies in Carey's entrapment in the basement. Another stems from the fact that the U.S. government in the postwar period urged Americans to convert their basements into bomb shelters. It is clearly ironic that Carey, who has been contaminated by nuclear fallout, finds himself trapped in a place where Americans were urged to seek protection from radiation. Returning to the issue of the film's submerged theme of racial devolution, one might also point out the irony in the fact that Carey's suburban basement is a conspicuously black space. In addition to the fact that Carey undergoes a racial degeneration there, the scenes in the cellar emphasize darkness and shadow and Scott dwells repeatedly on the blackness of the spider. The blackness of the basement world is ironic in light of the fact that suburbia in the fifties was conspicuously white—blacks and other minorities were systematically excluded from the newly built suburbs.)[62] More significant, the creator of the story, Richard Matheson, was also clearly aware of the undercurrents of misogyny in the narrative and played on them self-consciously. In the novel, for example, Carey hitches a ride home when his car blows a tire and, at three and a half feet tall, he finds himself unable to change it. The man who picks him up turns out to be gay, despondent over the loss of a lover, and considerably drunk. Before attempting to molest Scott, the man fulminates on the evils of women and marriage in a tirade clearly depicted as ridiculous but with obvious relations to the main plot of the novel. A married man, exclaims the unnamed driver, is "a creature of degradation, a lackey, a serf, an automaton. A—in short—lost and shriveled soul." "Women," he belches, "come into man's life a breath from the sewer" and destroy him "as secretly, as effectively, . . . as *hideously*" as cancer. A man's first experience with a woman, he expounds, "is analogous to turning your first rock and finding your first bug"—a statement that anticipates Carey's battles with the spider in the basement.[63]

Elements such as these have suggested to the critic Mark Jancovich that Matheson's fiction examines male anxieties of the fifties without endorsing them. In fact, Jancovich argues, Matheson's fiction often challenges patriarchal ideologies.[64] For Jancovich, the spider in the filmed version of Matheson's story represents a displacement of and focus for Carey's anxieties about fulfilling masculine ideals rather than a symbol of monstrous femininity.[65] This interpretation helps to explain why Carey identifies with the spider in the film. "I no longer felt hatred for the spider," he says at one point. "Like myself, it struggled blindly for the means to live." His actions in the cellar, Scott adds later, are founded on "reflex, as instinctive as the spider's." And like the spider, Scott repeatedly clambers up and down thread in search of food, as a means of exploring his world and as a tool for snaring other creatures (his first unsuccessful attempt to destroy the spider involved lassoing it and hurling it over a wall).

In the final analysis, both positions have merit. *The Incredible Shrinking Man,* like the novel upon which it is based, attempts to have it both ways. Competing ideologies find equal expression in the narrative; the conservative reaction against men's domestication in the fifties and the nascent feminism of the sixties coexist in uneasy tension and vie for dominance in the story.

The Incredible Shrinking Man ends soon after Scott destroys the spider. Having triumphed in his battle for the morsel of food, Carey discovers to his surprise that he no longer feels hunger. He ascends a dirt slope and, thanks to his continued diminution, slips through a mesh screen that had previously imprisoned him in the basement. Carey's physical liberation coincides with his mental emancipation. Previously his shrinking had inspired him with dread and stripped him of his feelings of self-worth as it deprived him of authority and power. As he steps out into the grass and leaves of his yard, the camera rises above him and then suddenly reverses its perspective to contemplate the night sky as Scott expresses his epiphany that, at any size, he still has significance in God's plan. "My fears melted away," he says to the ringing of church bells. "And in their place came acceptance. All this vast majesty of creation—it had to mean something. And then I meant something, too. Yes, smaller than the smallest, I meant something too. To God there is no zero. I still exist." In a reversal of the descending shot in the opening scene of the movie, the camera's perspective grows ever more expansive: first we look with Scott at the stars in the night sky, and then entire solar systems and galaxies unfold beneath our gaze until the universe itself (presumably) shines before us. In its final moments, then, the movie shares with turn-of-the-century texts an impulse toward visual transcendence that serves as an anodyne for the traumas of modernization. But as with everything in this film, the ending is laced with irony. The final image of the universe bears a striking resemblance to an atomic mushroom cloud. Whatever accommodation Scott makes to his condition—and whatever accommodation the movie's final sublime gesture offers for the travails of modernization—viewers are left with no sure grounds for faith in the dogma of millenialist progress in an atomic age.

If the nation still struggled to reconcile itself to a diminished masculinity in the middle of the twentieth century, it remained equally ambivalent about an enlarged and empowered femininity. Like *The Incredible Shrinking Man, Attack of the 50-Foot Woman* opens with an evocation of gender conflict. Nancy Archer's gold-digging husband, Harry (played by William Hudson), explains to his mistress, Honey Parker (Yvette Vickers), in the tavern that serves as their less-than-discreet love nest that he has remained married to his millionaire wife only because divorce laws prevent men from gaining alimony. "The community property routine only works for women," he laments. "A man hasn't got a chance." The movie cuts to a scene of Nancy (Allison Hayes) speeding home through the desert, where her flight is interrupted by the appearance of an alien satellite. Terrified, Archer returns to town and informs the gathered citizens that an alien spaceship has landed. She is hastily escorted back to the interstellar scene by the town's incredulous and condescending sheriff, who assumes she is drunk but plays along with her because she supplies the bulk of the county's taxes.

When Harry and Honey hear of Nancy's UFO sighting, they scheme to commit her to a sanitarium, where she has served time in the past as the result of a short-lived separation from Harry. Their marriage, we soon learn, has been doomed from the start; Nancy has stood by her philandering husband only because she can't force herself to leave him. Harry and Honey greedily look forward to enjoying Nancy's wealth without the messy entanglements of a marriage, and Nancy plays right into their hands when she continues to insist that the UFO is real and demands that Harry accompany her into the desert in search of it. To Harry's surprise and alarm, however, they find it. But, as far as Harry is concerned, an abduction of Nancy by aliens works just as well as a commitment to a sanitarium, if not better. After firing a few halfhearted shots at the alien with Nancy's revolver, Harry leaps into the car and roars off into the night, leaving Nancy in the gigantic clutches of the visitor from space.

Before Harry and Honey can escape from town, however, the sheriff's deputy arrives and escorts them back to his office; Nancy's disappearance has been reported by her paternalistically protective butler, Jess, and Harry is wanted for questioning. Meanwhile, Nancy turns up unconscious on the roof of her bathhouse with some scratches on her neck that turn out to be contaminated with radiation. Archer is returned to her home and sedated by her psychiatrist, and that's the last we hear from her for a while. Outside Nancy's mansion, the sheriff and his deputy diligently search the grounds and are rewarded by the discovery of a giant footprint. "Whatever it is, it wasn't made by a Japanese gardener," they deduce. Tracks from the alien lead the sheriff and Jess into the desert (the bumbling deputy is consigned to a desk job back at the station), where they find the spaceship and uncover the reason for the alien's interest in Nancy: it needs the enormous diamond she has been toting around to power its ship. But the alien discovers them, too, and after a brief, lopsided firefight in which the bald, transparent giant vents his frustrations on their unoffending car, they hoof it back to town.

In the meantime, Archer has grown to gargantuan proportions as a result of her radiation exposure, and her doctor orders elephant-sized restraints and enough morphine to put half of San Diego to sleep. Harry, who had entertained notions of overdosing Nancy with sedatives, admits defeat and retreats to the arms of Honey and a bottle in the place Nancy is most likely to come looking for him—the saloon. And there, indeed, she does find him. After the sedative wears off, Nancy escapes the chains and meat hooks keeping her in her place and lumbers over to the town, where she proceeds to tear the roof off the tavern (she is practiced at this maneuver, having already torn the roof off her own home), conveniently killing Honey in the process. In a scene that visually reverses King Kong's abduction of Fay Wray, the giant Nancy plucks her errant husband out of the wreckage of the bar. Ignoring all pleas to put Harry down, she strides off with him, at which point the sheriff fires his shotgun at her and somehow manages to hit the intervening power lines instead of the barn-sized Nancy. Nancy goes down in a pyrotechnic shower, and she and Harry die together. "She finally got Harry all to herself," Nancy's psychiatrist deadpans over her Amazonian corpse.

As with *The Incredible Shrinking Man,* critical appraisals of the movie have emphasized the contradictory elements of its gender politics. And justifiably so—in many respects the film seems uncertain about its position on the contemporary plight of women. On one hand, the movie is a forceful indictment of women's double bind in the fifties. As numerous historians have pointed out, the pressures to marry were intense for women at the time, a fact that helps to explain why Nancy remains in a marriage from which she clearly suffers.[66] Five years after the film's debut Betty Friedan would initiate the contemporary women's movement with her examination of the domestic mystique that pushed women into marriage, pulled them out of higher education, encouraged them to have children, and kept them tied to the home in unprecedented numbers during the fifties.[67] More recently the historian Elaine Tyler May has argued that the nation's foreign policy objectives during the early years of the cold war—the containment of communism—found a counterpart in an ideology of "domestic containment" that encouraged Americans in the fifties to seek personal fulfillment and security through domesticity, often at significant costs to their personal happiness.[68] What better symbol of the domestic trap and the containment of women than the image of Archer chained in her home and sedated with elephant-sized syringes of morphine? Consistently throughout the movie, moreover, Nancy is victimized by men and patriarchal authorities: her husband cheats on her; her psychiatrist urges her to stay in a marriage that is clearly abusive and has a ready hand with sedatives and the keys to the local mental institute; her butler, Jess, is complicit with the doctor; a television news anchor ridicules her; and the police condescend to her, deliberately keep her ignorant of Harry's philandering, and finally kill her. It is clearly significant that Nancy's first acts after growing to gargantuan proportions are to tear the roof off her house and experimentally shake the town's power lines. What better way to express female liberation than to represent Nancy's growth—a metaphor for feminine empowerment during the fifties just as it was at the turn of the century— as inimical to domesticity and an agent of disruption in conventional power lines?

One need not, moreover, view the alien invasion plot as a pointless diversion from the movie's primary theme of female liberation, as some

critics have been inclined to do, since the alien is clearly a materializa-
tion (and a magnified one at that) of Nancy's fears about her husband.[69]
Like Harry, the alien is after her wealth (at various points in the film
both Harry and the alien take possession of Nancy's Star of India diamond), and, like her relationship with Harry, Nancy escapes the alien
once only to return and be wounded by him.

But if elements of the film suggest that it is a "proto-feminist fantasy" of female liberation (to borrow the apt words of one recent critic),[70]
Nancy's defeat at the hands of the sheriff in the end of the movie—a
clear reassertion of patriarchal authority—implies the reverse: namely,
that her growth represents a monstrous femininity and her attack on
Harry and the town a frightful nightmare of unleashed feminine
vengeance that calls for violent suppression. Viewed in this light,
Nancy's last name (Archer) and the repeated associations between
Nancy and the moon (the deputy sheriff says Nancy drives "like she was
headed for the moon" and the TV reporter jokes that Nancy has seen the
proverbial "man in the moon") suggest that Nancy is a modern Artemis,
the goddess of hunting and the moon who is perhaps best known for
wreaking terrible vengeance on men—typically with less provocation
than Nancy and for reasons that seem, by today's standards at least,
capricious and irrational. Undeniably, the ending of the film posits feminine retribution as destructive to self and society, and consistently
throughout the movie Archer's actions are portrayed as hysterical and
impulsive (even if understandable in light of the condescension she suffers). Moreover, the camp qualities of the film, as several critics have
pointed out, undoubtedly have the effect of sapping the movie's more
serious feminist implications.[71]

Still, none of these things completely dissipates the film's more radical gestures, and we might justifiably conclude, as Jackie Byars does in
her recent essay on Hollywood cinema of the fifties, that *Attack of the
50-Foot Woman* expresses the "preemergent ideologies" of sixties' feminism even as the conclusion of the film, in typical fifties' fashion, finds
dominant ideologies ultimately prevailing against nascent oppositional
ones.[72] Like *The Incredible Shrinking Man,* in other words, *Attack of the
50-Foot Woman* contains the fault lines of contradictory impulses and
anticipates the social revolutions of the coming decade even as it
expresses obvious panic over its own prognostications. But more important for my purposes here, *Attack of the 50-Foot Woman* harbors patent
affinities with turn-of-the-century texts, most clearly in its ambivalence
about the feminine growth that it simultaneously portrays as a peculiar
consequence of modernity.[73]

The manifestations of America's culture of expansion in the fifties, and the responses to it, in other words, bear striking similarities to the same phenomena at the turn of the century. The notion of the Progressive American body that was forged in the late nineteenth century and that displaced the prior image of the degenerating American body remained intact well into the middle of the twentieth century—and, I would argue, into our own turn of the century. Nevertheless, the social and cultural forces surrounding and inflecting this body changed in significant ways.

The Incredible Shrinking Man and *Attack of the 50-Foot Woman* illustrate, for example, how containment anxieties were integrated into the bodily paradigm. Both films are nightmares of containment failure: Scott Carey's shrinkage occurs as the price of the failure to contain nuclear energy, and Nancy Archer's growth is an imagined outcome of the failure to contain women within traditional domestic arrangements. Thus, like their turn-of-the-century predecessors, the films explore gender hierarchies and changing gender roles through the symbolic medium of physical size; in the process they demonstrate a clear link between notions of gender and the size of the body. Unlike the Progressive era, however, gender hierarchies are not threatened by women's explicit demands in these films or in the decade as a whole. In characteristic cold war fashion, internal national tensions are projected outward onto real and imagined external enemies: aliens and errant radioactive clouds.

Like many of the Progressive-era texts examined in this book, Matheson's story is concerned with the fate of the Little Man and the associated, privileged American ideology of entrepreneurial capitalism. While observers at the turn of the century warned that the growth of corporations and the consolidation of industry threatened to crush the Little Man, Americans in the fifties were concerned with the New Little Man's adaptation to corporate culture. This might help to explain why corporations were no longer typically rendered in bodily images of giants ready to squeeze or stomp on the little guys. The corporation was now described in more abstract terms—as "the organization," for example—and the New Little Man no longer sought spectacular growth but, instead, sought to remain comfortably contained within familiar corporate structures. Thus, Scott Carey's shrinkage alienates him from the economic realm and undermines his ability to conform; it is not a consequence of his position among rising giants.

In characteristic fashion, the preoccupation with the fate of the Little Man leads to a contemplation of the effects of modernization for cherished American values like individualism, and here too the metaphor of physical size plays a key role in the imaginative exploration of the subject. Consumer products in the fifties, like corporate culture, suggested that individuals on a mass level could share in (or possess shares in) the cult of size; bigness could be possessed rather than merely worshiped or feared from below. The visual transcendence that was held out as an anodyne to modernization at the turn of the century was a sincere effort to endow individuals with a capacity equal to the expansive vision of the corporation. By the fifties, this fantasy could only be rendered ironically. In the age of an "organization society," a society fully steeped in corporate culture, transcendence seemed as likely as a revival of the bygone Jeffersonian-Wilsonian economy.

Finally, both films clearly harbor an interest in the relationship between social change and the body. Like the Progressive-era texts discussed earlier in this work, they contemplate the possibility that social evolution, the progress or decay of a civilization, might find expression in the bodies of a nation's citizens, and in this inquiry stature serves alternately as a code for race (as in *The Incredible Shrinking Man*) or as a component of race (as in turn-of-the-century texts). As biological determinism had lost much of its vogue following the Nazi atrocities of World War II, however, social changes were no longer seen as inextricably linked to biological changes, and the turn-of-the-century preoccupation with biological progress was replaced by a midcentury preoccupation with technological progress. Thus, Scott Carey's and Nancy Archer's bodies react to technological forces rather than racial-biological ones. At a time when Americans were more confident of their international prestige and power and thus less haunted by the racial degeneration fears of the turn of the century, and at a time when technological developments (particularly the atomic bomb) threatened and dwarfed individuals rather than enhanced their power (as turn-of-the-century inventions like the airplane, telephone, and automobile did), the myth of racial degeneration was replaced by a myth of nuclear extinction, and so it makes more sense, perhaps, to say that *The Incredible Shrinking Man* uses its audience's familiarity with the racial degeneration myth to elucidate the nuclear extinction myth. If size still played a role in the American self-image and in racial theories (exemplified by popular discourse on Japanese soldiers), the notion of growing and shrinking characters was now relegated principally to the pages of science fiction and imaginative children's literature and was treated humorously rather than seriously. Nevertheless, it remains significant that for midcentury Americans—and, arguably, for Americans today as well—smallness continued to signify degeneration and bigness represented a conflicted kind of progress.

Notes

INTRODUCTION

1. Brandeis, *Other People's Money,* 193.
2. I do not mean to be capricious here. Most historians regard the 1890s to 1917, roughly, as the Progressive era. I have designated the larger period the Progressive era because these are the years that saw the formation of the idea of the Progressive body.
3. Based on data from the U.S. Census Bureau.
4. Cremin, *American Education.*
5. Data acquired from the U.S. Census Bureau.
6. I have borrowed the term *island communities* from Wiebe, *Search for Order,* xiii.
7. See Hietala, *Manifest Design;* Onuf, *Jefferson's Empire;* Boorstin, *Americans: National Experience;* and Fisher, "Democratic Social Space."
8. It was also uncertain whether the western territories acquired during the nineteenth century would remain part of the Union. See Onuf, *Jefferson's Empire;* Hietala, *Manifest Design;* and Boorstin, *Americans: National Experience.* On the subject of the Revolutionary War and predictions about the future of the states, see Boorstin, *Americans: National Experience,* 404–6.
9. See Onuf, *Jefferson's Empire;* Owsley and Smith, *Filibusters and Expansionists;* Hietala, *Manifest Design;* and Boorstin, *Americans: National Experience.*
10. See Onuf, *Jefferson's Empire;* Owsley and Smith, *Filibusters and Expansionists;* Stephanson, *Manifest Destiny;* and Hietala, *Manifest Design.*
11. Boorstin, *Americans: National Experience,* 272.
12. Thanks to Bill Brown, who helped me articulate this idea.
13. Leuchtenburg, *Franklin D. Roosevelt,* 29.
14. Lippmann, *Drift and Mastery,* 211.
15. Starrett, *Skyscrapers,* 74.
16. Lloyd, *Wealth,* 2, 520.
17. Poole, *Harbor,* 88.
18. See Lutz, *American Nervousness;* Conn, *Divided Mind;* Harris, *Land of Contrasts;* Trachtenberg, *Incorporation of America;* and Banta, *Imaging American Women.*
19. This concise summary of Foucault's notion of discourse is taken from Bederman, *Manliness and Civilization,* 24. Note that in this book I also use the term *discourse* in its more conventional sense as the formal corpus of written material addressing a particular subject.
20. Fatness had quite different connotations beginning in this period.

See chapter 3 for a further discussion of the contradictory attitudes toward weight and height in the Progressive era.

21. See, for example, Burg, "Aesthetics of Bigness"; Van Leeuwen, *Skyward Trend;* Adams and Brock, *Bigness Complex;* Fine, "Goliath Effect"; and Chandler, *Scale and Scope.*

22. Wiebe, *Search for Order,* xiii.

23. Ibid., 40–43.

24. For further discussion, see Hacking, *Taming of Chance;* Seltzer, *Bodies and Machines* (particularly the chapter "Statistical Persons"); Poovey, *History of the Modern Fact;* Boorstin, *Americans: Democratic Experience* (particularly the chapter "Statistical Communities"); and chapter 2 of this book.

25. A striking example of the conscious embrace of the quantitative ethic can be found in an 1889 speech delivered by Francis A. Walker. Walker argues that bigness and growth are central to American national identity, that early Americans were reluctant to acknowledge this, and that "quantity has, with us, . . . determined and helped to constitute quality" ("Growth of the Nation," 195). Perhaps most important, he formulates his version of the quantitative ethic as a deliberate repudiation of an earlier transcendental ethic that regarded the celebration of bigness as crass, immoral philistinism.

26. There have been some excellent attempts to understand attitudes toward the body in the Progressive era, but as of yet little attention has been devoted specifically to height. Schwartz's *Never Satisfied,* Stearns's *Fat History,* and Bordo's "Reading the Slender Body" (in *Unbearable Weight*) all address the subject of weight. Gould's *Mismeasure of Man,* Terry and Urla's *Deviant Bodies,* Thomson's *Extraordinary Bodies* and *Freakery,* Wiegman's *American Anatomies,* and Fiedler's *Freaks* address race and various bodies constructed as deviant. Boscagli's *Eye on the Flesh,* Segel's *Body Ascendant,* Budd's *Sculpture Machine,* Kimmel's *Manhood in America,* Pleck and Pleck's *American Man,* Studlar's *This Mad Masquerade,* Dutton's *Perfectible Body,* and, to a more limited extent, Rotundo's *American Manhood* and Klein's *Little Big Men* all address the physical culture movement at the turn of the century. Armstrong's *Modernism* and Seltzer's *Bodies and Machines* examine the relationship between ideas about the body and technology at the turn of the twentieth century. A number of books addressing the general history of the body encompass the late nineteenth and early twentieth centuries; although a complete listing would be impossible here, some examples include Foucault's *Discipline and Punish,* Gallagher and Laqueur's *Making of the Modern Body,* Turner's *Body and Society,* and Laqueur's *Making Sex.*

27. For evidence of hiring and wage discrimination, see Loh, "Economic Effects"; Martel and Biller, *Stature and Stigma;* and Feldman, "Presentation of Shortness." For a discussion of the discrimination faced by little people, see Ablon, *Little People.* Ablon refers to others who examine discriminatory American voting practices. On the debate surrounding the use of growth hormone, see Que and Prakash, "Human Growth Hormone"; Barnard, "Concerns"; and Cronin, "It's a Tall."

According to statistics published in *Glamour* magazine and based on the research of consumer marketers for health and cosmetic companies, the height of the average American woman is 5′4″ and the height that the average woman *wishes* she were is 5'6" (Stanton, "Looking"). Similarly, sociology studies have indicated that the ideal height for men in this country is 6'2", well above the average (Martel and Biller, *Stature and Stigma,* 6).

It should be noted that height for women is somewhat more complex than my generalization suggests. Adolescent girls face problems if they are too short or too tall (see Phifer, *Growing Up Small*). The stigma against tallness presumably relates to the social expectation that women should be smaller than men, a phenomenon that one writer has labeled "sexual heightism" and that demonstrates the connection between sexism and stature prejudices (Gillis, *Too Tall*). Evidence from the medical literature confirms that tallness is a greater problem among girls and shortness among boys. Hormone therapy for increased growth is most often sought by parents of boys, whereas height reduction treatment is far more common among girls (Gillis, *Too Tall,* 90; and Gertner, "Short Stature").

28. See the texts referred to in note 27; Gilmore, *Manhood,* 86–88; and Smith, "Risking."

29. There have been some previous efforts in this direction, other than those cited previously, that deserve mention. In the field of cultural studies, two works in particular stand out. Fiedler's *Freaks* offers a cultural history of attitudes toward dwarfs and giants, and Bradford and Blume's *Ota* is a biography and cultural history of the life of Ota Benga, a pygmy who participated in the St. Louis World's Fair of 1904. A number of works have addressed themes of miniaturization and gigantification in literature and elsewhere, including Stewart's *On Longing,* Rugoff and Stewart's *At the Threshold,* Bachelard's *Poetics of Space,* Hunt's "Dwarf, Small World," Pace's "Body-in-Writing," Armstrong's "Gender," and Millhauser's "Fascination." A number of feminist and feminist-inspired texts have taken tentative steps in the direction of analyzing the relationship between size (exclusive of weight, which has received significantly more attention) and gender ideologies, including Brownmiller's *Femininity,* Modleski's *Feminism,* Armstrong's "Gender" and "'Here Little,'" Henley's *Body Politics,* Ostriker's *Stealing,* Moers's *Literary Women,* Goffman's *Gender Advertisements,* Lowe's "Dialectic," Bartky's "Foucault," Klein's *Little Big Men,* Banner's *American Beauty,* Banta's *Imaging American Women,* Marks's *Bicycles,* Meyer's "Rock Hudson's Body," and Dyer's "Don't Look Now." Finally, Lakoff attempts to explain the origins of our linguistic schema surrounding height and metaphors of verticality (*Metaphors*), and Tanner offers an important medical history of the study of human growth (*History*).

30. Foucault, *Discipline and Punish,* 24.

31. See Foucault, *Discipline and Punish* and *History of Sexuality,* vol. 1; Thomson, *Extraordinary Bodies;* Gallagher and Laqueur, *Making of the Modern Body;* Wiegman, *American Anatomies;* Turner, *Body and Society;* Terry and Urla, *Deviant Bodies;* and Bartky, "Foucault."

32. Gallagher and Laqueur, *Making of the Modern Body,* vii.

33. Several recent theorists have criticized social-constructionist approaches to the body on these grounds. See Turner, *Body and Society,* and Turner's introduction to Falk's *Consuming Society;* Williams and Bendelow, *Lived Body;* Ussher, *Body Talk;* and Grosz, *Volatile Bodies.*

34. This has been effectively demonstrated by the work of Mark Johnson and George Lakoff.

35. Bordo, *Unbearable Weight,* 35.

36. For further discussion of the role of visuality in science, see Terry and Urla, "Mapping Embodied Deviance," in *Deviant Bodies;* and Thomson, *Extraordinary Bodies,* chap. 1. For further discussion of the subject of vision in modern and postmodern culture generally, see Robyn Wiegman, *American Anatomies,* 2–4, and her bibliographic reference to major texts in the field (including Levin, *Modernity and the Hegemony of Vision;* Foster, *Vision and Visuality;* Berger, *Ways of Seeing;* Ellis, *Visible Fictions,* and others).

37. Brownmiller, *Femininity,* 28, 30.

38. One of the implications of Brownmiller's argument is that prejudices against short stature derive at least in part from prejudices against women, making an understanding of the gendered connotations of size even more crucial.

CHAPTER 1

1. I have placed the term *pygmies* in the title in quotation marks because I have reservations about the label. Many names exist for the people of the Congo commonly known today in the United States as pygmies. The name *pygmy* probably originated in ancient Greece, if not earlier; the *Iliad* refers to small "Pygmaian men," as does Aristotle. Herodotus also describes a group of small Africans assumed by nineteenth-century authorities to be the pygmies. The designation *pygmy* was first applied to several African groups, including the Akkas, the Batwa, the Obongos, and the Wambutti, and then later to peoples around the world who resembled them, like some Filipinos and Andaman Islanders, by American and European travelers and ethnologists who sought to classify the races of the world into manageable groups and to connect communities of small Africans to the ancient Greek authorities, thus demonstrating the historical permanence of the groups and the value of the racial classification. The term *pygmy* was also more widely known in the United States and Europe than names like Obongo and Akka, and authors often used the popular name in the titles of their works to ensure reader recognition and high sales. Before the term assumed importance in racial classification in the late 1880s, writers such as Paul Belloni Du Chaillu and Henry Stanley used the term *dwarf* more frequently. Ethnologists and anthropologists, on the other hand, favored academic labels like Negrito and Negrillo to wrest the discussion from the general public and to secure the authority of their disciplines over the matter of racial designation. Louis Sarno, author of the recent *Songs from the Forest,* says that "several major groups of Pygmies live in Central Africa. In the eastern Congo Basin in Zaire there are the Mbuti and the Twa. In the western Congo Basin, the Aka live. . . . The Baka live west of the Sangha, and the Bongo live . . . in Gabon. Within each group there are smaller clan divisions. The Ba-Benjellé are the westernmost clan of the Aka" (viii). It seems unlikely that any Africans refer to themselves as pygmies. While I do not wish to continue a tradition of imposing a name on people who have not chosen it for themselves, I have decided nevertheless to use the term *pygmy* in this book because I am dealing primarily with *representations* of Africans by Americans and Europeans, and that is the name by which small people of the Congo were and are commonly known in the United States and Europe.

2. Keane, *Man,* 7.

3. Evidence of Du Chaillu's influence can be seen, among other places, in Max Liniger-Goumaz's three-hundred-page 1968 bibliographic guide, *Pygmies and Other Short-Sized Races.*

4. Du Chaillu, *Explorations,* 378–79.

5. Evidence of the popular reaction to his work can be found in the bowdlerized, dime novel version of Du Chaillu's combined journeys, *Recent Remarkable Discoveries in Central Africa, by the Celebrated African Explorer M. De Challue* [sic], *with a Full Description of an Extraordinary Race of People, Supposed to Be the Connecting Link Between the Animal and the Human* (1867).

6. Du Chaillu, *Journey,* 315–16.

7. The episode with the pygmies also took on greater emphasis in the 1890 reprint of Du Chaillu's combined travel narratives, titled *Adventures in the Great Forest of Equatorial Africa and the Country of the Dwarfs.* In addition to the title that capitalized on the growing scientific attention to the pygmies, the nine pages from *A Journey to Ashango-Land* devoted to the Obongos formed an independent chapter.

8. It would always be the case that explanations were sought for observed differences in height among groups of people. Even differences of as little as an inch or two that could easily have been caused by sampling or measuring discrepancies or random variation received painstaking explanations that were more revealing of contemporary ideologies than of any objective "truth." At the turn of the century, height was a sign of many things, but inconsequential diversity was not one of them.

9. Du Chaillu, *Journey,* 320.

10. Du Chaillu, *Country,* 260. The possibility that such degeneration could occur was a source of anxiety among Americans and Europeans both, and it contributed to enthusiasm for the eugenics movement. In Britain, anxiety about degeneration led to the formation of the British interdepartmental committee on physical deterioration, which was especially active between 1904 and 1906, shortly after the Boer War. In the United States this same anxiety led to the formation of the Eugenics Record Office headed by Charles Davenport, whose duty it was, among other things, to track and interpret national data on stature. For a discussion of the role of height as a continuing sign of eugenic fitness and superiority in the middle of the twentieth century, see Cogdell, "Futurama Recontextualized."

11. Burrows, *Land of the Pygmies,* 173.

12. Cited in Bradford and Blume, *Ota,* 263.

13. Du Chaillu, *Country,* 258.

14. Stepan, *Idea of Race,* 86.

15. Du Chaillu, *Country,* 273.

16. See Fiedler, *Freaks.*

17. See Pearson and Lee, "Relative Variation."

18. Reed, *Negritos,* 13.

19. See, for example, Vanden Bergh, *On the Trail of the Pigmies,* who apologizes that "The title of this book is more or less misleading" (xiii).

20. See Vanden Bergh, *On the Trail,* 220.

21. Schweinfurth of Germany preceded Stanley, but he was less influential in the United States and England.

22. Stanley, *In Darkest Africa,* 1:352–53.

23. Stanley, "Pigmies," 3–4.

24. See Stanley, *In Darkest Africa,* 2:40.

25. Stanley, "Pigmies," 4.

26. Stanley, *Autobiography,* 367.

27. Seltzer, *Bodies and Machines,* 149–50.

28. Gates, "TV's Black World," 658.

29. Haller, *Outcasts,* 210.

30. Vanden Bergh, *On the Trail,* 238, 260.

31. Reed, *Negritos,* 33, 36.

32. Wollaston, *Pygmies,* 156–57.

33. Vanden Bergh, *On the Trail,* 237.

34. Ibid., 238–39.

35. For a further discussion of the synthesis of monogenism and polygenism, see Stepan, *Idea of Race.*

36. Stanley, *Autobiography,* 365, 367.

37. Vanden Bergh, *On the Trail,* preface.

38. Ibid., vi.

39. See Haller, *Outcasts,* 16–17.

40. As Stephen Jay Gould has pointed out, "the primary determinant of brain size is not mental capacity, but body size." Larger bodies, in other words, have larger brains (although the relationship between body size and brain size is not a linear one; "body size decreases more rapidly than brain size" so smaller bodies have larger brains relative to body size) (*Ever Since Darwin,* 187, 183). In using cranial capacity as evidence of the primitiveness of the pygmies, therefore, nineteenth-century anthropologists were simply repeating their view that the small body size of the pygmies indicated inferiority. Elsewhere, Gould explains that anthropologists like Paul Broca recognized the relationship between body size and brain size but ignored it when comparing the intelligence of women and blacks with that of white men. See Gould, *Mismeasure,* 103–7.

41. Flower, "Pygmy Races," 69.

42. Ibid., 44.

43. Races were routinely classified according to the height of men rather than women. This approach was also characteristic of the height studies carried out across Europe and the United States in the late nineteenth and early twentieth centuries.

44. Flower, "Pygmy Races," 44.

45. Keane, *Ethnology,* 187–89.

46. Ripley, *Races of Europe,* 98.

47. Schlichter, "Pygmy Tribes," 352–53.

48. Flower, "Pygmy Races," 69.

49. Keane, *Ethnology,* 242.

50. Tyson, *Anatomy,* 5 and Epistle.

51. For an excellent and more thorough discussion of Tyson's *Anatomy of a Pygmie,* see Stephen Jay Gould, "To Show an Ape," in *Flamingo's Smile.*

52. According to Douglas Futuyma, in *Evolutionary Biology,* Darwin recognized the problems inherent in this language. "The misrepresentation of evolution as progress was so apparent to Darwin that he reminded himself in his notebook 'never to say higher or lower' in reference to different forms of life, although he did not always follow his own admonition" (8).

53. The imagistic representation of evolution need not have been verti-

cal like a tree; it could easily have taken other, nonhierarchical shapes, like a wheel. In opposing this progressive view of evolution, Stephen Jay Gould has suggested that evolution is best characterized by the image of a bush: "Evolution forms a copiously branching bush, not a unilinear progressive sequence" (*Mismeasure*, 318). See also Gould, "Bushes and Ladders in Human Evolution," in *Ever Since Darwin*.

54. The vertical metaphors are equally apparent in Keane's written description of racial evolution. "Between the Negro and the Mongolo-American boughs," writes Keane, "the main stem passes upwards, developing a generalised Caucasic type—Homo Caucasicus—which also at an early date ramifies into three great branches, filling all the intervening central space, overshadowing the Negro, overtopping the Mongol, and shooting still upwards, one might say, almost into illimitable space. Such is the dominant position of this highest of the Hominidae, which seems alone destined to a great future, as it is alone heir to a great past" (*Ethnology*, 226).

55. Stepan, "Race and Gender," 274.

56. De Quatrefages, *Pygmies*, 162–63.

57. Ibid., 182–83.

58. Ibid., 48.

59. Haller argues that monogenists, "despite their insistence on man's single origin, . . . were not egalitarians. Races, during centuries of formation, acquired characteristics that, upon comparison, established an inequality 'impossible to deny.'" He suggests that de Quatrefages was among those monogenists who assumed the races had significantly different aptitudes and capabilities (see *Outcasts*, 73–74). Stepan, on the other hand, claims that de Quatrefages opposed evolutionary theory because he "associated evolutionism with the denigration of man and polygenism with the denigration of non-white races" (*Idea of Race*, 110).

60. No major ethnologists whose works I have read endorsed the theory that pygmies were degenerate, yet all addressed it in their writings, suggesting that it was a common popular view rather than a prevalent scientific one.

61. De Quatrefages, *Pygmies*, 184, 17.

62. Flower, "Pygmy Races," 67.

63. Ibid.

64. Ibid.

65. Keane, *Ethnology*, 238.

66. Ibid., 29.

67. Shepp, *Shepp's World's Fair*, 184.

68. Rydell, *All the World's a Fair*, 157.

69. Bradford and Blume, *Ota*, 152.

70. Rydell makes a similar argument. See *All the World's a Fair*, 5.

71. Ibid., 3–5.

72. Carnegie, *Gospel*, 90–91.

73. See Gage, "Finances"; Rydell, *All the World's a Fair*, 42–43.

74. Shepp, *Shepp's World's Fair*, 184.

75. Carnegie, *Gospel*, 94.

76. Shepp, *Shepp's World's Fair*, 186.

77. Foucault, *Discipline and Punish*, 25–28.

78. Quoted from a letter by fair organizers to the secretary of the U.S. treasury. See Rydell, *All the World's a Fair*, 56.

79. Quoted in ibid., 45.

80. Cited in Ellis, *Man and Woman*, 40.
81. "On the Elongation of Form," 33.
82. Sargent, "Physical Proportions," 17.
83. Sargent, "Physical Development," 174, 173.
84. See Rydell, *All the World's a Fair*, 60–63.
85. Starr, "Anthropology," 619.
86. See Rydell, *All the World's a Fair*, 65.
87. Quoted in ibid.
88. See Armstrong, "'A Jumble.'"
89. See Rydell, *All the World's a Fair*, 52–54.
90. Ibid., 159.
91. Ibid., 160.
92. Quoted in ibid., 159.
93. Quoted in ibid., 162.
94. McGee, "Anthropology," 822, 820.
95. McGee, "National Growth," 188–89, 204.
96. McGee, "Trend," 413.
97. McGee, "National Growth," 204.
98. The quotations, which come from a St. Louis newspaper and the *New York Sun*, are cited in Bradford and Blume, *Ota*, 98.
99. McGee, "Anthropology," 822.
100. See Rydell, *All the World's a Fair*, 183.
101. See Bradford and Blume, *Ota*, 115, 247–49.
102. Darwin, "Darwin on the Fuegians," 748.
103. Dastre, "Stature of Man," 24987.
104. Stepan, "Race and Gender," 274. Amy Kaplan adds that stereotypes of savages inevitably create instabilities that challenge the assumptions on which they are founded (*Anarchy*, 14).
105. See Ripley, *Races of Europe*, chap. 5, esp. 94–95. Karl Pearson and Alice Lee also take this approach in their article "On the Relative Variation and Correlation in Civilized and Uncivilized Races": "The increase in size with civilization seems, on the average, . . . incontestable" (49). They provide no evidence for the assertion.
106. Ripley, *Races of Europe*, 94–95.
107. Spencer, *Principles of Sociology, Volume 1*, 41.
108. Baxter, *Statistics*, 23. See also Baldwin, *Physical Growth*, 152–53. "Blond races are characterized by superior stature," wrote Baldwin. "The American Indian is a striking exception."
109. Dickson, "Statistics," 374.
110. Quoted in Bradford and Blume, *Ota*, 121.
111. Rydell, *All the World's a Fair*, 166.
112. Bennitt and Stockbridge, *History*, 573.
113. McGee, "Trend," 414, 447, 446.
114. McGee, "National Growth," 205.
115. Quoted in Rydell, *All the World's a Fair*, 162.
116. Quoted in ibid., 172.
117. Ibid.
118. Quoted in ibid., 176.
119. Quoted in ibid., 175.
120. I am indebted to Rydell for his description of this event. Amy Kaplan has recently pointed to an inherent contradiction in the American

imperialist agenda. While the ideology of American exceptionalism imagines a world steadily adopting the U.S. model of democratic capitalism, and while U.S. imperialism has sought to make this idea a reality, the very process of the Americanization of the world expands the boundaries of the nation in a way that "shatters the coherence of national identity" and introduces undesirable, alien elements into the national body (*Anarchy*, 16). One can see this anxiety in the anti-imperialist Democratic Party platform. Similarly, Kaplan refers to the Supreme Court's paradoxical definition of Puerto Rico as "foreign to the United States in a domestic sense" as emblematic of the semantic and ideological anarchy that arises from the desire to expand without diversifying (see the introduction to *Anarchy*). The case of the Philippines illustrated one way in which the paradox might be resolved and the integrity of the national body preserved even as it expanded. Those who were amenable to Americanization would be, if not embraced, at least invited onto the porch; those who were not would be sent packing. In this way, imperialist expansion could be regarded as merely the steady accretion of those who were destined to be Americans. America would remain for Americans only; the process of imperialism itself acted as the filter that separated the deserving from the undeserving.

121. Bennitt and Stockbridge, *History*, 676.

122. For a more detailed discussion of the pygmies' behavior at the fair, see Bradford and Blume, *Ota*.

123. Shepp, *Shepp's World's Fair*, 188.

124. Cited in Rydell, *All the World's a Fair*, 158–59.

125. Stewart, *On Longing*, xii, 102.

126. Ibid., 71, 172, 90.

127. See Trachtenberg, *Statue of Liberty*, 146. An equivalent trend in literature was the popularity of the promontory view in Victorian travel narratives. See Pratt, *Imperial Eyes*, 202–5.

CHAPTER 2

1. See Terry and Urla, *Deviant Bodies*, 8–10; and Robert Proctor's essay "The Destruction of 'Lives Not Worth Living'" in the same volume.

2. Ripley, *Races of Europe*, 103. Ripley's arguments were consistent with European authorities of his day, however. See Higham, *Strangers in the Land*, 154.

3. Conn, *Divided Mind*, 6; Trachtenberg, *Incorporation of America*, 88; and Higham, *Strangers in the Land*, 16.

4. Slotkin, *Fatal Environment*, 342.

5. See ibid., esp. chaps. 13–15 and 19. My discussion of Slotkin here, and my argument about the transference of imperialist techniques and ideologies to the metropolis, is not meant to suggest that the relationship between imperialist and metropolitan discourses was wholly one-directional. There was unquestionably back-and-forth interaction between the two. At times they were mutually reinforcing, while at other times they contradicted and destabilized one another. Amy Kaplan has recently criticized Slotkin and others for presenting imperialist ideologies as rigid and unilinear and for depicting Indian-white relations as the foundation for U.S. imperialist symbolism and politics (see *Anarchy of Empire*, 10, 17–18, 217–18n36). Slotkin's argument in *The Fatal Environment* is more complex

than her reading suggests, however. As the term *reversible metaphors* implies, Slotkin is aware of the back-and-forth, complex interactions among representations of Indians, the urban poor, blacks, and women (see, for example, *Fatal Environment,* 338–45). In any case, my argument in this and the previous chapter is congruent with Kaplan's, who writes, "domestic metaphors of national identity are intimately intertwined with renderings of the foreign and the alien, and . . . notions of the domestic and the foreign mutually constitute one another in an imperial context" (*Anarchy,* 4).

6. Jacobson, *Whiteness,* 167–68. Jacobson probably overstates his case, however. As explained previously, Ripley was defying American scientific dogma in 1899 when he divided whites into separate races. The example that Slotkin uses and Jacobson develops is popular responses to the 1877 railroad strike. While some of those responses indicated a literal use of racial divisions between the striking (white) workers and their opponents, the event occurred well before U.S. authorities on race sanctioned such divisions. Perhaps more than anything, Jacobson has revealed the widely differing uses and understandings of the term *race* in the late nineteenth century. It is more difficult than he acknowledges to distinguish metaphoric from literal uses of racial terminology in this period.

7. Haliburton, *Survivals,* 4; emphasis in original.

8. Chamberlain, "Robert Grant Haliburton," 63.

9. Haliburton, *Dwarf Survivals,* 7.

10. Ibid.

11. Ibid.; emphasis in original.

12. Ibid., 8.

13. See, for example, Pearson and Bell, *Study of the Long Bones.*

14. Kollmann, "Pygmies," 122.

15. Ibid.

16. Cited in Tanner, *History,* 4.

17. Ibid., 8.

18. See Aristotle, *Politics,* book VIII, chapter 4.

19. Aristotle, *Nicomachean Ethics,* book IV, chapter 3, 991.

20. Cited in Tanner, *History,* 10.

21. Cited in ibid., 468–69.

22. See Bondeson, "Giants"; Fiedler, *Freaks,* 98.

23. Cited in Tanner, *History,* 25.

24. Cited in ibid., 26.

25. Cited in ibid., 76.

26. Cited in ibid., 76–77.

27. Buffon's arguments are summarized by Jefferson, *Notes,* 47.

28. Ibid., 58–59.

29. Ibid., 47.

30. Ibid., 61.

31. On one occasion Jefferson delivered a large American panther skin to Buffon before meeting with him and trying to convince him of the error of his opinions regarding the size of American animals. When Buffon remained adamant in his views, Jefferson asked the governor of New Hampshire to obtain at great expense the skin, skeleton, and horns of a moose, which Jefferson then shipped to Buffon. See the notes provided by William Peden in Jefferson, *Notes,* 268.

32. Raynal's arguments are summarized by Jefferson, *Notes,* 64.

33. See Tanner, *History,* 161.

34. All of these studies were motivated by a desire to find ways to improve the stature of men in the nation (which entailed an assessment of the factors influencing stature) and thereby reduce the number of army rejects based on minimum height requirements. The historic variability of military height limits, on the other hand, reveals the arbitrary nature of such restrictions and suggests that they are based on norms of masculinity rather than military physiological demands. In France, for example, minimum height requirements in the eighteenth and nineteenth centuries varied between 5'1" and 5'4". In the United States, height requirements varied between 5'0" and 5'6". Not surprisingly, the lowest requirements corresponded to the times of greatest demand for soldiers; the Union imposed the lowest figure of 5'0" during the Civil War in 1864.

35. Cited in Tanner, *History,* 162.

36. Quetelet, *Treatise,* 99–100. Rosemarie Garland Thomson has discussed the disastrous consequences that Quetelet's views have had for the disabled. See *Extraordinary Bodies,* 63–66.

37. Following Quetelet, the study of human stature came to occupy a central place in the formation of modern statistics. Both Francis Galton and Karl Pearson used data on stature extensively, both to develop statistical theories and to determine the laws of human inheritance.

38. See the *Oxford English Dictionary.*

39. Quetelet, *Treatise,* 63.

40. "The men who fall, in respect of height, outside of the ordinary limits . . . may be regarded as monstrosities. . . . We must conceive the same distinctions in the moral world," wrote Quetelet, for example (*Treatise,* x).

41. Ibid.

42. In *The Taming of Chance,* Ian Hacking labels these two competing notions of progress—both common in the nineteenth century—the Quetelet-Durkheim model and the Galtonian model. Hacking claims both originated in statistical theory and reflect the inherent divisions in the concept of the "normal." The first view, which posits that the existing average, or normal figure, represents the ideal, is a preservationist, conservative notion of progress. The second view, championed by Francis Galton and eminently compatible with eugenics, is a forward-looking, ameliorative conception of progress that regards the average or normal as something to be improved (160–69). The American view was Galtonian in nature.

43. British Parliamentary Papers, *First Report,* 1.

44. Additional studies of factory children were carried out in England after the Factory Commission's, including Leonard Horner's study of fifteen thousand children in Manchester and Leeds in 1837. Horner conducted his research to develop standards of height-for-age to prevent what many believed was a widespread pattern of children falsifying their ages in order to gain industrial employment following the Factories Regulation Act of 1833. Tanner reviews the data of these early studies and offers a modern perspective. He concludes that inhalation or ingestion of toxic substances by the pregnant mother or newborn is the most likely explanation for the unusual smallness of factory children in the early nineteenth century, a phenomenon that attracted frequent comment by contemporary observers. Baby products like Godfrey's Cordial, Atkinson's Royal Infants Preservative, and Mrs. Wilkinson's Soothing Syrup, often used to pacify infants while their

mothers worked long hours, contained narcotics like laudanum, opium, and morphine. Although these products killed many infants, the practice of adding narcotics to infant products was not abolished until the 1890s. See Tanner, *History,* 156–59.

45. Quetelet, *Treatise,* 60–61; emphasis in original. Nancy Stepan has argued that "most British scientists shared by mid-century, almost unconsciously, Knox's belief that fixed and distinct racial types provided the key to human history and destiny" (*Idea of Race,* 4).

46. The theory of wartime selection on height would become a major concern in the United States at the turn of the century as well. David Starr Jordan was among those concerned about the elimination of the fittest during war. Jordan was president of Stanford University and a naturalist who espoused an odd combination of pacifism and eugenics. He wrote several books on eugenics and war, including *The Blood of the Nation; A Study of the Decay of Races Through Survival of the Unfit* (1902), *War's Aftermath; A Preliminary Study of the Eugenics of War as Illustrated by the Civil War of the United States and the Late Wars in the Balkans* (1914), and *War and the Breed: The Relation of War to the Downfall of Nations* (1922). In the latter, he described the effects of artificial selection during World War I on the British population as a warning against the dangers of U.S. military aggression. "It is a current theory that the fairy tales of Europe are based on persistent memories of prehistoric swarthy dwarf races which once lived on the continent," he wrote. "It is now claimed that these types, not yet extinct, are tending in the prevalence of military selection to reassert themselves and to 'congregate in their old haunts.' The 'pygmies of London,' under-sized, dark-skinned people, 'clothed in rags and begging an existence' are now increasing in relative numbers. . . . The increase of these dwarfs may be ascribed to their immunity from military selection" (17–18). See also Madison Grant, *Passing of the Great Race,* 66–67, 173, 178.

47. Cited in Tanner, *History,* 163.

48. Livermore, "American Physical Man," 118.

49. Ibid., 117–18.

50. Ibid., 133.

51. For a discussion of the typical methods of nineteenth-century science, see Gould, *Mismeasure.*

52. Gould, *Investigations,* 121.

53. See Tanner, "Relation," 194; and Sokoloff and Villaflor, "Early Achievement," 474.

54. Gould, *Investigations,* 126.

55. Whitman, *Leaves of Grass,* Modern Library College Edition, 622.

56. This passage comes from Whitman's *Democratic Vistas,* published just two years after Gould's report and the same year as Darwin's *Descent of Man.* Whitman, *Leaves of Grass,* Modern Library College Edition, 468.

57. From Whitman's "Song of the Redwood-Tree" in *Leaves of Grass,* Norton Critical Edition, 207–8.

58. Baxter, *Statistics,* 14.

59. Ibid., 15.

60. He neglected to consider that soldiers of American birth probably included fewer men from the upper classes since the rich could purchase substitutes, and therefore they could hardly be considered a random sample. There are many reasons to be suspicious of the findings of turn-of-the-cen-

tury science, not the least of which is unconscious or conscious manipulation of the results, a practice that Stephen Jay Gould discusses in *The Mismeasure of Man.*

61. Baxter, *Statistics,* 14.

62. Ibid., 18.

63. Ibid., 20.

64. Ibid., 23.

65. See Love and Davenport, *Defects,* 36.

66. The laws that were ultimately imposed—the Johnson Act of 1920 and the Johnson-Reed Act of 1924—discriminated particularly against Jews and Italians.

67. Love and Davenport, *Defects,* 37.

68. The powerful influence of the progressive myth continues today. Most people in the United States assume, for example, that human stature has gradually increased over time in the United States and Europe as a result of the improved conditions of modern society. In *A History of the Study of Human Growth,* Tanner explains how many people mistakenly assume that the secular trend (the scientific term for a change in average stature over time) is a unidirectional phenomenon.

> The word "trend" is really inappropriate as it usually denotes a change always in one direction, whereas there is no reason why the growth trend should not go the other way too. . . . Following the recovery from the Napoleonic Wars, stature rose in France . . . and a lively debate took place as to whether the wars had lowered stature from a pre-existing higher level to which it was again returning, or whether the trend was a new phenomenon. Van Wieringen (1978) . . . stresses how in a historical period of diminishing comfort and increasing misery, delay in growth and shortening of stature may return. Oppers (1966) believes this may have occurred in Holland in 1820–60, associated with the famines and increases in the price of rye. (116)

Moreover, recent investigations associated with a project on the history of nutrition sponsored by the National Bureau of Economic Research and the Center for Population Economics draw the presumed U.S. secular trend into question. "Contrary to the popular impression that there have been continuous secular improvements in nutrition and increases in height," write the authors of an article on the uses of height data for economic historians, "the evidence thus far analysed in the project indicates that there were cycles in the final heights of native-born whites and of U.S. blacks" (Fogel, Engerman, and Trussell, "Exploring," 416). The heights of full-grown American men, the authors claim, increased in the middle of the eighteenth century, leveled off during the American Revolution, increased slightly again in the first decades of the nineteenth century, declined during most of the century, and then increased at the beginning of the twentieth century. Additionally, the authors of an essay entitled "The Early Achievement of Modern Stature in America" from *Social Science History* use Revolutionary War data to show that "Native-born [male] Americans appear to have approached modern heights as long ago as two centuries" (Sokoloff and Villaflor, 474). If the data on which their study is based can be trusted, their figures also suggest that disparities in stature between social classes in the United States were widening between the Revolution and 1820 (see 474). The historical scope of the article is, unfortunately, too limited to indicate whether this remained the case later in the nineteenth century.

We should distinguish, therefore, factual secular trends and the associated myths of degeneration and progress that may or may not correspond to real phenomena. The American faith in progress informs our assumptions about contemporary heights despite the lack of reliable and widely publicized historical data. Contemporary assumptions about historical increases in American stature can almost certainly be traced to turn-of-the-century scientific studies on height.

It is also worthwhile to remember that, regardless of which myth presides in any period, both share a common premise: that body size is a sign of our social condition. Our assumptions about progress may differ in important ways from turn-of-the-century ones—we are more likely to assume, for example, that increasing height is a sign of economic rather than racial improvement—but we nevertheless retain the belief that the human body registers the tenor of the times and indicates the direction of the future. The consequence of this view is that we often attach an undeserved significance to human variation and the appearance of the body. Both myths also assume that increases in height are beneficial; only recently, with environmental problems increasing as a result of the global population explosion, have social commentators reversed this age-old tradition and suggested that increases in average adult height may not necessarily be advantageous, since they increase the demands placed on the earth's taxed resources. (For arguments of this kind, see Samaras, *Truth,* and Tanner, *History,* 399.) Finally, both myths connote that short stature is a "problem" to be corrected. The environmentalist view, while it seems more benign on the surface, is not incompatible with prejudices against short stature. Contemporary humanitarian scientists like J. M. Tanner who, in the tradition of Villermé, investigate the mean stature of various populations around the globe might argue that stature is merely a convenient marker for the biological effects of economic disparities; it is not short stature, per se, that they are hoping to correct but the associated nutritional and economic injustices. Conducting detailed studies of comparative growth and adult stature for different populations, however, is surely a circuitous and inefficient way to identify impoverished communities. If social and economic justice is the goal, it should be adequate simply to compare the income and living conditions of various groups. Clearly the impetus behind such studies is more complex than mere social justice.

69. For a more detailed discussion of Hall's influence on American education, see Cremin, *American Education,* 280.

70. Boas produced his composite North American growth curves by combining child growth data from the studies of Bowditch in Boston, Peckham in Milwaukee, Porter in St. Louis, his own studies in Worcester, and additional studies in Toronto and Oakland. The standard curves were derived from a disproportionate number of wealthy children.

71. Montgomery, "March Meeting," 508. Hall believed that humans developed from a "pigmoid" ancestor and were generally increasing in height (see *Adolescence,* chap. 1).

72. Montgomery, "March Meeting," 509–10.

73. My argument here is indebted to the work of Lawrence Cremin.

74. Seltzer, *Bodies and Machines,* 150.

75. Dunn, "Making Giants," 706.

76. See "Giants to be Grown."

77. My conclusions are different from those of Lucy Bending, who suggests that the discovery of growth hormone produced a "radical change in perception," a new awareness of the malleability of child growth that displaced a previous belief in the fixity of development ("From Stunted Child," 205). My research suggests that scientists and child growth experts were convinced of the malleability of child growth well before the discovery of growth hormone and sought a variety of ways to enhance height. Growth hormone represented just one more tool in this long-standing effort.

78. Bowditch, "Growth" (1877), 291.

79. Bowditch, "Physique," 300.

80. Bowditch, "Growth" (1891), 521.

81. Porter, "Relative Growth," 318, 311, 320, 324.

82. See Porter, "Percentile Charts."

83. Porter, "Seasonal Variation," 124.

84. Porter, "Physical Basis," 162.

85. Ibid., 177, 173.

86. For example, Winfield Hall, a medical examiner at Haverford College, examined two thousand Philadelphia schoolboys and college students aged nine to twenty-three between 1889 and 1893. The families of the boys were "with very few exceptions well-to-do," said Hall. Because they attended private schools with physical education programs, they also "presented a higher physical development than is usually found in city schools." Despite his awareness that these children represented a select and privileged group—or rather *because* he knew this was the case—Hall believed that his data established "a true American type" ("Changes," 21). The true American, for Hall, was economically comfortable and physically exceptional, and the selection of individuals for national standards should reflect this excellence.

87. Porter, "Growth," 345.

88. Porter, "Physical Basis," 161–62.

89. Ibid., 340.

90. Ibid., 346.

91. Baldwin, *Physical Growth,* 68.

92. Ibid., 90; emphasis in original.

93. Ibid., 96–97.

94. See Sargent, "Physique," 256.

95. Boas, "Growth of Children," *Science* 19, 256. Boas did, however, believe that different racial groups had different racial growth curves (see "Educational Research," 308). Within a particular racial group, the differences between one child's development and another's were due to "accidental causes," which apparently could include environmental factors and social class.

96. Boas, "On Dr. William," 227.

97. Ibid.

98. Boas, "Growth of Children," *Science* 20, 352.

99. Boas, "History of Anthropology," 521, and "Growth of Children," *Science* 20, 352.

100. See Gilbert, "Researches," for example.

101. Tyler, "What Teachers," 323.

102. Boas, "Educational Research," 305.

103. "New Educational Theories," 755.

104. See Gould, *Mismeasure*, 163–64.

105. Goddard, "Height and Weight," 217.

106. Ibid., 231.

107. Kline, "Truancy," 418.

108. Ibid., 395.

109. Ibid.

110. Ibid., 415.

111. Ibid., 411–12.

112. In *A Journey to Ashango-Land*, for example, Paul Du Chaillu describes his frustrations trying to measure African men and women. He succeeded in measuring the first pygmy woman he met only after lavishing her with gifts, but others were more obstinate.

113. Peckham, "Growth of Children," 30.

114. Porter, "Growth," 267.

115. Boas, *Changes*, 82.

116. See Antin, *Promised Land*, 83.

117. Boas's *Changes in Bodily Form of Descendants of Immigrants* was among the few scientific studies in the forty-seven-volume report that opposed immigration restriction.

118. Antin, *They Who Knock*, 10–11.

119. Antin, "The Lie," 181. All subsequent references are in parentheses in the text.

120. There are clear autobiographical elements to Antin's story. Antin's father also falsified her age in order to ensure that she would receive a public school education. Small for her age, Antin, like David, was advanced rapidly through the Chelsea school system. See Sollors, "Introduction," xxviii.

121. Antin makes the argument in more detail in her autobiography; see *Promised Land*, 16–23.

122. See Stepan, *Idea of Race*.

123. Emerson, "Physical," 362–64.

CHAPTER 3

1. Cited in Strum, *Louis D. Brandeis*, 152.

2. Stein and Brown, *Big Business*, 42.

3. See Brandeis, *Other People's Money*, chap. 7.

4. Brandeis, *Business*, 12.

5. Smith-Rosenberg, *Disorderly Conduct*, 44, 242–43.

6. Ibid., 244.

7. See Kline, "Goliath Effect."

8. See Adams and Brock, *Bigness Complex*.

9. Chandler, *Scale and Scope*, 52.

10. Ibid., 282.

11. Chandler, *Visible Hand*, 385, and *Coming of Managerial Capitalism*, 328.

12. Dawley, *Struggles for Justice*, 26–31.

13. Chandler, *Scale and Scope,* 21–24, 45, and *Essential Alfred Chandler,* 260–61.

14. Norris, *Advertising.* On the role of advertising in stimulating consumer demand in two industries, tobacco and automobiles, and thereby enabling manufacturers to exploit the economies of scale, see 129–30 and 147–48.

15. Williams, "Harmful Effects," 4.

16. Wilson, *New Freedom,* 25.

17. Chandler, *Scale and Scope,* 74–75.

18. Adams and Brock, *Bigness Complex,* 25.

19. Shaw, *Outlook,* 28.

20. Chandler, "Introduction to *The Visible Hand,*" in *Essential Alfred Chandler,* 394.

21. Norris, *Advertising,* 26, 32–33, 58.

22. *Chicago Conference on Trusts,* 124.

23. Dawley, *Struggles for Justice,* 99, 136.

24. Trachtenberg, *Incorporation of America,* 80.

25. Conn, *Divided Mind,* 10; Dawley, *Struggles for Justice,* 82.

26. Chandler, *Coming of Managerial Capitalism,* 513.

27. Dawley, *Struggles for Justice,* 171.

28. Godden, *Fictions of Capital,* 40–42; Dawley, *Struggles for Justice,* 158.

29. Weinstein, *Corporate Ideal,* 40.

30. Trachtenberg, *Incorporation of America,* 90.

31. Strum, *Brandeis on Democracy,* 125–26.

32. Ibid., 127.

33. Conn, *Divided Mind,* 13.

34. Wilson, *New Freedom,* 20–21.

35. *Chicago Conference on Trusts,* 333.

36. Williams, "Harmful Effects," 9.

37. Trachtenberg, *Incorporation of America,* 213.

38. Bellamy, *Looking Backward,* 63.

39. This debate is apparent, for example, in Graham Wallas's *The Great Society* and Walter Lippmann's *Drift and Mastery,* both published in 1914. Wallas believed that the expanded scale of modern life no longer accorded with human dimensions and psychology. Since human capacities were unlikely to change, institutions would have to.

> The change of social scale . . . has created the Great Society. If the fact that our present society is larger than any that has existed before merely meant that it contained the same number of individuals magnified as in the field of a microscope, no new problem of organisation would result. But it means that our society contains a larger number of individuals of the same size as before, and that therefore the relation of those individuals to each other is changed. The average citizen of twentieth-century London is of nearly the same height as the average citizen of modern Andorra or medieval France. . . . The Londoner and the Andorrist are both subject to similar inherited limitations. . . . The fact, therefore, that any particular institution works well in Andorra, or worked well in medieval Florence, creates no pre-

sumption that it will work well in London. (Wallas, *Great Society,* 239–40)

Walter Lippmann believed that human nature and thought would have to adjust to the enlarged modern world.

Bad as big business is to-day, it has a wide promise within it. . . . We don't imagine that the trusts are going to drift naturally into the service of human life. We think they can be made to serve if the American people compel them. We think that the American people may be able to do that if they can adjust their thinking to a new world situation. . . . Man as he is to-day is not big enough to master the modern world. . . . We shall have to . . . develop within men and women themselves the power they need. (Lippmann, *Drift and Mastery,* 144–47)

40. Bellamy, *Looking Backward,* 201–6.
41. Cited in Strum, *Brandeis,* 75, 194.
42. Ibid., 195–96.
43. Brandeis, "Trusts," 15.
44. Himmelberg, *Monopoly Issue,* xvi. An example of an unfair business practice would be local price cutting. This practice occurs when a large business, with outlets in multiple regions or states, reduces its prices for goods in one area below production costs so as to drive its local competitors out of business. A large business can make up for local losses with profits in other regions, while a small business cannot afford to lower prices indefinitely.
45. Roosevelt, *Roosevelt Policy,* 1:109.
46. Roosevelt, "Conservation of Business," 575.
47. Roosevelt, *Roosevelt Policy,* 1:80.
48. Moody, "Evolution of the Trust," 481.
49. Cited in Rozwenc, *Roosevelt,* 80.
50. Brandeis, *Curse of Bigness,* 80.
51. See Klebaner, "Potential Competition," 116; and Clark, *Control of Trusts,* 183, 194–95.
52. Wilson, *New Freedom,* 102, 108, 114–15, 109.
53. Sklar, "Woodrow Wilson," 304.
54. See Wiebe, *Search for Order,* and Pizer, "*Maggie,*" both of which argue that size is central to naturalist aesthetics.
55. Much of the discussion of the corporate form in this paragraph and those following is indebted to Trachtenberg, *Incorporation of America,* 82–83. I have also relied on Brandeis, *Brandeis on Democracy,* 149–53.
56. See Sklar, *Corporate Reconstruction,* 49; and Trachtenberg, *Incorporation of America,* 82–83.
57. Bryan, in *Chicago Conference on Trusts,* 510.
58. Ibid.
59. Norris, *Octopus,* 289, 345, 104, 571–72. All subsequent references are in parentheses in the text.
60. Bryan, in *Chicago Conference on Trusts,* 511.
61. Brandeis, *Brandeis on Democracy,* 150–51.
62. Carnegie, *Gospel of Wealth,* 4, 7, 15, 123, 88, 89.
63. Ibid., 94.
64. See Livesay, *Andrew Carnegie,* 24.

65. Cited in Livesay, *Andrew Carnegie,* 170; emphasis in original.

66. Garland, in *Chicago Conference on Trusts,* 350.

67. Gompers, "Labor," 881–82.

68. Trachtenberg, *Incorporation of America,* 99–100.

69. Gompers, "Labor," 882–83; emphasis in original.

70. Trachtenberg, *Incorporation of America,* 100.

71. Dawley, *Struggles for Justice,* 149.

72. See Gompers, in *Chicago Conference on Trusts,* 329–30.

73. See Buhle and Sullivan, *Images of American Radicalism,* 54.

74. See Kimmel, *Manhood in America,* chap. 1.

75. See Schwartz, *Never Satisfied;* Stearns, *Fat History;* Bordo, "Reading the Slender Body," in *Unbearable Weight;* and Banner, *American Beauty.*

76. See Schwartz, *Never Satisfied;* Stearns, *Fat History;* Bordo, "Reading the Slender Body," in *Unbearable Weight;* and Armstrong, "Disciplining the Corpus," in *American Bodies,* esp. 108–10.

77. Stearns, *Fat History,* 60.

78. See, for example, Dowe, in *Chicago Conference on Trusts.*

79. Lockwood, in *Chicago Conference on Trusts,* 379.

80. Cited in Dawley, *Struggles for Justice,* 239.

81. London, *Iron Heel,* 151.

82. Lloyd, *Wealth Against Commonwealth,* 6.

83. Some writers of the time, in fact, argued against this view. In *Drift and Mastery* (1914), for example, Walter Lippmann insisted that "the middle class has not disappeared: in this country it is the dominant power expressing itself through the Progressives, and through the Wilson administration" (310). The paradox of the contemporary response, it seems to me, is rooted in the changing nature of the middle class. Traditionally the middle class was characterized by—or conceived in terms of—independent ownership of small businesses. Increasingly it consisted of salaried white-collar workers in large corporations. Turn-of-the-century Americans simply did not see such workers as belonging to the middle class or capable of developing the traditional virtues of the class and therefore fostering the virtues of a middle-class nation: that is, self-sufficiency, freedom, independence, and so forth.

84. Zunz, *Making America Corporate,* 126–27; Blumin, *Emergence of the Middle Class,* 269, 290–95.

85. Wilson, *White Collar Fictions,* 5.

86. Banner, *American Beauty,* 189.

87. Wilson, *New Freedom,* 153.

88. Ibid., 104.

89. Ibid., 103.

90. Ibid., 31–32.

91. Sklar, "Woodrow Wilson," 305 (emphasis in original).

92. See Zunz, *Making America Corporate.*

93. McElrath, "Frank Norris," 388.

94. Michaels, *Gold Standard,* chapter 6. Michaels's point, of course, is somewhat different from my own. In demonstrating the "complicity between naturalism and the corporation" (213), and more specifically the similarity between Norris's conception of personhood and the corporate conception of personhood, Michaels emphasizes how Norris's work is a product of its (corporate) time—something that is inevitably true of any lit-

erary work. For Michaels, the corporate conception of personhood typified by *The Octopus* undermined the traditional distinction between natural and unnatural persons, between the "disembodied" body of the corporation and the "embodied" bodies of people, even as it depended on traditional notions of embodiment. Norris's conception of personhood, in other words, was structured by the same principles of internal difference and contradiction that were characteristic of the capitalist conception of personhood. What Michaels ignores, and what I am foregrounding in this chapter, is the alternative conceptions of embodiment and personhood that coexisted with the corporate one. As other scholars have pointed out, Michaels presumes a unitary, monolithic conception of cultures and the subjects they form. He ignores the internal contradictions within capitalism, the historic shifts between forms of capitalism, and the various ideologies that competed with or opposed corporate capitalism in one way or another.

95. John D. Rockefeller, for example, claimed that "The growth of a large business is merely a survival of the fittest, the working out of a law of nature and a law of God" (cited in Trachtenberg, *Incorporation of America,* 84–85).

96. Sherwood, "Influence of the Trust," 362; emphasis in original.

97. Lippmann, *Drift and Mastery,* 137–48, 166.

98. Poole, *Harbor,* 112. All subsequent references will be in parentheses in the text.

99. See Norris, *Octopus,* 4–5.

100. See 112, 120, 319. Regarding Sue, Bill says "she had grown tall and graceful" (97). "Her enthusiasm for all the new 'movements,' reforms and ideas that she had heard of God-knows-where and felt she must gather into herself to expand herself—it was wonderful" (112). Similarly, although Eleanore remains "rather small and demurely feminine," she strikes Bill "as having grown tremendously" (120) in part, no doubt, because she participates in suffrage marches. And Bill sees Nora Ganey "grow amazingly" (319) through her involvement in the dock workers' strike.

CHAPTER 4

1. Steffens, "Modern Business Building."
2. Marin, "Water-Colors."
3. Mumford, *Sticks and Stones,* 177.
4. Roberts [Giles Edgerton], "How New York," 458.
5. Mumford, *Sticks and Stones,* 177.
6. Gilder, "City of Dreadful Height," 139.
7. "Regulation of Building Heights."
8. Adam, "Titan's Tower"; emphasis in original.
9. Schleier, *Skyscraper in American Art,* 72.
10. "American Skyscraper," 3.
11. Zunz, *Making America Corporate,* 122–23.
12. Cecilia Tichi has argued that modernist writers like Lewis, Dos Passos, Hemingway, and Williams adapted skyscraper aesthetics to literature beginning in the 1920s. See Tichi, *Shifting Gears,* 290–93.
13. Fenske, "'Skyscraper Problem,'" 220, 226.
14. Sears, "Introduction," xii.
15. Ibid., xi.

16. James, *American Scene,* 172. Subsequent page numbers are in parentheses in the text.

17. "American Skyscraper," 3.

18. Haviland, *Henry James's Last Romance,* 160. Even further, James feared that the nation was forsaking its entire literary culture. See Brown, *Material Unconscious,* 2.

19. Cited in Bogardus, *Pictures and Texts,* 113–14.

20. Cather, "Behind the Singer Tower," 46.

21. Immigrants were not, of course, housed in skyscrapers. Skyscrapers were built for a variety of complicated reasons, such as to facilitate land speculation, to advertise particular businesses, to house the expanding middle management and clerical classes in American industry, to represent business rivalries (there was fierce competition among competing newspapers in New York for the tallest building, for example), and to celebrate the American love of bigness. The building of skyscrapers was not tied to population size, as is clear from the fact that large European cities like London and Paris did not erect the tall buildings.

22. O. Henry, *Complete Works of O. Henry,* 1217.

23. Edwin Cochran, manager of the Woolworth Building, estimated that 375,000 tourists ascended to the top of the building annually between 1913 and 1920 (Mitchell, "Human Nature," 58).

24. Bill Brown has gone even further in suggesting that James has virtually "abandon[ed] the visible" in *The American Scene* (*Sense of Things,* 178).

25. Dawley, *Struggles for Justice,* 65. The term *rush hour* was coined in the late 1890s to describe the dense new urban traffic (Corn, *Great American Thing,* 160).

26. For a discussion of how, alternatively, this practice of having buildings speak may represent an effort to resist commodity fetishism, see Brown, *Sense of Things,* 177–88.

27. Mumford, *Sticks and Stones,* 176.

28. Sears, "Introduction," xvi.

29. It was commonplace among magazine writers in the 1890s and early 1900s to address the change in values from spiritualism to materialism implicit in this architectural shift.

30. Most novelists at the time chose etchings for their books. Many still did not regard photography as a genuine art form. See Bogardus, *Pictures and Texts.*

31. See ibid.

32. Sears, "Introduction," xviii.

33. See Schleier, *Skyscraper in American Art;* and Domosh, "Imagining New York's First Skyscrapers."

34. Schleier, *Skyscraper in American Art,* 1, 7.

35. Domosh, "Imagining New York's First Skyscrapers," 235.

36. Ibid., 241.

37. Sullivan, "Tall Office Building," 406.

38. Coburn, "Relation of Time to Art," 72.

39. Van Dyke, *New New York,* 18.

40. Mumford, *Sticks and Stones,* 174–75.

41. Coburn, "New York from Its Pinnacles."

42. Coburn, "Relation of Time to Art," 72.

43. Coburn, *Alvin Langdon Coburn,* 48.
44. Ibid., 120.
45. See "Crown of the Skyscraper."
46. Starrett, *Skyscrapers,* 100–101.
47. For further discussion of this point, see Seltzer, *Bodies and Machines.*
48. "Trinity Church from Above" is a notable exception to this rule. In that photo, the motion of the pedestrians at the lower foreground poses a striking contrast to the immobility of the tombstones behind the church. This contrast is relevant to the meaning of the photograph. For one thing, it situates Trinity literally between life and death, codifying visually the threats to the building's future at a time when many churches were demolished to make way for skyscrapers. The vantage point of the photograph, which traps the church between two skyscrapers in the foreground and a row of tall buildings in the rear, similarly emphasizes the building's precarious position. The inclusion of the pedestrians so close to Trinity also serves to create an association between the two, just as James argued that the church, unlike skyscrapers, appealed to the "patient pedestrian sense." In many regards, the photograph is a perfect visualization of James's eulogy for the church.
49. Poole, "Cowboys," 642.
50. "Visits Woolworth Tower."
51. Saltus, "New York from the Flatiron," 382.
52. Cited in Kaplan, *Lewis Hine in Europe,* 34. One might further the comparison of Coburn with his contemporaries by pointing to the example of Joseph Stella, an Italian immigrant. Stella's "Battle of Lights, Coney Island" (1913) was among the first modernist paintings in the United States, and, like Coburn, Stella continued to labor in the vanguard of modernism with such compositions as "Brooklyn Bridge" (1919) and "New York Interpreted" (1920–22). The immense central panel of the latter painting, in fact, was devoted to New York's skyscrapers; like Coburn, Stella recognized the effects that modern architecture and urban existence were having on social life and modern consciousness. "From the domes of your temples dedicated to commerce one is treated to a new view, a prospect stretching out into the infinite," he wrote (cited in Jaffe, *Joseph Stella,* 78). (In this he was clearly using the Woolworth Building, dubbed the "Cathedral of Commerce" soon after it was built, to stand generically for New York's skyscrapers; the tallest of the buildings in the central panel of "New York Interpreted," in fact, is likely the Woolworth Building depicted from the rear. See Corn, *Great American Thing,* 156.) Like Coburn, Stella's work was influenced by modern architecture and his experiences in New York, a city whose "growth and expansion proceed[ed] parallelly to the development of my own life" and which he described as "like a huge steel bolt flashing with streaks of lightning. The vertical line dominates, triumphs" (cited in Jaffe, *Joseph Stella,* 68, 72). As critics of his work have pointed out, verticality is a consistent and insistent feature of his work (see Jaffe, *Joseph Stella,* 22, 127; and Haskell, *Joseph Stella,* 175. Wanda Corn adds that "Stella's paintings are the most . . . vertiginous that anyone . . . painted of Manhattan in the 1920s" [*Great American Thing,* 135]). Stella himself acknowledged that his art was influenced at times by modern architecture; referring to the composition of "Brooklyn Bridge," he wrote in 1928, "It was the time when I was awaken-

ing in my work an echo of the oceanic poliphony . . . expressed by the steely orchestra of modern constructions: the time when, in rivalry to the new elevation in superior spheres as embodied by the skyscrapers and the new fearless audacity in soaring above the abyss of the bridge, I was planning to use all my fire to forge with a gigantic art illimited and far removed from the insignificant frivolities of easel pictures" (cited in Haskell, *Joseph Stella*, 206). Despite his rapid conversion to modernist aesthetics, despite his enduring interest in modern architecture, despite his fascination with the verticality of twentieth-century American cities, despite even the absence of human subjects in much of his modernist urban compositions, Stella nevertheless maintained close ties with the humanitarian, documentary tradition of Lewis Hine and others. Between 1905 and 1924 Stella accepted numerous commissions from Progressive reform organizations. His illustrations appeared in Progressive periodicals like the *Outlook, Charities and the Commons,* and the *Survey;* in Ernest Poole's first documentary novel *The Voice of the Street;* and Mary Antin's pro-immigration tract *They Who Knock at Our Gates.* He documented the effects of the Monongah mining explosion in 1907 for *Charities and the Commons,* and in 1908 he traveled, along with Lewis Hine, to Pennsylvania, where he produced over one hundred drawings for the Pittsburgh Survey, most of which were striking individual portraits of industrial workers.

53. See Foucault, *Discipline and Punish;* Stewart, *On Longing;* Wallach, "Making a Picture."

54. Trachtenberg, *Reading American Photographs,* 209–30. Allan Sekula, examining two remarkably similar Hine and Stieglitz photographs of immigrants arriving in the United States (Hine's "Immigrants Going Down Gangplank" and Stieglitz's "The Steerage"), concludes that the main difference between the two photographers is not their work but the manner in which their work was exhibited and received and the intentions of the photographers. All photographs, he argues, can be viewed in documentary or artistic terms. Part of the inevitable difficulty of interpreting photographs is determining which mode to emphasize—the realistic, documentary quality of the photograph or its artistic, metaphoric quality (see Sekula, "On the Invention"). What I wish to emphasize here is the historical context in which Coburn was working and how his photographs aligned themselves with particular political and social aims that he himself may not have been fully aware of. In seeking an aesthetic realm outside politics, Coburn was unwittingly reinforcing a particular, class-based political vision.

55. Lehman, *New York Skyscraper,* 130.

56. Bayne, "Woolworth Building."

57. Schuyler, "Woolworth Building" (1913), in *American Architecture II,* 608.

58. Bragdon, *Frozen Fountain,* 30.

59. See McAtamney, *Dinner,* 15.

60. Woolworth maintained a rigid two-tiered employment ladder. He hired women as salesclerks in his stores and deliberately kept their wages low—far lower, in fact, than that of average clerks. He was able to suppress wages so aggressively because he also developed new sales practices that reduced the responsibilities of clerks from active salespeople to passive cashiers. He instructed his managers to fire clerks who demanded wages above a strict cutoff; in most stores, the minimum wage for clerks was also

the maximum wage. Woolworth hired men to manage his stores, and with his aggressive program of expansion he offered many opportunities for his male employees to ascend the management hierarchy. See Winkler, *Five and Ten.*

61. See ibid.

62. For Wilson's opposition to this practice, see Wilson, *New Freedom,* 108. For Woolworth's use of this practice, see Winkler, *Five and Ten,* 165–67.

63. McAtamney, *Dinner,* 30.

64. Ibid., 58.

65. Ibid., 79–80.

66. Ibid., 80.

67. Ibid., 50, 49.

68. Ibid., 23.

69. Cited in Goldberger, *Skyscraper,* 44.

70. Tittle, "Creator of the Woolworth Tower," 101.

71. Schleier, *Skyscraper in American Art,* 80.

72. Schuyler, "Woolworth Building" (1913), in *American Architecture II,* 606.

73. Schuyler, "Towers of Manhattan," 103.

74. Cochran, *Cathedral of Commerce* (no pagination supplied).

75. Schuyler, "Woolworth Building" (1913), in *American Architecture II,* 606, 617.

76. Crane, *Complete Poems,* 102.

77. See Giles, *Hart Crane,* 49.

78. Wentworth and Flexner, *Dictionary of American Slang.* The subsequent reference is from the same source.

79. Brunner, *Splendid Failure,* 148.

80. Gibbs, *Business Architectural Imagery,* 146.

81. Ibid., 97. See also Kostof, *America by Design,* 245–46.

82. Fenske, "'Skyscraper Problem.'"

83. McAtamney, *Dinner,* 79.

84. Zunz, *Making America Corporate,* 114.

85. See Winkler, *Five and Ten,* 102–3, 118.

86. See, for example, Sennett, *Flesh and Stone;* and Grosz, "Bodies-Cities."

87. Sennett, *Flesh and Stone,* 24.

88. I am aware of recent criticism on *The American Scene* that seeks to redeem James from charges of anti-Semitism and nativist prejudice by claiming that he expresses an "unflinching sense of affinity with the alien" (Posnock, "Affirming the Alien," 227) and an "openness to otherness" (Blair, *Henry James,* 172) for which he has not traditionally been given credit (see Blair, *Henry James;* Haviland, *Henry James's Last Romance;* and Posnock, "Affirming the Alien"). I confess that I do not find these arguments very persuasive. It is true, as these critics point out, that James offers a compelling "critique of the logic of Americanization" (Blair, *Henry James,* 172), and it is also true that he interrogates the meaning of the word *alien,* exposing the ways that all Americans are in some sense "aliens." These elements of *The American Scene* appear to temper the bigotry that is so arresting and that has been the subject of so much attention in the critical discourse (for recent examples, see Sears, "Introduction"; and Conn, *Divided Mind*). Yet his prej-

udices are nonetheless palpable, and I do not think they are incompatible with a critique of the processes of Americanization. James interrogates the word *alien* not to identify with the immigrants he disdains but rather to demonstrate that alienation is a common predicament in the United States at a time when the nation is changing so swiftly. (In this sense, as in others, his work clearly anticipates modernism. See Conn, *Divided Mind,* for further discussion of James's contributions to modernism.) To argue that all Americans are alienated does not necessarily mean that native-born Americans are similar in other ways to immigrants—nor is it incompatible with prejudices toward immigrants.

CHAPTER 5

1. Gilman, *Women and Economics,* 148.
2. Cahan, *Rise of David Levinsky,* 354–55.
3. Antin, *Promised Land,* 83. All subsequent references to the book are in parentheses in the text.
4. Among those critiques that view Antin's autobiography as an unambivalent tale of assimilation are Dearborn, *Pocahontas's Daughters;* Proefriedt, "Education of Mary Antin"; Cohen, "Mary Antin's"; Rosenfeld, "Inventing the Jew"; Tuerk, "Youngest"; and Uffen, *Strands.* Dearborn claims *The Promised Land* thoroughly reflects dominant ideologies and lacks any voice of protest. Cohen argues that Antin was so eager to become assimilated that she "cast off the albatross of Judaism so she could have smooth sailing as an American" ("Mary Antin's," 34). Rosenfeld contends that Antin, whose self-image was "unambiguously American" ("Inventing the Jew," 136), allowed herself the "fiction" that America was Eden. Tuerk says Antin had a naive "optimism about the virtues of America and Americanization" ("Youngest," 33). Uffen claims that Antin thoroughly rejected her history and people. The nostalgia and ambiguity in her autobiography, says Uffen, are unintentional; "there is no apparent critical consciousness at work. . . . Antin seems unaware of any ambiguity of vision" (*Strands,* 21).

Rubin, "Style and Meaning"; Parrish, "Whose Americanization?"; Wasson, "Mary Antin"; Bergland, "Rereading Photographs"; Buelens, "New Man"; Zaborowska, *How We Found America;* Smith, "Cheesecake"; and Antler, "Sleeping with the Other," argue that *The Promised Land* is a more complicated text than these critics suggest. Rubin claims that the spirit of nostalgia, regret, and ambivalence that suffuses the autobiography contradicts the book's apparent optimism about assimilation and conditions in America. Smith, Wasson, Antler, and Buelens take a similar position. Bergland says the photographs included in the original edition of *The Promised Land* "contradict the prevailing message of the narrative" and "expose the contradictions of the American Dream" ("Rereading Photographs," 75–76). In the most thorough analysis of the ambiguity and multivocality of Antin's autobiography, Zaborowska argues that the book contains a dominant narrative and a subtext "in which the woman writer describes her frustration and disillusionment with the Promised Land" (*How We Found America,* 6–7).

5. Roosevelt, "Applied Idealism," 476.
6. Antin, "Woman," 485.
7. Antin's work on behalf of workingwomen has never been fully acknowledged in the critical discussion of her work. In fact, some critics

have denounced her for her lack of consideration for the plight of her sister Fetchke in *The Promised Land*. Evidence of Antin's participation in the fight for improved conditions for workingwomen can be found in the *Survey*'s "Keeping the Promise of the Promised Land." Her concern for working-women also suggests that Antin allied herself with the female *veltlickhe yidn* ("secular Jews") or *radikaln*. These women wrote in Yiddish for the Jewish socialist, anarchist, and communist presses. Predominantly drawn from tradespeople, teachers, and artists, they rejected Orthodox Judaism and were committed to cultural pluralism, the preservation of the Yiddish language and Jewish holidays, the fight for the working class, and Jewish communal loyalties. They were also patriotically American. See Pratt, "Culture and Radical Politics."

8. Downey, *Portrait of an Era*, 194. See also "On the Elongation of Form."

9. Banner, *American Beauty*, 154.

10. Downey, *Portrait of an Era*, 200–203; and Meyer, *America's Great Illustrators*, 212, 225.

11. Banta, *Imaging American Women*, 507, 755.

12. See Banner, *American Beauty*, 156–74.

13. Patterson, "Survival of the Best Fitted," 74. See also Banta, *Imaging American Women*, 214.

14. Banner, *American Beauty*, 326n33; Downey, *Portrait of an Era*, 194.

15. Banta, *Imaging American Women*, xxviii. Although taller than the Republic, the Statue of Liberty was built in France.

16. Ibid., chap. 12; Trachtenberg, *Statue of Liberty*, 9, 100; Banner, *American Beauty*, 168.

17. See Banner, *American Beauty*.

18. Banta, *Imaging American Women*, 515.

19. Ibid., 509.

20. Mosher, "Height of College Women," 5, 10–11.

21. Gilman, *Women and Economics*, 148–49.

22. Ibid., 182–83.

23. Ibid., 3–4, 44–47, 168.

24. See Gilman, *Herland*, 84. As the male narrator of the story remarks, he and his male comrades "began to rather prize those beards of ours; they were almost our sole distinction among those tall and sturdy women, with their cropped hair and sexless costume."

25. Smith-Rosenberg, *Disorderly Conduct*, 246.

26. Ibid., 258–59.

27. Bowditch, "Growth" (1877), 277, 286.

28. See Marks, *Bicycles, Bangs, and Bloomers*, 174; and Rotundo, *American Manhood*, 269.

29. See Ellis, *Man and Woman*, 4, 13, 16–17, 54; and Gilman, *Women and Economics*, 44–47, 147–49, 168, 330.

30. Smith-Rosenberg, *Disorderly Conduct*, 40.

31. See Marks, *Bicycles, Bangs, and Bloomers*, 2, 147; and Smith-Rosenberg, "New Woman as Androgyne," in *Disorderly Conduct*.

32. For some of those statistics, see Smith-Rosenberg, *Disorderly Conduct*, 253, 281.

33. See Tichi, "Women Writers," 593–97; and Rzepka, "'If I Can Make It,'" 58–59.

34. Marks, *Bicycles, Bangs, and Bloomers*, 176. Christophe Den Tandt has also suggested that twin figures emerged at the turn of the century in response to changes in gender roles: the amazon, a New Woman figure with masculine characteristics, and the "corporate androgyne," a male figure with feminine characteristics ("Amazons and Androgynes").

35. To demonstrate this point fully would require an additional chapter. But I can provide some interesting examples of the gendered treatment of size. Surveys conducted by the psychologists Martel and Biller indicate that short men are regarded as more feminine than tall and average men (*Stature and Stigma*, 59, 75–76). Alicia Ostriker has observed that literary critics tend to reserve large adjectives for male writers and small ones for women. "We seldom encounter, in praise of women poets, terms like *great, powerful, forceful, masterly, violent, large,* or *true.* The language used to express literary admiration in general presumes the masculinity of the author, the work, and the act of creation—but not if the author is a woman. Complimentary adjectives of choice then shift toward the diminutives: *graceful, subtle, elegant, delicate, cryptic,* and, above all, *modest*" (*Stealing the Language*, 3). Brownmiller has observed that consumer marketers often reinforce the association between masculinity and largeness. "A man-size portion puts more food on the plate and the Man-Size Kleenex packs more tissues in the box" (*Femininity*, 28).

36. Marks, *Bicycles, Bangs, and Bloomers*, 179.

37. Gilman, *Herland*, 19.

38. Downey, *Portrait of an Era*, 193–94.

39. Davis, "How the World Looks," 66.

40. Klein, *Little Big Men*, 34–36.

41. Brownmiller, *Femininity*, 28.

42. Rotundo, *American Manhood*, chap. 10; Klein, *Little Big Men*, 32–37; and Banner, *American Beauty*, chap. 11.

43. See Banner, *American Beauty*, 226–30.

44. Gillis, *Too Tall, Too Small*, 50, 130. Carroll Smith-Rosenberg has made a similar argument about the man-on-top sexual position favored by Victorians (see *Disorderly Conduct*, 286).

45. Raub, "New Woman," 127.

46. Mosher, "Height of College Women," 11. See also Gilman, *Women and Economics*, 158–59.

47. Banta, *Imaging American Women.*

48. Patterson, *Beyond the Gibson Girl.*

49. See Sollors, "Introduction," xv. The criticism was equally common at the time Antin wrote her autobiography. See, for example, the review "Mary Antin's 'They Who Knock at Our Gates'" from the *Bookman*.

50. Dearborn, *Pocahontas's Daughters*, 42.

51. See Zaborowska, *How We Found America.*

52. Antin, *They Who Knock*, 95.

53. Ripley, *Races of Europe*, 349, 383, 380, 372–73.

54. Grant, *Passing*, 14.

55. Hall, *Immigration*, 51.

56. Ross, *Old World*, 289–90.

57. Walker, "Restriction," 824, 828.

58. Walker, "Immigration," 644.

59. Hall, *Immigration*, 105.

60. Grant, *Passing*, 80.

61. Hall, *Immigration*, 99–101.

62. See Grant, *Passing*, 25.

63. See McLaughlin, "How Immigrants are Inspected."

64. See Hall, *Immigration*, 259, 243–44n8, 260–61n7; and Ward, "Higher Mental and Physical Standards," 544–47.

65. Efron, *Defenders of the Race*, 8–9, 176–79.

66. Jacobs, *Jewish Statistics*, xi.

67. Ibid., i.

68. See Jacobs and Spielman, "On the Comparative Anthropometry."

69. Boas, *Changes in Bodily Form*, 5.

70. Ibid., 5.

71. Fishberg, *Jews*, vii.

72. Fishberg, "Materials," 40.

73. Ibid., 44–45.

74. Antin was undoubtedly aware of Boas's findings in the Dillingham Commission report. In *They Who Knock at Our Gates*, she urged her readers to ignore the anthropological reports of the Dillingham Commission.

75. "Tells of Race Characteristics."

76. See Dearborn, *Pocahontas's Daughters*, 33–42.

77. On the latter, see "Keeping the Promise."

78. Gaines, "Black Americans," 450.

79. Antin, "A Confession of Faith."

80. Critics have offered various explanations for Antin's motives in writing *The Promised Land*. Rosenfeld takes her at her word when she says in the preface to her autobiography that she wants to forget the past. "To jettison the past so as to reach some stasis of identity in a normal, less perplexed present, to weld a unity of self out of the confusions of doubleness— these were the impulses that led Mary Antin to autobiographical invention," he writes ("Inventing the Jew," 134). Sally Ann Drucker agrees that this was one of Antin's motives (see "'It Doesn't Say So,'" 63). While a desire to reconcile her separate identities may have played a role in Antin's decision to write the book, whatever unity she did imagine was self-consciously performed for an audience with specific expectations, a factor that we must take into account when analyzing her treatment of double consciousness. In any case, it is clear from the contemporary reception of the book that readers took it primarily as a call for open immigration. "The argument for immigration," wrote a reviewer for the *New York Times* in 1912, "is implicit in every chapter of 'The Promised Land'" ("The Immigrant").

81. Butler, *Gender Trouble*, viii.

82. Butler, *Bodies That Matter*, 139.

83. Ibid., 107.

84. See ibid., 94–95, 234.

85. See Butler, *Gender Trouble* and *Bodies That Matter*.

86. Cited by Sollors in "Introduction," xxxvii.

87. Butler, *Gender Trouble*, 139.

88. See Sollors's Explanatory Notes to the Penguin edition of *The Promised Land*, 303.

89. Dearborn, *Pocahontas's Daughters*, 38.

90. See Adams, *Telling Lies*; and Eakin, *Fictions in Autobiography*.

91. See Sollors's Explanatory Notes to the Penguin edition of *The Promised Land,* 303.

CHAPTER 6

1. See Stewart, *On Longing;* Rugoff and Stewart, *At the Threshold;* Bachelard, *Poetics of Space;* Brown, "Science Fiction"; Pace, "Body-in-Writing"; Armstrong, "Gender and Miniaturization" and "'Here Little'"; Liebs, "Between *Gulliver* and *Alice*"; and Millhauser, "Fascination of the Miniature."

2. Hunt, "Dwarf, Small World," 116.

3. Dreiser, *Sister Carrie,* 433, 431.

4. Ibid., 609.

5. London, *Sea Wolf,* 35, 246, 220.

6. Hunt, "Dwarf, Small World," 133.

7. Filene, *Him/Her/Self,* 32–33.

8. Hantover, "Boy Scouts," 292.

9. James, *Bostonians,* 283.

10. Dreiser, *Sister Carrie,* 625.

11. Ibid., 558.

12. Between the Civil War and 1910, the percentage of men who were self-employed diminished from nine in ten to less than one in three, according to the historians Michael Kimmel and Michael Kaufman ("Weekend Warriors," 278).

13. Bederman, *Manliness and Civilization,* 12; Rotundo, *American Manhood,* 178–79; Grossberg, "Institutionalizing Masculinity," 138.

14. From *Varieties of Religious Experience,* cited in Lears, *No Place of Grace,* 179.

15. See, for example, Bederman, *Manliness and Civilization,* 10–15; and Kimmel, *Manhood in America,* 124.

16. Baron, "Acquiring Manly Competence."

17. See Barrett, *Work and Community.*

18. Cited in Kimmel, *Manhood in America,* 84.

19. London, *People of the Abyss,* 45–46, 7, 220, 285.

20. Rotundo, *American Manhood,* 17.

21. Martel and Biller, *Biopsychosocial Development,* 39–40.

22. Norris, *McTeague,* 71 passim. Dreiser's Hurstwood relies on a similar mantra: "I'm not down yet," he says repeatedly (Dreiser, *Sister Carrie,* 473 passim).

23. The term *physical imperative* comes from Segel, *Body Ascendant.*

24. *Physical Culture* magazine's special issue "Making the Body Taller" appeared in June 1912. Earlier issues occasionally included articles on the same subject. See, for example, Garland, "Exercises for Increasing the Height." In an editor's note to that article, Bernarr McFadden said the magazine had "received hundreds of inquiries in reference to the methods extensively advertised recently for increasing the height." One of those ads is shown in figure 39.

25. Citations come from Boy Scouts promotional literature and are quoted in Hantover, "Boy Scouts," 293, 196.

26. The phrase "cult of the body" comes from Studlar, *This Mad Masquerade,* 29.

27. Greene, *America's Heroes,* 127. For a comparison to earlier descriptions of heroes in popular American magazines, see 46–47.

28. Gaines, *Yours in Perfect Manhood,* 19, 70–71.

29. Roosevelt, *Autobiography,* 30.

30. Ibid., 31–32, 43.

31. Ibid., 84 passim.

32. Rotundo, *American Manhood,* 222.

33. Solomon-Godeau, "Male Trouble," 70; and Modleski, *Feminism Without Women,* 7.

34. A classic articulation of the crisis theory can be found in Dubbert, "Progressivism." Filene in *Him/Her/Self* and Kimmel in *Manhood in America* support slightly modified versions of the crisis theory (see Filene, where he argues that "manliness was suffering strain in all its dimensions" [74] at the turn of the century, and Kimmel, who suggests that "manhood was widely *perceived* to be in crisis" [78]). Both Griffen in "Reconstructing Masculinity" and Bederman in *Manliness and Civilization* contest the crisis theory and argue instead that gender norms were simply undergoing rapid transformation (see Griffen, 183–85, and Bederman, 10–15; both writers offer useful summaries of the debates over the crisis theory).

35. Sinclair, *The Jungle,* 20. All subsequent references are in parentheses in the text.

36. Barrett, *Work and Community,* 56.

37. Sullivan, *Autobiography,* 307–8.

38. See Mitchell, *Determined Fictions,* for an excellent formulation of this argument.

39. Ibid., 6.

40. Derrick, "What a Beating," 88, 94–95.

41. See Howard, *Form and History;* and Den Tandt, *Urban Sublime.*

42. Howard, *Form and History,* 95–103.

43. The inspiration for *Sister Carrie,* for example, came during Theodore Dreiser's experience of proletarianization. Frustrated with work as a newspaper reporter, Dreiser quit the profession and entered a period of temporary unemployment and poverty. While sitting idly on a park bench he conceived the Hurstwood character. Of the major naturalist writers— Dreiser, Norris, Crane, and London—only London was not born in the middle class.

44. Howard, *Form and History,* 159.

45. Ibid., chap. 3.

46. Ibid., 158.

47. Ibid., 159 (emphasis in original).

48. Michael Folsom confirms that "The *Appeal to Reason* had a larger working-class Socialist readership than any publication in the history of the American left." What is more important, however, is Sinclair's assumptions about his audience ("Upton Sinclair's Escape," 246).

49. Harris, *Upton Sinclair,* 151.

50. See, in addition to Howard, Folsom, "Upton Sinclair's Escape"; and Dembo, "Socialist and Socialite Heroes."

51. Folsom, "Upton Sinclair's Escape," 237.

52. Muncy, "Trustbusting," 22.

53. Ibid., 27–31.

54. Accordingly, literary and cultural narratives of shrinkage and

growth are, to my knowledge, always sharply gendered at the turn of the century. While men are depicted as capable of shrinking or growing, women always grow or remain in stasis. Female degeneration is rendered in terms other than bodily shrinkage; typically degeneration has sexual implications (e.g., the "womb trouble" that Ona suffers).

55. Muncy, "Trustbusting," 21.

56. On Sinclair's advocacy of nonviolent revolution, see *The Jungle*, 313; Yoder, *Upton Sinclair*; and Harris, *Upton Sinclair*.

57. London, *Sea Wolf*, 168, 201.

58. For a general discussion of the white slavery crusade, see Filene, *Him/Her/Self*, 91–99. For a fascinating discussion of the popular white slavery tract genre and its influence on other forms of literature (notably Zane Grey's *Riders of the Purple Sage*), see Mitchell, *Westerns*, chap. 5.

59. Filene, *Him/Her/Self*, 96–97.

60. The danger of changing the gender order is apparent in naturalism as a repeated and ominous trope of male dependence on women. Frank Norris and Theodore Dreiser, respectively, link McTeague's and Hurstwood's degeneration and ultimate destruction to the loss of their careers and consequent dependence on their wives. Dreiser goes further than Norris, linking male dependence fears with prostitution anxieties. When Carrie suggests that she will seek acting work as a way of bringing in some money during Hurstwood's unemployment, he listens in "horror" (Dreiser, *Sister Carrie*, 496), immediately conjuring images of Carrie sleeping with a theater manager in the supposedly typical way chorus girls secured and maintained their positions. Reaching the very nadir of his degeneration in *The Jungle*, Jurgis faces the ultimate perversion of his manhood when Marija, now a prostitute, offers to support him through her labor. As a way of imagining the consequences of gender role reversals, naturalist texts seem locked into a fearful vision of male deterioration related simultaneously to their unemployment and their dependence on women. To put this another way, one could say that threats to the gender order are integral to the naturalist proletarianization plot. Male dependence on women, male failure to protect women, and the specters of prostitution and white slavery are all direct consequences of downward mobility (including Hump's impressment as a sailor, Hooven's loss of his farm, McTeague's loss of his dental practice, Hurstwood's unemployment, and Jurgis's loss of his manufacturing job).

61. See *The Jungle*, 333, where Sinclair, repeating the arguments of feminist socialists like Charlotte Perkins Gilman, briefly suggests that the majority of women endure lives of prostitution under the current social system—either the middle-class form of prostitution known as marriage or the more familiar form of lower-class prostitution.

62. See Solomon-Godeau, "Male Trouble"; Modleski, *Feminism Without Women*; Cook, "Masculinity in Crisis?"; and Ross, "Great White Dude."

63. This is a reference to Jurgis's embrace of unionism, but it describes equally well his later conversion to socialism.

64. As an example, one might consider a passage from late in the book after Jurgis's conversion to socialism. "You would begin talking to some poor devil," Sinclair writes (Jurgis's thoughts and the narrator's voice merge here), "and when you started to tell him about Socialism he would sniff and say, 'I'm not interested in that—I'm an individualist!' And then he would go

on to tell you that Socialism was 'paternalism.' . . . [Such people] really thought that it was 'individualism' for tens of thousands of them to herd together and obey the orders of a steel magnate, and produce hundreds of millions of dollars of wealth for him" (324–25). The idea that the alternative to capitalist individualism is socialist "paternalism" is suggestive of the way antisocialists presumed that men would be placed in a feminized or dependent position in a socialist state.

EPILOGUE

1. Diggins, *Proud Decades,* 178–83; Reeves, *Twentieth-Century America,* 156; and O'Neill, *Years of Confidence,* 1.

2. Reeves, *Twentieth-Century America,* 156; Belton, *Widescreen Cinema,* 81.

3. Mills, *White Collar,* xiv. See also 64, where Mills estimates that the percentage of white-collar workers rose from 15 to 56 percent of the middle class between 1870 and 1940.

4. Ibid., 13.

5. Whyte, *Organization Man,* 68, 131.

6. Ibid., 69.

7. Ibid., 72–73.

8. Goldberger, *Skyscraper,* 103.

9. "The formal differences between a Chevrolet sedan and a Frigidaire refrigerator were often all but undetectable," writes Karal Ann Marling (*As Seen on TV,* 261). See also Baughman, "Frustrated Persuader," 29.

10. Shapiro, *Americans* (unpaginated). There is a curious degree of dissembling—one might even say self-deception—that occurs in the pages of Shapiro's article, first published in *Natural History* magazine in 1945 and later reprinted as a monograph by the American Museum of Natural History. Shapiro insists repeatedly that Americans have undergone a progressive, secular increase in stature since measurements were first taken in the middle of the nineteenth century, and he claims that Sargent's statues of Adam and Eve "were shorter than their modern counterparts." Yet both Eve and Norma measured 5'3" (to be more precise, Norma represented an individual who was 5'3"; Norm and Norma were half-life-size statues) (see Robertson, "Theater Cashier," 1; and chap. 1 of this book). In addition, Shapiro contradicts himself in saying that average American women of 1940 were taller than college women of 1920; the data he exhibits indicate that women in the 1940 study averaged 5'3.6", whereas college women in the 1920 studies averaged 5'4.8" (see *Americans,* unpaginated text). Whether Norm was taller (in adjusted terms) than Adam is difficult to judge from the pages of *Americans,* since, curiously, Shapiro does not provide Norm's or Adam's measurements (Norma's and Eve's measurements are omitted as well, but they are available from other sources, as indicated previously). The fact that Shapiro does include data indicating an increase in stature among male Harvard students during the years 1856 to 1915 suggests that Norm was no taller than Adam—and possibly shorter (that is to say, it seems likely that Shapiro would have included the measurements of Adam and Norm had they supported his argument). As if to underscore the unreliability of the Harvard data for their indication of average American male stature, by the way, Shapiro's article includes data from the Davenport-Love study of

American men drafted in World War I, which give an average height for American men well below the figures given by the Harvard study. In other words, Shapiro's repeated claims about the secular increases in stature among American men and women are not sufficiently supported by his data and are, in fact, contradicted by the data.

For further discussion of Norm and Norma and the publicity surrounding the creation of the models, see Urla and Swedlund, "Anthropometry of Barbie."

11. The preoccupation with the height of Japanese soldiers can be found throughout the wartime media. A 1943 War Department Orientation Film designed to educate U.S. recruits about Japan and the Japanese entitled *Know Your Enemy—Japan,* for example, begins a wide-ranging discussion of Japanese history, politics, geography, economy, education, and religion with a discussion of the physical characteristics of the Japanese soldier.

> First, let's examine a typical Japanese soldier. His average height is 5 feet 3 inches, his average weight 117 pounds. He and his brother soldiers are as much alike as photographic prints off the same negative. . . . His appearance [is] unsoldierly, even comic, according to Western standards. . . . He has been trained to be a soldier almost from birth, and into his tough, little mind has been drilled and hammered the fanatical belief that Japanese are descendants of Gods and destined to rule the earth and all who live on it.

A writer for *National Geographic* in 1942 expressed the confidence in ultimate victory that was deduced from comparisons of Japanese and American physical characteristics. "We see [the Japanese] as being like us—on a smaller scale. . . . And we take it for granted that we can lick a smaller version of ourselves" (Price, "Unknown Japan," 225). See also "How to Tell Japs" and Abend, "Japan's Soldier's."

12. Kallen, *The 1950s,* 24; Diggins, *Proud Decades,* 181; and Reeves, *Twentieth-Century America,* 155.

13. O'Neill, *American High,* 288.

14. For further discussion of these innovations in the film industry, see Belton, *Widescreen Cinema;* and Cohan, *Masked Men,* chap. 4. Although the title of Belton's book suggests that lateral expansion was the chief characteristic of fifties' cinematic innovations, Paramount's VistaVision expanded the frame in the vertical dimension and enabled what Cohan describes as a "vertical aesthetic" (*Masked Men,* 158; see also Belton, *Widescreen Cinema,* 126).

15. See May, *Homeward Bound,* 13–14.

16. Hendershot, "Darwin and the Atom," 319.

17. May, *Homeward Bound,* 14.

18. Mills, *White Collar,* 111.

19. Whyte, *Organization Man,* 11; emphasis in original.

20. Mills, *White Collar,* xv.

21. Ibid., xv–xvii, 297.

22. Ibid., xvi–xvii, 263–64.

23. Ibid., xv–xvii, 206, 272–307.

24. Filene, *Him/Her/Self,* 173.

25. Diggins, *Proud Decades,* 212; O'Neill, *American High,* 43.

26. O'Neill, *American High,* 43; Harvey, *The Fifties,* xix.

27. Filene, *Him/Her/Self,* 175.

28. Ibid., 208.

29. *Decline of the American Male,* 18–19.

30. Mills, *White Collar,* 200, 228, 263–64; Kimmel, *Manhood in America,* 241–42; May, *Homeward Bound,* 87; and Cohan, *Masked Men,* xii.

31. Kimmel, *Manhood in America,* 245–46.

32. Ibid., 255.

33. See Friedan, *Feminine Mystique,* 190–93; and Kimmel, *Manhood in America,* 229.

34. Cohan, *Masked Men,* xii, 56–57; Kimmel, *Manhood in America,* 224–25.

35. Cohan, *Masked Men,* x–xi.

36. In addition to the films discussed here, shrinking men and growing women can be found in Jim Thompson's 1953 novel *Savage Night* (in the character of Charles Bigger), John Okada's 1957 novel *No-No Boy* (in the character of Kenji), and the illustrations accompanying *Look* magazine's special issue "The Decline of the American Male" (see fig. 42).

37. For further discussion of the incident, see Kallen, *The 1950s,* 92–93; and Diggins, *Proud Decades,* 327.

38. Mills, *White Collar,* xviii, ix.

39. Ibid., xii.

40. Ibid., 257.

41. See, for example, Matheson, *Shrinking Man,* 67.

42. This is not to say, as Tania Modleski does, that the "preoccupation with size" is "eminently masculine" (*Feminism Without Women,* 95). Clearly, as I argued in chapter 5, women have been preoccupied with size as well. Rather, I am suggesting, as I did in chapter 6, that narratives of shrinkage often codify masculine anxieties in addition to whatever else they may signify.

43. See Matheson, *Shrinking Man,* 20–21; and Jancovich, *Rational Fears,* 159–60.

44. In the novel this character performs under the sobriquet Mrs. Tom Thumb, the turn-of-the-century celebrity.

45. For further discussion and analysis of the freak show, see Fiedler, *Freaks;* and Thomson, *Freakery* and *Extraordinary Bodies.*

46. Matheson, *Shrinking Man,* 18, 68.

47. For further discussion of this idea, see Bederman, *Manliness and Civilization;* and Rotundo, *American Manhood,* 227–39.

48. Tarratt, "Monsters from the Id." See also Wells, who offers a similar reading of the film in his witty essay "The Invisible Man."

49. Modleski, *Feminism Without Women,* 93–95.

50. Matheson, *Shrinking Man,* 22.

51. See Marling, *As Seen on TV,* chap. 1; May, *Homeward Bound,* 112; and Harvey, *Fifties,* xi.

52. These features of the story have suggested to Cyndy Hendershot that Scott's descent into the basement represents a "fall into matriarchy." Unlike Tarratt and Modleski, however, Hendershot does not believe the film depicts the matriarchal cellar world or the spider as inherently evil, although she does agree that the narrative is deeply invested in the "reassertion of patriarchal dominance" ("Darwin and the Atom," 329–30).

53. Examples include Lehman, *Running Scared;* Schehr, *Parts of an Andrology;* and Bordo, *Male Body.*

54. Examples include Dyer, "Don't Look Now"; Tasker, *Spectacular Bodies;* Klein, *Little Big Men;* and Dutton, *Perfectible Body.*

55. Race was also initially given scant attention in studies of masculinity, but that omission has been rectified recently.

56. In his preface to *American Manhood,* for example, Rotundo briefly suggests that the size of his uncles—one of whom was under five feet and one of whom was "tall and strong"—must surely have affected their adaptation to "codes of manhood" (x). He pursues this subject later in the book when he addresses the significance attached to differences of physical size in nineteenth-century boy culture, noting that "smaller boys became victims in various kinds of organized games" and bigness "earned a boy respect among his peers" (see 40–42). He offers no discussion of the importance of height among adult men, however. In a cross-cultural study of masculinity, Gilmore points out that tallness has dramatic social benefits for men among the Mehinaku while short men suffer various forms of abuse and discrimination, circumstances that indicate an affinity with U.S. culture (*Manhood in the Making,* 86–88). The only sustained attention to the relationship between physical stature and gender has come from works outside the field of masculinity studies. These include Keyes, *Height of Your Life;* Gillis, *Too Tall, Too Small;* Feldman, "Presentation of Shortness"; and Brownmiller, *Femininity.* Although it does not engage with much of the recent critical discourse on masculinity, Martel and Biller's *Stature and Stigma* is the only text that might be considered to fall within the contemporary field of masculinity studies.

57. Lehman, *Running Scared,* 85–86.

58. Ibid., 86.

59. These problems are also evident in Modleski's "Incredible Shrinking He(r)man" (in *Feminism Without Women*) and Wells's "Invisible Man." Both are inclined to read images of shrinking men in sexual terms, and neither relates such images to stature prejudices. Only Wells, in fact, seems to recognize that such prejudices exist (see 189).

60. Martel and Biller, *Stature and Stigma,* 89.

61. Husbands often converted cellars into workshops in the fifties. This is what Robert Moskin has in mind in his essay on women's domination of men in *Look* magazine's special issue "The Decline of the American Male." "For a while the male fled to the basement and busied himself sawing, painting and sandpapering" as a defensive response to the domestic mystique of the fifties, says Moskin. "But the women followed him, and today they are hammering right along with him. No place to hide there" (*Decline of the American Male,* 19–20).

62. See Kallen, *The 1950s,* 16, 142; O'Neill, *American High,* 19; and Diggins, *Proud Decades,* 181–83. In this light, Carey's entrapment in the basement and his invisibility to others bear a certain resemblance to the plight of the main character in Ellison's *Invisible Man,* published just four years before Matheson's *Shrinking Man.* One might argue that Carey's story is, on some level, a narrative of racial passing and that the basement is a metaphor for the nation's politics of segregation.

63. Matheson, *Shrinking Man,* 61–62; emphasis in original.

64. Other stories by Matheson, Jancovich points out, "challenge

assumptions about women," critique male privilege, and examine "the exploitation of women by men" (*Rational Fears,* 136–38). Paul Wells also emphasizes the ways *The Incredible Shrinking Man* critiques dominant notions of masculinity (see "Invisible Man").

65. See Jancovich, *Rational Fears,* chap. 4.

66. See, for example, May, *Homeward Bound;* Harvey, *The Fifties;* Diggins, *Proud Decades;* Filene, *Him/Her/Self;* and O'Neill, *American High.*

67. See Friedan, *Feminine Mystique.* Coincidentally, Friedan was preoccupied, like her feminist forebears at the turn of the century and *Attack of the 50-Foot Woman,* with female growth and the inhibition of women's growth in a patriarchal society. "It is my thesis," she argues, "that the core of the problem for women today is . . . a stunting or evasion of growth that is perpetuated by the feminine mystique" (77).

68. See May, *Homeward Bound,* esp. 184–85.

69. See, for example, Jancovich, who regards the alien satellite as "an irrelevant and pointless diversion from the central story" of the film (*Rational Fears,* 206). In the opposing camp is Tony Williams, who, like me, views the alien as a symbol of Nancy's fears about her husband and of Nancy's oppression ("Female Oppression," 269–70).

70. Jancovich, *Rational Fears,* 205. Jancovich examines both readings of the film—the one emphasizing its feminist impulses and the other accentuating its male paranoiac traits—and finds both insufficient, not because there are inherent flaws in the positions but because in his view the film never achieves complete coherence (see 205–6).

71. See Williams, "Female Oppression," 265, 270–71; and Wells, "Invisible Man," 194.

72. Byars, "Prime of Miss Kim Novak," 200, 216. Both Williams ("Female Oppression") and Wells ("Invisible Man") come to similar conclusions about the film.

73. That is to say, Nancy's transformation is an effect of an era that witnessed the advent of satellites and nuclear energy. Hers is "a case not infrequent in this supersonic age," says the psychiatrist called in by Nancy's doctor to consult on her amazing growth.

Bibliography

Abend, Hallett. "Japan's Soldiers—Unsoldierly Yet Fanatic." *New York Times Magazine,* January 11, 1942, 12.

Ablon, Joan. *Little People in America: The Social Dimensions of Dwarfism.* New York: Praeger, 1984.

Adam, Paul. "The Titan's Tower." *Independent* 60 (May 24, 1906): 1200.

Adams, Bluford. *E Pluribus Barnum: The Great Showman and the Making of U.S. Popular Culture.* Minneapolis: University of Minnesota Press, 1997.

Adams, Timothy Dow. *Telling Lies in Modern American Autobiography.* Chapel Hill: University of North Carolina Press, 1990.

Adams, Walter, and James Brock. *The Bigness Complex: Industry, Labor, and Government in the American Economy.* New York: Pantheon Books, 1986.

"The American Skyscraper: The Giant in Architecture: Its Purpose, Beauty and Development." *Craftsman* 24 (April 1913): 3–10.

Antin, Mary. "The Amulet." *Atlantic Monthly,* January 1913, 31–41.

———. "A Confession of Faith." *Jewish Advocate,* February 15, 1917, 5.

———. "The Lie." *Atlantic Monthly,* August 1913, 177–90.

———. *The Promised Land.* 1912. Reprint, New York: Penguin Books, 1997.

———. *They Who Knock at Our Gates: A Complete Gospel of Immigration.* Boston and New York: Houghton Mifflin, 1914.

———. "A Woman to Her Fellow-Citizens." *Outlook* 102 (1912): 482–86.

Antler, Joyce. "Sleeping with the Other: The Problem of Gender in American-Jewish Literature." In *Feminist Perspectives on Jewish Studies,* ed. Lynn Davidman and Shelly Tenenbaum. New Haven: Yale University Press, 1994.

Aristotle. *The Basic Works of Aristotle.* Ed. Richard McKeon. New York: Random House, 1941.

Armstrong, Frances. "Gender and Miniaturization: Games of Littleness in Nineteenth-Century Fiction." *English Studies in Canada* 16, no. 4 (December 1990): 403–16.

———. "'Here Little, and Hereafter Bliss': *Little Women* and the Deferral of Greatness." *American Literature* 64, no. 3 (September 1992): 453–74.

Armstrong, Meg. "'A Jumble of Foreignness': The Sublime Musayums of Nineteenth-Century Fairs and Expositions." *Cultural Critique* 23 (winter 1992–93): 199–250.

Armstrong, Tim. *Modernism, Technology, and the Body: A Cultural Study.* Cambridge: Cambridge University Press, 1998.

———, ed. *American Bodies: Cultural Histories of the Physique.* New York: New York University Press, 1996.

Attack of the 50-Foot Woman. Dir. Nathan Juran. Allied Artists, 1958.

Atwan, Robert, Donald McQuade, and John Wright. *Edsels, Luckies, and Frigidaires: Advertising the American Way.* New York: Dell Publishing, 1979.

Bachelard, Gaston. *The Poetics of Space.* 1958. Trans. Maria Jolas, Boston: Beacon Press, 1994.

Baldwin, Bird Thomas. *Physical Growth and School Progress: A Study in Experimental Education.* U.S. Bureau of Education Bulletin No. 10. Washington: Government Printing Office, 1914.

Banner, Lois. *American Beauty.* New York: Alfred A. Knopf, 1983.

Banta, Martha. *Imaging American Women: Ideas and Ideals in Cultural History.* New York: Columbia University Press, 1987.

Barnard, Neal, et al. "Concerns about Growth Hormone Experiments in Short Children." In *Physicians Committee for Responsible Medicine, Research Controversies and Issues, Ethics in Human Research.* Visited May 21, 2004. <http://www.pcrm.org/issues/Ethics_in_Human_Research/ethics_human_growthhormone.html>.

Baron, Ava. "Acquiring Manly Competence: The Demise of Apprenticeship and the Remasculinization of Printers' Work." In *Meanings for Manhood: Constructions of Masculinity in Victorian America,* ed. Mark Carnes and Clyde Griffen. Chicago: University of Chicago Press, 1990.

Barrett, James R. *Work and Community in the Jungle: Chicago's Packing-house Workers, 1894–1922.* Urbana: University of Illinois Press, 1987.

Bartky, Sandra Lee. "Foucault, Femininity, and the Modernization of Patriarchal Power." In *Writing on the Body: Female Embodiment and Feminist Theory,* ed. Katie Conboy, Nadia Medina, and Sarah Stanbury. New York: Columbia University Press, 1997.

Baughman, James. "The Frustrated Persuader: Fairfax M. Cone and the Edsel Advertising Campaign, 1957–59." In *The Other Fifties: Interrogating Midcentury American Icons.* Ed. Joel Foreman. Urbana: University of Illinois Press, 1997.

Baxter, J. H. *Statistics, Medical and Anthropological, of the Provost-Marshal-General's Bureau.* Vol. 1. Washington: Government Printing Office, 1875.

Bayne, S. G. "The Woolworth Building." *New York Times,* June 6, 1913, 10.

Bean, Robert Bennett. "Stature Throughout the World." *Science* 67, no. 1723 (January 6, 1928): 1–5.

Bederman, Gail. *Manliness and Civilization: A Cultural History of Gender and Race in the United States, 1880–1917.* Chicago: University of Chicago Press, 1995.

Bellamy, Edward. *Looking Backward.* 1888. Reprint, New York: Penguin Books, 1984.

Belton, John. *Widescreen Cinema.* Cambridge, MA: Harvard University Press, 1992.

Bending, Lucy. "From Stunted Child to 'New Woman': The Significance of Physical Growth in Late-Nineteenth-Century Medicine and Fiction." *Yearbook of English Studies* 32 (2002): 205–16.

Bennitt, Mark, and Frank Parker Stockbridge, eds. *History of the Louisiana Purchase Exposition: St. Louis World's Fair of 1904.* St. Louis: Universal Exposition Publishing, 1905.

Berger, John. *Ways of Seeing*. London: British Broadcasting Company and Penguin, 1972.

Berger, Maurice, Brian Wallis, and Simon Watson, eds. *Constructing Masculinity*. New York: Routledge, 1995.

Bergland, Betty. "Rereading Photographs and Narratives in Ethnic Autobiography: Memory and Subjectivity in Mary Antin's *The Promised Land*." In *Memory, Narrative, and Identity: New Essays in Ethnic American Literature*, ed. Amritjit Singh, Joseph Skerrett, and Robert Hogan. Boston: Northeastern University Press, 1994.

Bird, Stewart, Dan Georgakas, and Deborah Shaffer, eds. *Solidarity Forever: An Oral History of the IWW*. Chicago: Lake View Press, 1985.

Blair, Sara. *Henry James and the Writing of Race and Nation*. Cambridge: Cambridge University Press, 1996.

Blumin, Stuart. *The Emergence of the Middle Class: Social Experience in the American City, 1760–1900*. Cambridge: Cambridge University Press, 1989.

Boas, Franz. *Changes in Bodily Form of Descendants of Immigrants*. Washington: Government Printing Office, 1911.

———. "On Dr. William Townsend Porter's Investigation of the Growth of the School Children of St. Louis." *Science*, n.s., 1 (March 1, 1895): 225–30.

———. "Educational Research and Statistics: The Growth of Children as Influenced by Environmental and Hereditary Conditions." *School and Society* 17 (March 17, 1923): 305–8.

———. "The Growth of Children." *Science* 19 (1892): 256–57.

———. "The Growth of Children." *Science* 20 (December 23, 1892): 351–52.

———. "The History of Anthropology." *Science*, n.s., 20 (October 21, 1904): 513–24.

———. *Materials for the Study of Inheritance in Man*. New York: Columbia University Press, 1928.

Bogardus, Ralph. *Pictures and Texts: Henry James, A. L. Coburn, and New Ways of Seeing in Literary Culture*. Michigan: UMI Research Press, 1984.

Bondeson, Jan. *A Cabinet of Medical Curiosities*. New York: Cornell University Press, 1997.

Boorstin, Daniel. *The Americans: The Democratic Experience*. New York: Random House, 1973.

———. *The Americans: The National Experience*. New York: Vintage Books, 1965.

Bordo, Susan. *The Male Body: A New Look at Men in Public and in Private*. New York: Farrar, Straus, and Giroux, 1999.

———. *Unbearable Weight: Feminism, Western Culture, and the Body*. Berkeley: University of California Press, 1993.

Boscagli, Maurizia. *Eye on the Flesh: Fashions of Masculinity in the Early Twentieth Century*. Boulder, CO: Westview Press, 1996.

Bowditch, Henry. "The Growth of Children." In *Eighth Annual Report of the State Board of Health of Massachusetts*, 275–327. Boston: Wright, 1877.

———. "The Growth of Children Studied by Galton's Method of Percentile Grades." In *22nd Annual Report of the State Board of Health of Massachusetts*, 479–525. Boston: Wright and Potter, 1891.

———. "The Physique of Women in Massachusetts." In *21st Annual Report of the State Board of Health of Massachusetts,* 287–304. Boston: Wright and Potter, 1890.

Bradford, Phillips Verner, and Harvey Blume. *Ota: The Pygmy in the Zoo.* New York: St. Martin's Press, 1992.

Bragdon, Claude. *Architecture and Democracy.* 2d ed. New York: Alfred A. Knopf, 1926.

———. *The Frozen Fountain: Being Essays on Architecture and the Art of Design in Space.* New York: Alfred A. Knopf, 1932.

Brandeis, Louis. *Brandeis on Democracy.* Ed. Philippa Strum. Lawrence: University Press of Kansas, 1995.

———. *Business—A Profession.* 1914. Reprint, New York: Augustus M. Kelley, 1971.

———. *The Curse of Bigness.* Ed. Osmond Fraenkel. New York: Viking Press, 1934.

———. *Other People's Money and How the Bankers Use It.* 1914. Reprint, New York: Frederick A. Stokes, 1933.

———. "Trusts, Efficiency, and the New Party." *Collier's,* September 14, 1912, 14–15.

British Parliamentary Papers. Reports from Commissioners 4:20. *First Report into the Employment of Children in Factories.* 1833. Reprint, Dublin: Irish University Press, 1968.

Brown, Bill. *The Material Unconscious: American Amusement, Stephen Crane, and the Economies of Play.* Cambridge, MA: Harvard University Press, 1996.

———. "Science Fiction, the World's Fair, and the Prosthetics of Empire, 1910–1915." In *Cultures of United States Imperialism,* ed. Amy Kaplan and Donald Pease. Durham: Duke University Press, 1993.

———. *A Sense of Things: The Object Matter of American Literature.* Chicago: University of Chicago Press, 2003.

Brown, Susan Jenkins. *Robber Rocks: Letters and Memories of Hart Crane, 1923–32.* Middletown, CT: Wesleyan University Press, 1968.

Brownmiller, Susan. *Femininity.* New York: Fawcett Columbine, 1984.

Bruce, H. Addington. *Above the Clouds and Old New York: An Historical Sketch of the Site and a Description of the Many Wonders of the Woolworth Building.* New York: Hugh McAtamney Munder-Thomsen Press, 1913.

Brunner, Edward. *Splendid Failure: Hart Crane and the Making of* The Bridge. Urbana: University of Illinois Press, 1985.

Budd, Michael Anton. *The Sculpture Machine: Physical Culture and Body Politics in the Age of Empire.* New York: New York University Press, 1997.

Buelens, Gert. "The New Man and the Mediator: (Non-)Remembrance in Jewish-American Immigrant Narrative." In *Memory, Narrative, and Identity: New Essays in Ethnic American Literature,* ed. Amritjit Singh, Joseph Skerrett, and Robert Hogan. Boston: Northeastern University Press, 1994.

Buhle, Paul, and Edmund B. Sullivan. *Images of American Radicalism.* Hanover, MA: Christopher Publishing House, 1998.

Bullock, Charles J. "Trust Literature: A Survey and a Criticism." *Quarterly Journal of Economics* 15 (February 1901): 167–217.

Burg, David. "The Aesthetics of Bigness in Late Nineteenth Century American Architecture." In *Popular Architecture,* ed. Marshal Fishwick and J. Meredith Neil. Bowling Green, OH: Bowling Green Popular Press, 1974.

Burrows, Guy. *The Land of the Pygmies.* New York: Thomas Y. Crowell, 1898.

Butler, Judith. *Bodies that Matter: On the Discursive Limits of "Sex."* New York: Routledge, 1993.

———. *Gender Trouble: Feminism and the Subversion of Identity.* New York: Routledge, 1990.

Byars, Jackie. "The Prime of Miss Kim Novak: Struggling Over the Feminine in the Star Image." In *The Other Fifties: Interrogating Midcentury American Icons,* ed. Joel Foreman. Urbana: University of Illinois Press, 1997.

Cahan, Abraham. *The Rise of David Levinsky.* 1917. Reprint, New York: Harper and Row, 1960.

Carnegie, Andrew. *The Gospel of Wealth and Other Timely Essays.* New York: Century, 1901.

Cather, Willa. "Behind the Singer Tower." In *Willa Cather's Collected Short Fiction, 1892–1912,* ed. Virginia Faulkner. Lincoln: University of Nebraska Press, 1970.

Chamberlain, Alex. F. "Robert Grant Haliburton." *Journal of American Folk-Lore* 14 (January–March 1901): 62–64.

Chandler, Alfred. *The Coming of Managerial Capitalism.* Homewood, IL: R. D. Irwin, 1985.

———. *The Essential Alfred Chandler: Essays Toward a Historical Theory of Big Business.* Ed. Thomas McCraw. Boston: Harvard Business School Press, 1988.

———. *Scale and Scope: The Dynamics of Industrial Capitalism.* Cambridge: Belknap Press of Harvard University, 1990.

Chicago Conference on Trusts. Chicago: Civic Federation of Chicago, 1900.

Clark, John Bates, and John Maurice. *The Control of Trusts.* New York: MacMillan, 1912.

Coburn, Alvin Langdon. *Alvin Langdon Coburn, Photographer: An Autobiography.* New York: Frederick A. Praeger, 1966.

———. "New York from Its Pinnacles." In *Camera Pictures.* London: Goupil Gallery, 1913.

———. "The Relation of Time to Art." *Camera Work* 36 (1911): 72–73.

Cochran, Edwin. *The Cathedral of Commerce.* New York: Woolworth Building, 1916.

Cogdell, Christina. "The Futurama Recontextualized: Norman Bel Geddes's Eugenic 'World of Tomorrow.'" *American Quarterly* 52, no. 2 (June 2000): 193–245.

Cohan, Steven. *Masked Men: Masculinity and the Movies in the Fifties.* Bloomington: Indiana University Press, 1997.

Cohen, Sarah Blacher. "Mary Antin's *The Promised Land:* A Breach of Promise." *Studies in American Jewish Literature* 3, no. 2 (1977–78): 28–35.

Conn, Peter. *The Divided Mind: Ideology and Imagination in America, 1898–1917.* Cambridge: Cambridge University Press, 1983.

Cook, Pam. "Masculinity in Crisis?" *Screen* 23, no. 3–4 (September–October 1982): 39–46.

Corn, Wanda. *The Great American Thing: Modern Art and National Identity, 1915–1935.* Berkeley: University of California Press, 1999.

Crane, Hart. *Complete Poems and Selected Letters and Prose of Hart Crane.* New York: Liveright Publishing, 1966.

Cremin, Lawrence. *American Education: The Metropolitan Experience 1876–1980.* New York: Harper and Row, 1988.

Crichton-Browne, Harold. "Dwarfs and Dwarf Worship." *Nature* 45 (January 21, 1892): 269–71.

Cronin, Brian. "It's a Tall, Tall World." *Discover,* January 1994, 83–84.

"The Crown of the Skyscraper." *Architectural Record* 27 (May 1910): 431–34.

Darwin, Charles. "Darwin on the Fuegians and Patagonians." *Popular Science Monthly,* April 1890, 744–50.

———. *The Descent of Man and Selection in Relation to Sex.* 2d ed. New York: D. Appleton, 1896.

Dastre, A. "The Stature of Man at Various Epochs." *Scientific American,* Supplement, November 18 and 25, 1905, 24986–87, 24998–99.

Davis, J. Frank. "How the World Looks to a Short Man." *American Magazine,* July 1920, 66–67+.

Dawley, Alan. *Struggles for Justice: Social Responsibility and the Liberal State.* Cambridge, MA: Belknap Press of Harvard University, 1991.

Dearborn, Mary. *Pocahontas's Daughters: Gender and Ethnicity in American Culture.* New York: Oxford University Press, 1986.

Decline of the American Male. New York: Random House, 1958.

Dembo, L. S. "The Socialist and Socialite Heroes of Upton Sinclair." In *Toward a New American Literary History,* ed. Louis Budd, Edwin Cady, and Carl Anderson. Durham: Duke University Press, 1980.

Den Tandt, Christophe. "Amazons and Androgynes: Overcivilization and the Redefinition of Gender Roles at the Turn of the Century." *American Literary History* 8, no. 4 (winter 1996): 639–64.

———. *The Urban Sublime in American Literary Naturalism.* Urbana: University of Illinois Press, 1998.

Denison, George. "Robert Grant Haliburton." *Canadian Magazine,* June 1901, 126–30.

Derrick, Scott. "What a Beating Feels Like: Authorship, Dissolution, and Masculinity in Sinclair's *The Jungle.*" *Studies in American Fiction* 23, no. 1 (spring 1995): 85–100.

Dickson, S. Henry. "Statistics of Height and Weight." *American Journal of the Medical Sciences* 52 (1866): 373–80.

Diggins, John Patrick. *The Proud Decades: America in War and in Peace, 1941–1960.* New York: W. W. Norton, 1988.

Domosh, Mona. "Imagining New York's First Skyscrapers, 1875–1910." *Journal of Historical Geography* 13, no. 3 (1987): 233–48.

Downey, Fairfax. *Portrait of an Era as Drawn by C. D. Gibson.* New York: Charles Scribner's Sons, 1936.

Dreiser, Theodore. *Sister Carrie.* New York: Modern Library, 1999.

Drucker, Sally Ann. "'It Doesn't Say So in Mother's Prayerbook': Autobiographies in English by Immigrant Jewish Women." *American Jewish History* 79, no. 1 (autumn 1989): 55–71.

Du Chaillu, Paul Belloni. *Adventures in the Great Forest of Equatorial Africa and the Country of the Dwarfs.* New York: Harper and Brothers, 1890.

———. *The Country of the Dwarfs.* 1872. Reprint, New York: Negro Universities Press, 1969.

———. *Explorations and Adventures in Equatorial Africa.* London: John Murray, 1861.

———. *A Journey to Ashango-Land and Further Penetration into Equatorial Africa.* London: John Murray, 1867.

Dubbert, Joe L. "Progressivism and the Masculinity Crisis." In *The American Man,* ed. Elizabeth Pleck and Joseph Pleck. Englewood Cliffs, NJ: Prentice-Hall, 1980.

Dunn, H. H. "Making Giants Out of Mice and Men." *Popular Mechanics,* May 1925, 705–6.

Dutton, Kenneth R. *The Perfectible Body: The Western Ideal of Male Physical Development.* New York: Continuum Publishing, 1995.

Dyer, Richard. "Don't Look Now: The Instabilities of the Male Pin-Up." In *Only Entertainment.* New York: Routledge, 1992.

Eakin, Paul John. *Fictions in Autobiography: Studies in the Art of Self-Invention.* Princeton: Princeton University Press, 1985.

Efron, John. *Defenders of the Race: Jewish Doctors and Race Science in Fin-de-Siecle Europe.* New Haven: Yale University Press, 1994.

Ehrenreich, Barbara. *The Hearts of Men: American Dreams and the Flight from Commitment.* New York: Doubleday, 1983.

Ellis, Havelock. *Man and Woman: A Study of Human Secondary Sexual Characters.* 4th ed. New York: Charles Scribner's Sons, 1904.

Ellis, John. *Visible Fictions: Cinema, Television, and Video.* London: Routledge, 1982.

Emerson, Wm. R. P. "Physical and Mental Unfitness in Children." *School and Society* 20 (September 20, 1924): 361–65.

England, George Allan. *The Afterglow.* 1912–13. Reprint, New York: T. Bouregy, 1967.

———. *Beyond the Great Oblivion.* 1912–13. Reprint, New York: T. Bouregy, 1965.

———. *Darkness and Dawn.* 1912–13. Reprint, New York: T. Bouregy, 1964.

———. *Out of the Abyss.* 1912–13. Reprint, New York: T. Bouregy, 1967.

———. *People of the Abyss.* 1912–13. Reprint, New York: T. Bouregy, 1966.

Falk, Pasi. *The Consuming Body.* London: SAGE Publications, 1994.

Feldman, Saul. "The Presentation of Shortness in Everyday Life—Height and Heightism in American Society: Toward a Sociology of Stature." In *Life Styles: Diversity in American Society,* ed. Saul Feldman and Gerald Thielbar, 2d ed. Boston: Little, Brown, 1975.

Fenske, Gail. "The 'Skyscraper Problem' and the City Beautiful: The Woolworth Building." Ph.D. diss., Massachusetts Institute of Technology, 1988.

Fiedler, Leslie. *Freaks: Myths and Images of the Secret Self.* New York: Simon and Schuster, 1978.

Filene, Peter G. *Him/Her/Self: Gender Identities in Modern America.* 3d ed. Baltimore: Johns Hopkins University Press, 1998.

Fine, Gary Alan. "The Goliath Effect: Corporate Dominance and Mercantile Legends." *Journal of American Folklore* 98 (1985): 63–84.

Fishberg, Maurice. *The Jews: A Study of Race and Environment.* New York: Charles Scribner's Sons, 1911.

———. "Materials for the Physical Anthropology of the Eastern European Jews." *Memoirs of the American Anthropological Association* 1 (1905): 1–141.

Fisher, Philip. "Democratic Social Space: Whitman, Melville, and the Promise of American Transparency." In *The New American Studies: Essays from Representations,* ed. Philip Fisher. Berkeley: University of California Press, 1991.

Flower, William Henry. "The Pygmy Races of Men." *Nature* 38 (May 10 and 17, 1888): 44–46, 66–69.

Fogel, Robert, Stanley Engerman, and James Trussell. "Exploring the Uses of Data on Height: The Analysis of Long-Term Trends in Nutrition, Labor Welfare, and Labor Productivity." *Social Science History* 6, no. 4 (fall 1982): 401–21.

Folsom, Michael Brewster. "Upton Sinclair's Escape from *The Jungle:* The Narrative Strategy and Suppressed Conclusion of America's First Proletarian Novel." *Prospects* 4 (1979): 236–66.

Foreman, Joel, ed. *The Other Fifties: Interrogating Midcentury American Icons.* Urbana: University of Illinois Press, 1997.

Foster, Hal, ed. *Vision and Visuality.* Seattle: Bay Press, 1988.

Foucault, Michel. *Discipline and Punish: The Birth of the Prison.* New York: Vintage Books, 1977.

———. *The History of Sexuality.* Vol. 1, *An Introduction.* New York: Vintage Books, 1980.

Friedan, Betty. *The Feminine Mystique.* New York: W. W. Norton, 1963.

Futuyma, Douglas. *Evolutionary Biology.* 2d ed. Sunderland, MA: Sinauer Associates, 1986.

Gage, Lyman J. "The Finances of the Exposition." *Cosmopolitan,* December 1893, 201–6.

Gaines, Charles. *Yours in Perfect Manhood, Charles Atlas.* New York: Simon and Schuster, 1982.

Gaines, Kevin. "Black Americans' Racial Uplift Ideology as 'Civilizing Mission': Pauline Hopkins on Race and Imperialism." In *Cultures of United States Imperialism,* ed. Amy Kaplan and Donald Pease. Durham: Duke University Press, 1993.

Gallagher, Catherine, and Thomas Laqueur, eds. *The Making of the Modern Body: Sexuality and Society in the Nineteenth Century.* Berkeley: University of California Press, 1987.

Garland, C. M. "Exercises for Increasing the Height." *Physical Culture* 12, no. 4 (October 1904): 312–14.

Gates, Henry Louis. "TV's Black World Turns—But Stays Unreal." In *Rereading America: Cultural Contexts for Critical Thinking and Writing,* ed. Gary Colombo, Robert Cullen, and Bonnie Lisle, 2d ed., 653–60. Boston: Bedford Books, 1992.

Gertner, Joseph. "Short Stature in Children." *Medical Aspects of Human Sexuality* 20 (August 1986): 36–42.

"Giants to be Grown with Super-Medicine." *Literary Digest,* May 11, 1929, 32.

Gibbs, Kenneth. *Business Architectural Imagery in America, 1870–1930.* Michigan: UMI Research Press, 1984.

Gilbert, J. Allen. "Researches Upon School Children and College Students." *University of Iowa Studies in Psychology* 1 (1897): 1–39.

Gilder, Joseph. "The City of Dreadful Height." *Putnam's,* November 1908, 139.

Giles, Paul. *Hart Crane: The Contexts of* The Bridge. Cambridge: Cambridge University Press, 1986.

Gillis, John. *Too Tall, Too Small.* Champaign, IL: Institute for Personality and Ability Testing, 1982.

Gilman, Charlotte Perkins. *Herland.* 1915. Reprint, New York: Pantheon Books, 1979.

———. *Women and Economics: A Study of the Economic Relation Between Men and Women as a Factor in Social Evolution.* 1898. Reprint, ed. Carl Degler, New York: Harper and Row, 1966.

Gilmore, David. *Manhood in the Making: Cultural Concepts of Masculinity.* New Haven: Yale University Press, 1990.

Gilmore, Paul. *The Genuine Article: Race, Mass Culture, and American Literary Manhood.* Durham: Duke University Press, 2001.

Goddard, Henry H. "The Height and Weight of Feeble-Minded Children in American Institutions." *Journal of Nervous and Mental Disease* 39, no. 4 (April 1912): 217–35.

Godden, Richard. *Fictions of Capital: The American Novel from James to Mailer.* Cambridge: Cambridge University Press, 1990.

Goffman, Erving. *Gender Advertisements.* Cambridge, MA: Harvard University Press, 1979.

Goldberger, Paul. *The Skyscraper.* New York: Alfred A. Knopf, 1981.

Gompers, Samuel. "Labor, and Its Attitude Toward Trusts." *American Federationist* 14 (1907): 880–86.

Gould, B. A. *Investigations in the Military and Anthropological Statistics of American Soldiers.* New York: U.S. Sanitary Commission, Riverside Press, 1869.

Gould, Stephen Jay. *Ever Since Darwin: Reflections in Natural History.* New York: W. W. Norton, 1977.

———. *The Flamingo's Smile: Reflections in Natural History.* New York: W. W. Norton, 1985.

———. *The Mismeasure of Man.* New York: W. W. Norton, 1981.

Grant, Madison. *The Passing of the Great Race: Or The Racial Basis of European History.* New York: Charles Scribner's Sons, 1916.

Greene, Theodore. *America's Heroes: The Changing Models of Success in American Magazines.* New York: Oxford University Press, 1970.

Grey, Zane. *Riders of the Purple Sage.* New York: Grosset and Dunlap, 1912.

Griffen, Clyde. "Reconstructing Masculinity from the Evangelical Revival to the Waning of Progressivism: A Speculative Synthesis." In *Meanings for Manhood: Constructions of Masculinity in Victorian America,* ed. Mark Carnes and Clyde Griffen. Chicago: University of Chicago Press, 1990.

Grossberg, Michael. "Institutionalizing Masculinity: The Law as a Masculine Profession." In *Meanings for Manhood: Constructions of Masculinity in Victorian America,* ed. Mark Carnes and Clyde Griffen. Chicago: University of Chicago Press, 1990.

Grosz, Elizabeth. "Bodies-Cities." In *Places Through the Body,* ed. Heidi Nast and Steve Pile. New York: Routledge, 1998.

———. *Volatile Bodies: Toward a Corporeal Feminism.* Bloomington: Indiana University Press, 1994.

Hacking, Ian. *The Taming of Chance.* Cambridge: Cambridge University Press, 1990.

Haliburton, Robert Grant. "Dwarfs and Dwarf Worship." *Times* (London), September 14, 1891.

———. *Dwarf Survivals, and Traditions as to Pygmy Races.* Salem, MA: publisher unknown, 1895. Personal copy.

———. *Survivals of Dwarf Races in the New World.* From *Proceedings of the American Association for the Advancement of Science,* Vol. XLIII, 1894.

Hall, G. Stanley. *Adolescence: Its Psychology and Its Relations to Physiology, Anthropology, Sociology, Sex, Crime, Religion, and Education.* New York: D. Appleton, 1904.

Hall, Prescott. *Immigration and Its Effects Upon the United States.* 2d ed. New York: Henry Holt, 1906.

Hall, Winfield S. "The Changes in the Proportions of the Human Body During the Period of Growth." *Journal of the Anthropological Institute* 25 (February 1895): 21–46.

Haller, John. *Outcasts from Evolution: Scientific Attitudes of Racial Inferiority, 1859–1900.* Urbana: University of Illinois Press, 1971.

Hantover, Jeffrey P. "The Boy Scouts and the Validation of Masculinity." In *The American Man,* ed. Elizabeth Pleck and Joseph Pleck. Englewood Cliffs, NJ: Prentice-Hall, 1980.

Harris, Leon. *Upton Sinclair: American Rebel.* New York: Thomas Y. Crowell, 1975.

Harris, Neil. *The Land of Contrasts: 1880–1901.* New York: G. Braziller, 1970.

Harvey, Brett. *The Fifties: A Women's Oral History.* New York: Harper Perennial, 1993.

Haskell, Barbara. *Joseph Stella.* New York: Whitney Museum of American Art, 1994.

Haviland, Beverly. *Henry James's Last Romance: Making Sense of the Past and the American Scene.* Cambridge: Cambridge University Press, 1997.

Hendershot, Cyndy. "Darwin and the Atom: Evolution/Devolution Fantasies in *The Beast From 20,000 Fathoms, Them!,* and *The Incredible Shrinking Man.*" *Science-Fiction Studies* 25 (1998): 319–35.

Henley, Nancy. *Body Politics.* Englewood Cliffs, NJ: Prentice-Hall, 1977.

Hietala, Thomas. *Manifest Design: Anxious Aggrandizement in Late Jacksonian America.* Ithaca: Cornell University Press, 1985.

Higham, John. *Strangers in the Land: Patterns of American Nativism 1860–1925.* New York: Atheneum, 1965.

Himmelberg, Robert, ed. *The Monopoly Issue and Antitrust 1900–1917.* New York: Garland Publishing, 1994.

"How to Tell Japs From the Chinese." *Life,* December 22, 1941, 81–82.

Howard, June. *Form and History in American Literary Naturalism.* Chapel Hill: University of North Carolina Press, 1985.

Hunt, Caroline C. "Dwarf, Small World, Shrinking Child: Three Versions of Miniature." *Children's Literature* 23 (1995): 115–36.

"The Immigrant." Review of *The Promised Land. New York Times,* April 14, 1912, 228.

Incredible Shrinking Man. Dir. Jack Arnold. Universal, 1957.

Jacobs, Joseph. *Studies in Jewish Statistics, Social, Vital and Anthropometric.* London: David Nutt, 1891.

Jacobs, Joseph, and Isidore Spielman. "On the Comparative Anthropology of English Jews." *Journal of the Anthropological Institute* 19 (1889): 76–88.

Jacobson, Matthew Frye. *Whiteness of a Different Color: European Immigrants and the Alchemy of Race.* Cambridge, MA: Harvard University Press, 1998.

Jaffe, Irma B. *Joseph Stella.* Rev. ed. New York: Fordham University Press, 1988.

James, Henry. *The American Scene.* New York: Penguin Books, 1994.

————. *The Bostonians.* New York: Dial Press, 1945.

Jancovich, Mark. *Rational Fears: American Horror in the 1950s.* Manchester: Manchester University Press, 1996.

Jefferson, Thomas. *Notes on the State of Virginia.* 1785. Reprint, New York: W. W. Norton, 1982.

Jenks, Jeremiah. *The Trust Problem.* New York: McClure, Phillips, 1900.

Johnson, Mark. *The Body in the Mind: The Bodily Basis of Meaning, Imagination, and Reason.* Chicago: University of Chicago Press, 1987.

Johnson, T. Broadwood. *Tramps Round the Mountains of the Moon and Through the Back Gate of the Congo State.* London: T. Fisher Unwin, 1908.

Jordan, David Starr. *War and the Breed: The Relation of War to the Downfall of Nations.* New York: World Book, 1922.

Kallen, Stuart, ed. *The 1950s.* San Diego: Greenhaven Press, 2000.

Kaplan, Amy. *The Anarchy of Empire in the Making of U.S. Culture.* Cambridge, MA: Harvard University Press, 2002.

————. *The Social Construction of American Realism.* Chicago: University of Chicago Press, 1988.

Kaplan, Daile. *Lewis Hine in Europe: The Lost Photographs.* New York: Abbeville Press, 1988.

Keane, Arthur H. J. "Anthropological Curiosities: The Pygmies of the World." *Scientific American,* Supplement, August 17, 1907, 99.

Keane, Augustus H. *Ethnology.* 2d ed. Cambridge: University Press, 1909.

————. *Man: Past and Present.* Cambridge: University Press, 1899.

"Keeping the Promise of the Promised Land." *Survey* 29 (February 8, 1913): 637–38.

Keyes, Ralph. *The Height of Your Life.* Boston: Little, Brown, 1980.

Kimmel, Michael. *Manhood in America: A Cultural History.* New York: Free Press, 1996.

Kimmel, Michael, and Michael Kaufman. "Weekend Warriors: The New Men's Movement." In *Theorizing Masculinities,* ed. Harry Brod and Michael Kaufman. Thousand Oaks: Sage Publications, 1994.

King, Moses. *King's Views of New York, 1896–1915 and Brooklyn 1905.* Reprint, New York: Arno Press, 1977.

Klebaner, Benjamin. "Potential Competition and the American Antitrust Legislation of 1914." In *The Monopoly Issue and Antitrust, 1900–1917.* Ed. Robert Himmelberg. New York: Garland, 1994.

Klein, Alan M. *Little Big Men: Bodybuilding Subculture and Gender Construction.* Albany: State University of New York Press, 1993.

Kline, Linus W. "Truancy as Related to the Migrating Instinct." *Pedagogical Seminary* 5 (January 1898): 381–420.

Know Your Enemy—Japan. War Department Orientation Film, 1943. Available through Academic Industries Video Division, LOC #824.

Kollmann, J. "Pygmies in Europe." *Journal of the Anthropological Institute* 25 (April 1895): 117–22.

Kostof, Spiro. *America by Design.* New York: Oxford University Press, 1987.

Lakoff, George. *Women, Fire, and Dangerous Things.* Chicago: University of Chicago Press, 1987.

Lakoff, George, and Mark Johnson. *Metaphors We Live By.* Chicago: University of Chicago Press, 1980.

Laqueur, Thomas. *Making Sex: Body and Gender from the Greeks to Freud.* Cambridge, MA: Harvard University Press, 1992.

Lears, T. J. Jackson. *No Place of Grace: Antimodernism and the Transformation of American Culture 1880–1920.* New York: Pantheon Books, 1981.

Lehman, Arnold. "The New York Skyscraper: A History of Its Development, 1870–1939." Ph.D. diss., Yale University, 1974.

Lehman, Peter. *Running Scared: Masculinity and the Representation of the Male Body.* Philadelphia: Temple University Press, 1993.

Leuchtenburg, William. *Franklin D. Roosevelt and the New Deal.* New York: Harper and Row, 1963.

Leverenz, David. *Manhood and the American Renaissance.* Ithaca: Cornell University Press, 1989.

Levin, David Michael, ed. *Modernity and the Hegemony of Vision.* Berkeley: University of California Press, 1993.

Liebs, Elke. "Between *Gulliver* and *Alice:* Some Remarks on the Dialectic of Great and Small in Literature." *Phaedrus: An International Annual of Children's Literature Research* 13 (1988): 56–60.

Liniger-Goumaz, Max. *Pygmies and Other Short-Sized Races (Bushmen, Hottentots, Negritos, Etc.): General Bibliography.* Geneva: Les Editions Du Temps, 1968.

Lippmann, Walter. *Drift and Mastery: An Attempt to Diagnose the Current Unrest.* 1914. New York: Henry Holt, 1917.

Livermore, A. A. "The American Physical Man." *Unitarian Review and Religious Magazine* 7, no. 2 (February 1877): 117–34.

Livesay, Harold. *Andrew Carnegie and the Rise of Big Business.* Boston: Little, Brown, 1975.

Lloyd, Albert. *In Dwarf Land and Cannibal Country: A Record of Travel and Discovery in Central Africa.* New York: Charles Scribner's Sons, 1900.

Lloyd, Henry Demarest. *Wealth Against Commonwealth.* 1894. New York: Harper and Brothers, 1898.

Loh, Eng Seng. "The Economic Effects of Physical Appearance." *Social Science Quarterly* 74, no. 2 (June 1993): 420–38.

London, Jack. *The Iron Heel.* 1907. Reprint, New York: MacMillan, 1937.

———. *The People of the Abyss.* New York: Macmillan, 1903.

———. *The Sea Wolf.* 1904. Reprint, New York: Bantam Books, 1981.

Love, Albert, and Charles Davenport. *Defects Found in Drafted Men.* Washington: Government Printing Office, 1920.

Lowe, Marian. "The Dialectic of Biology and Culture." In *Woman's Nature: Rationalizations of Inequality,* ed. Marian Lowe and Ruth Hubbard. New York: Pergamon Press, 1983.

Lutz, Tom. *American Nervousness, 1903: An Anecdotal History.* Ithaca: Cornell University Press, 1991.

Marin, John. "Water-Colors by John Marin." *Camera Work* 42–43 (April–July 1913): 18.

Marks, Patricia. *Bicycles, Bangs, and Bloomers: The New Woman in the Popular Press.* Lexington: University of Kentucky Press, 1990.

Marling, Karal Ann. *As Seen on TV: The Visual Culture of Everyday Life in the 1950s*. Cambridge, MA: Harvard University Press, 1994.

Martel, Leslie, and Henry Biller. *Stature and Stigma: The Biopsychosocial Development of Short Males*. Lexington, MA: D.C. Heath, 1987.

"Mary Antin's 'They Who Knock at Our Gates.'" Review. *Bookman* 39 (June 1914): 458–59.

Matheson, Richard. *The Shrinking Man*. New York: Fawcett Publications, 1956.

May, Elaine Tyler. *Homeward Bound: American Families in the Cold War Era*. New York: Basic Books, 1988.

McAtamney, Hugh. *Dinner Given to Cass Gilbert, Architect, by Frank W. Woolworth*. New York: Munder-Thomsen Press, 1913.

McClelland, John. *Wobbly War: The Centralia Story*. Tacoma: Washington State Historical Society, 1987.

McCullough, David. *The Great Bridge*. New York: Simon and Schuster, 1972.

McElrath, Joseph. "Frank Norris." *Dictionary of Literary Biography*. Vol. 12. Detroit: Gale Research, 1982.

McGee, W. J. "Anthropology at the Louisiana Purchase Exposition." *Science*, n.s., 22 (December 22, 1905): 811–26.

———. "National Growth and National Character." *National Geographic*, June 1899, 185–206.

———. "The Trend of Human Progress." *American Anthropologist*, n.s., 1, no. 3 (July 1899): 401–47.

McLaughlin, Allan. "How Immigrants are Inspected." *Popular Science Monthly*, February 1905, 357–61.

Meyer, Richard. "Rock Hudson's Body." In *Inside/Out: Lesbian Theories, Gay Theories*, ed. Diana Fuss. New York: Routledge, 1991.

Meyer, Susan. *America's Great Illustrators*. New York: Harry N. Abrams, 1978.

Meyerowitz, Joanne, ed. *Not June Cleaver: Women and Gender in Postwar America, 1945–1960*. Philadelphia: Temple University Press, 1994.

Michaels, Walter Benn. *The Gold Standard and the Logic of Naturalism*. Berkeley: University of California Press, 1987.

Miller, Arthur. *Death of a Salesman*. New York: Penguin Books, 1949.

Millhauser, Steven. "The Fascination of the Miniature." *Grand Street* 2, no. 4 (1983): 128–35.

Mills, C. Wright. *White Collar: The American Middle Classes*. New York: Oxford University Press, 1953.

Mitchell, Hannah. "Human Nature—as Seen in a Great Office Building." *American Magazine*, November 1920, 58–138.

Mitchell, Lee Clark. *Determined Fictions: American Literary Naturalism*. New York: Columbia University Press, 1989.

———. *Westerns: Making the Man in Fiction and Film*. Chicago: University of Chicago Press, 1996.

Modleski, Tania. *Feminism Without Women: Culture and Criticism in a "Postfeminist" Age*. New York: Routledge, 1991.

Moers, Ellen. *Literary Women*. Garden City, NY: Doubleday, 1976.

Montgomery, Mrs. Frank Hugh. "The March Meeting of the Parents' Association." *Elementary School Teacher* 5 (April 1905): 508–10.

Moody, John. "The Evolution of the Trust: Its Evil Element and the True Remedy." *Arena* 37 (1907): 477–84.

Mosher, Clelia Duel. "The Height of College Women (Second Note)." Reprint from *The Medical Woman's Journal,* November 1921.

———. "Some of the Causal Factors in the Increased Height of College Women (Third Note)." Reprint from *Journal of the American Medical Association* 81 (August 18, 1923): 535–38.

Mumford, Lewis. *Sticks and Stones: A Study of American Architecture and Civilization.* New York: Horace Liveright, 1924.

Muncy, Robyn. "Trustbusting and White Manhood in America, 1898–1914." *American Studies* 38, no. 3 (fall 1997): 21–42.

"New Educational Theories and Practices in Connection with the Weighing and Measuring of Children." *Hygeia* 8 (August 1930): 754–55.

Norris, Frank. *McTeague: A Story of San Francisco.* 1899. Reprint, New York: Holt, Rinehart, & Winston, 1966.

———. *The Octopus: A Story of California.* 1901. Reprint, New York: A. Wessels, 1906.

Norris, James. *Advertising and the Transformation of American Society, 1865–1920.* New York: Greenwood Press, 1990.

Nott, Josiah Clark, and George R. Gliddon. *Types of Mankind.* Philadelphia: Lippincott, Grambo, 1854.

O. Henry. "Psyche and the Pskyscraper." In *Complete Works of O. Henry.* New York: Doubleday, Doran, 1931.

Okada, John. *No-No Boy.* 1957. Reprint, Seattle: University of Washington Press, 1976.

"On the Elongation of Form." *Camera Work* 10 (April 1905): 27–35.

O'Neill, William. *American High: The Years of Confidence, 1945–1960.* New York: Free Press, 1986.

Onuf, Peter. *Jefferson's Empire: The Language of American Nationhood.* Charlottesville: University Press of Virginia, 2000.

Ostriker, Alicia. *Stealing the Language: The Emergence of Women's Poetry in America.* Boston: Beacon Press, 1986.

Owsley, Frank, and Gene Smith. *Filibusters and Expansionists: Jeffersonian Manifest Destiny, 1800–1821.* Tuscaloosa: University of Alabama Press, 1997.

Pace, Patricia. "The Body-in-Writing: Miniatures in Mary Norton's *Borrowers.*" *Text and Performance Quarterly* 11, no. 4 (October 1991): 279–90.

Parrish, Timothy. "Whose Americanization? Self and Other in Mary Antin's *The Promised Land.*" *Studies in American Jewish Literature* 13 (1994): 27–38.

Patterson, Martha. *Beyond the Gibson Girl: Reimagining the American New Woman, 1895–1915.* Urbana: University of Illinois Press, 2005.

———. "'Survival of the Best Fitted': Selling the American New Woman as Gibson Girl, 1895–1910." *American Transcendental Quarterly* 9, no. 2 (June 1995): 73–87.

Pearson, Karl, and Alice Lee. "On the Relative Variation and Correlation in Civilized and Uncivilized Races." *Science* 6 (July 1897): 49–50.

Pearson, Karl, and Julia Bell. *A Study of the Long Bones of the English Skeleton.* London: Cambridge University Press, 1919.

Peckham, George W. "The Growth of Children." *Annual Report of the Wisconsin State Board of Health* 6 (1881): 28–73.

Phifer, Kate. *Growing Up Small.* Middlebury, VT: Paul Eriksson, 1979.

Pizer, Donald. "*Maggie* and the Naturalistic Aesthetic of Length." *American Literary Realism* 28, no. 1 (1995): 58–65.

Pleck, Elizabeth, and Joseph Pleck. *The American Man.* Englewood Cliffs, NJ: Prentice-Hall, 1980.

Poole, Ernest. "Cowboys of the Skies." *Everybody's Magazine,* November 1908, 641–53.

———. *The Harbor.* 1915. Reprint, New York: MacMillan, 1921.

Poovey, Mary. *A History of the Modern Fact: Problems of Knowledge in the Sciences of Wealth and Society.* Chicago: University of Chicago Press, 1998.

Porter, William T. "The Growth of St. Louis School Children." *Transactions of the Academy of Science of St. Louis* 6 (1894): 263–426.

———. "Percentile Charts of the Height and Weight of Boston School Children." *Boston Medical and Surgical Journal* 188, no. 17 (April 26, 1923): 639–44.

———. "The Physical Basis of Precocity and Dullness." *Transactions of the Academy of Science of St. Louis* 6 (1893): 161–81.

———. "The Relative Growth of Individual Boston School Boys." *American Journal of Physiology* 61 (1922): 311–25.

———. "The Seasonal Variation in the Growth of Boston School Children." *American Journal of Physiology* 52 (1920): 121–31.

Posnock, Ross. "Affirming the Alien: The Pragmatist Pluralism of *The American Scene.*" In *The Cambridge Companion to Henry James,* ed. Jonathan Freedman. Cambridge: Cambridge University Press, 1998.

Pratt, Mary Louise. *Imperial Eyes: Travel Writing and Transculturation.* London and New York: Routledge, 1992.

Pratt, Norma Fain. "Culture and Radical Politics: Yiddish Women Writers in America, 1890–1940." In *Women of the Word: Jewish Women and Jewish Writing,* ed. Judith Baskin. Detroit: Wayne State University Press, 1994.

Price, Willard. "Unknown Japan." *National Geographic,* August 1942, 225.

Proctor, Robert. "The Destruction of Lives 'Not Worth Living.'" In *Deviant Bodies: Critical Perspectives on Difference in Science and Popular Culture,* ed. Jennifer Terry and Jacqueline Urla. Bloomington: Indiana University Press, 1995.

Proefriedt, William. "The Education of Mary Antin." *Journal of Ethnic Studies* 17, no. 4 (winter 1990): 81–100.

———. "The Immigrant or 'Outsider' Experience as Metaphor for Becoming an Educated Person in the Modern World: Mary Antin, Richard Wright and Eva Hoffman." *MELUS* 16, no. 2 (summer 1989–90): 77–89.

Quatrefages de Breau, Armand de. *The Pygmies.* Trans. Frederick Starr. New York: D. Appleton, 1895.

Que, Vicky, and Snigdha Prakash, "Human Growth Hormone: FDA Approves Drug for Use in Healthy, Short Children." Three-part Report, August 12–14, 2003. National Public Radio. May 21, 2004. <http://discover.npr.org/features/feature.jhtml?wfId=1392897>.

Quetelet, Lambert A. J. *Anthropométrie.* Bruxelles: C. Muquardt, 1870.

———. *A Treatise on Man and the Development of his Faculties.* 1842. Reprint, Gainsville, FL: Scholars' Facsimiles and Reprints, 1969.

Raub, Patricia. "A New Woman or an Old-Fashioned Girl? The Portrayal of the Heroine in Popular Women's Novels of the Twenties." *American Studies* 35, no. 1 (spring 1994): 109–30.

Recent Remarkable Discoveries in Central Africa, With a Full Description of an Extraordinary Race of People Supposed to be the Connecting Link Between the Animals and the Human. Philadelphia: Barclay, 1867.

Reed, William Allan. *Negritos of Zambales.* Manila: Bureau of Public Printing, 1904.

Reeves, Thomas. *Twentieth-Century America: A Brief History.* New York: Oxford University Press, 2000.

"The Regulation of Building Heights." *American City,* December 1913, 513.

Ripley, William Z. *The Races of Europe: A Sociological Study.* New York: D. Appleton, 1899.

Roberts, Mary Fanton [Giles Edgerton]. "How New York Has Redeemed Herself from Ugliness." *Craftsman* 11 (January 1907): 458–71.

Robertson, Josephine. "Theater Cashier, 23, Wins Title of 'Norma,' Besting 3,863 Entries." *Cleveland Plain Dealer,* September 23, 1945, A1, A4.

Roosevelt, Theodore. "Applied Idealism: The Fifth Installment of Chapters of a Possible Autobiography." *Outlook,* June 28, 1913, 461–78.

———. "The Conservation of Business—Shall We Strangle or Control It?" *Outlook* 100 (March 16, 1912): 574–78.

———. *The Roosevelt Policy.* Vol. 1. New York: Current Literature Publishing, 1908.

———. "The Strenuous Life." 1899. In *The Works of Theodore Roosevelt,* 13:319–31. New York: Charles Scribner's Sons, 1926.

———. *Theodore Roosevelt: An Autobiography.* 1913. In *The Works of Theodore Roosevelt,* vol. 20. New York: Charles Scribner's Sons, 1926.

Rosenfeld, Alvin. "Inventing the Jew: Notes on Jewish Autobiography." In *The American Autobiography: A Collection of Critical Essays,* ed. Albert Stone. Englewood Cliffs, NJ: Prentice-Hall, 1981.

Ross, Andrew. "The Great White Dude." In *Constructing Masculinity,* ed. Maurice Berger, Brian Wallis, and Simon Watson. New York: Routledge, 1995.

Ross, Edward Alsworth. *The Old World in the New: The Significance of Past and Present Immigration to the American People.* New York: Century, 1913.

Rotundo, E. Anthony. *American Manhood: Transformations in Masculinity from the Revolution to the Modern Era.* New York: Basic Books, 1993.

Rozwenc, Edwin, ed. *Roosevelt, Wilson and the Trusts.* Boston: D. C. Heath, 1950.

Rubin, Steven. "American-Jewish Autobiography, 1912 to the Present." In *Handbook of American-Jewish Literature: An Analytical Guide to Topics, Themes, and Sources,* ed. Lewis Fried, Gene Brown, Jules Chametzky, and Louis Harap. Westport, CT: Greenwood Press, 1988.

———. "Style and Meaning in Mary Antin's *The Promised Land:* A Reevaluation." *Studies in American Jewish Literature* 5 (1986): 35–43.

Rugoff, Ralph, and Susan Stewart. *At the Threshold of the Visible: Miniscule and Small-Scale Art, 1964–96.* New York: Independent Curators, 1997.

Rydell, Robert W. *All The World's a Fair: Visions of Empire at American International Expositions, 1876–1916.* Chicago: University of Chicago Press, 1984.

Rzepka, Charles. "'If I Can Make It There': Oz's Emerald City and the New Woman." *Studies in Popular Culture* 10, no. 2 (1987): 54–66.

Saltus, Edgar. "New York from the Flatiron." *Munsey's Magazine,* July 1905, 381–90.

Samaras, Thomas. *The Truth About Your Height: Exploring the Myths and Realities of Human Size and Its Effects on Performance, Health, Pollution, and Survival.* San Diego: Tecolote Publications, 1994.

Sargent, D. A. "The Physical Development of Women." *Scribner's Magazine,* February 1889, 172–85.

———. "The Physical Proportions of the Typical Man." *Scribner's Magazine,* July 1887, 3–17.

———. "The Physique of Scholars, Athletes, and the Average Student." *Popular Science Monthly,* September 1908, 248–56.

Sarno, Louis. *Song from the Forest: My Life Among the Ba-Benjellé Pygmies.* Boston: Houghton Mifflin, 1993.

Schehr, Lawrence. *Parts of an Andrology: On Representations of Men's Bodies.* Stanford: Stanford University Press, 1997.

Schleier, Merrill. *The Skyscraper in American Art, 1890–1931.* Michigan: UMI Research Press, 1986.

Schlichter, Henry. "The Pygmy Tribes of Africa." *Scottish Geographical Magazine,* June 1892, 289–356.

Schuyler, Montgomery. *American Architecture and Other Writings.* Vol. 2. Ed. William Jordy and Ralph Coe. Cambridge, MA: Harvard University Press, 1961.

———. "The Towers of Manhattan and Notes on the Woolworth Building." *Architectural Record* 33, no. 2 (February 1913): 98–122.

Schwartz, Hillel. *Never Satisfied: A Cultural History of Diets, Fantasies and Fat.* London: Collier Macmillan Publishers, 1986.

Sears, John F. "Introduction." In *The American Scene,* Henry James. New York: Penguin Books, 1994.

Segel, Harold B. *Body Ascendant: Modernism and the Physical Imperative.* Baltimore: Johns Hopkins University Press, 1998.

Sekula, Allan. "On the Invention of Photographic Meaning." In *Photography Against the Grain: Essays and Photo Works, 1973–1983.* Halifax: Press of the Nova Scotia College of Arts and Design, 1984.

Seltzer, Mark. *Bodies and Machines.* New York: Routledge, 1992.

Sennett, Richard. *Flesh and Stone: The Body and the City in Western Civilization.* New York: W. W. Norton, 1994.

Shapiro, Harry. *Americans: Yesterday, Today, Tomorrow.* Man and Nature Publications (Science Guide No. 126). New York: American Museum of Natural History. Reprinted from *Natural History,* June 1945.

Shaw, Albert. *The Outlook for the Average Man.* New York: MacMillan, 1907.

Shepp, James. *Shepp's World's Fair Photographed.* Chicago: Globe Bible Publishing, 1893.

Sherwood, Sidney. "Influence of the Trust in the Development of Undertaking Genius." *Yale Review* 8 (February 1900): 362–72.

Sinclair, Upton. *The Jungle.* 1906. Reprint, New York: Bantam Books, 1981.

Sklar, Martin. *The Corporate Reconstruction of American Capitalism, 1890–1916: The Market, the Law, and Politics.* New York: Cambridge University Press, 1988.

————. "Woodrow Wilson and the Political Economy of Modern United States Liberalism." In *The Monopoly Issue and Antitrust, 1900–1917.* Ed. Robert Himmelberg. New York: Garland, 1994.

Slotkin, Richard. *The Fatal Environment: The Myth of the Frontier in the Age of Industrialization 1800–1890.* New York: Atheneum, 1985.

Slusser, George. "Pocket Apocalypse: American Survivalist Fictions from *Walden* to *The Incredible Shrinking Man.*" In *Imagining Apocalypse: Studies in Cultural Crisis,* ed. David Seed. New York: St. Martin's Press, 2000.

Smith, Craig. "Risking Limbs for Height, and Success in China." *New York Times,* May 5, 2002, International Section, 3.

Smith, Sidonie. "Cheesecake, Nymphs, and 'We the People': Un/National Subjects about 1900." *Prose Studies* 17, no. 1 (April 1994): 120–40.

Smith-Rosenberg, Carroll. *Disorderly Conduct: Visions of Gender in Victorian America.* New York: Oxford University Press, 1985.

Sokoloff, Kenneth, and Georgia Villaflor. "The Early Achievement of Modern Stature in America." *Social Science History* 6, no. 4 (fall 1982): 453–81.

Sollors, Werner. "Introduction." In *The Promised Land* by Mary Antin. 1912. Reprint, New York: Penguin Books, 1997.

Solomon-Godeau, Abigail. "Male Trouble." In *Constructing Masculinity,* ed. Maurice Berger, Brian Wallis, and Simon Watson. New York: Routledge, 1995.

Spencer, Herbert. *The Principles of Sociology.* Vol. 1. 3d ed. 1885. Reprint, New York: D. Appleton, 1916.

Stanley, Henry M. *Autobiography of Sir Henry Morton Stanley.* Boston: Houghton Mifflin, 1909.

————. *In Darkest Africa.* 2 vols. London: Sampson Low, Marston, Searle and Rivington, 1890.

————. "The Pigmies of the Great African Forest." *Scribner's Magazine,* January 1891, 3–17.

————. *Through the Dark Continent.* London: Sampson Low, Marston, Searle and Rivington, Limited, 1878.

Stanton, Melissa. "Looking After Your Looks." *Glamour,* August 1993, 233.

Starr, Frederick. "Anthropology at the World's Fair." *Popular Science Monthly,* September 1893, 610–21.

Starrett, W. A. *Skyscrapers and the Men Who Build Them.* New York: Charles Scribner's Sons, 1928.

Stearns, Peter. *Fat History: Bodies and Beauty in the Modern West.* New York: New York University Press, 1997.

Steffens, Lincoln. "The Modern Business Building." *Scribner's Magazine,* July 1897, 38.

Stein, Leon, and Gene Brown, eds. *Big Business.* New York: New York Times Press, 1978.

Steinorth, Karl, ed. *Alvin Langdon Coburn: Photographs 1900–1924.* Zurich: Edition Stemmle, 1998.

————. *Lewis Hine: Passionate Journey.* Zurich: Edition Stemmle, 1996.

Stepan, Nancy. *The Idea of Race in Science: Great Britain 1800–1960.* London: Macmillan Press, 1982.

————. "Race and Gender: The Role of Analogy in Science." *Isis* 77 (June 1986): 261–77.

Stephanson, Anders. *Manifest Destiny: American Expansionism and the Empire of Right.* New York: Hill and Wang, 1995.

Stewart, Susan. *On Longing: Narratives of the Miniature, the Gigantic, the Souvenir, the Collection.* Durham: Duke University Press, 1993.

Strum, Philippa. *Brandeis: Beyond Progressivism.* Lawrence: University Press of Kansas, 1993.

———. *Louis D. Brandeis: Justice for the People.* Cambridge, MA: Harvard University Press, 1984.

Studlar, Gaylyn. *This Mad Masquerade: Stardom and Masculinity in the Jazz Age.* New York: Columbia University Press, 1996.

Sullivan, Louis. *Autobiography of an Idea.* New York: Press of the American Institute of Architects, 1924.

———. "The Tall Office Building Artistically Considered." *Lippincott's,* March 1896, 403–9.

Tanner, J. M. *A History of the Study of Human Growth.* Cambridge: Cambridge University Press, 1981.

———. "Relation of Body Size, Intelligence Test Scores, and Social Circumstances." In *Trends and Issues in Developmental Psychology,* ed. Paul Mussen et al. New York: Holt, Rinehart, and Winston, 1969.

Tarratt, Margaret. "Monsters from the Id." *Films and Filming* 17 (December 1970): 38–42 and (January 1971): 40–42.

Tasker, Yvonne. *Spectacular Bodies: Gender, Genre and the Action Cinema.* New York: Routledge, 1993.

"Tells of Race Characteristics Altered by Residence in America." Review of *The Promised Land. Christian Science Monitor,* April 22, 1912, 4.

Terry, Jennifer, and Jacqueline Urla, eds. *Deviant Bodies: Critical Perspectives on Difference in Science and Popular Culture.* Bloomington: Indiana University Press, 1995.

Thomas, Nicholas. *Colonialism's Culture: Anthropology, Travel and Government.* Princeton, NJ: Princeton University Press, 1994.

Thompson, Jim. *Savage Night.* New York: Vintage Books, 1953.

Thomson, Rosemarie Garland. *Extraordinary Bodies: Figuring Physical Disability in American Culture and Literature.* New York: Columbia University Press, 1997.

———, ed. *Freakery: Cultural Spectacles of the Extraordinary Body.* New York: New York University Press, 1996.

Tichi, Cecilia. *Shifting Gears: Technology, Literature, Culture in Modernist America.* Chapel Hill: University of North Carolina Press, 1987.

———. "Women Writers and the New Woman." In *Columbia Literary History of the United States,* ed. Emory Elliott. New York: Columbia University Press, 1988.

Tittle, Walter. "The Creator of the Woolworth Tower." *World's Work,* May 1927, 96–102.

Trachtenberg, Alan. *The Incorporation of America: Culture and Society in the Gilded Age.* 1982. Reprint, New York: Hill and Wang, 1997.

———. *Reading American Photographs: Images as History, Mathew Brady to Walker Evans.* New York: Hill and Wang, 1989.

Trachtenberg, Marvin. *The Statue of Liberty.* New York: Penguin Books, 1986.

Tuerk, Richard. "The Youngest of America's Children in *The Promised Land.*" *Studies in American Jewish Literature* 5 (1986): 29–34.

Turner, Bryan S. *The Body and Society: Explorations in Social Theory.* 2d ed. London: Sage Publications, 1996.

Turner, Frederick Jackson. "The Significance of the Frontier in American History." 1893. Reprint, New York: Continuum Publishing, 1991.

Tyler, Dr. John M. "What Teachers Ought to Know About the Physical Growth of Children." *National Education Association Addresses and Proceedings* 56 (1918): 323–26.

Tyson, Edward. *Orang-Outang, Sive Homo Sylvestris: or The Anatomy of a Pygmie Compared with that of a Monkey, an Ape, and a Man. To Which is Added a Philological Essay Concerning the Pygmies . . . Wherein It Will Appear that They are Either Apes or Monkeys, and Not Men, as Formerly Pretended.* 1699. Reprint, London: Dawsons of Pall Mall, 1966.

Uffen, Ellen. *Strands of the Cable: The Place of the Past in Jewish American Women's Writing.* New York: Peter Lang, 1992.

Urla, Jacqueline, and Alan Swedlund. "The Anthropometry of Barbie: Unsettling Ideals of the Feminine Body in Popular Culture." In *Deviant Bodies: Critical Perspectives on Difference in Science and Popular Culture,* ed. Jennifer Terry and Jacqueline Urla. Bloomington: Indiana University Press, 1995.

Ussher, Jane, ed. *Body Talk: The Material and Discursive Regulation of Sexuality, Madness and Reproduction.* London: Routledge, 1997.

Van Dyke, John. *The New New York.* New York: MacMillan, 1909.

Van Leeuwen, Thomas. *The Skyward Trend of Thought: The Metaphysics of the American Skyscraper.* Cambridge, MA: MIT Press, 1988.

Vanden Bergh, Leonard John. *On the Trail of the Pigmies.* 1921. Reprint, New York: Negro Universities Press, 1969.

Vaucaire, Michel. *Paul Du Chaillu: Gorilla Hunter.* Trans. Emily Pepper Watts. New York: Harper and Brothers, 1930.

"Visits Woolworth Tower." *New York Times,* October 20, 1912, sec. 3, p. 6.

Walker, Francis A. "Growth of the Nation." In *Discussions in Economics and Statistics,* vol. 2. New York: Henry Holt, 1899.

———. "Immigration and Degradation." *Forum,* August 1891, 634–44.

———. "Restriction of Immigration." *Atlantic Monthly,* June 1896, 822–29.

Wallach, Alan. "Making a Picture of the View from Mount Holyoke." In *American Iconology: New Approaches to Nineteenth-Century Art and Literature,* ed. David Miller. New Haven: Yale University Press, 1993.

Wallas, Graham. *The Great Society: A Psychological Analysis.* 1914. Reprint, New York: MacMillan, 1919.

Ward, Robert. "Higher Mental and Physical Standards for Immigrants." *Scientific Monthly,* November 1924, 533–47.

Warshaw, Steven. *The Gibson Girl: Drawings of Charles Dana Gibson.* Berkeley, CA: Diablo Press, 1968.

Wasson, Kirsten. "Mary Antin." In *Jewish American Women Writers: A Bio-Bibliographical and Critical Sourcebook,* ed. Ann Shapiro et al. Westport, CT: Greenwood Press, 1994.

Weinstein, James. *The Corporate Ideal in the Liberal State: 1900–1918.* Boston: Beacon Press, 1968.

Weir, James. "The Pygmy in the United States." *Popular Science Monthly,* May 1896, 47–56.

Wells, Paul. "The Invisible Man: Shrinking Masculinity in the 1950s Science Fiction B-Movie." In *You Tarzan: Masculinity, Movies and Men*, ed. Pat Kirkham and Janet Thumim. London: Lawrence and Wishart, 1993.

Wentworth, Harold, and Stuart Flexner. *Dictionary of American Slang*. New York: Thomas Y. Crowell, 1960.

Whitman, Walt. *Leaves of Grass and Selected Prose*. Modern Library College Edition. Ed. Lawrence Buell. New York: McGraw-Hill, 1981.

———. *Leaves of Grass*. Norton Critical Edition. Ed. Sculley Bradley and Harold Blodgett. New York: W. W. Norton, 1973.

Whyte, William. *The Organization Man*. New York: Simon and Schuster, 1956.

Wiebe, Robert. *The Search for Order, 1877–1920*. New York: Hill and Wang, 1967.

Wiegman, Robyn. *American Anatomies: Theorizing Race and Gender*. Durham: Duke University Press, 1995.

Williams, John. "Harmful Effects of Industrial Combinations on Labor Conditions." *Annals of the American Academy of Political and Social Science* 42 (1912): 3–9.

Williams, Simon, and Gillian Bendelow. *The Lived Body: Sociological Themes, Embodied Issues*. London: Routledge, 1998.

Williams, Tony. "Female Oppression in *Attack of the 50-Foot Woman*." *Science Fiction Studies* 12 (1985): 264–72.

Wilson, Christopher. *White Collar Fictions: Class and Social Representation in American Literature, 1885–1925*. Athens: University of Georgia Press, 1992.

Wilson, Woodrow. *The New Freedom*. 1913. Reprint, Englewood Cliffs, NJ: Prentice-Hall, 1961.

Winkler, John. *Five and Ten: The Fabulous Life of F. W. Woolworth*. New York: Robert McBride, 1940.

Wiseman, Carter. *Shaping a Nation: Twentieth-Century American Architecture and Its Makers*. New York: W. W. Norton, 1998.

Wollaston, A. F. R. *Pygmies and Papuans: The Stone Age To-day in Dutch New Guinea*. New York: Sturgis and Walton, 1912.

Woodward, R. S. "Beneficial Effects of Industrial Combinations on Labor Conditions." *Annals of the American Academy of Political and Social Science* 42 (1912): 20–24.

Yoder, Jon A. *Upton Sinclair*. New York: Frederick Ungar Publishing, 1975.

Zaborowska, Magdalena. *How We Found America: Reading Gender Through East European Immigrant Narratives*. Chapel Hill: University of North Carolina Press, 1995.

Zunz, Olivier. *Making America Corporate, 1870–1920*. Chicago: University of Chicago Press, 1990.

Zurier, Rebecca. *Art for the Masses: A Radical Magazine and Its Graphics, 1911–1917*. Philadelphia: Temple University Press, 1988.

Index

Above the Clouds and Old New York (Bruce), 171
abundance, culture of, 119
"Accident Case in Steel Mills" (Hine), 164
Adam, Paul, 141
Adam and Eve, 49, 236, 284n10
advertising, 1, 103, 191; in magazines, 104–5; Woolworth Building as, 166, 169
AFL. *See* American Federation of Labor
African Americans, 195, 219, 227; American body and, 236; education of, 83; height studies of, 77; political policies and, 30–31; as U.S. citizens, 63; vertical metaphor and, 40; writers, 206–7. *See also* race; whites
Akka, 35, 37, 256n1; children in, 42
aliens, 247, 248, 249–50; immigrants as, 276n88
Allis engine, 44, 47
altitude, 75, 77
Amalgamated Association of Iron and Steel Workers, 114
Amazonian women, 189
America. *See* United States
American Anti-Trust League, 122
American dream, 175
American Federation of Labor (AFL), 105, 115; labor reform and, 121; racial democracy and, 136; Unionized Body and, 121
American Indians, 262n5; adoption of civilization and, 57; at Chicago World's Fair, 50; degeneracy and, 70–71; education and Christianization of, 83; height studies of, 77; stature of, 54–55, 79, 260n108; at

St. Louis World's Fair, 52; as U.S. citizens, 63; vertical metaphor and, 40
American Scene, The (James), 142–50, 174, 176–77, 276n88
American Tobacco, 103, 104
Anatomy of a Pygmie Compared with that of a Monkey, an Ape, and a Man . . . , The (Tyson), 38, 40
Andamanese people, 37, 38, 42, 43, 66
animals, size of American, 69–70, 262n31
anthropologists: Ripley, 36–37; travel writers and, 35. *See also* pygmies
Anthropology Building, 49–50
Anthropology Days, 56, 57
anthropometric measurements, 29, 78; of Civil War soldiers, 28, 54, 76; of fairgoers, 49, 55; of Jews, 197–98, 200–203, 204; of pygmies, 20, 28; race and, 55, 64, 66; in schools, 85, 87, 88–89; on truants, 90–91; urban communities and, 64; of U.S. citizens, 28, 29; of women, 188. *See also* stature
anti-Darwinism, 26
Antin, Mary, 13, 92–95, 181–84, 194–97, 200, 277n4, 277n7; cooperation and, 205–6; Dillingham Commission Report and, 280n74; education and, 195–97; growth of, 182–84, 196, 203, 205, 208, 268n120; immigration and, 195, 203–11; lying and, 211–13; motives of in *The Promised Land,* 280n80; parody and, 209–10; rhetorical elements in writing of, 211–14; science and, 203–4, 207, 214. See also *Promised Land, The* (Antin)
anti-Semitism, 201, 276n88

311

savages, 260n104

Scarlet Street (film), 244

Schlichter, Henry, 37–38

scholiocentric vs. pedocentric school, 82

school, 56, 82; anthropometric measurements in, 85, 87, 88–89; for the feeble-minded, 83, 89. *See also* education

schoolchildren, studies of, 87; in Massachusetts, 84–85, 85–86, 90–91; in Milwaukee, 84–85; in St. Louis, 85–86

Schuyler, Montgomery, 166, 169, 170

science, 9, 10, 188, 192, 196, 214; Antin and, 203–4, 207, 214; Jewish scientists and, 200–203; size of bodies and, 197

Search for Order, 1877–1920, The (Wiebe), 6

Sea Wolf, The (London), 216, 228

Second Industrial Revolution, 102

Seltzer, Mark, 30

Senate Interstate Commerce Committee, 109

Sennett, Richard, 175, 176

Sergi, 66–67

setback design, 159, 169, 173

sexual heightism, 192, 255n27

sexual promiscuity, 68

Shapiro, Harry, 236, 284n10

shareholders, 112

Shaw, Albert, 104

Sherman Antitrust Act (1890), 106, 108, 116

Sherwood, Sidney, 129

shortness, 198, 200–201; altitude and, 75, 77; atavism and, 62, 65–66; degeneration and, 21–22; economic class and, 72; as hereditary vs. environmental phenomenon, 33–34, 36; immoral practices and, 68; moral decline and, 71; nutrition and, 68–69, 70, 72, 74–75; physical exercise and, 68; role of deficiencies in, 67; sexual promiscuity and, 68; tender upbringing and, 69. *See also* stature

shrinking man, 12–13, 189, 215–33, 286n36; *The Incredible Shrinking Man* and, 14, 240–47, 288n64; *The Jungle* and, 13, 216, 222–30; labor

and, 218–19; in naturalist fiction, 13, 215–16, 225–27; New Woman and, 189, 190, 215, 216–18; physical culture movement and, 220–21; race and, 219, 220; sexual terms of, 287n59; *Sister Carrie* and, 215–16, 217–18

Shrinking Man, The (Matheson), 241–42, 243, 251

Sinclair, Upton, 110, 131, 216, 223, 225–33; class and, 226; shrinking man and, 13. See also *Jungle, The* (Sinclair)

Sister Carrie (Dreiser), 215–16, 217–18, 242, 282n43, 283n60

size, 1, 197; of American animals, 69–70, 262n31; as criterion of value, 6–7; cult of, 45; discourses of, 5; gender and, 12–13, 14, 251, 256n38, 279n35; hierarchies of, 54, 120–21, 122; intelligence and, 192. *See also* stature

Skiff, F. J. V., 51

Sklar, Martin, 109, 124–25

skyscrapers, 2, 10, 104, 140–77, 234–35, 272n12; body and, 11; Coburn and, 150–66; immigrants and, 273n21; James, Henry, and, 142–50; roofs on, 159; Woolworth Building, 166–75

Slotkin, Richard, 63, 261n5

small-scale business, 103, 123

Smith, F. Hopkinson, 168

Smith-Rosenberg, Carroll, 102, 188–89

Snider, Denton, 50

socialism, 110, 119, 125, 127, 175; Brandeis and, 107–8; class consciousness and, 136; collectivism and, 107; iconography and, 117–18; institutions and, 121; *The Jungle* and, 231–33, 283n64; in literature, 131, 227, 230, 231–33; revolution of, 116; Unionized Body and, 116–18, 120–21

Socialist Party, 105

social programs, 108

social transformations, 102, 107, 110, 269n39

Society of Italian Geography, 42

soldiers, 69, 72; Civil War, 13, 28, 54, 76–79; WWI, 80, 81, 85, 88; WWII, 285n11

Wilson, Woodrow, 11, 104, 106,
122–23, 167–69, 175; corporate culture and, 124–25, 137; middle class
and, 124–25; trusts and, 109
"With Only a Glance Now and Then
Down Into the Tangle of Civilization" (Hewitt and Clarke), 162
Wollaston, A. F. R., 30, 33
women, 181, 188, 189; *Attack of the
50-Foot Woman* and, 249–52; college, 187, 239, 284n10; economics
and, 114; effect of education on,
82–83, 249; evolution and, 85;
growing, 12–13, 194, 197, 213–14,
286n36, 288n67; height of, 182,
245, 254n27; *Incredible Shrinking
Man* and, 288n64; industrial labor
and, 228–30; male autonomy and,
232; male dependence on, 283n60;
race and, 227; in 1950s, 238–40;
shrinking vs. growing, 283n54;
unions and, 120; in workforce,
216–17. *See also* gender; men; New
Woman
Women and Economics (Gilman), 187
Woolworth Building, 11, 141, 142,
159, 166–75, 234, 273n22; builders
of, 173; praise of, 166–67; upward
mobility and, 169–75, 176; Wilson
and, 167–69, 175
"Woolworth Building, The" (Coburn),
153, 154

Woolworth Company, 167
Woolworth, Frank, 167–70, 173–75,
275n60
workers, 234, 238; white-collar, 119,
241
working conditions, 105, 115,
163–64
workingwomen, 216–17, 239, 277n7
World's Fair of 1893. *See* Chicago
World's Columbian Exposition of
1893
World's Fair of 1904. *See* St. Louis
Louisiana Purchase Exposition of
1904
world's fairs: anthropologists and ethnologists at, 49; economy of scale
and, 46–47; political investment of
body and, 49; pygmies and, 44–61;
racial differences and, 45; upward
gaze and, 47. *See also* Chicago
World's Columbian Exposition of
1893; St. Louis Louisiana Purchase
Exposition of 1904
World War I, 80, 81, 85, 88, 285n10
World War II, 236, 240, 285n11

xenophobia, 81

"Young Widow, The" (Gibson), 185
youth, 146

Zaborowska, Magdalena, 195